THE
KEY IDEAS
BIBLE HANDBOOK

RON RHODES

HARVEST HOUSE PUBLISHERS
EUGENE, OREGON

Cover by Dugan Design Group

THE KEY IDEAS BIBLE HANDBOOK
Copyright © 2016 Ron Rhodes
Published by Harvest House Publishers
Eugene, Oregon 97402
www.harvesthousepublishers.com

ISBN 978-0-7369-6435-7 (pbk.)
ISBN 978-0-7369-6436-4 (eBook)

Library of Congress Cataloging-in-Publication Data
    Names: Rhodes, Ron, author.
    Title: Key ideas Bible handbook / Ron Rhodes.
    Description: Eugene, Oregon : Harvest House Publishers, 2016.
    Identifiers: LCCN 2015050565 (print) | LCCN 2016018403 (ebook) | ISBN
      9780736964357 (pbk.) | ISBN 9780736964364 ()
    Subjects: LCSH: Bible—Criticism, interpretation, etc.
    Classification: LCC BS511.3 .R494 2016 (print) | LCC BS511.3 (ebook) | DDC
      220.6/1—dc23
    LC record available at https://lccn.loc.gov/2015050565

Printed in the United States of America

16 17 18 19 20 21 22 23 24 /VP-JC/ 10 9 8 7 6 5 4 3 2 1

To my beloved wife, Kerri

Acknowledgments

Having now written more than 70 books over a span of 35 years, I can say without reservation that no author is an island—no author accomplishes his or her task without the continued support of multiple other people. In my case, my primary support team has always been my family—my wife, Kerri, and my two grown children, David and Kylie. With every year that passes I grow in appreciation for these three. As I have stated on many occasions, the sun always seems to shine a little bit brighter with them in my world. What a blessing from God!

I am also hugely appreciative of my ongoing relationship with the fine team at Harvest House Publishers—especially with Bob Hawkins Jr., the president of the company. A special thanks also goes to Steve Miller and Terry Glaspey for their helpful suggestions in the early stages of the book, and to Janelle Coury for her excellent layout and design work on the book. Also...Gene Skinner, where would I be without you? You've edited so many of my books that I've lost count. But all the books are better because of your involvement.

Last but certainly not least, I bow before the Lord Jesus Christ in humble appreciation for the opportunity to serve Him through the written word. What a privilege and joy!

—Ron Rhodes
Frisco, Texas

Contents

The New Testament

The Gospels

A Historical Book

The Pauline Epistles

The General Epistles

An Apocalyptic Book

The Key Ideas Bible Handbook

Thank you for joining me on this exciting journey through *The Key Ideas Bible Handbook,* a book brimming with the applicational "big ideas" from Genesis to Revelation. By its very nature, this book is designed to help bring about life-change in your walk with God and to produce a spiritual transformation in your daily life. That means you should not read this book thinking it will only fill your head with more intellectual knowledge. It will enlighten your mind, yes, but it will also touch your heart—*and deeply.*

My hope and prayer is that as you read *The Key Ideas Bible Handbook,* you will attain

- a thorough understanding of the power of God's Word to change your life;
- an appreciation for how the Word of God can be exciting and liberating;
- an awareness that God is a personal being who desires to personally interact with you;
- an awareness that God not only makes promises to you in His Word, but is also a relentless promise keeper;
- a conviction that God will bless you when you choose to live righteously;
- an understanding of the need for unwavering faith in the midst of life's troubles;
- a thorough understanding of God's sovereignty in your life;
- a deep appreciation for the wondrous salvation you have in Jesus;
- an experience of daily intimacy with Jesus like never before;
- an ever-increasing understanding of God's marvelous grace as He

works in your life; and an eternal perspective that will enable you to see life's problems and difficulties from heaven's vantage point.

As you peruse *The Key Ideas Bible Handbook*, you will notice that it sifts a wide variety of applicational concepts from the biblical text. I use the phrase "applicational concepts" by design, for such concepts involve life-changing truths. An example might be this: "It's not merely *what* you know that brings salvation, but *who* you know—Jesus Christ the divine Savior." *The Key Ideas Bible Handbook* is loaded with such life-changing truths, from the creation account in the early chapters of Genesis to the eternal state in the latter chapters of Revelation.

To illustrate further, a traditional heading of Philippians 1:20-26 in a study Bible might be something like this: "Paul lives for Jesus Christ." In place of such a generalized heading, here is an applicational concept: "When Christ is your life, living becomes vibrantly productive and death is nothing to fear." *That* is a life-changing, transformational truth!

Likewise, a traditional heading of Colossians 1:15-19 in a study Bible might be something like this: "Christ is supreme." In place of such a generalized heading, here is an applicational concept: "Because Christ is supreme in reality, He must become supreme experientially in your life." *That* is a life-changing, transformational truth!

A traditional heading of Psalm 1 in a study Bible might be, "The righteous versus the wicked." In place of such a heading, here is an applicational concept: "God wants to bless you, but you must first become bless-able by being obedient to Him." Again, *that* is a life-changing, transformational truth!

The Key Ideas Bible Handbook is ultimately a tool that provides an applicational framework from Genesis to Revelation. It will enable you as a Christian to understand not only what the Bible means, but also what the Bible means *to you* in terms of life-changing truths. Used hand in hand with a Bible, this tool can be truly transformational.

I believe this approach to the Bible reflects the nature of God's intention for Scripture. In 2 Timothy 3:16, for example, we are told Scripture is intended to be "profitable for teaching, for reproof, for correction, and for training in righteousness." Or, as The Expanded Bible renders the verse, all Scripture "is useful for teaching, for showing people what is wrong in their lives [refuting error; rebuking], for correcting faults, and for teaching how to live right [training in righteousness]."

Some Christians might be tempted to think only the New Testament contains the primary applicational concepts for today's believers. First Corinthians 10:11

reveals, however, that events that transpired in Old Testament times were written down for our instruction. That means the whole Bible—both the Old and New Testaments—contains applicational concepts to guide and enrich us.

You will notice a number of unique features in *The Key Ideas Bible Handbook*. I devote one chapter to each biblical book. At the head of each chapter is a super-concept—a guiding theme that runs throughout the entire biblical book. This sets the context for all that is to come in that chapter. Then, following a brief historical introduction of the book, are thematic summaries, short word studies, quotes from famous Christians, Bible promises, exhortations, applicational ideas, short outline lists of important teachings, verses to remember, and more. It is all designed to yield a truly enriching and uplifting experience in your Bible study. Flipping through its pages before beginning formal Bible study will whet your appetite for what is to come. Exciting times are ahead!

To get the most out of this book, I suggest you pray something like this whenever you use it alongside the Word of God:

> *Lord, I ask You to open my eyes and enhance my understanding so I can grasp what You want me to learn today [Psalm 119:18]. I also ask You to enable me, by Your Spirit, to apply the applicational concepts I learn to my daily life. I ask You to guide me moment by moment by Your Word [Psalm 119:105; 2 Timothy 3:15-17]. I thank You in Jesus's name, amen.*

Let's begin our journey!

Genesis

God created humanity. Though human sin caused alienation with God, God's merciful plan of salvation was set in motion from the very beginning. The plan began with a man of faith (Abraham) who gave rise to a nation of promise (Israel).

Timeline

2166—Abram is born.

2091—Abram enters into Canaan.

2080—Ishmael is born.

2066—Isaac is born.

2006—Jacob and Esau are born.

1915—Joseph is born.

1898—Joseph is sold into slavery.

1885—Joseph begins ruling in Egypt.

1876—Jacob and his family go to Egypt.

1805—Joseph dies.

1529—Aaron is born.

1526—Moses is born.

1445–1405—Moses writes Genesis.

"Thus says the LORD, your Redeemer, who formed you from the womb: 'I am the LORD, who made all things, who alone stretched out the heavens, who spread out the earth by myself.'"

—Isaiah 44:24

The book of Genesis was written by Moses between 1445 and 1405 BC and is foundational to a proper understanding of the rest of the Bible. After all, Genesis not only tells us about the origins of the universe and humankind, it also informs us of the origins of human sin, suffering, and death. God's work of redemption, as recorded throughout the rest of Scripture, would make little sense if we did not first understand these foundational truths in the book of Genesis. We might say Genesis sets the stage for all that follows in the rest of Scripture. The word "genesis" literally means "beginnings."

Following are key applicational concepts in Genesis:

God is your Creator, so have some creaturely respect.

Genesis 1:1 tells us, "In the beginning, God created the heavens and the earth." God also created human beings upon the earth (1:26-27; see also 5:1; 9:6). As creatures, you and I are responsible to obey the Creator. The psalmist—reflecting back on the book of Genesis—put it this way: "Know that the LORD, he is God! It is he who made us, and we are his; we are his people, and the sheep of his pasture" (Psalm 100:3). Indeed, "Come, let us worship and bow down;

let us kneel before the LORD, our Maker! For he is our God, and we are the people of his pasture, and the sheep of his hand" (Psalm 95:6-7).

You and I are made in the image of God. Live accordingly!

Genesis 1:27 tells us, "God created man in his own image, in the image of God he created him; male and female he created them." Elsewhere in Scripture, we learn man was created in God's image in the sense that he is a finite reflection of God in his rational nature (Colossians 3:10), in his moral nature (Ephesians 4:24), and in his dominion over creation (Genesis 1:27-28). In the same way the moon reflects the brilliant light of the sun, so finite man—as created in God's image—is a reflection of God in these aspects.

My friend, since part of being created in God's image relates to our rational nature, doesn't it make sense to fill our minds with God's Word (Colossians 3:16)? And since part of being created in God's image relates to our moral nature, doesn't it make sense to follow the moral injunctions in God's Word (James 1:22-23)? Let's do it!

God created you as a social being. Don't try to go it alone in life.

God affirmed, "It is not good that the man should be alone" (Genesis 2:18). God accordingly gave Adam a wife named Eve. She became his "helper"—a word that carries the idea "one who supports." When you think about it, all of us need support. All of us need companionship with other people. So don't try to go it alone in life. We need each other.

Sin brings alienation between humans and God, but confession of sin brings restoration.

When Adam and Eve sensed the approach of God in the garden of Eden after they partook of the fruit, they "hid themselves from the presence of the LORD God among the trees of the garden" (Genesis 3:8). This hiding was rooted in the shame, remorse, confusion, guilt, and fear that accompany rebellion against God. We tend to respond in the same way.

Of course, there is no place to hide from God (Psalm 139:1-2,7-8). The best step to take after succumbing to sin is to confess it to God so that fellowship with Him can be restored (Psalm 32:3,5; 51:4; Proverbs 28:13; 1 John 1:9).

No Hiding from God

"Where shall I go from your Spirit? Or where shall I flee from your presence? If I ascend to heaven, you are there! If I make my bed in Sheol, you are there" (Psalm 139:7-8).

"'Can a man hide himself in secret places so that I cannot see him?' declares the Lord" (Jeremiah 23:24).

Sin brings about both spiritual death and physical death.

God warned Adam that he would die the same day he ate of the forbidden fruit (Genesis 2:17). This does not contradict Genesis 5:5, which tells us Adam lived to the age of 930 years. When Adam and Eve sinned, they did not die that day physically, but they did die spiritually. The word "death" carries the idea of separation. Spiritual death involves the separation of the human being from God. When Adam and Eve partook of the forbidden fruit, they were immediately separated from God in a spiritual sense—"dead…in trespasses and sins" (Ephesians 2:1). Their spiritual separation from God eventually led to their physical deaths (Genesis 5:5).

> "Sin is always at work in the heart; a temporary lull in its assaults means not that it is dead, but that it is very much alive…Sin's strategy is to induce a false sense of security as a prelude to a surprise attack."
>
> —J. I. Packer

Good news: Jesus overcame death for us (Hebrews 2:14-15). Those who trust in Him for salvation are recipients of eternal life (John 3:14-16,36; 10:28; 1 John 5:11-13,20). Rejoice!

People often make excuses when they sin.

> "A sin is two sins when it is defended."
>
> —Henry Smith (1560–1591)

When Adam was confronted by God about his sin, he said, "The woman whom you gave to be with me, she gave me fruit of the tree, and I ate" (Genesis 3:12). When Eve was confronted by God, she said, "The serpent deceived me, and I ate" (verse 13). Both passed the buck. Both made excuses.

We tend to make excuses as well (Luke 14:16-24). When we sin, let's be honest with God and admit our failures (Psalm 51:3,4,6; 32:5; 1 John 1:9). Only then will we be restored into proper fellowship with God.

Walk with God each and every day.

> "What does the LORD require of you but to do justice, and to love kindness, and to walk humbly with your God?"
>
> —Micah 6:8

"Enoch walked with God" (Genesis 5:22), as did Noah (Genesis 6:9). You and I may not walk with God in the exact same sense as Enoch and Noah, but Scripture says much about our spiritual walk with God. We ought to walk honestly (1 Thessalonians 4:11-12), and in a way that is worthy of the Lord (Colossians 1:10). We should walk humbly with God (Micah 6:8). We should have a godly walk characterized by integrity (Proverbs 20:7). We should walk in dependence on the Holy Spirit

(Galatians 6:8) and seek to walk as Jesus Himself walked (1 John 2:6). Walk with God!

God is holy and responds in sudden judgment in the face of unrepentant sin.

We often find sudden destruction falling upon the wicked in the Bible. The unrepentant people living during Noah's time experienced a sudden and catastrophic flood (Genesis 6–9). They had 120 years to repent as Noah preached to them, but they ignored him, and irrevocable judgment suddenly fell (6:3-7).

> **Cross-References: God as a Judge**
> Genesis 16:5 • 18:25 • 30:6 • 31:53 • 1 Chronicles 16:33 • Psalm 7:8 • 50:4 • 58:11 • 67:4 • 75:7 • Ecclesiastes 12:14 • Isaiah 2:4 • Micah 4:3 • 1 Peter 1:17 • Revelation 20:11-15

Sudden judgment is a common theme in Scripture. Proverbs 6:15 issues this warning about the wicked: "Therefore calamity will come upon him suddenly; in a moment he will be broken beyond healing." Isaiah 47:11 warns sinners that "ruin shall come upon you suddenly, of which you know nothing."

God doesn't mess around. He means business when it comes to sin.

God's favor falls on those who live His way.

Many people in biblical times found favor with God. The Genesis account reveals that "Noah found favor in the eyes of the LORD" (Genesis 6:8). A bit later, we are told that "the LORD was with Joseph" and "gave him favor" (39:21).

> "It's not great talent that God blesses so much as likeness to Jesus."
>
> —*Robert Murray M'Cheyne (1813–1843)*

Elsewhere in Scripture we read that "the boy Samuel continued to grow both in stature and in favor with the LORD" (1 Samuel 2:26). "David became greater and greater, for the LORD, the God of hosts, was with him" (2 Samuel 5:10). The angel said to Mary, "Do not be afraid, Mary, for you have found favor with God" (Luke 1:30).

How 'bout it, my friend? Do you seek God's favor? If so, then imitate the people I just mentioned by living righteously and in obedience to God (Proverbs 12:2).

God rescues His own people before sending judgment upon the rebellious.

God is often seen rescuing His people before His judgment falls upon the rebellious (2 Peter 2:5-9). Enoch was transferred to heaven before the judgment of the flood (Genesis 5:24). Noah and his family were in the ark before the judgment of the flood (Genesis 7:1,6-7). Lot was taken out of Sodom before judgment was poured out on Sodom and Gomorrah (Genesis 19:1-22). The firstborn among the Hebrews in Egypt were sheltered by the blood of the Paschal lamb before judgment fell (Exodus 12:7,13). The spies were safely out of Jericho and Rahab was secured before judgment fell on Jericho (Joshua 2). One day, the church will be rescued by the rapture before judgment falls during the tribulation period (1 Thessalonians 4:13-17; 1 Corinthians 15:51-52).

God is a relentless promise keeper. You can take Him at His word.

Generation after generation, the evidence mounts that God is a relentless promise keeper. The Abrahamic covenant is a perfect example. God in this covenant made unconditional promises to Abraham. Among other things, God promised Abraham and his descendants, "Look toward heaven, and number the stars, if you are able to number them...So shall your offspring be" (Genesis 15:5). Later in Genesis, we read that the Israelites "were fruitful and multiplied greatly" (47:27). The promise was already beginning to be fulfilled.

God also promised Abraham that all the people of the earth would be blessed by one of his descendants (Genesis 12:3). Fast-forward to New Testament times. Jesus is the descendant from the physical line of Abraham, through whom all the families of the earth are to be blessed (Matthew 1:1-2).

All this gives us boldness in believing that all the other promises in the Bible about our Savior are just as reliable. There is good reason to anchor ourselves on the promises of God.

God's Promises Never Fail
"God is not man, that he should lie, or a son of man, that he should change his mind. Has he said, and will he not do it? Or has he spoken, and will he not fulfill it?" (Numbers 23:19). "You know with all your heart and soul that not one of all the good promises the LORD your God gave you has failed. Every promise has been fulfilled; not one has failed" (Joshua 23:14 NIV).

God uses flawed human beings in the outworking of His plan of salvation.

God uses imperfect humans to accomplish His purposes. God used Noah even though he got drunk (Genesis 9:21). God used Abraham even though he lied on several occasions (20:2). God used Sarah even though she laughed at the suggestion that God would enable her to have a son in old age (18:12-13). God used Jacob even though he was a deceiver (25:19-34; 27:1-41). This gives us confidence that God can use us too!

Trusting God against all odds brings phenomenal blessing.

A number of the people mentioned in Genesis are heroes of faith. Perhaps the best example is Abraham, who showed unflinching faith when obeying God's command to sacrifice his own son Isaac (Genesis 22:1-19). Of course, God stopped him just in the nick of time.

You and I also encounter tests of our faith. James 1:2 urges us to "count it all joy, my brothers, when you meet trials of various kinds, for you know that the testing of your faith produces steadfastness" (see also 1 Peter 1:6-7). I urge you: trust God no matter what!

Never forget: with God all things are possible.

Even though Abraham and Sarah were too old to have a baby, the Lord said to Abraham, "Is anything too hard for the LORD?" (Genesis 18:14). God can do anything He desires: "My purpose will stand, and I will do all that I please" (Isaiah 46:10 NIV).

Are you facing an insurmountable problem? Turn to the God who can do the impossible.

Good news: you are justified (declared righteous) by faith alone.

Abram "believed the LORD, and he counted it to him as righteousness" (Genesis 15:6). We call this "justification by faith." The word "justified" is a legal term. Negatively, the word means one is once-for-all pronounced not guilty before God. Positively, the word means one is once-for-all pronounced righteous. You and I are justified by faith in Christ (Romans 3:25,28,30).

Warning: sin can lead to the domino effect.

Joseph's brothers sold him into slavery (Genesis 37:18-36). In so doing, they sinned greatly and then encountered the "domino effect." By "domino effect," I am referring to how one sin can easily lead to another. In this case, the ten brothers initially sinned against their father by selling his beloved Joseph into slavery.

Trusting God When Life Hurts

Joseph trusted God even when his life was full of trouble. God greatly blessed him (Genesis 50:20).

"Call upon me in the day of trouble; I will deliver you, and you shall glorify me" (Psalm 50:15).

"Trust in him at all times...God is a refuge for us" (Psalm 62:8).

"Faith does not operate in the realm of the possible. There is no glory for God in that which is humanly possible. Faith begins where man's power ends."

—*George Muller (1805–1898)*

"In no case must we permit sin to find a lodging in our mind. Learn to say 'no' right in the moment sin approaches you. Only thus is victory possible."

—*Erich Sauer (1898–1959)*

This quickly led to another sin involving spilling blood on Joseph's coat to deceive their father into thinking Joseph was dead. They allowed the deception to continue for decades.

Sin is like a cancer. Unless checked, it can grow and grow. Better to nip it in the bud.

Never forget: God has the amazing ability to bring good out of evil.

God can bring good out of evil. A great example is Joseph's story (Genesis 45:1–50:26). He was sold into slavery by his own brothers. Once he was brought down to Egypt, he was eventually falsely accused by an immoral woman and then thrown into prison. All the while, God was sovereignly working behind the scenes. In the end, He used these circumstances to elevate Joseph to a position of great authority in Egypt so Joseph could then save many people from famine.

Cross-References: God's Sovereignty

Exodus 15:18 • Deuteronomy 4:39 • 10:14 • 2 Chronicles 20:6 • Psalm 9:7 • 29:10 • 33:8-11 • 47:2 • 83:18 • 103:19 • Isaiah 40:21-26 • 46:10 • Daniel 4:34-35 • Romans 14:11 • Ephesians 1:20-22

Here's a great Bible promise: "We know that for those who love God all things work together for good, for those who are called according to his purpose" (Romans 8:28).

Don't hold grudges. Forgiveness is the better path.

Once Jacob died, Joseph's brothers worried that Joseph would seek retribution for the sin they committed decades ago (selling him into slavery). But Joseph urged them, "Do not fear" (Genesis 50:19). He said God was the one who ultimately brought him down to Egypt (50:20). Joseph had completely forgiven his brothers.

Cross-References: Forgiveness

Genesis 50:17 • Matthew 5:39 • 5:43-44 • 6:14 • Mark 11:25 • Luke 6:27,37 • Romans 12:17,19 • Ephesians 4:32 • Colossians 3:13

My friend, forgiving others is one of the most important lessons we can learn. Colossians 3:13 instructs, "As the Lord has forgiven you, so you also must forgive."

A Thought to Anchor in Your Heart

Don't compromise. Walk with God and experience His favor.

Exodus

God does whatever is necessary to bring deliverance and redemption to His people.

Exodus is one of the most loved books in the Old Testament. One reason for this is that it has all the elements of a great story—strong personalities, powerful drama, great dialogue, and victorious underdogs. But more important, it is a true story about how God redeemed His people from bondage.

This book, written by Moses in about 1440 BC, is a continuation of the story that began in Genesis—particularly chapters 37–50. This is clear not only in the fact that the first seven verses of Exodus 1 repeat information from Genesis, but the first word of verse 1 in the Hebrew text of Exodus is the word "And." This little word connects the books of Exodus and Genesis to each other.

In the Hebrew Bible, Exodus is titled "And these are the names." This title is based on the opening words of the book (Exodus 1:1). The ancients often titled a book according to its first words.

When the Hebrew Bible was translated into the Greek language, the book was given a new title. It was called Exodus, from the Greek word *exodos*. This is a compound word that joins two Greek words: *ek* (meaning "out of") and *odos* (meaning "a road"). Taken together, the word "exodus" means "a road out of" or "departure." This title describes the central event in the book: Israel's departure from Egypt as a result of the ten plagues God inflicted on Pharaoh and the Egyptians.

The book also deals with God's establishment of a theocratic (God-ruled) nation under Moses by means of a new "constitution" called the Sinai covenant (Exodus 16–40). In this covenant, God gave instructions for the ordering of life

Timeline

1885— Joseph begins ruling in Egypt.

1876— Jacob and his family go to Egypt.

1529— Aaron is born.

1526— Moses is born.

1486— Moses flees to Midian from Egypt.

1446— The first Jewish Passover is celebrated; the Jews leave Egypt.

1446— Pharaoh and the Egyptians are defeated at the Red Sea.

1445— The Ten Commandments are given.

1445— The tabernacle is built and dedicated.

1444— Israel camps at Mount Sinai.

1440— Moses writes the book of Exodus.

Exodus

among the Hebrew people through the commandments given to Moses at Mount Sinai. Exodus also provides detailed information about the tabernacle and the ministry of the priests.

From the time of Joseph's death at the end of Genesis to the time of the book of Exodus, nearly 300 years had passed. The Israelites had once been favored and privileged guests of Pharaoh and Joseph, but now they had become a nation of slaves. The ruler who had been favorably disposed toward Joseph had died. And Egypt had forgotten its indebtedness to Joseph.

The new king, unfamiliar with Joseph, departed from his predecessor's graciousness. He introduced a harsh policy against the Hebrews designed to guarantee the national security of Egypt and alleviate fears of a possible Israelite rebellion.

The backdrop of Pharaoh's fear was that the Israelite population had grown at an incredible pace. Pharaoh feared that if a foreign invader made war with Egypt, the Israelites might join forces with them and overrun Egypt (Exodus 1:10). So Pharaoh decided to initiate a policy that would exploit their labor potential (by slavery) while at the same time check their growing population. He did this by consigning the Israelites to hard labor in building treasure cities.

The Israelites suffered cruel bondage in this way for 400-plus years. But God had not forgotten the promise He made to the patriarchs. He "remembered his covenant with Abraham, with Isaac, and with Jacob" (Exodus 2:24). He would send a deliverer.

Following are key applicational concepts in Exodus:

God's people are not exempt from bad things happening—even for an extended time.

Bad things sometimes happen to God's people—and sometimes the bad circumstances can last a long, long time. The Lord had previously warned Abraham about this: "The LORD said to Abram, 'Know

---

Biblical Covenants

A covenant is an agreement between two parties. In Bible times God made covenants with

- Noah (Genesis 9:8-17);
- Abraham (Genesis 15:12-21; 17:1-14);
- The Israelites at Mount Sinai (Exodus 19:5,6);
- David (2 Samuel 7:13; 23:5); and
- God's people in the New Covenant (Hebrews 8:6-13).

"God is not man, that he should lie, or a son of man, that he should change his mind. Has he said, and will he not do it? Or has he spoken, and will he not fulfill it?"

—Numbers 23:19

God Can Bring Good out of Evil

"We know that for those who love God all things work together for good, for those who are called according to his purpose" (Romans 8:28).

for certain that your offspring will be sojourners in a land that is not theirs and will be servants there, and they will be afflicted for four hundred years'" (Genesis 15:13). This is a rounded-off number. Exodus 12:40 provides the exact time: "The time that the people of Israel lived in Egypt was 430 years." (See also Acts 7:6.)

We are not exempt from bad things happening today either. In fact, Scripture warns us, "Through many tribulations we must enter the kingdom of God" (Acts 14:22).

God cares about the oppressed in the world.

When Joseph brought his family to Egypt, he had no idea a subsequent ruler would end up enslaving them—indeed, his entire people (Exodus 1:1-14). What was intended to be a blessing turned out to be the curse of oppression.

God, of course, does not countenance slavery. From the very beginning, God declared that all humans are created in His image (Genesis 1:26-27). The apostle Paul also declared that we are all "God's offspring" (Acts 17:29), and that God "made from one man every nation of mankind to live on all the face of the earth" (Acts 17:26).

Moreover, despite the fact that slavery was countenanced in the Semitic cultures of the day, the law in the Bible demanded that slaves eventually be set free (Exodus 21:2; Leviticus 25:40). Likewise, servants had to be treated with respect (Exodus 21:20,26). Israel, itself in slavery in Egypt for a prolonged time, was constantly reminded by God of this (Deuteronomy 5:15), and their emancipation became the model for the liberation of all slaves (Leviticus 25:40).

> **One in Christ**
> Paul declared that in Christ "there is neither Jew nor Greek, there is neither slave nor free, there is no male and female, for you are all one in Christ Jesus" (Galatians 3:28).
> All social classes are broken down in Christ; we are all equal before God.

Though the apostle Paul urged bondservants to obey their earthly masters (Ephesians 6:5; Colossians 3:22), he was not approving of the institution of slavery but was simply alluding to the de facto situation in his day. He was instructing servants to be good workers, just as believers should be today, but he was not commending slavery. Paul also instructed all believers to be obedient to government (even if unjust) for the Lord's sake (Romans 13:1; see also Titus 3:1; 1 Peter 2:13). But this in no way condones oppression and tyranny, which the Bible repeatedly condemns (Isaiah 10:1; Exodus 2:23-25). We must stand against all forms of oppression in the world today.

Training for serving God can sometimes take a long time.

God heard the cry of His people and raised up Moses to deliver them. Though Moses grew up in Egypt, and was trained and cultured as an Egyptian, he witnessed the unfair treatment of his own Hebrew people and did not like it. After killing an Egyptian taskmaster for treating a Hebrew harshly, he was driven into the wilderness, where he became a shepherd (Exodus 2:11-15). How quickly circumstances changed. This happened when Moses was 40 years old (Acts 7:23-29).

Moses spent the next 40 years as a shepherd in the land of Midian (Exodus 2:11-15). This served to be a time of education for him. Previously, he had studied under the Egyptians. Now God taught him how to survive in the desert and how to be a good shepherd. These are skills he would need in shepherding the Israelites out of Egypt toward the Promised Land.

Eventually God appeared to Moses in a burning bush and commanded him to go to Egypt to deliver His people (Exodus 3:2). Moses was hesitant at first, but God assured him He would be with him and that he would succeed in his task. God had thoroughly prepared him.

When God assigns you to a task, excuses are not acceptable.

When God commissioned Moses to deliver His people from Egyptian bondage, Moses responded, "Oh, my Lord, I am not eloquent, either in the past or since you have spoken to your servant, but I am slow of speech and of tongue" (Exodus 4:10).

God responded to Moses, "Who has made man's mouth? Who makes him mute, or deaf, or seeing, or blind? Is it not I, the LORD? Now therefore go, and I will be with your mouth and teach you what you shall speak" (Exodus 4:11-12).

God would not allow this or any other excuse from Moses. When God assigns a person to a task, excuses are not acceptable. Obedience is the only option.

Examples of Excuses

- Adam's excuse—Genesis 3:12
- Eve's excuse—Genesis 3:13
- Moses's excuse—Exodus 4:1,10
- A potential disciple's excuse—Matthew 8:21
- A potential disciple's excuse—Luke 9:59
- No excuses—Romans 1:20

You can learn much about God by the names He uses for Himself.

In the ancient world a name was not a mere label as it is today. A name was considered equivalent to whomever or whatever bore it. Knowing a person's name amounted to knowing his essence and being. With that in mind, God ascribes the name Yahweh to Himself ("the LORD") when speaking to Moses (Exodus 3:15). This name indicates God is eternally self-existent. He never came into being at a point in time. He has always existed. He is the eternal God. The name also points to God's covenant faithfulness.

Later in Exodus, God is called Yahweh-Nissi—a term meaning "the Lord Our Banner." Israel could not defeat her enemies in her own strength. The battles were to be the Lord's because He was Israel's banner—her source of victory (Exodus 17:15).

Today you and I are privileged to call God "Abba"—an Aramaic term of great intimacy, loosely meaning "daddy" or "papa" (Romans 8:15).

God's servants are sometimes thrown into very difficult situations, but God always remains in providential control.

Moses appeared before Pharaoh and proclaimed, "Thus says the LORD, the God of Israel, 'Let my people go.'" Pharaoh said he did not know the God of the Jews. Pharaoh then defiantly added to the burden of the Jews by commanding that they make bricks without any straw (Exodus 5). God reassured Moses that He would yet deliver the Jews. Moses communicated this to the Jews, but they were too disheartened to listen (6:1-9). The Lord promised to stretch out His hand against the Egyptians and bend their will (6:10–7:13). But the Jews remained discouraged. This was not an easy experience for Moses.

This brings to mind how the apostle Paul in New Testament times often found himself in uneasy circumstances in service to the Lord. In fact, the Lord Jesus said this of Paul: "He is a chosen instrument of mine to carry my name before the Gentiles and kings and the children of Israel. For I will show him how much he must suffer for the sake of my name" (Acts 9:15-16).

It is entirely possible that we may be called to serve Christ in some capacity that is way outside our comfort zone and proves to be very difficult. But relax. Jesus has promised, "I am with you always, to the end of the age" (Matthew 28:20).

God can and does use miraculous power to accomplish His sovereign purposes.

Pharaoh was not about to listen to reason. He was arrogant and prideful, defying the God of Israel. God therefore empowered Moses to inflict ten plagues upon the Egyptians: (1) Nile turned to blood (Exodus

---

Notable Divine Deliverances

- Daniel's friends were rescued from the fiery furnace (Daniel 3).
- Daniel was rescued from the lions' den (Daniel 6).
- Jesus was rescued from death through the resurrection (Luke 24).

7:14-25); (2) swarm of frogs (8:1-15); (3) swarm of gnats (8:16-19); (4) swarm of flies (8:20-32); (5) diseased livestock (9:1-7); (6) outbreak of boils (9:8-12); (7) hail from sky (9:13-35); (8) swarm of locusts (10:1-20); (9) land engulfed in darkness (10:21-29); and (10) killing of firstborn among Egyptians (11:1–12:36). These judgments brought Egypt to its knees, and the Jews were released from bondage.

Yahweh is incomparable. There is no one like Him.

> **Two Means of Expressing Yahweh's Incomparability**
>
> *Negation:* "There is no one like the LORD our God" (Exodus 8:10).
>
> *Rhetorical questions:* "Who is like you, O LORD, among the gods?" (Exodus 15:11).

In Egyptian religion, the god at the very top of the totem pole was the sun god, Re. Next in line was Pharaoh, the ruler of Egypt, who was considered to be the son of Re. So Pharaoh was himself considered a god in his own right. Because Re was considered superior to all other gods, his son—Pharaoh, the king—was also considered to possess unmatched power as a god. This adds a whole new dimension to the Exodus account.

It is as though a contest occurs between the true God on the one side and the false gods of Egypt's mystery religions on the other side (see Numbers 33:4).

Pharaoh was unable to turn back the mighty plagues of Yahweh. The Egyptian Nile River god Nilus was unable to respond when Yahweh turned the whole river to blood (Exodus 7:17-21). The Egyptian sun god, Re, was unable to respond when Yahweh turned the entire land dark (Exodus 10:21-22). The Egyptian pantheon was impotent before Yahweh. (This is not unexpected, since other so-called gods do not really exist.)

Today there are many pretenders to the divine throne. Don't be fooled. Truly, there is no one like God in all the universe. He is incomparable.

Victories sometimes entail a level of final resistance that must be overcome.

The Egyptians had let the Israelites go, and God led them into the wilderness near the Red Sea (Exodus 13:17-22). The Egyptians then *re-pursued* them (14:1-9). Seeing their sudden danger, the Israelites rebelled against Moses and God (14:1-12). God, however, quickly opened the Red Sea so the Israelites could go across. The Egyptians continued to pursue, but God caused the waters of the Red Sea to close upon and destroy them (14:13-31). The fickle Israelites then thanked God (15:1-21).

Here's an important lesson to remember: we must never give up in our service to God. "With us is the LORD our God, to help us and to fight our battles" (2 Chronicles 32:8). God promises, "I will never leave you nor forsake you" (Hebrews 13:5).

God is the Sustainer of the universe. That means He is also your personal Sustainer.

In the wilderness, God preserved His people from thirst (Exodus 15:22-27; 17:1-7), hunger (16), defeat (17:8-16), and from potential chaos through effective governing (18). In short, God took care of His people.

> **God as Sustainer**
>
> "If God maintains sun and planets in bright and ordered beauty, He can keep us."
>
> —F. B. Meyer (1847–1929)

Jesus is the Sustainer of the universe. "He upholds the universe by the word of his power" (Hebrews 1:3). The word "upholds" does not refer to a mere passive support—like an Atlas supporting the weight of the world in his hands. Nor does it merely indicate the idea of maintenance. The word carries the idea of movement toward a final goal, toward an appointed course. Scripture reveals that Jesus sustained the Israelites during the wilderness sojourn following their deliverance from Egypt (1 Corinthians 10:1-4). He also sustains you and me (Colossians 1:17).

God provides His people with behavioral parameters to guide their living day to day.

God instituted a covenant with His people, the Jews (Exodus 19:1-25). This covenant necessitated obedience to the Ten Commandments (20:1-26). The Ten Commandments can be broken down into two basic categories. The first four commandments pertain to the Israelites' relationship with God: (1) Have no other gods; (2) Have no graven images of God; (3) Do not take the Lord's name in vain; and (4) Keep the Sabbath. The next six commandments deal with the Israelites' relationships with each other: (5) Honor parents; (6) Do not kill; (7) Do not commit adultery; (8) Do not steal; (9) Do not bear false witness; and (10) Do not covet.

In view of this, the total content of the Ten Commandments can be summarized in two briefer commandments: (1) Love God; and (2) Love your neighbor (Deuteronomy 6:5; Leviticus 19:18). For this reason, Jesus said the greatest commandment is "Love the Lord your God," while the second is "Love your neighbor as yourself" (Matthew 22:37-39).

Exodus

God's commandments were given to Israel not to place a burden on the people, but to set them apart and distinguish them from surrounding pagan nations. They were provided to make the Israelites wise, great, and pleasing to a holy God. Those who obeyed the commandments reaped great blessing. Those who disobeyed brought discipline upon themselves (Exodus 19:3-25).

A Thought to Anchor in Your Heart

Just as Moses delivered the Israelites from physical slavery, so Jesus—the greater Deliverer—has delivered you from slavery to sin. Rejoice!

Leviticus

God is holy. He desires His people to be holy as well.

Leviticus was written by Moses between 1445 and 1405 BC. The book contains multiple ceremonial and ritual rules and regulations designed to govern every imaginable aspect of life among the ancient Israelites. Following the exodus of the Israelites from Egypt, Israel was called to a new way of life, involving priests, tabernacle worship, sacrifices, and the like, making such rules and regulations necessary. So Leviticus contains laws about offerings and sacrifices (Leviticus 1–7); laws on the appointment and conduct of priests (8–10); laws about ritual cleansing, personal hygiene, and food (11–15); instructions regarding the Day of Atonement (16); and information and laws regarding Israel's festivals (17–27).

Timeline

1526—Moses is born.

1446—The first Jewish Passover is celebrated; the Jews leave Egypt.

1445—The Ten Commandments are given.

1445—The tabernacle is built and dedicated.

1445–1405—Moses writes Leviticus.

This book takes its name from the Levites, the priestly tribe in ancient Israel. Leviticus literally means "pertaining to the Levites." It was written essentially for the priests, who were then to instruct God's people on these laws.

> "A true love to God must begin with a delight in his holiness."
>
> —*Jonathan Edwards (1703–1758)*

Perhaps the most pivotal statement in the book of Leviticus is this: "I am the LORD your God. Consecrate yourselves therefore, and be holy, for I am holy" (Leviticus 11:44). A bit later in the book, the Lord repeated, "Speak to all the congregation of the people of Israel and say to them, You shall be holy, for I the LORD your God am holy" (19:2). All the laws, rules, and regulations contained in this book are merely an outgrowth of the call to be holy. The Israelites were to be holy (or separate) from the pagan nations around them. And since God, as the divine Ruler, had made a covenant with the Israelites, the Israelites were obligated to obey the holiness stipulations of the covenant.

> "I believe the holier a man becomes, the more he mourns over the unholiness which remains in him."
>
> —*Charles Spurgeon (1834–1892)*

The regulations regarding the tabernacle and sacrificial system are no longer binding on us today, for Christ's sacrifice was once-for-all, rendering the entire

Leviticus

Old Testament sacrificial system obsolete (Hebrews 9:13–10:18). Nor are the food laws about hygiene binding on us today (Colossians 2:16-17). What *does* remain is God's holiness and His call on His followers to live in holiness (1 Peter 1:15-16).

Following are key applicational concepts in Leviticus:

God's holiness has profound implications for how you live.

The underlying theme of Leviticus is God's holiness: "I am the LORD your God...I am holy" (Leviticus 11:44). "I the LORD your God am holy" (19:2).

Biblically, God's holiness means not just that He is entirely separate from evil but also that He is absolutely righteous. He is pure in every way. He is separate from all that is morally imperfect.

A key ramification of this is that if we want to fellowship with God, we have to take personal holiness seriously. Walking daily with God in fellowship necessarily involves living in a way that is pleasing to Him. And that is the secondary emphasis in the book of Leviticus. Because God is holy, God's people must be holy: "Be holy, for I am holy" (Leviticus 11:44). "You shall be holy, for I the LORD your God am holy" (19:2).

We find the need for God's people to be holy repeated in the New Testament: "As he who called you is holy, you also be holy in all your conduct" (1 Peter 1:15). "God has not called us for impurity, but in holiness" (1 Thessalonians 4:7). "Strive for peace with everyone, and for the holiness without which no one will see the Lord" (Hebrews 12:14; see also 1 John 1:5,7). My friend, I urge you to take this seriously. Holiness is a big deal to God.

God Is Holy
- "Majestic in holiness" (Exodus 15:11)
- "There is none holy like the Lord" (1 Samuel 2:2)
- "The Lord our God is holy" (Psalm 99:9)
- His "name is Holy" (Isaiah 57:15)
- "Holy, holy, holy" (Isaiah 6:3; Revelation 4:8)
- "The Holy One in your midst" (Hosea 11:9)

There is a right way and a wrong way to worship God.

In the context of the book of Leviticus, the right way of worship hinged on God's laws regarding offerings and sacrifices—including general laws on the burnt offering (Leviticus 1:1-17), grain offering (2:1-16), peace offering (3:1-17), sin offering (4:1–5:13), and guilt offering (5:14–6:7). We also find *specific* laws on the burnt offering (6:8-13), grain offering (6:14-23), sin offering (6:24-30), guilt offering (7:1-10), and peace offering (7:11-38). Careful attention to these ritual requirements was necessary for all the people.

Today we no longer follow such ceremonial laws on worship, for they passed away with the coming of Jesus Christ (Romans 10:4). The New Testament—along with supplementary insights from Psalms—tells us all we need to know about proper worship today.

The New Testament teaches that God alone is to be worshiped—not human beings, not angels, not idols, not anything else (Matthew 4:10; Acts 14:11-18; Revelation 19:10). Worship involves reverencing God, adoring Him, praising Him, venerating Him, and paying homage to Him, not just outwardly in a corporate setting, but in our hearts as well.

The church is a place of worship. The Hebrew word for worship, *shaha*, means "to bow down" or "to prostrate oneself" (Genesis 22:5; 42:6). Likewise, the New Testament word for worship, *proskuneo*, means "to prostrate oneself" (Matthew 2:2,8,11). In Old English, "worship" was rendered "worthship," pointing to the worthiness of the God we worship. Such worship is the proper response of a creature to the divine Creator (Psalm 95:6). Worship can be congregational in nature (1 Corinthians 11–14) or individual (Romans 12:1). Worship does not stop on earth, but continues in heaven when believers enter into glory (Revelation 4–5).

> "God is not moved or impressed with our worship until our hearts are moved and impressed by Him."
>
> —*Kelly Sparks*

The backdrop to combining praise and song in worship of God is found in the psalms. Psalm 28:7 says, "My heart exults, and with my song I give thanks to him." Psalm 69:30 says, "I will praise the name of God with a song." Psalm 95:2 says, "Let us come into his presence with thanksgiving; let us make a joyful noise to him with songs of praise!" Psalm 149:1 says, "Praise the LORD! Sing to the LORD a new song."

The New Testament continues the emphasis on praise and song. Ephesians 5:19-20 says we should address "one another in psalms and hymns and spiritual songs, singing and making melody to the Lord with your heart, giving thanks always and for everything to God the Father in the name of our Lord Jesus Christ." Colossians 3:16 likewise instructs, "Let the word of Christ dwell in you richly, teaching and admonishing one another in all wisdom, singing psalms and hymns and spiritual songs."

Jesus accepted worship from

- Thomas (John 20:28);
- the angels (Hebrews 1:6);
- wise men (Matthew 2:11);
- a ruler (Matthew 9:18);
- a blind man (John 9:38);
- Mary Magdalene (Matthew 28:9); and
- the disciples (Matthew 28:17).

Of course, because Jesus is the heart of Christianity, much of our worship should center on Him. Jesus—as God—is to be worshiped just as the Father is worshiped (Revelation 4–5). He was worshiped (Greek: *proskuneo*) as God many times according to the Gospel accounts—and He always accepted such worship as perfectly appropriate.

The sacrificial system shows the heavy cost to be paid for sin: a life for a life.

The Day of Atonement was annually celebrated on the tenth day of the seventh month of the Jewish calendar—the month of Tishri (September/October). Only once a year could Aaron (or the high priest) enter into the Holy of Holies, the innermost part of the tabernacle, where the Ark of the Covenant was located. Before doing this, however, he had to secure forgiveness for his own sins. He did this by sacrificing a bull as a sin offering for himself, and he would sprinkle some of the blood in front of the Ark of the Covenant (Leviticus 4:5; 16; 23:27).

Only after the high priest's sin had been forgiven could he then go on to offer sacrifices on behalf of the people of Israel. He would first kill a goat for the sins of the people. Then hands were laid on a second goat, and the high priest would symbolically transfer the guilt of the people to it, after which it was driven into the desert to symbolize that their sins had been carried away.

Since these sacrifices took place annually, the Israelites were reminded year in and year out that sin cut them off from God, so there was a regular need for atonement. This makes the sacrifice of Christ all the more important, for His sacrifice was once-for-all (Hebrews 9:9; 10:10). He gave His life for us! What an awesome Savior we have in Jesus.

Obedience to God brings blessing. Disobedience brings chastisement.

> "It might be well if we stopped using the words 'victory' and 'defeat' to describe our progress in holiness. Rather we should use the words 'obedience' and 'disobedience.'"
>
> —*Jerry Bridges*

A theme found not only in Leviticus but throughout the Bible is that obedience brings blessing whereas disobedience brings chastisement. In Leviticus, God instructs, "If you walk in my statutes and observe my commandments and do them, then I will give you your rains in their season, and the land shall yield its increase, and the trees of the field shall yield their fruit" (Leviticus 26:3-4). Other blessings would come as well, including dwelling securely in the land, peace in the land, and victory over all enemies.

By contrast, dire consequences would result "if you will not listen to me and will not do all these commandments, if you spurn my statutes, and if your soul abhors my rules, so that you will not do all my commandments, but break my covenant" (Leviticus 26:14-15). The people would suffer disease, defeat at the hands of their enemies, failed crops, and much more.

Once we get to New Testament times, a primary emphasis is that we show our love for Christ by our obedience to Him. "If you love me, you will keep my commandments" (John 14:15). "Whoever has my commandments and keeps them, he it is who loves me. And he who loves me will be loved by my Father, and I will love him and manifest myself to him" (John 14:21). "This is the love of God, that we keep his commandments" (1 John 5:3). Those who obey Christ are even called Christ's friends: "You are my friends if you do what I command you" (John 15:14).

A Thought to Anchor in Your Heart

Make every effort to be best friends with Jesus.

Numbers

God's people sometimes experience divine purging and discipline in preparation for great blessing. Unbelief is the big hindrance to watch out for.

Timeline

1526—Moses is born.

1444—Israel camps at Mount Sinai.

1443—The spies check out Canaan.

1445–1405—Moses writes Numbers.

1406—Moses dies; Joshua is appointed; Israel enters into Canaan.

Cross-References: Censuses

Exodus 38:26 • Numbers 26:51 • 2 Samuel 24:9 • 1 Chronicles 21:5 • 2 Chronicles 2:17-18 • Ezra 2:64 • Luke 2:1

Moses wrote the book of Numbers between 1445 and 1405 BC (see Numbers 33:2; 36:13). Numbers documents the 40-year period from the giving of the Law at Sinai up until the conquest of Canaan.

The title of this book derives from the two censuses recorded in the book, one at Mount Sinai (the original Exodus generation) and one on the plains of Moab (the generation that grew up in the wilderness and conquered Canaan—see Numbers 1 and 26). Obviously, censuses involve "numberings" or countings of people.

Aside from these censuses, the book also contains a listing of the tribes of Israel (Numbers 2), regulations for the priests and Levites (3–8), information about the Passover (9), a chronicle of Israel moving from Mount Sinai to Moab on the border of Canaan (10–21), a record of Balaam and Balak (22–32), and the Israelites' journey coming to an end (33–36).

One thing in this book that stands out with practical value for believers today is that God blesses obedience to His laws but brings discipline to those who are disobedient. While the people of Israel initially had faith in God as they were delivered from Egyptian bondage, their faith soon gave way to perpetual grumbling and rebellion, and, as a result, this brought God's disciplinary judgment. This judgment caused an 11-day journey (about 220 miles) to expand to a lifetime of travel—40 years' worth. Had they been obedient, the trip would have been short, and the majority of the original Exodus generation would have entered the Promised Land instead of a mere handful. As it was, it was mostly the children of

these grumblers who entered the land and enjoyed the promises that had originally been made.

Following are key applicational concepts in Numbers:

Being organized is good, but sanctification is more important.

Numbers begins with a census of the people (Numbers 1:1–4:49). Instructions are then given regarding the position of the
tribes in camp and on the march (2:1-34). The plac-
ing of the Levites is discussed (3:1–4:49). Things were
well organized. More important, however, Moses
urged sanctification—that is, keeping away from
defiled things (5:1-31), taking a Nazirite vow (6:1-27),
giving offerings (7:1-89), ensuring the consecration of
the Levites (8:1-26), observing the Passover (9:1-14),
and following God (9:15–10:10). The wilderness
sojourn, despite being well organized, would fail
unless there was true spiritual commitment among the people.

> **Verses to Remember**
>
> "The LORD bless you and keep you; the LORD make his face to shine upon you and be gracious to you; the LORD lift up his countenance upon you and give you peace."
>
> —*Numbers 6:24-26*

Numbers

God is a promise keeper.

Recall God's promise to Abraham in Genesis 15:5:
"Look toward heaven, and number the stars, if you are
able to number them…. So shall your offspring be."
When Joseph brought Jacob's family to Egypt, they
numbered just 70 persons (Genesis 46:27). Numbers
1:46 tells us the Jewish people now numbered 603,550. Balaam would later ask,
"Who can count the dust of Jacob or number the fourth part of Israel?" (Numbers 23:10). God is a promise keeper!

> "Not one word of all the good promises that the LORD had made to the house of Israel had failed; all came to pass."
>
> —*Joshua 21:45*

Keep God at the center of your life.

Numbers 2 tells us about the layout of the various
tribes. Notice that the tabernacle was placed at the
very center of the camp, with the various tribes being
placed around the tabernacle. We can infer from this
placement that God was supposed to be at the heart
and center of the Jewish community. Certainly the Lord ought to be at the heart
and center of our lives, our families, and our churches.

> "Seek first the kingdom of God and his righteousness, and all these things will be added to you."
>
> —*Matthew 6:33*

Numbers

Two key verses point to the wisdom of centering our lives on the Lord. Jesus said, "Apart from me you can do nothing" (John 15:5). The apostle Paul affirmed, "I can do all things through him who strengthens me" (Philippians 4:13).

It is unwise to break your commitments to God.

The backdrop to much of what we see happening throughout Numbers relates to the establishment of the Sinai Covenant. God's covenant with Israel at Mount Sinai constituted the formal basis of the redemptive relationship between God and the Israelites (Exodus 19:3-25). This covenant was couched in terms of ancient Hittite suzerainty treaties made between a king and his subjects. In such treaties, there would always be a preamble naming the author of the treaty, a historical introduction depicting the relationship between the respective parties, a list of required stipulations explaining the responsibilities of each of the parties, a promise of either blessing or judgment invoked depending on faithfulness or unfaithfulness to the treaty, a solemn oath, and a religious ratification of the treaty. In such treaties, the motivation for obedience to the stipulations was the undeserved favor of the king making the treaty. Out of gratitude, the people were to obey the stipulations.

Such parallels between ancient treaties and God's covenant with Israel show that God communicated to His people in ways they were already familiar with. Key parallels between such treaties and the Sinai Covenant are that God gave stipulations to the people explaining their responsibilities (the Law, Exodus 20:1-17), and then gave a promise of blessing for obeying the law and a promise of judgment for disobeying the law (Deuteronomy 28). Tragically, Israel was often disobedient to God's covenant (Exodus 32:1-31). In this covenant, blessing was conditioned on obedience.

As we consider the book of Numbers, we see that death often resulted from

The Gist of the Book

"Then the Lord said, 'I will pardon them as you have requested. But as surely as I live, and as surely as the earth is filled with the Lord's glory, not one of these people will ever enter that land. They have all seen my glorious presence and the miraculous signs I performed both in Egypt and in the wilderness, but again and again they have tested me by refusing to listen to my voice. They will never even see the land I swore to give their ancestors. None of those who have treated me with contempt will ever see it.'"

—*Numbers 14:20-23* NLT

Israel's Three Big Problems

- Fear (Numbers 14:9)
- Unbelief (Numbers 20:12)
- Complaining (Numbers 11:1)

"Complaining about our lot in life may seem quite innocent in itself, but God takes it personally."

—*Erwin Lutzer*

the covenant failures of God's people, whether on an individual or group basis (Numbers 15:32-36; 25:6-9). Moses himself was barred from entering the Promised Land because of his disobedience (20:10-13). Nevertheless, God in His grace eventually saw to it that the faithful among His people made it to the Promised Land.

It's simple—complaining displeases God.

Numbers 11:1 tells us, "The people complained in the hearing of the LORD about their misfortunes." This understandably angered the Lord. God had provided them everything they needed, and yet they complained about everything. Such complaints were like a slap in the face of God, telling Him, "You haven't done good enough." Had they been a thankful people, events would have turned out much differently for them.

Scripture often speaks of the importance of being thankful. One of the more famous verses is Psalm 100:4: "Enter his gates with thanksgiving, and his courts with praise! Give thanks to him; bless his name!"

Thankfulness to God
- Give thanks forever—Psalm 30:12
- Honor God with thanksgiving—Psalm 69:30
- Come before God with thanksgiving—Psalm 95:2
- Sacrifice of thanksgiving—Psalm 116:17
- Always give thanks—Ephesians 5:20
- Overflow with thanksgiving—Colossians 2:7

Numbers

The majority is not necessarily right. Going along with the crowd can get you into trouble.

In Kadesh, Jewish scouts were dispatched into the land of Canaan to report on the fortifications of the enemies (Numbers 13:1-24). The majority of the scouts—all but two—wimped out with their reports (13:25-33). We might translate their words in modern vernacular this way: "Forget it. No can do. It's a no-go. The enemy will squash us like bugs. We're outta here." The problem was, the majority was in the wrong. Only two spies proved faithful, ready to depend on God and His promises. Everyone else panicked.

Continue to trust in God, even when the odds appear to be heavily stacked against you.

Granted, the Israelite spies saw a major opponent ahead of them: "There we saw the Nephilim (the sons of Anak, who come from the Nephilim), and we seemed to ourselves like grasshoppers, and so we

"Trusting God means looking beyond what we can see to what God sees."

—*Charles Stanley*

seemed to them" (Numbers 13:33). Their mistake, however, was leaving God out of the picture. Here are the two possible outcomes:

Israelites ALONE against the enemy = defeat.

Israelites WITH GOD against the enemy = victory.

Unfortunately, the majority of the spies held to option 1. They became fearful and succumbed to unbelief, an unbelief that cost them dearly. Had they trusted in God—despite the odds being stacked against them—they would have had an entirely different outcome.

Beware: unbelief is highly contagious. It spreads like wildfire.

As soon as the majority of the spies gave a negative report, unbelief spread like wildfire among the camp. We here witness the domino effect—the people went down like dominoes, full of fear and unbelief. "All the congregation raised a loud cry, and the people wept that night. And all the people of Israel grumbled against Moses and Aaron" (Numbers 14:1-2).

Cross-References: Unbelief

Numbers 20:12 • Psalm 78:32 • 95:8 • Matthew 13:58 • Mark 9:24 • 16:14,16 • Luke 8:12,18 • 18:8 • 24:25-36 • John 6:64 • 7:5 • 10:25 • 12:37 • 20:27 • Acts 19:9 • Romans 11:20 • 2 Corinthians 6:14 • Hebrews 3:12 • 11:6 • 12:25 • James 1:6 • 2 Peter 3:4

The New Testament consistently urges believers against fear (John 14:27; Romans 8:31; 2 Timothy 1:7). A great antidote to fear is to meditate on Bible verses that speak of God's absolute control of all things: Deuteronomy 10:14; 1 Chronicles 29:12; 2 Chronicles 20:6; Job 42:2; Psalm 33:8-11; 47:2; Isaiah 46:10; Ephesians 1:20-22; and John 14:1-3.

A short-term lack of trusting God can have long-term negative consequences.

After the spies gave a gloomy report, fear and unbelief spread among Israel's camp. They trusted in the naysayers instead of trusting in God's promises. As a result of their unbelief, God sentenced them to wandering in the desert for 40 years. Their short-term unbelief brought about long-term negative consequences. During this time, the original generation died out and hope grew as a new generation emerged.

A New Testament Application

In Old Testament times, unbelief and hardened hearts kept people out of the Promised Land (Numbers).

Unbelief and hardened hearts can also keep modern Christians out of the abundant life of rest (Hebrews 3:7-19).

It may be sobering for some to reach old age and then look back over their lives, asking, "How might my life have turned out differently had I not succumbed to fear and unbelief throughout my life?"

Life on earth can be hard, but your reward awaits you in the afterlife.

Moses did not enter the Promised Land because of his sin against God (Numbers 20:10-13). God instructed Moses, "Go up into this mountain of Abarim and see the land that I have given to the people of Israel. When you have seen it, you also shall be gathered to your people, as your brother Aaron was" (27:12-13). Death is a universal experience. Like all of his ancestors before him, Moses died and was "gathered" to his people in heaven. You and I, too, will one day be gathered to our people—that is, Christians in heaven (1 Thessalonians 4:13-17).

> **A Thought to Anchor in Your Heart**
> Beware of fear, unbelief, and complaining.
> They will bring you down!

Deuteronomy

Each new generation of people needs to hear the
Word of God with a challenge to obey it.

Timeline

1526—Moses is born.

1446—The Jews depart Egypt
under Moses's leadership.

1444—Israel camps at Mount
Sinai.

1410—Moses writes the book
of Deuteronomy.

1406—Moses dies; Joshua is
appointed; Israel enters into
Canaan.

The book of Deuteronomy, written by Moses in about 1410 BC, contains the words Moses spoke to the Israelites as they were camped in the plains of Moab, preparing to enter into the Promised Land (Deuteronomy 1:1). This was Moses's farewell address, and he was passing the mantle on to Joshua.

Some scholars have argued that Moses could not have written Deuteronomy, for the last chapter in the book records his death. It appears that another person—likely Joshua—penned the last chapter of Deuteronomy and appended it to what Moses had already written. It was not uncommon in biblical days for a person to append an obituary to the work of a great man (Deuteronomy 1:5; 31:9,22,24; 1 Kings 2:3; 8:53; 2 Kings 14:6; 18:12; Matthew 19:7-8).

In any event, the word "deuteronomy" literally means "second law," and accurately describes some of the book's contents. Indeed, the Ten Commandments recorded in Exodus 20 are repeated in Deuteronomy 5, with minor variations. Other laws recorded in Exodus are also repeated in Deuteronomy.

The book also contains a restatement and reaffirmation of the covenant God made with the Israelites at Sinai (Deuteronomy 1–30). The covenant is couched in terms of ancient Hittite suzerainty treaties made between a king and his subjects. In such treaties, there would always be a preamble naming the author of the treaty, a historical introduction depicting the relationship between the respective parties, a list of required stipulations explaining the responsibilities of each of the parties, a promise of either blessing or judgment invoked depending on faithfulness or unfaithfulness to the treaty, a solemn oath, and a religious ratification of the treaty. Such parallels between ancient treaties and God's covenant with Israel show that God communicated with His people in ways familiar to them.

Following are key applicational concepts in Deuteronomy:

It is helpful to periodically review your past victories and defeats, as well as God's past acts of faithfulness.

In the opening chapters of Deuteronomy, Moses provided a historical review of the wilderness sojourn, focusing heavily on God's mighty acts. He reviewed the sending out of the spies (Deuteronomy 1:19-25), the murmuring of the Israelites (1:26-46), the conquest of Transjordan (2:26–3:20), the division of the land (3:12-20), and his being forbidden to cross the Jordan (3:21-29). He exhorted his people to learn from their past and obey the Lord (4). It is always wise to learn lessons from our past experiences.

> "History is a story written by the finger of God."
>
> —*C. S. Lewis (1898–1963)*

Review God's Word on a consistent basis.

Moses reviewed with his people the stipulations of God's covenant. He reiterated the Ten Commandments (Deuteronomy 5:1-33) and the command to love the Lord (6:1-25), and gave instructions about loving each other in the Promised Land (7:1-26). He exhorted the people to not forget the Lord (8:1-20), issued a warning based on past infidelities (9:1–10:11), and exhorted all to revere the Lord (10:12–11:32). Moses then set forth covenant stipulations on proper worship (12:1–16:17), running the nation (16:18–19:21), warfare (20), interpersonal relationships (21:1–25:19), and firstfruits and tithes (26).

Moses provided this review as the Israelites were camped in the plains of Moab, preparing to enter into the Promised Land. This review was critically important because it would keep their priorities straight in their new land.

A continual reviewing of God's Word is beneficial to us as well. Let us never forget what Paul said about God's Word in 2 Timothy 3:16-17: "All Scripture is breathed out by God and profitable for teaching, for reproof, for correction, and for training in righteousness, that the man of God may be complete, equipped for every good work." Reviewing God's Word will keep you equipped and on track!

> "I have stored up your word in my heart, that I might not sin against you."
>
> —*Psalm 119:11*

Don't ever be deceived: there is only one true God.

Deuteronomy 6:4 tells us, "Hear, O Israel: The LORD our God, the LORD is one." I believe the text is best rendered from the Hebrew, "Hear, O Israel! The Lord is our God, the Lord alone." It is an affirmation that despite the multiple alleged deities of paganism, there is truly only one God, and that is the God of whom Moses spoke.

This affirmation of faith was known as the Shema among the ancient Jews. When we consider that the Israelites had been delivered from Egypt—a land brimming with false gods and idols—the importance of the Shema is obvious. The Jews made a habit of reciting this affirmation twice a day—once in the morning and once in the evening. They also required children to memorize it at an early age.

Cross-References: One True God
Deuteronomy 4:35,39 • 6:4 • James 2:19 • 1 Corinthians 8:4 • 1 Kings 8:60

Obedience brings blessing from the Lord. Disobedience brings chastisement.

Moses described the terms of the covenant and called for obedience, which would bring blessing. Abandoning God's covenant, by contrast, would bring severe consequences (Deuteronomy 29). Prosperity comes only in staying close to the Lord (30:1-10). A covenant offer of life or death was given to the people (30:11-20). Moses urged them to choose life by obeying God.

Consequences of Sin
• Separation from God—Ephesians 4:17-19
• Wages of sin is death—Romans 6:23
• Causes us to do what we don't want to do—Romans 7:14-15

As we consult the rest of Scripture, we find that obedience to God has many benefits. Obedience to God brings blessing (Luke 11:28), long life (1 Kings 3:14; John 8:51), happiness (Psalm 112:1; 119:56), peace (Proverbs 1:33), and a state of well-being (Jeremiah 7:23; see also Exodus 19:5; Leviticus 26:3-4; Deuteronomy 4:40; 12:28; 28:1; Joshua 1:8; 1 Chronicles 22:13; Isaiah 1:19).

"Family life is a school for character."

—Martin Luther (1483–1546)

"The home is God's built-in training facility."

—Charles Swindoll

Parents ought to always impress God's Word upon their children.

Deuteronomy 6:6-7 tells us, "These words that I command you today shall be on your heart. You shall teach them diligently to your children, and shall talk of them when you sit in your house, and when you walk by the way, and when you lie down, and when you rise." The phrase "teach them diligently to your children" can also be rendered "*impress* them on your

Deuteronomy (side tab)

children." The term *impress* literally means "to whet." We are to whet our children's appetites for the things of God. Our goal is to make the things of God palatable to our children so they will grow in their appetite of it.

The word "impress" is also a present tense word. This means the "impressing" is to be a continuous and ongoing activity. It's not only a Sunday thing. It's a seven-day-a-week thing.

A secondary meaning of the Hebrew word for impress is "to sharpen." We are to sharpen our children's minds with God's Word so their thinking patterns will reflect His will. As we continue to impress the things of God upon our children's minds, they will increasingly build a Christian worldview—a grid through which they will see and interpret everything around them.

The method we are to use in teaching our children about God and loving God is to relate what the Scriptures say to the context of all of life—when you sit down, when you walk around, when you lie down, and when you rise up. As you go about your day in the normal circumstances of life, teach your children what you have been taught and have learned and discovered in your own experience.

> "If you neglect to instruct children in the way of holiness, will the devil neglect to instruct them in the way of wickedness? No; if you will not teach them to pray, he will to curse, swear, and lie; if ground be uncultivated, weeds will spring."
>
> —*John Flavel (1627–1691)*

You can only pass on to your children what you already possess.

Notice that God's instruction about impressing the things of God upon our children *follows* the command to "love the LORD your God with all your heart and with all your soul and with all your might" (Deuteronomy 6:5). It's not just that we teach our kids to love God supremely. First and foremost, parents themselves must love God supremely. We cannot pass a love for God on to our children that we ourselves do not already possess. We model for our children what it means to love God.

> "If Christendom is to be helped, one must begin with the children."
>
> —*Martin Luther (1483–1546)*

As God's people, we are to both *fear the Lord* and *love the Lord*.

Deuteronomy 10:12-13 instructs, "And now, Israel, what does the LORD your God require of you, but to fear the LORD your God, to walk in all his ways, to love him, to serve the LORD your God with all your heart and with all your soul, and to keep the commandments and statutes of the LORD, which I am commanding you today for your good?" Though it might sound a bit contradictory, God's people are called to both *fear the Lord* and *love the Lord*. Of course, to "fear" the Lord does not mean we are to have the emotional feeling of being afraid of Him. Rather, the term points to reverence for God—showing Him what might be called "religious awe." There is no conflict in loving God and showing Him great reverence.

Beware: false prophets could lead you astray.

Deuteronomy 18:10-22 warns God's people against false prophets. Verses 21-22 indicate that false prophets are those who give false prophecies that do not come true. As we consult the rest of the Bible, we find that false prophets also sometimes cause people to follow false gods or idols (Exodus 20:3-4; Deuteronomy 13:1-3); deny the deity of Jesus Christ (Colossians 2:8-9); deny the humanity of Jesus Christ (1 John 4:1-2); advocate abstaining from certain foods and/or meats for spiritual reasons (1 Timothy 4:3-4); deprecate or deny the need for marriage (1 Timothy 4:3); promote immorality (Jude 4-7); and encourage legalistic self-denial (Colossians 2:16-23).

Here is a basic rule of thumb: if a so-called prophet says anything that clearly contradicts any part of God's Word, his teachings should be rejected (Acts 17:11; 1 Thessalonians 5:21).

Beware of false religions—they often involve destructive practices and can easily contaminate God's people.

The primary false religious system faced by the Israelites was that of Canaanite paganism (Deuteronomy 7). The Canaanites were polytheists who were intent on spreading their false religion as far as they could. They believed that behind the world of nature were numerous gods and goddesses that controlled

Fear of the Lord Motivates
- obedience to God—Deuteronomy 5:29; Ecclesiastes 12:13;
- service to God—Deuteronomy 6:13; and
- the avoidance of evil—Proverbs 3:7; 8:13; 16:6.

Definition: False Prophets
False prophets are individuals who pretend to be genuine spokesmen for God but in fact propagate false doctrine (Matthew 7:15-16; 2 Corinthians 11:2-3; Acts 20:28-30). For this reason, the Bible exhorts believers to test those who claim to be prophets (1 John 4:1-2).

God's Abhorrence of False Religions
Again and again the Bible implies and states that God hates, despises, and utterly rejects anything associated with heathen false religions and practices.

Those who follow such idolatry are not regarded as groping their way to God but rather as having turned their backs on Him, following the ways of darkness.

various events. El was considered the chief among the Canaanite deities. Likened to a bull in a herd of cows, the people referred to him as "father bull" and regarded him as creator. Asherah was the wife of El.

Chief among the 70 gods and goddesses considered offspring of El and Asherah was Hadad, more commonly known as Baal, meaning "Lord." As reigning king of the gods, Baal controlled heaven and earth. As god of rain and storm, he was responsible for vegetation and fertility, and so his blessing was critical to the Canaanites in obtaining good harvests. Anath, the goddess who loved war, was his sister as well as his spouse. These and many other gods were part and parcel of the Canaanite pantheon.

The Canaanites often gave sacrifices to their gods—sometimes involving an animal, but at other times humans (Hosea 13:2). This, of course, was considered an abomination to God (Deuteronomy 12:13).

God therefore warns His people to avoid being contaminated by such false religion: "You shall not intermarry with them, giving your daughters to their sons or taking their daughters for your sons, for they would turn away your sons from following me, to serve other gods" (Deuteronomy 7:3-4). God's will is clear: Come out and be separate (2 Corinthians 6:17).

Jesus is the greater prophet of whom Moses spoke. Jesus must always be your top authority.

In Deuteronomy 18:15-18 Moses said, "The Lord your God will raise up for you a prophet like me from among you, from your brothers—it is to him you shall listen," and God said of this greater prophet, "I will put my words in his mouth, and he shall speak to them all that I command him."

Jesus perfectly fulfilled these verses, since (1) He was from among His Jewish brethren (Galatians 4:4). (2) He fulfilled the affirmation in Deuteronomy 18:18 that this prophet speaks only what God commands of Him. After all, Jesus said, "I do nothing on my own authority, but speak just as the Father taught me" (John 8:28). And, "I have not spoken on my own authority, but the Father who sent me has himself given me a commandment—what to say and what to speak" (John 12:49). (3) He called Himself a "prophet"

Three Offices of Jesus

As a *Prophet*, Jesus gave the Upper Room Discourse (John 14–16), the Olivet Discourse (Matthew 24–25), and the Sermon on the Mount (Matthew 5–7).

As our divine *High Priest*, Jesus represents the Father to us and represents us to the Father (2 Timothy 2:5; Hebrews 7:25,27).

Jesus is also the messianic *King* (2 Samuel 7:16; Psalm 2:6; 110; Daniel 7:13-14).

(Luke 13:33), and the people considered Him a prophet (Matthew 21:11; Luke 7:16). More broadly, Scripture reveals Jesus was a *Prophet* (speaking to men for God), a *Priest* (speaking to God for men, Hebrews 7–10), and a *King* (reigning over men for God, Revelation 19–20).

Deuteronomy 18:15 prophesied that this prophet would be "like" Moses. Interestingly, as babies, both Moses and Jesus had death plots initiated against them (Exodus 1:15-16,22, Matthew 2:13-15); both of them were rescued as a result of divine intervention (Exodus 2:2-10, Matthew 2:13-15); both of them were authenticated by signs and wonders (Exodus 7:10,19,20; 8–12; Matthew 8:14-17; 14:13; Luke 7:11); Moses liberated the Israelites from bondage in Egypt, while Christ liberated believers from the bondage of sin (Exodus; Isaiah 53; John 8:32-36; Romans 6:18-22, 8:2; Galatians 5:1); Moses spoke to God "face to face," as did Christ on the Mount of Transfiguration (Exodus 33:11, Matthew 17:3); and Moses was the mediator of the old covenant, whereas Christ was the mediator of the new covenant (Exodus 19 and 20, Hebrews 12:24).

We can also observe that in Acts 3:19-23 the apostle Peter indicates Jesus is the fulfillment of the prophet prophesied in Deuteronomy 18. No wonder Jesus said to some Jewish critics, "If you believed Moses, you would believe me; for he wrote of me" (John 5:46). Now, here is a point not to miss: since Jesus is the great prophet—indeed, since He is the very Son of God (John 3:16)—it is incumbent on us to listen to Him and obey Him in all things.

Don't be disappointed if you don't always get all the answers you want on this side of eternity.

Deuteronomy 29:29 tells us, "The secret things belong to the LORD our God, but the things that are revealed belong to us and to our children forever, that we may do all the words of this law." Such a statement is understandable in view of the fact that God is omniscient (all-knowing) while man has finite understanding. We will never fully understand God's thoughts: "My thoughts are not your thoughts, neither are your ways my ways, declares the LORD. For as the heavens are higher than the earth, so are my ways higher than your ways and my thoughts than your thoughts" (Isaiah 55:8-9).

> "Oh, the depth of the riches and wisdom and knowledge of God! How unsearchable are his judgments and how inscrutable his ways!"
>
> —Romans 11:33

Despite God's forgiveness of sin, the temporal consequences of sin may yet remain.

God said to Moses, "This is the land of which I swore to Abraham, to Isaac, and to Jacob, 'I will give it to your offspring.' I have let you see it with your eyes, but you shall not go over there" (Deuteronomy 34:4). We are then told, "So Moses the servant of the LORD died there in the land of Moab, according to the word of the LORD" (34:5). Moses, of course, went straight to heaven. But the temporal consequences of one particular sin remained (Numbers 20:7-13). He therefore died, not being permitted to enter the Promised Land. This is a good lesson for all of us.

A Thought to Anchor in Your Heart

Make it a daily habit to both fear the Lord and love the Lord.

Deuteronomy

Joshua

God has made wondrous promises to His people. His people can either hasten fulfillment of these promises by doing things God's way or throw up a roadblock by engaging in sin or unbelief.

Timeline

1446—The first Jewish Passover is celebrated; the Jews leave Egypt.

1445—The Ten Commandments are given.

1444—Israel camps at Mount Sinai.

1443—The spies check out Canaan.

1406—Moses dies; Joshua is appointed; Israel enters into Canaan.

1405–1385—Joshua writes the book of Joshua.

Jewish tradition affirms that Joshua wrote this book. Parts of the book actually identify Joshua as the author (Joshua 8:32; 24:1-26). Supporting this is the fact that the author was an eyewitness (5:1,6; 18:9; 24:26) who wrote the book close in time to the actual events (6:25; 15:63). An assistant to Joshua—or perhaps the high priest Eleazar—attached comments about Joshua's death, and the events that took place after his death (24:29-33). The book was written between 1405 and 1385 BC.

Joshua was Moses's assistant leader during the Exodus and the desert wanderings (Joshua 1:1). He was an extremely effective military commander and leader, and for this reason, he was a natural successor to Moses (Deuteronomy 34; Joshua 1:1-18). This would have been when Joshua was about 90 years old.

Joshua was one of the only original Israelites who left Egypt to have the faith and courage to enter into the Promised Land (Caleb was the other, Numbers 14:38). Joshua would certainly need this kind of faith and courage in leading the Israelites in conquering Canaan. His name is a shortened form of *Yehoshua*, which literally means "the Lord is salvation." The Lord's "salvation" would be evident in bringing victory over the inhabitants of Canaan. The Canaanites were an evil people, engulfed in such things as religious prostitution, many kinds of sexual perversion, and human sacrifice.

The book of Joshua focuses on Israel's entering the land of Canaan (Joshua 1:1–5:15), Israel's conquering of the land of Canaan (6:1–12:24), and the dividing of the land of Canaan among the 12 tribes of Israel (13:1–24:33), all under the effective leadership of Joshua. All of this is rooted in the land promises given to Abraham and his descendants (Genesis 15:7; 26:2). (Ultimate fulfillment of the land promises comes in Christ's future millennial kingdom.)

Following are key applicational concepts in Joshua:

Regular meditation on the Word of God brings success in life.

Joshua 1:8 instructs, "This Book of the Law shall not depart from your mouth, but you shall meditate on it day and night, so that you may be careful to do according to all that is written in it. For then you will make your way prosperous, and then you will have good success."

Biblical meditation involves pondering God's Word and His faithfulness (Joshua 1:8; Psalm 119:148). The Hebrew word for "meditate" can mean "to utter, imagine, speak, roar, mutter, meditate, and muse." The word is used in Isaiah 31:4 to express the roar of a lion. It is used in Isaiah 38:14 in reference to the sound of the mourning of doves. In both cases, the idea seems to be that outward expression is an outgrowth of strong inner emotions and thought.

> "Meditation is holding the Word of God in the mind until it has affected every area of one's life and character."
>
> —Andrew Murray (1828–1917)

When used of humans, the term carries the basic idea of "murmuring." It portrays a person who is deep in thought, mumbling with his lips as though talking to himself. It is as though strong feelings build up in the innermost depths of his soul, and the pressure is finally released (like steam) in verbal expression. When one meditates on God's Word, one concentrates so intensely that murmuring with the lips can occur.

Such meditation "will make your way prosperous, and then you will have good success" (Joshua 1:8). Contextually, this refers not to financial prosperity but rather to military victory. In the conquest of the Promised Land, God promised Joshua that his military efforts would prosper if he and his followers maintained a commitment to meditate upon and obey God's Word. Of course, we can draw a broader application, recognizing that our endeavors in life will be successful to the extent that we stay rooted in God's Word and obey it (compare with Psalm 1).

Life-saving carries more ethical weight than truth-telling.

Joshua sent in spies to check out Jericho. They lodged at Rahab's house. The pagan king became aware of this and commanded Rahab, "Bring out the men who have come to you, who entered your house, for they have come to search out all the land" (Joshua 2:3).

Rahab lied: "True, the men came to me, but I did not know where they were from. And when the gate was about to be closed at dark, the men went out. I do not know where the men went. Pursue them quickly, for you will overtake them" (Joshua 2:4-5). For this, Rahab was commended in the Hebrews Faith Hall of Fame (Hebrews 11:31).

> "Absolute moral laws sometimes run into inevitable conflict. In such cases it is our moral duty to do the lesser evil. We must break the lesser law and plead mercy. For instance, we should lie to save the life and then ask for forgiveness for breaking God's absolute moral law."
>
> —Norman Geisler

Rahab was faced with a moral dilemma. Should she lie to her government, or save the lives of the spies? Since life-saving is a higher obligation than truth-telling, God did not hold her responsible for the lie but rather honored her in the Hebrews Faith Hall of Fame.

Of course, this was a unique situation that should not be taken to mean it is okay for Christians to go around telling lies. Scripture forbids lying (Exodus 20:16). It is an abomination to God (Proverbs 12:22; see also Psalm 59:12). Righteous men hate lying (Proverbs 13:5). In the present case, lying was a last resort engineered to save lives.

Some people are so heinously wicked and evil that to protect the broader pool of innocent humanity it becomes necessary for good people to use lethal force against them.

God instructed Joshua and his army to drive out and destroy the Canaanites (Joshua 3:10). God's command was issued not because God is cruel and vindictive, but because the Canaanites were so horrible, so evil, so oppressive, and so cancerous to society that, like a human cancer, the only option was complete removal.

God's Wrath

- God is a God of love (Psalm 33:5; 86:5; Jeremiah 31:3; 1 John 4:8).
- Yet He is also a holy God (Leviticus 11:44; Psalm 99:9; Isaiah 6:3).
- He therefore shows wrath against sin (Revelation 20:11-15).

These were people who were burning their children alive in honor of their false gods, engaging in sex with animals, and all sorts of other loathsome practices (Leviticus 18:23-24; 20:3). They were unrepentant in all these activities. Human society itself would have been poisoned without the utter removal of the cancerous Canaanites. God would have been showing utter disregard for the broader pool of innocent humanity if He had not acted to stop this gangrenous nation from taking over all society.

One must keep in mind that the Canaanites had had plenty of time to repent. The biblical pattern is that when nations repent, God withholds promised judgment (Jeremiah 18:7-8). This principle is clearly illustrated for us in the case of the Ninevites, who repented and averted promised judgment (Jonah 3). God is often seen showing mercy where repentance is evident (Exodus 32:14; 2 Samuel 24:16; Amos 7:3,6).

The Canaanites were not acting blindly. They had heard of the God of the Israelites and knew what was expected of them, but they defied Him and continued in their sinful ways. They were ripe for judgment.

God is a God of miracles. He can do things beyond all imagination.

Joshua 6 describes the miraculous fall of the walls of Jericho. God's instructions to Joshua and his people were to walk around the city of Jericho for six days in a row, and then on the seventh day walk around the city seven times. God promised, "The priests shall blow the trumpets. And when they make a long blast with the ram's horn, when you hear the sound of the trumpet, then all the people shall shout with a great shout, and the wall of the city will fall down flat" (Joshua 6:4-5). The people did as instructed. The walls of Jericho fell flat. My friend, we must get used to the idea that God can do things beyond all imagination. He can do the seemingly impossible (Matthew 19:26).

We find another example of God's mighty miracles in Joshua 10. Sunlight was waning as Joshua and his army were doing battle against the Amorites. Joshua therefore commanded the sun to stand still (10:12-13). We are told, "The sun stopped in the midst of heaven and did not hurry to set for about a whole day. There has been no day like it before or since, when the LORD heeded the voice of a man, for the LORD fought for Israel" (10:13-14).

Miracles

- C. S. Lewis defines a miracle as "an interference with nature by supernatural power."
- J. Gresham Machen defines a miracle as "an event in the external world that is wrought by the immediate power of God."
- J. I. Packer says a miracle is "an observed event that triggers awareness of God's presence and power."

Don't Put God in a Box

- Don't limit God with your preconceived notions about what He can and cannot do.
- God is able to "do far more abundantly than all that we ask or think" (Ephesians 3:20).

Joshua

God stopped the earth's rotation on its axis. Such a miracle poses no problem for the Almighty God of the universe. Performing a mighty miracle (stopping the earth's rotation) is no more difficult for Him than performing a minor miracle (withering a fig tree). Interestingly, the Amorites worshiped the sun and the moon as deities. The true God brought about the defeat of the Amorites through the agency of their own supposed deities.

> "If there is a God who can act, then there can be acts of God. The only way to show that miracles are impossible is to disprove the existence of God."
>
> —Norman Geisler

God is a promise keeper.

Joshua 6:17 tells us all of Jericho was marked for destruction except Rahab's dwelling: "The city and all that is within it shall be devoted to the LORD for destruction. Only Rahab the prostitute and all who are with her in her house shall live, because she hid the messengers whom we sent." Interestingly, at an archaeological site located at the northern section of biblical Jericho, a portion of the lower city wall has been discovered that did not fall as it did everywhere else. This still-standing portion of wall is up to eight feet high, with houses built against it that are still intact. This lends support to the biblical account of Rahab's deliverance (Joshua 6:17-25).

> "We cannot rely on God's promises without obeying his commandments."
>
> —John Calvin (1509–1564)

We find another example of God being a promise keeper later in the book: "Thus the LORD gave to Israel all the land that he swore to give to their fathers. And they took possession of it, and they settled there. And the LORD gave them rest on every side just as he had sworn to their fathers. Not one of all their enemies had withstood them, for the LORD had given all their enemies into their hands. Not one word of all the good promises that the LORD had made to the house of Israel had failed; all came to pass" (Joshua 21:43-46). Are *you* trusting in God's promises?

Beware of overconfidence. It can bring you down.

Joshua and his army had just won a major victory over a major city—Jericho (Joshua 6). They were basking in glory. Then they got overconfident.

They now needed to face Ai, a much smaller city, and decided to send a much smaller army, confident of success (Joshua 7:1-5). Surprise! They were

> "He who sings his own praise is usually off-key."
>
> —Anonymous

defeated. Following the unexpected defeat, Joshua mournfully prayed to the Lord. Of course, it would have been wiser for Joshua to pray *before* the attack on Ai to obtain the Lord's blessing.

We learn a good lesson here. It is better to place our confidence not in ourselves but in the Lord. Scripture affirms that the Lord is our confidence (Proverbs 3:26; see also Philippians 4:13). Indeed, the fear of the Lord brings *strong* confidence (Proverbs 14:26).

It's always best to do things God's way—especially after your own way has failed so miserably.

Joshua's army had attacked Ai and been defeated. They had done things their own way and failed. Now they did things God's way and obtained victory over Ai. God affirmed to Joshua, "Do not fear and do not be dismayed. Take all the fighting men with you, and arise, go up to Ai. See, I have given into your hand the king of Ai, and his people, his city, and his land" (Joshua 8:1). God's blessing makes all the difference. My advice: It is always to our advantage to do all things God's way (Proverbs 3:5-6).

Beware of the sin of coveting. It can bring you down.

God had instructed that none of the cursed items of their enemies were to be taken. Achan violated God's instructions and confessed to Joshua, "Truly I have sinned against the LORD God of Israel, and this is what I did: when I saw among the spoil a beautiful cloak from Shinar, and 200 shekels of silver, and a bar of gold weighing 50 shekels, then I coveted them and took them. And see, they are hidden in the earth inside my tent, with the silver underneath" (Joshua 7:20-21).

> "One can be covetous when he has little, much, or anything between, for covetousness comes from the heart, not from the circumstances of life."
>
> —Charles Ryrie

Notice the three pivotal words: *saw...coveted...took.* Sin escalated quickly in Achan. He *saw* something that appealed to him, he *coveted* it, and then he *took* it for himself. In this case, Achan paid the ultimate price for his sin against God. Scripture warns us to beware of coveting (Exodus 20:17; Romans 7:7-8; 13:9; James 4:2). It is best to be content with what we have (Philippians 4:11-12; 1 Timothy 6:6,8).

We are reminded of the words of Jesus: "Take care, and be on your guard against all covetousness, for one's life does not consist in the abundance of his possessions" (Luke 12:15). He urged His followers to have an eternal perspective:

"Do not lay up for yourselves treasures on earth, where moth and rust destroy and where thieves break in and steal, but lay up for yourselves treasures in heaven, where neither moth nor rust destroys and where thieves do not break in and steal" (Matthew 6:19-20). Wise advice!

Joshua challenges God's people with a God-centered Life Plan.

Joshua imparted to his people a wise Life Plan: "Be very careful to observe the commandment and the law that Moses the servant of the Lord commanded you, to love the Lord your God, and to walk in all his ways and to keep his commandments and to cling to him and to serve him with all your heart and with all your soul" (Joshua 22:5). This sounds similar to Jesus's suggested Life Plan: "You shall love the Lord your God with all your heart and with all your soul and with all your mind. This is the great and first commandment" (Matthew 22:37-38). Does your Life Plan need any adjustments?

A Thought to Anchor in Your Heart

God's people are instructed, "Fear the Lord and serve him in sincerity and in faithfulness" (Joshua 24:14). Notice the three critical components: (1) fear the Lord; (2) serve God in sincerity; and (3) be faithful. Go thou and do likewise!

Joshua

Judges

Succumbing to moral relativism and sinful rebellion yields God's judgment. Even then, God continues to show grace and guide His people.

The book of Judges was written by an unidentified author between 1043 and 1000 BC. Jewish tradition in the Talmud (Tractate Baba Bathra 14b) says the author was the prophet Samuel. The book covers the time beginning with Joshua's death and ending with the rise of the prophet Samuel (Judges 2:6-9).

Primary attention is placed on the judges of Israel at that time. While the book is called Judges, the Hebrew term for the title (*Shophet*) can mean "Deliverers" or "Saviors." This points to the intended role of these judges. As Judges 2:16 puts it, "Then the LORD raised up judges, who saved them out of the hand of those who plundered them."

Timeline

1375—The period of the judges begins.

1367—Othniel begins judging.

1209—Deborah begins judging.

1162—Gideon begins judging.

1105—Samuel is born.

1080—Saul is born.

1075—Samson begins judging.

1043–1000—The book of Judges is written.

Judges

The backdrop is that Joshua's conquest, while effective, still left pockets of resistance that continued to cause trouble for the Israelites. The judges were raised up specifically as military champions to lead the tribes of Israel against these culprits and to bring about final and complete conquest. These judges were needed, for at that time the 12 tribes of Israel had no central leadership. Four of the judges are listed in the Faith Hall of Fame in Hebrews 11—Gideon, Barak, Sampson, and Jephthah (Judges 6:1–8:32; 4:1-11; 10:6–12:7; 13:1–16:31).

Unfortunately Israel was anything but faithful to God during this time, even giving allegiance to some of the false local gods of paganism. Despite the fact that God had repeatedly blessed them, they always seemed to revert to going their own way instead of God's way (Judges 3:7; 6:1; 10:6; 13:1). The primary problem of the people during this time was that they did what they considered to be right in their own eyes (Judges 21:25). This is moral relativism.

Following are key applicational concepts in Judges:

Continued rebellion against God's commands leads to continued chastisement.

Israel's continued dire condition was due to her continued sin against God, which seemed to go from bad to worse: "The people of Israel did what was evil in the sight of the LORD and served the Baals. And they abandoned the LORD, the God of their fathers, who had brought them out of the land of Egypt. They went after other gods, from among the gods of the peoples who were around them, and bowed down to them. And they provoked the LORD to anger" (Judges 2:11-12; see also 3:6-7,12; 4:1; 6:1,10; 8:24-27,33; 10:6; 13:1; 17:6; 21:25). As bad as their forefathers had been in the wilderness, the present generation was even worse.

> **Better to Repent**
>
> It is better to kneel in repentance than to stand in judgment. Judgment always comes when repentance is lacking (Ezekiel 18:32; Luke 13:3; Acts 3:19; 2 Peter 3:9; Isaiah 55:6-7).

Tears over sin is not enough. There must be genuine repentance.

Judges 2:4-5 tells us, "As soon as the angel of the LORD spoke these words to all the people of Israel, the people lifted up their voices and wept. And they called the name of that place Bochim. And they sacrificed there to the LORD." *So far, so good.* The people wept when confronted about their sin. But their sorrow was short-lived. The people remained unfaithful to God (2:11-23). Their tears did not lead to ongoing repentance. They felt bad for a while, got over it, and then plummeted right back into sin. May this *never* be true of you and me.

If you are a parent, tell your children about the great things God has done. This will encourage them to stay strong in the faith.

Judges 2:10 tells us, "All that generation also were gathered to their fathers. And there arose another generation after them who did not know the LORD or the work that he had done for Israel." In other words, the generation that experienced such great victories under Joshua's leadership died, and the next generation was unaware of the great things God had done. They were oblivious to God's miraculous work in the previous generation. They ended up spiritually lethargic and were unfaithful to God (2:11-23). If only the first generation had taught the second generation about God's wonders.

God continues to remain faithful, even when His people are perpetually unfaithful.

Despite the ongoing sin and rebellion of His people, God remained ever faithful toward them. Judges 2:16 tells us that "the LORD raised up judges, who saved them out of the hand of those who plundered them." Moreover, "Whenever the LORD raised up judges for them, the LORD was with the judge, and he saved them from the hand of their enemies all the days of the judge. For the LORD was moved to pity by their groaning because of those who afflicted and oppressed them" (2:18). The people did not deserve this benevolence from God, but God nevertheless helped them. God was resolved to fulfill the promises He had made to Abraham and his descendants (Genesis 12:7; 15:7,18-21; 26:2-3; 35:12). This reminds us of Paul's description of God as the "Father of mercies and God of all comfort" (2 Corinthians 1:3).

> **Father of Mercies**
>
> Paul describes God as the "Father of mercies and God of all comfort."
>
> —2 Corinthians 1:3

Learn from your past mistakes.

Judges 3:7-11 describes a cycle we see repeated throughout the book of Judges: (1) The people commit great evil; (2) they forget all about God; (3) they fall into idolatry; (4) God chastises them by allowing them to go into slavery under a foreign king; (5) the people cry out to God; (6) God delivers them; and then (7) the cycle repeats all over again. People need to learn from their past mistakes!

> Those who cannot remember the past are condemned to repeat it.

Judges

Don't offer excuses when God calls you to service.

We find people giving excuses all through the Bible (for example, Genesis 3:12-13; Luke 14:16-24). In Judges 6:15, Gideon said to the Lord, "Please, Lord, how can I save Israel? Behold, my clan is the weakest in Manasseh, and I am the least in my father's house." The Lord responded, "I will be with you, and you shall strike the Midianites as one man" (6:16). Gideon was focused more on his weakness and limitations than on the power of God.

> **Divine Empowerment**
>
> When God calls us to service, He empowers us for that service. The apostle Paul affirmed, "I can do all things through him who strengthens me" (Philippians 4:13).

God's peace is always available to His servants.

Gideon thought he was going to die. But the Lord said to him, "Peace be to you. Do not fear; you shall not die" (Judges 6:23). God promises His followers a supernatural peace. As Jesus put it, "Peace I leave with you; my peace I give to you. Not as the world gives do I give to you. Let not your hearts be troubled, neither let them be afraid" (John 14:27). Trusting in God naturally leads to this peace. Isaiah 26:3 affirms, "You keep him in perfect peace whose mind is stayed on you, because he trusts in you."

> "Do not be anxious about anything, but in everything by prayer and supplication with thanksgiving let your requests be made known to God. And the peace of God, which surpasses all understanding, will guard your hearts and your minds in Christ Jesus."
>
> —Philippians 4:6-7

When leaders are corrupt, it is no wonder those who follow them are corrupt as well.

It is a sad commentary of the spiritual state of affairs in the period of the judges that major judges like Gideon (Judges 8:24-27), Jephthah (11:30-31,34-40), and Samson (14–16) all fell into sin. They not only failed to be a consistently positive influence on the nation; they actually contributed to its becoming worse. The only judge who was a consistent bright light in the overwhelming darkness of the nation was the female judge, Deborah (4:6,14; 5:7).

God's people can offer themselves up as living sacrifices.

Judges 11:30-39 is an extremely controversial passage. Scholars have different opinions on how it is to be interpreted. One view is that Jephthah actually did offer his own daughter as a burnt sacrifice to the Lord. If this is the case, it does not in any way mean God endorsed what Jephthah did. He was certainly not under orders from God to do that. God had earlier revealed that human sacrifice was absolutely forbidden (Leviticus 18:21; 20:2-5; Deuteronomy 12:31; 18:10).

We must also keep in mind that simply because something is recorded in the Bible does not mean God agrees with it. God certainly does not agree with the words or actions of Satan, but the Bible nevertheless accurately reports on his words and actions. In the present case, the author of Judges may have just provided an objective account of the event without passing judgment.

> **A Verse to Remember**
> "In those days there was no king in Israel. Everyone did what was right in his own eyes."
>
> —Judges 21:25

One must also remember that the book of Judges deals with a period in human history when everyone was doing what was right in his or her own eyes (Judges 21:25). It is very possible that Jephthah was doing what was right in his own eyes, thereby victimizing his own daughter. If Jephthah actually committed this act, we can only conclude that he was acting in great folly and was going against the will of God, despite his good motives and apparent desire to please the Lord.

Another possible interpretation of the passage is that Jephthah may have offered up his daughter in the sense of consecrating her for service at the tabernacle for the rest of her life and devoting her to celibacy. This would involve offering up his daughter in a spiritual way instead of physically offering her as a burnt offering. As the apostle Paul said in Romans 12:1, people can be offered to God as "a living sacrifice."

If his daughter was indeed offered as a living sacrifice, this necessarily would involve a life of perpetual virginity, which was a tremendous sacrifice in the Jewish context of the day. She would not be able to bring up children to continue her father's lineage.

This may explain why his daughter responded by saying, "Let this thing be done for me: leave me alone two months, that I may go up and down on the mountains and weep for my virginity, I and my companions" (Judges 11:37). Note that she did not weep because of an impending death. She wept because she would never marry and would remain a virgin.

In any event, Christian believers today are privileged to offer themselves as living sacrifices to God (Romans 12:1). After all, as Paul puts it in 1 Corinthians 6:19-20, "Your body is a temple of the Holy Spirit" and "You are not your own, for you were bought with a price." (See also Romans 8:9.) That price was the sacrificial death of Jesus Christ. Because Jesus died sacrificially for us, it is right and proper that we live sacrificially for Him.

God can providentially bring good out of evil.

Samson was not entirely committed to God. His lustful lifestyle makes that clear (Judges 14:3; 16:1,4). His problem with lust shows that he was self-focused, seeking gratification of fleshly desires. In the context of Judges 14, it is obvious that Samson had no intention of battling the Philistines out of a spiritual commitment to God. God therefore used Samson's self-interests to incite his anger against the Philistines, which ultimately resulted in Israel's deliverance.

Samson: the Bad and the Good

- The *bad*: Samson had a problem with lust (Judges 14: 2-3,7; 16:1,4).
- The *good*: Samson was a man of faith (Judges 15:18-19), and he is listed in the Faith Hall of Fame (Hebrews 11:32,34).

Judges

This is yet another example of how God can providentially bring good out of evil. Samson had improper motives, but God nevertheless used his actions—regardless of motives—for the good of Israel. Spend a little time meditating on Romans 8:28.

Don't be foolish!

Samson kept feeding Delilah bogus information on how to make him weak (Judges 16). Every time he informed her of a means to weaken him, an attempt was made to weaken him by that means. How, then, could Samson have been so foolish as to reveal the *true* means of weakening him—cutting his hair? It boggles the mind. Samson acted foolishly.

Contextually, of course, Samson's strength was rooted in his unique relationship with God, based on the Nazirite vow he had taken. His long hair was a sign of that vow, and so the cutting of his hair essentially amounted to breaking that vow. This highlights Samson's folly even more.

Let us learn from Samson's mistake. Don't be foolish. Don't be shortsighted. A practical step is to spend regular time in the book of Proverbs.

> **Wisdom**
> - rebukes sin (Proverbs 1:8-33);
> - richly rewards those who seek it (2–3);
> - keeps one from dangerous paths (4);
> - warns against sensuality (5);
> - represses lustful desires (6:20-35); and
> - warns against evil women (7).

Greater love has no one than this, that he lay down his life for his friends.

Some people have wondered if Samson committed suicide (Judges 16:26-30). Contextually, Judges 16 seems clear that Samson did not commit suicide. Rather, he sacrificed his life for a greater cause. Recall that Jesus Christ Himself said, "Greater love has no one than this, that someone lay down his life for his friends" (John 15:13). This is precisely what Samson did. He laid down his life for his people. As a result, many more Philistines (enemies of Israel) died with his death than during his life (Judges 16:30).

Moral relativism is insufficient as a workable philosophy of life.

Judges 21:25 tells us, "In those days there was no king in Israel. Everyone did what was right in his own eyes." Everyone made up their own rules. Each person was a law unto him—or herself. This is the idea that anything can be true for the individual, but nothing can be true for everyone. In other words, there are no absolute truths.

The "all truth is relative" position is not logically satisfying. One might understand "all truth is relative" as meaning it is an absolute truth that all truth is relative. Of course, such a statement is self-defeating (since there are supposedly no absolute truths) and is therefore false.

Second, one could understand this as saying it is a relative truth that all truth is relative. But such a statement is ultimately meaningless.

No matter how you understand this statement, it should be rejected because it is not a workable philosophy of life. As people accelerate down the road where moral relativity takes us, there is no center stripe on the highway of life. There are many casualties along this highway.

Moral Absolutes

- Absolute morals are grounded in the absolutely moral God of the Bible. Scripture affirms, "You therefore must be perfect, as your heavenly Father is perfect" (Matthew 5:48).
- Moral law flows from the moral Law-giver of the universe—God.
- God therefore stands against the moral relativist whose behavior is based on "whatever is right in his own eyes" (Deuteronomy 12:8; Judges 17:6; 21:2).

A Thought to Anchor in Your Heart

Absolute morals are grounded in the absolutely moral God of the Bible. Don't fall prey to moral relativism.

Judges

Ruth

God blesses those who are kind, generous, and faithful.

Timeline

1100–1000—The events recorded in the book of Ruth transpire.

1000—The book of Ruth is written.

The book of Ruth was likely written during the time of the judges in about 1000 BC. Some scholars believe the book was written by the prophet Samuel, but there is no hard proof of this. The word "Ruth" is probably a derivative of the Hebrew term *reuit*, which means "friendship." The word is appropriate, for it describes Ruth's character as a loyal friend.

According to this book, Elimelech and his wife, Naomi, migrated from Bethlehem to Moab during a time of famine. (Moab is northeast of the Dead Sea.) They were accompanied by Elimelech's two sons, who both married Moabite women. Eventually the father and sons died in Moab, and this left Naomi in a predicament. In biblical times women were dependent upon men for provisions in life. A woman without a father or husband or son was in a dire situation. Naomi decided to return to Bethlehem, and her Moabite daughter-in-law, Ruth, decided to go with her (Ruth 1:6-18).

Upon their arrival, they found themselves in poverty (Ruth 1:19-22). In God's providence, however, Ruth met a distant relative of her first husband's family named Boaz (2:1-7). Boaz ended up fulfilling his family duty—his "kinsman-redeemer" duty—and married Ruth, despite the fact that Ruth was not an Israelite (4:1-12). Problem solved!

Providence

Providence refers to God's preserving and governing of all things. See Acts 17:28, Colossians 1:17, and Hebrews 1:3.

It is noteworthy that Ruth, the Moabite, was the great-grandmother of David, the king of Israel, and so an ancestress of Jesus (Matthew 1:1,5). Even though Ruth did not know it at the time, her lineage was important to the unfolding plan of God. It is also noteworthy that this is one of two books in the Bible named after a woman. (The other is Esther.)

Following are key applicational concepts in the book of Ruth:

When tragedy strikes, you feel all alone, and are out of options, don't be surprised if you discover that God has been providentially working behind the scenes to rescue you the whole time.

Naomi's husband, Elimelech, died and she was left with two sons to care for. The sons eventually took Moabite wives, lived ten years, and then died. Naomi was now all alone (Ruth 1:1-5).

Naomi and Ruth, a daughter-in-law, returned together to Bethlehem. Ruth—a woman of honor, generosity, and integrity—expressed a heartfelt pledge to accompany Naomi (Ruth 1:6-18). They arrived in Bethlehem at the beginning of the barley harvest (1:19-22).

> **A Verse to Remember**
>
> "Where you go I will go, and where you lodge I will lodge. Your people shall be my people, and your God my God."
>
> —*Ruth 1:16*

Ruth and Naomi were very poor. God's law, however, made provisions for the poor. Leviticus 19:9-10 stipulated that the outer perimeters of the harvest field were to be left for the poor to glean. God's providence led Ruth to glean from Boaz's field. (Boaz was Elimelech's kinsman.) Boaz showed grace and kindness far beyond what the law required (Ruth 2:9,14-16), providing for and protecting Ruth. It is clear that God was guiding Ruth's rescue (and, consequently, Naomi's rescue) from beginning to end. God showed Himself strong on their behalf (see also Psalm 1:6).

> **Kinsman-Redeemer**
>
> A kinsman-redeemer is a next-of-kin relative who—if able—could redeem or rescue a family member.
>
> Boaz was Elimelech's kinsman. Ruth (and Naomi) found redemption in Boaz.

God's blessings and provisions can far exceed human expectations.

A redeeming romance emerged between Boaz and Ruth. Naomi gave instructions to Ruth on pursuing Boaz as her kinsman-redeemer (Ruth 3:1-4). Ruth followed these instructions (3:5-9). Boaz responded affirmatively and pledged to be her kinsman-redeemer (3:10-18). There was, however, a kinsman closer to Ruth than Boaz was. So Boaz had to first approach this kinsman to discuss the matter.

The kinsmen engaged in discussion at the city gate, where most legal business was conducted. The other kinsman declared himself unwilling to take on the responsibility, for it would not have been

> **Business and Gates**
>
> In biblical times, business often took place at the gates of various cities. At these gates vendors would set up shop, selling such products as fruit, vegetables, pottery, and clothing. Legal contracts were also negotiated near the gates. In the book of Ruth, kinsman-redeemer negotiations took place at the city gate.

Ruth

advantageous to him. Boaz and Ruth were then able to marry (Ruth 4:1-12) and Ruth gave birth to a son (4:13-17)—all this because of the marvelous providential grace of God.

Naomi found solace in her grandson. This grandson's lineage eventually led to the birth of David (4:18-22), from whose line the Messiah was to be born. Glorious!

Faithfulness has a reciprocal effect.

Faithfulness is like a thread that runs through the entire book of Ruth. Ruth, Naomi, and Boaz showed themselves faithful to God and His law. Ruth showed herself faithful in her treatment of her mother-in-law, Naomi. Boaz showed himself faithful in caring for Ruth. The result? God showed Himself faithful in meeting all their needs and taking care of them. Faithfulness has a reciprocal effect in the book of Ruth. My friend, show faithfulness to others and receive faithfulness in return.

Be Faithful
- God preserves the faithful—Psalm 31:23
- God guards the faithful—Psalm 97:10 (NLT)
- God does not forsake the faithful—Psalm 37:28

Treat others with kindness, and kindness will be returned upon you.

Kindness is another thread that seems to run through the book of Ruth. Ruth was kind to Naomi (Ruth 1:16-17; 2:11,18,23). Boaz was kind to Ruth (2:20; 4:9-10,13). And God was kind to Ruth, Naomi, and Boaz by bringing them all together (4:1-17).

God's kindness is a common theme throughout all of Scripture. God is said to be full of loving-kindness (Jeremiah 31:3 NASB), rich in kindness (Romans 2:4), and have everlasting kindness (Isaiah 54:8). Best of all, God showed "kindness toward us in Christ Jesus" (Ephesians 2:7).

Human kindness actually reflects the greater kindness (or "steadfast love") the Lord shows to His people (Exodus 15:13; Deuteronomy 7:8-9; Psalm 103:4; 106:7,10; 136:10-15). As God floods us with kindness, the overflow of that kindness enables us to show kindness to others. Our vertical relationship with God affects our horizontal relationships with other people.

Acting in integrity and trusting God creates a rich soil where God's blessings can blossom.

Ruth and Naomi were poor and in a dire situation, especially since women in biblical times depended upon men for their support—whether from a father,

Ruth

a husband, or a son. Ruth and Naomi had no such support. They were without means and without any obvious solutions to their situation.

They had not been forgotten by God, however. Through Ruth's marriage to Boaz—a marriage providentially arranged by God—they found more than abundant support to meet their needs.

Dear Christian, one thing we learn from this account is that even when things look their bleakest, we can rest assured that we are not forgotten by God, and that God can come through in ways we never could have imagined. A good passage to anchor ourselves on is Proverbs 3:5-6: "Trust in the LORD with all your heart, and do not lean on your own understanding. In all your ways acknowledge him, and he will make straight your paths."

Acting in Integrity

Ruth showed great integrity in leaving her former land to accompany Naomi. Boaz showed great integrity as a man of morality, honesty, and benevolence toward others.

God desires integrity of each of us (Psalm 26:1; Proverbs 10:9; 20:7; Luke 6:31; Philippians 4:8).

"Faith expects from God what is beyond all expectation."

—Andrew Murray (1828–1917)

A Thought to Anchor in Your Heart

Do unto others as you would have them do unto you.

Ruth

1 Samuel

Heart commitment to the true King of the universe brings great blessing.

The prophet Samuel was the author of 1 Samuel 1:1–24:22. Samuel's death is recorded in 1 Samuel 25:1, however, so he could not have written that chapter or those that follow (or 2 Samuel). Perhaps it is best to say that 1 and 2 Samuel were written by Samuel and others known only to God. Both books were written about 931 BC.

Samuel was the last and greatest of the judges of Israel, and was a wonderful prophet in his own right. He ruled Israel his entire life, and is noted for bringing the Israelites back to God's laws. He was a bright light in Old Testament times.

The two books of Samuel chronicle Israel's history from the time of the judges through the reign of King David (who reigned from 1011 to 971 BC)—about 135 years of history. It was during this time that Israel demanded a king like the nations around them, and it was Samuel who anointed the first king, Saul, who reigned from 1050 to 1011 BC. These books, then, chronicle the transition in leadership from judges to kings in the life of Israel.

Originally, 1 and 2 Samuel were a single book, known as the "Book of Samuel." But the translators of the Septuagint—the Greek translation of the Hebrew Old Testament that predates the time of Christ—divided it into two parts.

One observation we can make regarding these books is that God is the true King. So long as the human kings—in the present case, Saul or David—obey the divine King's orders, they prosper and succeed. If, however, they depart from the will of God, as did Saul, they are judged and even dethroned. We learn from this that earthly kings, no matter how powerful they may seem in themselves, are nothing next to the power of the divine King.

Following are key applicational concepts in 1 Samuel:

Those fully committed to the Lord can accomplish mighty feats on His behalf.

Samuel was born to a prayerful Hannah (1 Samuel 1), who dedicated him to the Lord (2). Raised by Eli in the tabernacle, and responding positively to God's call on his life, Samuel became a great and faithful prophet who was mightily used of the Lord (3). He faithfully proclaimed the Word of God (9:27), was an upright man, thereby setting a great example (12:1-5), and continually exhorted Israel to follow the ways of the Lord (7:3; 12:14-16; 12:20-25).

Sexual sin among spiritual leaders is a heinous offense against God.

Eli's sons were priests, and yet sinned grossly by engaging in sexual relations with women who served in the tabernacle (1 Samuel 2:22). God's response was severe: "It was the will of the LORD to put them to death" (2:25).

It is a tragic reality that sexual sin still occurs today among some spiritual leaders. Even if a physical affair has not taken place, some have nevertheless fallen victim to Internet pornography. God calls His people to sexual purity (1 Thessalonians 4:3-8).

> **Sexual Sin**
> - Abstain from fornication (Acts 15:20).
> - Flee fornication (1 Corinthians 6:13,18).
> - It should not even be named among Christians (Ephesians 5:3).

A sacred object ought to never be used as a talisman among God's people.

In 1 Samuel 4:3 we read, "When the people came to the camp, the elders of Israel said, 'Why has the LORD defeated us today before the Philistines? Let us bring the ark of the covenant of the LORD here from Shiloh, that it may come among us and save us from the power of our enemies.'"

The Israelites had come to believe that if the ark were present during a battle, Yahweh (God) was in battle with them, and so they would surely win. They believed the presence of the ark would ensure victory. Such misguided thinking essentially amounted to using the ark as a talisman. (A talisman is an object believed to contain certain magical properties that provide good luck for the possessor, or possibly offer

> **Seeking God's Actual Presence**
> "Our fellowship is with the Father and with his Son Jesus Christ" (1 John 1:3).
>
> "Behold, I stand at the door and knock. If anyone hears my voice and opens the door, I will come in to him and eat with him, and he with me" (Revelation 3:20).

1 Samuel

protection from harm.) Israel needed to learn the lesson that having the paraphernalia of God is not the same as having God Himself.

A lack of faith in God can drive you to do unwise things.

Israel was a theocracy—that is, a God-ruled nation. God had taken care of the Israelites ever since He delivered them from Egyptian bondage. But a time came when they wanted a real flesh-and-blood human king, like all the other nations around them had (1 Samuel 8). They were intent on grumbling until they got their way.

Samuel tried to talk to them about the downsides of a human king (1 Samuel 8:10-18), but they would not listen. In their blindness, all they saw were positive benefits. Ultimately this desire for a human king stemmed from a lack of faith in God, their true King. They sought to trade a God who loved them for a human king, who would end up exploiting them. They got what they wanted, but the nation was injured in the process, as the rest of 1 Samuel attests. My advice: Always trust in your true King (God), and He'll keep your path smooth, no matter what human leaders may do (Proverbs 3:5-6).

Cross-References: Unbelief
Psalm 95:8 • Hebrews 3:12 • 11:6 • 12:25 • Mark 16:14 • John 12:37 • 20:27 • Romans 11:20 • James 1:6

Human beings fixate on people's external features. The Lord looks at the heart.

The people of Israel were demanding a king, like the other nations around them had. Israel's first king was appointed by the prophet Samuel (1 Samuel 10–11). His name was Saul, and he was considered the stateliest man in all Israel. He was said to be "a handsome young man," and "from his shoulders upward he was taller than any of the people" (9:2). After Saul became king, however, he was not fully obedient to the Lord, and he sinned by wrongly assuming the role of a priest (13:13-14; 2 Chronicles 26:18).

Because of David's growing fame, King Saul became increasingly jealous of him, and even sought to kill him. This resulted in David having to live as an outlaw for a number of years. It is to David's credit that he did not respond in like manner and seek to take Saul's life. Meanwhile, David developed a close friendship with Saul's son, Jonathan (1 Samuel 20).

Cross-References: God Looks at the Heart
1 Kings 8:38 • 1 Chronicles 28:9 • Psalm 7:9 • Jeremiah 11:20 • 17:10 • 20:12 • Acts 1:24

When it came time for David to be selected as Israel's new king, God reminded Samuel of an important factor: "The Lord sees not as man sees: man looks on the outward appearance, but the LORD looks on the heart" (1 Samuel 16:7). "The LORD has sought out a man after his own heart" (13:14), and that man was David.

My friend, perhaps this is a good time for self-examination (2 Corinthians 13:5). Since God cares so much about the state of our hearts, it might be wise to deal with any heart issues in your life that may not be pleasing to Him. Do it today!

Partial obedience is not enough. God demands full obedience.

God had commanded Saul, "Go and strike Amalek and devote to destruction all that they have. Do not spare them, but kill both man and woman, child and infant, ox and sheep, camel and donkey" (1 Samuel 15:3). Saul, however, was only partially obedient: "Saul and the people spared Agag and the best of the sheep and of the oxen and of the fattened calves and the lambs, and all that was good, and would not utterly destroy them" (15:9).

> **Psalm 119: Total Obedience**
> "Blessed are those whose way is blameless...who seek him with their whole heart, who also do no wrong...You have commanded your precepts to be kept diligently" (verses 1-4).

Because of Saul's partial obedience, God lamented, "I regret that I have made Saul king, for he has turned back from following me and has not performed my commandments" (1 Samuel 15:11). Partial obedience amounts to disobedience.

Good news: the Holy Spirit permanently indwells all believers today. He's your power source for living the Christian life.

In 1 Samuel 16:14 we are told "the Spirit of the LORD departed from Saul, and a harmful spirit from the LORD tormented him." In Old Testament times,

> "We do not use the Holy Spirit; He uses us."
> —*Warren Wiersbe*

the Holy Spirit came upon people to enable them to accomplish special tasks and often only for a limited time (10:5-6; Judges 15:14). In Saul's case, the Holy Spirit came upon him to empower him to accomplish the task of being a good leader. But Saul sinned and turned away from God. His leadership days were over, and the Holy Spirit departed from him.

Starting in New Testament times, the Holy Spirit began to *permanently* indwell believers (Romans 8:9; 1 Corinthians 12:13). The indwelling presence and empowerment from the Holy Spirit enables Christ's followers to live the Christian life (Acts 2:4; 1 Corinthians 6:19-20; Galatians 5:22-23; Ephesians

3:16,20). Ephesians 5:18 instructs us to be perpetually "filled" with—*or controlled by*—the Holy Spirit.

The size of the obstacle is not important. Rather, the power and blessing of God are what is important.

David became instantly famous for killing Goliath, the giant Philistine warrior (1 Samuel 17). The fact that David would go up against such a gargantuan warrior as a young boy shows tremendous trust in God on his part. Of course, during his years as a shepherd boy, David had become increasingly proficient in using a slingshot, which he was able to providentially use with God's blessing in defeating Goliath. It seems obvious, then, that even in David's younger years God was already preparing him for his future role, though David was unaware of it at the time. The important thing for us to remember is that the size of the obstacle (Goliath) is not what is important. Rather, the power and blessing of God are what is important. Are you presently facing an obstacle? Turn to God this moment!

> "Nothing will be impossible with God."
>
> —Luke 1:37

God's people must never succumb to any form of occultism or divination.

In 1 Samuel 28, we witness King Saul with the medium at Endor seeking to summon up the dead—that is, the prophet Samuel. Bible expositors have different opinions on the meaning of this passage.

> "There shall not be found among you anyone who [is]…a medium or a necromancer or one who inquires of the dead, for whoever does these things is an abomination to the Lord."
>
> —Deuteronomy 18:10-12

A minority believe the medium worked a miracle by demonic powers and actually brought Samuel back from the dead. In support of this view, certain passages seem to indicate demons have the power to perform lying signs and wonders (Matthew 7:22; 2 Corinthians 11:14; 2 Thessalonians 2:9,10; Revelation 16:14). This view is unlikely, however, since Scripture also reveals that death is final (Hebrews 9:27), the dead cannot return (2 Samuel 12:23; Luke 16:24-27), and demons cannot usurp or overpower God's authority over life and death (Job 1:10-12).

A second view is that the medium did not really bring up Samuel from the dead, but a demonic spirit simply impersonated the prophet. Those who hold to this view note that certain verses indicate that demons can deceive people who try to contact the dead (Leviticus 19:31; Deuteronomy 18:11; 1 Chronicles 10:13). This view is unlikely, however, because the passage affirms that Samuel did in fact return from the dead, that he provided a prophecy that actually came to pass,

> **Cross-References: Occultism Condemned**
> Exodus 22:18 • Leviticus 19:26,31 • 20:27 • 1 Samuel 28:3 • Acts 19:19

and that it is unlikely that demons would have uttered God's truth since the devil is the father of lies (John 8:44).

A third view (my view) is that God sovereignly and miraculously allowed Samuel's spirit to appear to rebuke Saul for his sin. Samuel's spirit did not appear as a result of the medium's powers (for indeed, no human has the power to summon dead humans—see Luke 16:24-27; Hebrews 9:27), but only because God sovereignly brought it about. This view is supported by the fact that Samuel actually returned from the dead (1 Samuel 28:14), and this caused the medium to shriek with fear (see verse 12). The medium's cry of astonishment indicates that this appearance of Samuel was not the result of her usual tricks.

That God allowed Samuel's spirit to appear on this one occasion should not be taken to mean that mediums have any real power to summon the dead. God had a one-time purpose for this one-time special occasion. This passage is therefore descriptive, not prescriptive. That is, it simply *describes* something that happened historically. It does not *prescribe* something that people should expect in the future.

Life and death are in the hands of our sovereign God.

First Samuel 31:4-5 tells us, "Saul took his own sword and fell upon it. And when his armor-bearer saw that Saul was dead, he also fell upon his sword and died with him." Apparently, then, Saul took his own life. But this was done according to God's sovereign will. In 1 Chronicles 10:13-14 we are told, "So Saul died for his breach of faith. He broke faith with the LORD in that he did not keep the command of the LORD, and also consulted a medium, seeking guid-

> **God Is Sovereign**
> • His purpose will stand— Isaiah 46:10
> • His plans alone stand— Psalm 33:8-11
> • He rules over all—Psalm 103:19

ance. He did not seek guidance from the LORD. Therefore the LORD put him to death and turned the kingdom over to David the son of Jesse."

1 Samuel

Though Saul committed suicide, it was ultimately the Lord who put him to death. Recall God's words in Deuteronomy 32:39: "See now that I, even I, am he, and there is no god beside me; I kill and I make alive; I wound and I heal; and there is none that can deliver out of my hand." (See also Psalm 139:16.) Our God is a sovereign God.

God is the true King of the universe.

Despite the people of Israel's desire to have a human king, the true King of the universe is God Himself. God's reign from the heavenly throne is evident throughout Scripture. God as King is sovereign over all earthly kings. In 1 Samuel 12:14-15, for example, Samuel instructed the people, "If you will fear the Lord and serve him and obey his voice and not rebel against the commandment of the Lord, and if both you and the king who reigns over you will follow the Lord your God, it will be well. But if you will not obey the voice of the Lord, but rebel against the commandment of the Lord, then the hand of the Lord will be against you and your king."

God is not only enthroned over the entire universe (Psalm 102:12); He ought also to be enthroned upon our hearts. We ought to follow the psalmist's lead, who said, "I delight to do your will, O my God" (Psalm 40:8).

A Thought to Anchor in Your Heart

God is your true King. Obey Him, no matter what.

---

1 Samuel

2 Samuel

Godly people can still do ungodly things.
When they do so, they can be forgiven by God,
but temporal consequences may yet remain.
There is much grief in life. But we can all look forward
to the day when the divine messianic King comes and
sets up His perfect kingdom.

Samuel's death is recorded in 1 Samuel 25:1, so 2 Samuel could not have been written by him. The author is anonymous, but was perhaps an apprentice or close associate trained by Samuel. It is still appropriate that the book be titled 2 Samuel, for it was titled after the man God used to establish the kingship in Israel—Samuel the prophet. The book was written about 931 BC.

Second Samuel continues the historical record that began in 1 Samuel. It records the history of David's reign as Israel's king—including both the highs (such as his military victories) and the lows (such as his sin with Bathsheba). During this time, Jerusalem became the political and religious heart of the nation.

Following are key applicational concepts in 2 Samuel:

It is good to seek unity among people.

David was crowned as king (2 Samuel 5:1-4) and his kingdom extended over Judah (2:1-7). He sought to include other tribes (2:8–4:12), and was eventually enthroned over all the tribes, encompassing all of Israel (5:1-6). David consolidated the kingdom,

Timeline

1040—David is born.

1010—Saul dies; David becomes king of Judah.

1003—David becomes king of all Israel.

1000—David captures Jerusalem.

997—David captures Rabbah; David sins with Bathsheba.

991—Solomon is born.

980—David takes a census of Israel.

931—The book of 2 Samuel is written.

Cross-References: Unity

Psalm 133:1 • Acts 4:32 • Romans 12:16 • 14:19 • 15:5-6 • 1 Corinthians 1:10 • 2 Corinthians 13:11 • Ephesians 4:3 • Philippians 1:27 • 2:2 • 1 Peter 3:8

2 Samuel

established his government in Jerusalem (5:7-25), and brought the ark to Jerusalem (6:1-23).

Seeking unity is a noble goal for all of us. Psalm 133:1 says, "How good and pleasant it is when brothers dwell in unity." The apostle Paul urges us to walk "with all humility and gentleness, with patience, bearing with one another in love, eager to maintain the unity of the Spirit in the bond of peace" (Ephesians 4:2-3). Be a unifier, not a divider.

Despite human power-plays, the Lord will ultimately accomplish all His purposes.

It was God's sovereign purpose for David to be king over all His people (2 Samuel 1:1-27). But General Abner had other plans in mind (2–4). Abner made Saul's son Ish-bosheth king. Abner's resistance to God ultimately led to much bloodshed—including that of his own. David did in fact become king over all God's people. Let us not forget God's words in Isaiah 46:10: "My counsel shall stand, and I will accomplish all my purpose."

Fear of the Lord is the beginning of wisdom.

> "As the embankment keeps out the water, so the fear of the Lord keeps out uncleanness."
>
> —*Thomas Watson (1620–1686)*

In 2 Samuel 6:6-9 we read, "When they came to the threshing floor of Nacon, Uzzah put out his hand to the ark of God and took hold of it, for the oxen stumbled. And the anger of the LORD was kindled against Uzzah, and God struck him down there because of his error, and he died there beside the ark of God...David was afraid of the LORD that day." Perhaps David didn't have sufficient fear of the Lord prior to this time. But he certainly learned to fear the Lord very quickly.

Fearing God—that is, *reverencing* God—is important for all God's children. Fear of the Lord is true wisdom (Job 28:28; Psalm 111:10) and is the beginning of knowledge (Proverbs 1:7). David learned true wisdom that fateful day. Fear of the Lord motivates obedience to God (Deuteronomy 5:29; Ecclesiastes 12:13) and the avoidance of evil (Proverbs 3:7; 8:13; 16:6).

Good news: the messianic King will come from the line of David. A promise is a promise.

God made a covenant with David. He promised that one of his descendants would rule forever on the throne of David (2 Samuel 7:12-13; 22:51). This is an

2 Samuel

example of an unconditional covenant. It did not depend on David in any way for its fulfillment. David realized this when he received the promise from God, and responded with an attitude of humility and a recognition of God's sovereignty over the affairs of human beings.

The three key words of the covenant are "kingdom," "house," and "throne." Such words point to the political future of Israel. The word "house" here carries the idea of "royal dynasty."

This covenant finds its ultimate fulfillment in Jesus Christ, who was born from the line of David (Matthew 1:1), and in the millennial kingdom will rule from the throne of David in Jerusalem (Ezekiel 36:1-12; Micah 4:1-5; Zephaniah 3:14-20; Zechariah 14:1-21). This reign of Christ during the millennial kingdom will extend beyond the Jews to include the Gentile nations as well.

One might recall that when the angel Gabriel appeared to the young virgin Mary to inform her that the Messiah was to be born through her womb, he spoke to her in Davidic terms: "Do not be afraid, Mary, for you have found favor with God. And behold, you will conceive in your womb and bear a son, and you shall call his name Jesus. He will be great and will be called the Son of the Most High. And the Lord God will give to him the throne of his father David, and he will reign over the house of Jacob forever, and of his kingdom there will be no end" (Luke 1:30-33).

Definition: Millennial Kingdom

The millennial kingdom is a 1000-year kingdom Christ will set up on earth following His second coming (Revelation 20:2-7; see also Psalm 2:6-9; Isaiah 65:18-23; Jeremiah 31:12-14,31-37; Ezekiel 34:25-29; 37:1-13; 40–48; Daniel 2:35; 7:13-14; Joel 2:21-27; Amos 9:13-14; Micah 4:1-7; Zephaniah 3:9-20).

The three key words used by the angel to describe the future rule of Christ were "throne," "house," and "kingdom." It is significant that each of these words is found in the covenant God made with David when God promised one from David's line would rule forever (2 Samuel 7:16).

Gabriel's words must have immediately brought these Old Testament promises to mind for Mary, a devout young Jew. Indeed, Gabriel's words constituted a clear announcement that Mary's Son would come into this world to fulfill the promise given to David that one of David's sons would sit on David's throne and rule over David's kingdom. Glorious!

2 Samuel

Good leaders are characterized by justice, equity, kindness, and loyalty.

David was an effective leader. He "administered justice and equity to all his people" (2 Samuel 8:15), took the initiative in showing kindness (9:1,3,7), and openly displayed loyalty (10:2). Modern politicians could learn a thing or two from David.

Even men after God's own heart can break God's heart.

Though David was a man after God's own heart (Acts 13:22), in middle age he fell deeply into sin and remained in sin for almost a full year. God had no choice but to discipline him, after which David, in desperation, finally confessed his sin to God and repented.

The progression of sin in David's life is heart-rending. David saw Bathsheba bathing from his roof, sent for her, slept with her, and impregnated her (2 Samuel 11:1-5). How easily and how quickly a great man can fall. And what pain is caused when great men fail to repent. David could have saved himself a lot of trouble and pain by repenting and confessing his sin immediately to God. He still would have had consequences to deal with, but at least he could have gotten on the healing path immediately instead of waiting almost a year.

Second Samuel 11:6-17 indicates David ended up greatly compounding his problem, digging his hole ever deeper. He caused himself more pain by his subsequent sinful actions. More specifically, he connived and tried to get Bathsheba's husband, Uriah, to sleep with her. He even got Uriah drunk in an effort to get him to go home and have sexual relations with his wife. But he didn't do so.

> "No marvel that our sorrows are multiplied when our sins are."
>
> —Matthew Henry (1662–1714)

In the morning David wrote a letter to the commander Joab and sent it with Uriah. In it he wrote, "Set Uriah in the forefront of the hardest fighting, and then draw back from him, that he may be struck down, and die" (11:15).

In obedience, Joab put Uriah at a place where he knew the strongest fighters were. When the men of the city came out and fought against Joab, some of the men in David's army fell; moreover, Uriah the Hittite died.

> "Sins are like circles in the water when a stone is thrown into it; one produces another."
>
> —Philip Henry (1631–1696)

Over the course of this episode, David ended up breaking four of the Ten Commandments: "You shall not murder" (Exodus 20:13); "You shall not commit

2 Samuel

adultery" (verse 14); "You shall not steal" (verse 15); "You shall not covet your neighbor's wife" (verse 17). David grievously sinned against God. And in the process, he committed one sin to cover up another sin.

God's people are always best served to flee immorality.

As noted previously, 2 Samuel 11:2 tells us David was walking around on his roof and saw Bathsheba bathing. Instead of averting his attention, he watched her long enough to see she was beautiful. The rest is history. David sinned by sleeping with her.

> "Learn to say no right in the moment sin approaches you. Only thus is victory possible."
>
> —*Erich Sauer (1898–1959)*

David should have turned from sin immediately. Indeed, he should have followed Joseph's lead. Joseph immediately fled from the advances of Potiphar's wife when she tried to seduce him (Genesis 39). He had learned the lesson that would later be recorded in 2 Timothy 2:22: "Flee youthful passions and pursue righteousness." (See also 2 Corinthians 6:16.)

Our sins look horrible when we see them in someone else.

In 2 Samuel 12:1-7 we read about how David got "Nathanized." Nathan described a particular man's horrible crime, and David's anger was kindled against the man. "You are the man," Nathan told him. How ugly our sins look when we behold them in other people. Someone said we tend to condemn in others what we ourselves are most guilty of.

Ultimately our sins are against God, even when we've injured human beings in the process.

We find David's repentance after he sinned with Bathsheba recorded in Psalm 51. In that psalm, David affirmed to God, "For I know my transgressions, and my sin is ever before me. Against you, you only, have I sinned and done what is evil in your sight" (verses 3-4).

The good news is, when we go to God in confession, there is forgiveness of sins: "I acknowledged my sin to you, and I did not cover my iniquity; I said, 'I will confess my transgressions to the LORD,' and you forgave the iniquity of my sin" (Psalm 32:5). First John 1:9 tells us, "If we confess our sins, he is faithful and just to forgive us our sins and to cleanse us from all unrighteousness."

2 Samuel

Even though God forgives your sin, you may yet experience temporal consequences for your sin.

> "If a man gets drunk and goes out and breaks his leg so that it must be amputated, God will forgive him if he asks it, but he will have to hop around on one leg all his life."
>
> —Dwight L. Moody (1837–1899)

David's sin was forgiven by God (2 Samuel 12:13). Nevertheless, David would subsequently experience severe temporal consequences: (1) The sword would never depart from his house; (2) Because of the evil he inflicted on another man's family, David's family would now experience great evil; and (3) the child that was to be born would die. Let us never forget: choices have consequences.

In heaven, we will see our children who have died.

When his baby was dying, David prayed and fasted and wept on his behalf. Once the baby died, David stopped fasting. He said, "While the child was still alive, I fasted and wept, for I said, 'Who knows whether the LORD will be gracious to me, that the child may live?' But now he is dead. Why should I fast? Can I bring him back again? I shall go to him, but he will not return to me" (2 Samuel 12:22-23). This last part of the passage shows David's belief that he would be reunited with his dead son in the afterlife: "I will go to him"—that is, I will go to heaven where he is.

> "O death, where is your victory?"
>
> —1 Corinthians 15:55

Scripture has other evidences for the salvation of babies and infants: (1) No descriptions of hell mention infants or young children. (2) No descriptions of the great white throne judgment mention infants or young children (Revelation 20:11-15). (3) The basis of the last judgment is "according to what they had done" (Revelation 20:11-13), and infants are not responsible for their actions. And (4) Children quite obviously have a special place in Jesus's heart, and Jesus said we must become like children to enter God's kingdom (Matthew 18).

You reap what you sow.

Anyone who sows good will reap good. A person who sows evil will reap evil. Absalom, David's son, is a good example. Absalom was vengeful and became a murderer (2 Samuel 13:20-33). He was vain and arrogant (14:25-28). He undercut his father, David, while seeking to cultivate loyalty to himself throughout Israel (15:1-12). He had a significant military force and sought to usurp David's throne (16–17). David's army attacked Absalom's forces, though David explicitly ordered that Absalom be spared. Joab disobeyed David and killed Absalom (18). We are reminded of Galatians 6:7: "Whatever one sows, that will he also reap."

God's people are not immune to experiencing great grief.

Among the greatest pains faced by human beings is grief when a friend or loved one dies. David grieved greatly at the death of his friend Jonathan (2 Samuel 1:17-27). He lamented aloud, "I am distressed for you, my brother Jonathan" (verse 26). David cared deeply for him.

David also grieved over the death of his son Absalom, who rebelled against him and even tried to usurp his throne, almost successfully. Despite Absalom's rebellion against David, David loved him. When Absalom died in a battle, David was overwhelmed with grief. Second Samuel 18:33 tells us, "The king was deeply moved and went up to the chamber over the gate and wept. And as he went, he said, 'O my son Absalom, my son, my son Absalom! Would I had died instead of you, O Absalom, my son, my son.'" (See also 19:1-8.)

God's people are not immune to the pain of grief. Even though Christ has taken the "sting" out of death (1 Corinthians 15:55), it is nevertheless extremely painful when a family member or friend dies (1 Thessalonians 4:13). Even the great apostle Paul considered death an "enemy" yet to be conquered (1 Corinthians 15:26).

> "We are healed of grief only when we express it to the full."
>
> —Charles Swindoll

Watch out for pride. It will bring you down!

Second Samuel 24 portrays David taking a census. David was measuring the size of his army—apparently in a prideful way. David wanted to glory in the size of his fighting force. This resulted in God's chastisement. Let us never forget: "Pride goes before destruction, and haughtiness before a fall" (Proverbs 16:18 NLT).

A Thought to Anchor in Your Heart

Flee youthful passions and pursue righteousness.

2 Samuel

1 Kings

Earthly leaders who obey God bring blessing upon their nation. Those who disobey forfeit God's blessing for their nation.

First Kings derives its title from the first word in the Hebrew text—"Kings" (1:1). It focuses on 40 kings in Israel (the northern kingdom) and Judah (the southern kingdom).

Jewish tradition holds that Jeremiah wrote 1 and 2 Kings. Other traditions claim Ezra or Ezekiel wrote the books. This unnamed prophet lived in exile with Israel in Babylon, and he wrote the books around 550 BC.

The two books were originally a single book. They were divided into two books by the translators of the Septuagint—the Greek translation of the Hebrew Old Testament that predates the time of Christ.

These books focus heavy attention on how Israel divided into two kingdoms. Early in 1 Kings, we find a stable kingdom under the leadership of King Solomon (1 Kings 1–9). During this time the kingdom was united, and it was characterized by glory and splendor. As an outworking of the covenant promises God had made to Israel in the book of Deuteronomy, the nation was truly blessed by God so long as the nation continued to obey His laws.

When the nation turned from God, however, it weakened religiously, morally, economically, and politically. As the nation strayed further and further from the worship of the one true God, things went from bad to worse. Internal strife weakened the kingdom and it eventually split into two kingdoms—the northern kingdom (retaining the name Israel) and the southern kingdom (called Judah).

The two sets of kings and their kingdoms remained indifferent to God's laws and His prophets. They were thoroughly disobedient, and this ultimately led to

Israel's fall in 722 BC and the crushing Babylonian captivity for Judah in 587 BC. The author clearly communicates that this dire situation was a direct result of the people's long-term disobedience to God (1 Kings 9:3-9). Even so, God's mercy was always still available if there was repentance.

Following are key applicational concepts in 1 Kings:

Death is not the end. An afterlife awaits each of us.

David was now an old man, and Solomon was anointed king (1 Kings 1). "Then David slept with his fathers and was buried in the city of David" (2:10). The phrase "slept with his fathers" is one of many ways the Bible describes death and burial. A famous person (or king) like David would typically be buried with family members in a tomb—family members like a father, grandfather, great-grandfather, and so on. So David literally did sleep in death "with his fathers." Bible expositors point out, however, that the word "sleep" implies a future awakening—a resurrection of the body (1 Corinthians 15).

> "Time is short. Eternity is long. It is only reasonable that this short life be lived in the light of eternity."
>
> —*Charles Spurgeon (1834–1892)*

It is important to grasp that the term "sleep" refers only to the body and not to the soul or spirit. The term is appropriate for the body since the body takes on the appearance of sleep at death. One's spirit or soul, however, survives death and goes either to heaven or a place of punishment, depending on whether one is a believer.

Scripture is clear that the souls of both believers and unbelievers are fully conscious between death and the future day of resurrection. For example, Lazarus, the rich man, and Abraham—all of whom had died—were fully conscious and fully aware of all that was transpiring around them (Luke 16:19-31). Moses and Elijah (who had died long ago) were conscious on the Mount of Transfiguration with Jesus (Matthew 17:3). Jesus promised the repentant thief that he would be with Him (consciously) in paradise the very day he died (Luke 23:43). The "souls" of martyrs are portrayed as being conscious in heaven, talking to God (Revelation 6:9-10).

Jesus, in speaking about the Old Testament saints Abraham, Isaac, and Jacob, said God "is not God of the dead, but of the living" (Luke 20:38). In effect, Jesus was saying, "Abraham, Isaac, and Jacob, though they died physically many years ago, are actually living

> "Eternity to the godly is a day that has no sunset; eternity to the wicked is a night that has no sunrise."
>
> —*Thomas Watson (1620–1686)*

1 Kings

today. For God, who calls Himself the God of Abraham, Isaac, and Jacob, is not the God of the dead but of the living." In summary, believers who die are in conscious bliss in heaven (2 Corinthians 5:8; Philippians 1:21-23) while unbelievers are in conscious woe (Luke 16:22-23; Mark 9:47-48; 2 Peter 2:9).

God is always willing to give wisdom to those who ask for it.

Solomon was now Israel's king. As a young man, he prayed for God's wisdom:

> "The fear of the LORD is the beginning of wisdom; all those who practice it have a good understanding."
>
> —Psalm 111:10

"Give your servant therefore an understanding mind to govern your people, that I may discern between good and evil, for who is able to govern this your great people" (1 Kings 3:9). God granted his request: "I now do according to your word. Behold, I give you a wise and discerning mind, so that none like you has been before you and none like you shall arise after you" (3:12). We are told, "God gave Solomon wisdom and understanding beyond measure, and breadth of mind like the sand on the seashore, so that Solomon's wisdom surpassed the wisdom of all the people of the east and all the wisdom of Egypt" (4:29-30).

You and I can ask God for wisdom too. James 1:5 says, "If any of you lacks wisdom, let him ask God, who gives generously to all without reproach, and it will be given him." The word "generously" here means "without reserve, liberally, ungrudgingly." Just ask and it will be given.

God is present among us.

David had sought to build the first temple for God, though it was not to happen, for David was a warrior, and this served to disqualify him. It was through his son Solomon that the temple was eventually built (1 Kings 6–7).

Built in Jerusalem, the temple was rectangular in shape, running east and west, and measured about 87 by 30 feet. It was 43 feet high. The walls of the temple were made of cedar wood, and carved into the wood were cherubim angels, flowers, and palm trees. The walls were overlaid with gold. The floor was made of cypress.

Solomon's temple had a holy place and a Holy of Holies. Double doors led into the Holy of Holies, where the Ark of the Covenant was found. God manifest Himself in the Holy of Holies in a cloud of glory (1 Kings 8:10-11).

The temple was the heart and center of religious worship for the Jews. It was

God's dwelling place—His glory inhabited it (Ezekiel 10:4). In Bible times Jews outside of Jerusalem would pray toward Jerusalem because the temple (God's dwelling place) was located there. In a very real sense, then, God was "among" His people in Old Testament times via the temple.

In New Testament times, an awesome new truth was taught by the apostle Paul. Every Christian's body is a temple of the Holy Spirit: "Do you not know that you are God's temple and that God's Spirit dwells in you?" (1 Corinthians 3:16). "Do you not know that your body is a temple of the Holy Spirit within you, whom you have from God?" (1 Corinthians 6:19). God is "among" us in a whole new way, for now God is within us.

> "Do you not know that your body is a temple of the Holy Spirit within you, whom you have from God? You are not your own, for you were bought with a price. So glorify God in your body."
>
> —1 Corinthians 6:19-20

One of Paul's points about the body being a temple of the Holy Spirit is that the body must never be used for sinful purposes. That would amount to defiling God's temple. The big idea: Live righteously!

God is both immanent and transcendent—both right here with us, but also high above us.

Though Solomon built a temple for God, he knew God could not be contained by an earthly temple: "Will God indeed dwell on the earth? Behold, heaven and the highest heaven cannot contain you; how much less this house that I have built" (1 Kings 8:27). The biblical teaching is that God is both immanent and transcendent.

A number of verses in the Bible teach both God's transcendence and His immanence. Deuteronomy 4:39 says, "Know therefore today, and lay it to your heart, that the LORD is God in heaven above and on the earth beneath; there is no other." Isaiah 57:15 affirms, "For thus says the One who is high and lifted up, who inhabits eternity, whose name is Holy: 'I dwell in the high and holy place, and also with him who is of a contrite and lowly spirit.'" In Jeremiah 23:23-24 we read, "Am I a God at hand, declares the LORD, and not a God far away?...Do I not fill heaven and earth? declares the LORD." Our God is an awesome God!

God's Immanence
How comforting to know that no matter where we go, we will never escape the presence of our beloved God. He is always immanent—always right here with us. Like a good shepherd never leaves his sheep, so God never leaves His children alone (Psalm 23; John 10:1-15).

1 Kings

Beware: even wise people can act foolishly.

Solomon was the wisest man on planet Earth. God gave him this wisdom (1 Kings 3:9,12). And yet, Solomon acted like a fool in disobeying God by marrying many foreign women. These women seduced Solomon into worshiping false gods (11:1-8). This ought to be a warning to each of us. Just because we are Bible-believing Christians who love Jesus does not mean we are incapable of falling into ungodliness. Christian, beware!

> **Be Wise**
> - The wise control their anger—Proverbs 14:29
> - The wise keep their cool—Proverbs 29:11
> - The wise are hungry for truth—Proverbs 15:14
> - The wise listen—Proverbs 12:15
> - The wise take advice—Proverbs 13:10
> - The wise are cautious—Proverbs 14:16

Monogamy has always been God's will for marriage.

First Kings 11:1-3 tells us, "King Solomon loved many foreign women...He had 700 wives, who were princesses, and 300 concubines." Contrary to Solomon's lifestyle, monogamy is God's standard for the human race. This is clear from numerous scriptural facts:

1. From the beginning God set the pattern by creating a monogamous marriage relationship with one man and one woman, Adam and Eve (Genesis 1:27; 2:21-25).

2. Following from this God-established example of one woman for one man, this was the general practice of the human race (Genesis 4:1) until interrupted by sin (4:23).

3. The Law of Moses clearly commands that the king "shall not acquire many wives for himself, lest his heart turn away" (Deuteronomy 17:17).

4. The warning against polygamy is repeated in the very passage where it numbers Solomon's many wives: "You shall not enter into marriage with them, neither shall they with you, for surely they will turn away your heart after their gods" (1 Kings 11:2).

5. Our Lord reaffirmed God's original intention, noting that God created one "male and female" for each other (Matthew 19:4).

6. The New Testament stresses that "because of the temptation to sexual immorality, each man should have his own wife and each woman her own husband" (1 Corinthians 7:2).

7. Paul insisted that a church leader should be "the husband of one wife" (1 Timothy 3:2,12).

8. Monogamous marriage is a prefiguration of the relationship between Christ and His bride, the church (Ephesians 5:31-32).

Why, then, did Solomon take so many wives? History reveals that Solomon was aggressive in his foreign policy. In sealing treaties in ancient days, it was customary for a lesser king to give his daughter in marriage to the greater king (in this case, Solomon). Every time a new treaty was sealed, Solomon ended up with yet another wife. These wives were considered tokens of friendship and "sealed" the relationship between the two kings. It may be that Solomon was not even personally acquainted with some of these wives, even though he was married to them.

> "Each man should have his own wife and each woman her own husband."
> —1 Corinthians 7:2

In the process of doing all this, Solomon was disobedient to the Lord. He was so obsessed with power that it overshadowed his spiritual life and he ended up falling into apostasy—worshiping some of the false gods of the women who became married to him. What a tragedy.

You can be "wholly true to the Lord" and yet fall into sin.

First Kings 15:3 says of Abijam, "His heart was not wholly true to the LORD his God, as the heart of David his father." In this verse we read the heart of David had been fully devoted ("wholly true") to the Lord. We recall, however, that David committed a heinous sin in his adulterous relationship with Bathsheba (2 Samuel 11).

Of course, David had a sin nature like all the rest of us. (He said, "I was brought forth in iniquity, and in sin did my mother conceive me"—Psalm 51:5.) David was not perfect. But the overall orientation of his life was consistently God-ward. And when he did fall into sin, he confessed his sin to God and was

Confession of Sin
- Refuse to confess, misery results—Psalm 32:3
- Confession brings forgiveness—Psalm 32:5
- Confession brings mercy—Proverbs 28:13
- Confession restores fellowship—1 John 1:9

restored in his relationship with Him (Psalm 51). It is in this sense that David's heart is said to have been "wholly true" to the Lord. He was wholly true even in recognizing his fallenness.

Personally I'm glad the Bible gives us the "full scoop" on the frailties and warts of the biblical saints. It gives me hope that despite my own frailties, I can continue in my pursuit of being wholly true to God (see Philippians 1:6).

1 Kings

Our God is incomparable. False gods don't stand a chance against Him.

Elijah the prophet challenged the 850 priests of Baal and Asherah to prove the existence of their god (1 Kings 18:21). A sacrifice was set up, and the priests of Baal were challenged to have Baal burn the sacrifice, which would prove his existence. If, however, he was unable to do this, and Israel's God was able to burn up the sacrifice, this would prove that the God of Israel was the one true God.

> "I am God, and there is no other; I am God, and there is none like me."
>
> —Isaiah 46:9

Baal's prophets did their best, calling on Baal all day long, dancing around the altar. But it was to no avail. Baal did not reply. Elijah then quickly called on the one true God of Israel, and the altar was immediately consumed by fire. The God of Israel was mightily vindicated on that day. Baal's impotence (nonexistence) was obvious to all. As a judgment, the prophets of Baal were then slaughtered at Elijah's command (1 Kings 18:40).

Our God truly is incomparable. In the Old Testament, God's incomparability is expressed in two ways. The first is by negation: "There is none like God" (Deuteronomy 33:26). The second is by rhetorical questions, such as, "Who is like you, O LORD, among the gods?" (Exodus 15:11). The implied answer is "No one in all the universe." Our God is an awesome God!

A Thought to Anchor in Your Heart

Never forget—even wise people can act foolishly. The best safeguard is to daily stay rooted in God's Word and obey Him in all things.

2 Kings

Earthly leaders who obey God bring blessing upon their nation. Those who disobey forfeit God's blessing for their nation.

Second Kings naturally follows 1 Kings, both having previously been part of a single book. Please consult the previous chapter on 1 Kings for background information on both books. Following are key applicational concepts in 2 Kings:

Bad leadership can bring a nation down—and keep a nation down.

A pattern we witness in 2 Kings is the preponderance of bad kings who ruled God's people—whether in the northern kingdom (Israel) or the southern kingdom (Judah) (2 Kings 3–17). These leaders caused a trickle-down effect—that is, evil trickled down from the throne to the general populace. The people took on *and maintained* the wicked character of their leadership. No wonder Israel went into captivity (17:7-41).

This is one good reason to vote in presidential elections. We should seek to bring into office those who best represent our values and goals. They'll cause a trickle-down effect for good.

Music can open the heart to spiritual things.

Elisha the prophet experienced God's anointing at the sound of music: "When the musician played, the hand of the LORD came upon him [Elisha]" (2 Kings 3:15). Music also played a significant role in worship. Indeed, various musical instruments were used in producing music as a part of worship in the temple

Timeline

848— Prophetic mantle passes from Elijah to Elisha.
841— Jehu becomes king of Israel.
835— Joash becomes king of Judah.
798— Jehoash becomes king of Israel.
793— Jeroboam becomes king of Israel.
722— The northern kingdom is taken into exile by the Assyrians.
715— Hezekiah becomes king of Judah.
640— Josiah becomes king of Judah.
605— The southern kingdom is taken into exile by the Babylonians.
550— The books of 1 and 2 Kings are written (these were originally one book).

"Leaders need to cultivate two things: a righteous heart and rhinoceros skin."

—*Charles Swindoll*

2 Kings

(1 Chronicles 25). Many of the psalms were originally designed for musical accompaniment (for example, Psalms 4 and 5).

> "Next to theology I give to music the highest place and honor. Music is the art of the prophets, the only art that can calm the agitations of the soul; it is one of the most magnificent and delightful presents God has given us."
>
> —Martin Luther (1483–1546)

Scripture reveals that "David and all the house of Israel were celebrating before the LORD, with songs and lyres and harps and tambourines and castanets and cymbals" (2 Samuel 6:5). We are told that "4,000 shall offer praises to the LORD with the instruments...made for praise" (1 Chronicles 23:5). The Levites were stationed "in the house of the LORD with cymbals, harps, and lyres, according to the commandment of David" (2 Chronicles 29:25). The psalmist proclaims, "I will praise you with the lyre, O God, my God" (Psalm 43:4). He exults, "I will also praise you with the harp for your faithfulness, O my God; I will sing praises to you with the lyre, O Holy One of Israel" (Psalm 71:22). He further exults, "Praise him with trumpet sound; praise him with lute and harp! Praise him with tambourine and dance; praise him with strings and pipe! Praise him with sounding cymbals; praise him with loud clashing cymbals" (Psalm 150:3-5). Instrumental music and singing continued to be common in the postexilic period (Ezra 3:10-11; Nehemiah 12:27-47). Long story short: Music has consistently played a role in opening people's hearts to the things of the spirit.

God's angels are His invisible helpers who watch after us.

> "The deer of the forest far surpass our human capacity in their keenness of smell. Bats possess a phenomenally sensitive built-in radar system. Some animals can see things in the dark that escape our attention. Swallows and geese possess sophisticated guidance systems that appear to border on the supernatural. So why should we think it strange if men fail to perceive the evidences of angelic presence?"
>
> —Billy Graham

In 2 Kings 6:15-17 we read about how angels invisibly protected Elisha and his servant: "When the servant of the man of God rose early in the morning and went out, behold, an army with horses and chariots was all around the city. And the servant said, 'Alas, my master! What shall we do?' He said, 'Do not be afraid, for those who are with us are more than those who are with them.' Then Elisha prayed and said, 'O LORD, please open his eyes that he may see.' So the LORD opened the eyes of the young man, and he saw, and behold, the mountain was full of horses and chariots of fire all around Elisha.'" God's heavenly host was protecting them.

2 Kings

The reason Elisha never got worried was his "assurance of things hoped for, the conviction of things not seen" (Hebrews 11:1). The eye of faith recognizes that God acts on our behalf—as do His angels—even when we don't perceive their presence with our physical senses.

Like the servant, you and I are typically unaware of angelic presence in our midst. They're actually all around us, even though we do not perceive them. There is no telling just how many times God has kept us safe through the work of angels without us having known anything about it.

This brings to mind Psalm 91:11: "He will command his angels concerning you to guard you in all your ways." The angels were guarding Elisha and his servant in all their ways. The angels have the same ministry among us.

Other verses reveal that angels are sometimes used by God in answering the prayers of God's people (Acts 12:5-10), escorting believers into heaven following the moment of death (Luke 16:22), and ministering to us in a variety of ways (Hebrews 1:14).

God is full of amazing grace.

In 2 Kings 9:6 we find Jehu being anointed as king. God spoke through the prophet Elisha: "Thus says the LORD, the God of Israel, I anoint you king over the people of the LORD, over Israel."

Despite the fact that the people had fallen deep into sin, and that this sin had been going on for generations, God *still* referred to the people as "the people of the Lord." God could have just annihilated them for their relentless sin. But He still held on to them as His precious people—*the people of the Lord*. That's amazing grace!

The word "grace" literally means "unmerited favor." "Unmerited" means this favor cannot be earned. Grace, theologically speaking, refers to the undeserved, unearned favor of God. God's people—Israel—did not deserve to be the people of the Lord, but they were. Likewise, you and I don't deserve to be saved, but we are by the grace of God. Romans 5:1-11 tells us God gives His incredible salvation to those who actually deserve the opposite—that is, condemnation.

True grace is sometimes hard for people to grasp. After all, our society is

God's Grace
- Grace comes from Jesus—John 1:14-17
- We are justified by God's grace—Romans 3:24
- God's grace is sufficient—1 Corinthians 15:10
- God's grace abounds for every need—2 Corinthians 9:8

performance-oriented. Good grades in school depend on how well we perform in school. Climbing up the corporate ladder at work depends on how well we perform at work. Nothing of any real worth is a "free ticket" in our society. But God's gift of salvation is a grace-gift. It is free. We cannot attain it by a good performance. Ephesians 2:8-9 assures us, "For by grace you have been saved through faith. And this is not your own doing; it is the gift of God, not a result of works, so that no one may boast." Titus 3:5 likewise tells us God "saved us, not because of works done by us in righteousness, but according to his own mercy." Praise God!

Always be open to good advice from respected spiritual leaders. It can keep you spiritually on track.

In 2 Kings 12:2 we are told that "Jehoash did what was right in the eyes of the LORD all his days, because Jehoiada the priest instructed him." King Jehoash received good spiritual advice from the priest Jehoiada, and he acted upon it. Jehoash made himself accountable to Jehoiada.

We are wise to make ourselves accountable to a more mature spiritual person. Perhaps it's a pastor or elder in the church. Perhaps it's just a more mature Christian who knows a lot about the Bible. The truth is, spiritual accountability leads to spiritual maturity.

Listening to Advice

- Son listens to father—Proverbs 1:8
- Wise man listens—Proverbs 12:15
- Listening makes one wise—Proverbs 19:20
- Be quick to listen—James 1:19

God doesn't always heal His people.

In 2 Kings 13:14 we read, "Now when Elisha had fallen sick with the illness of which he was to die, Joash king of Israel went down to him and wept before him." It is clearly not always God's will to heal His children—not even great prophets like Elisha.

As we consult the rest of Scripture, we find that the apostle Paul couldn't heal Timothy's stomach problem (1 Timothy 5:23), nor could he heal Trophimus at Miletus (2 Timothy 4:20) or Epaphroditus (Philippians 2:25-27). Paul spoke of "a bodily ailment" he had (Galatians 4:13-15). He also suffered a thorn in the flesh that God allowed him to retain (2 Corinthians 12:7-9). God certainly allowed Job to go through a time of physical suffering (Job 1–2). In all cases, these individuals accepted their situations and trusted in God's grace for sustenance.

Numerous verses in Scripture reveal that our physical bodies are continuously running down and suffering various ailments. Our bodies are said to be

2 Kings

perishable and weak (1 Corinthians 15:42-44). Paul said "our outer self is wasting away" (2 Corinthians 4:16). Death and disease will be a part of the human condition until we receive resurrection bodies—that is, body upgrades—that are immune to such frailties (1 Corinthians 15:51-55).

An afterlife awaits each of us.

In 2 Kings 14:29 we read that "Jeroboam slept with his fathers, the kings of Israel." "Sleep" is an appropriate figure of speech for the death of the body since death is only temporary, awaiting the resurrection when the body will be awakened from its sleep (1 Corinthians 15). Further, both sleep and death have the same posture—lying down.

> **The Afterlife in Heaven**
>
> "We would rather be away from the body and at home with the Lord" (2 Corinthians 5:8).
>
> "My desire is to depart and be with Christ" (Philippians 1:23).
>
> "In your presence there is fullness of joy; at your right hand are pleasures forevermore" (Psalm 16:11).

The Bible is very clear that the believer's spirit survives death (Luke 12:4), and is consciously present with the Lord (2 Corinthians 5:8) in a better place (Philippians 1:23) where other souls are talking (Matthew 17:3) and even praying (Revelation 6:9-10). Likewise, the unbeliever's soul is in a place of conscious torment (Luke 16:22-26; Revelation 19:20–20:15).

Don't play games with God. Fear Him and follow only Him.

In 2 Kings 17:33 we read of those who "feared the LORD but also served their own gods." What absolute folly! Anyone who has a proper fear of the Lord will follow the Lord alone, and not insult Him by serving other gods (Deuteronomy 5:29; 6:13; Job 28:28; Psalm 111:10; Proverbs 1:7; 3:7; 8:13; 16:6; Ecclesiastes 12:13).

> "You shall have no other gods before me."
>
> —Exodus 20:3 (1st of the Ten Commandments)

Avoid all forms of idolatry. It will bring you down.

Every evil king in both Israel and Judah encouraged idolatry (2 Kings 17:12,15; 21:11,21; 23:24). Their continual trafficking with false gods staggers the mind.

Modern Christians find it easy to condemn such ancient forms of idolatry. The scary thing is that we have our own modern idols that are often unrecognized as idols. Idolatry involves worshiping other things in place of God, such as

2 Kings

money, materialism, the pursuit of fame, and sexual immorality. The New Testament consistently urges Christians to beware of idolatry (1 Corinthians 5:11; 10:7,14; 2 Corinthians 6:16; Galatians 5:20).

God answers prayers!

Hezekiah was told to get his house in order because his life was about to end (2 Kings 20:1). He then turned to God in prayer: "Now, O LORD, please remember how I have walked before you in faithfulness and with a whole heart, and have done what is good in your sight" (20:3). The Lord responded, "I have heard your prayer; I have seen your tears. Behold, I will heal you...I will add fifteen years to your life" (20:5-6). Never forget that our God answers prayers (Philippians 4:6-7).

> **Advice on Prayer**
> - Sin hinders prayer being answered (Psalm 66:18).
> - Righteousness opens the door to prayer being answered (Proverbs 15:29).

Don't compromise. Stay fully committed to the Lord in all things.

In 2 Kings 22:2 we find a great model in the person of Josiah: "He did what was right in the eyes of the LORD and walked in all the way of David his father, and he did not turn aside to the right or to the left." In other words, Josiah was not a compromiser. He wouldn't budge an inch from God's chosen path. He walked the straight and narrow way, and was resolved to continue doing so. May we all follow his example.

God sometimes disciplines His people harshly for their own good.

In the book of Deuteronomy, God through Moses promised great blessings if the nation lived in obedience to the Sinai covenant. God also warned that if the nation disobeyed His commands, it would experience the punishments listed in the covenant—including exile from the land (Deuteronomy 28:15-68).

Old Testament history is replete with illustrations of how unfaithful Israel was to the covenant. The two most significant periods of exile for the Jewish people involved the fall of Israel to the Assyrians in 722 BC, and the collapse of Judah to the Babylonians in 605 BC. Just as God promised, disobedience brought exile to God's people.

As a backdrop, it is interesting to observe that the

> **A Failure to Repent Brings Discipline**
> A failure to repent of sin always brings God's discipline (Psalm 32:3-5; 51). "If we judged ourselves truly, we would not be judged" (1 Corinthians 11:31).

first chapter of Isaiah takes the form of a courtroom lawsuit against Judah. Judah was indicted by the Lord (through Isaiah) because of Judah's "breach of contract" in breaking the Sinai covenant, which had been given to the nation at the time of the exodus from Egypt.

The Lord indicted Judah for rebelling against Him. The Hebrew word for "rebel" in Isaiah 1:2 was often used among the ancients in reference to a subordinate state's violation of a treaty with a sovereign nation. In Isaiah 1, the word points to Judah's blatant violation of God's covenant. Hence, Judah went into captivity.

The Babylonian captivity was therefore God's means of chastening Judah (2 Kings 24–25). This punishment, of course, was intended as a corrective. Just as an earthly father disciplines his children, so God the Father disciplines His children to train and educate them (Hebrews 12:1-5; see also Job 5:17; 33:19; Proverbs 3:11-12).

A Thought to Anchor in Your Heart

Judge yourself and minimize the need for God's discipline in your life.

2 Kings

1 Chronicles

There is always hope for the future despite
a dire past. God's promises energize us.

Timeline

First and 2 Chronicles were written by an unidentified author between 450 and 425 BC. They were originally a single book, but were separated around 200 BC when the Septuagint translators divided the long scroll into two books. (The Septuagint is a Greek translation of the Hebrew Old Testament that predates the time of Christ.)

These books draw most of their information from the books of Samuel and the books of Kings, covering the period from the time of the Judges to the time of the exile. As was true in the previous books, 1 and 2 Chronicles emphasize that the nation is blessed by God when it is obedient to Him, but it is punished by Him when it is disobedient. While the material is essentially the same as in these other books, it is presented from the vantage point of Jewish exiles returning from Babylon to Jerusalem.

The problem for these returning exiles was that the future looked bleak, especially in contrast to Israel's glorious past (the David-Solomon years). On the one hand, they were glad to be back in the Promised Land. On the other hand, they were grieved at the hurtful memories of what they had lost as a result of their ancestors' sins. It is in this context that the books of Chronicles become so meaningful, for they served to give hope back to the Jews by reminding them of truths about God's promises to them, their land, their temple, their priesthood, and especially the fact that they were from the line of David and were therefore God's chosen people. Being reminded of these things was engineered to encourage the Jews to remain faithful to God during these difficult times. God's covenant was still in force with them, so they should be obedient to Him.

Following are key applicational concepts in 1 Chronicles:

Comparing Scripture with Scripture points to the glorious coming of the divine Messiah, born as a man so He could rescue us from sin.

In 1 Chronicles 1–2 we find a genealogy from Adam to David. One significant aspect of this genealogy relates to the fact that the Old Testament makes clear that Jesus had to be both God and man as the Messiah (Isaiah 7:14; 9:6). Considering the genealogy in 1 Chronicles 1–2 alongside the genealogies of Jesus in Matthew 1:1-16 and Luke 3:23-38 provides proof that, indeed, Jesus the divine Messiah *did* become a man, and has a human ancestry to prove it.

> "O for a thousand tongues to sing my great Redeemer's praise!"
>
> —*Charles Wesley (1707–1788)*

This relates directly to our salvation, for by becoming a man, Jesus became our Kinsman-Redeemer. In Old Testament times the next of kin—one related by blood—always functioned as the kinsman-redeemer of a family member who needed redemption from jail. Jesus became related to us by blood (He became a man) so He could function as our Kinsman-Redeemer and rescue us from the bondage of sin.

God answers prayer!

In 1 Chronicles 4:10 we find Jabez praying, "Oh that you would bless me and enlarge my border, and that your hand might be with me, and that you would keep me from harm so that it might not bring me pain!" We are then told, "God granted what he asked."

Our God is a God who answers the prayers of His people. As we consult other Scriptures, we find that there should be at least five components to prayer:

Thanksgiving. In prayer we ought to always give thanks to God for everything we have (Ephesians 5:20; Colossians 3:15). We should "enter his gates with thanksgiving" (Psalm 100:4; see also Psalm 95:2).

Praise. Praise for God should always be on our lips (Psalm 34:1; 103:1-5,20-22). We should "continually offer up a sacrifice of praise to God" (Hebrews 13:15).

> "Nothing lies beyond the reach of prayer except that which lies outside the will of God."
>
> —*Anonymous*

Worship. Like the psalmist, we should bow down in worship before the Lord our Maker (Psalm 95:6; Revelation 14:7), and do so with "reverence and awe" (Hebrews 12:28). We should worship Him alone (Exodus 20:3-5).

Confession. Confession in prayer is wise, for "whoever conceals his transgressions will not prosper, but he who confesses and forsakes them will obtain mercy" (Proverbs 28:13; see also 1 John 1:9).

1 Chronicles

Requests. In the Lord's Prayer, we are exhorted to pray for our daily needs (Matthew 6:11). The apostle Paul wrote, "Do not be anxious about anything, but in everything by prayer and supplication with thanksgiving *let your requests be made known to God*" (Philippians 4:6, emphasis added). This is what Jabez did. It's what we should do too.

Avoid idolatry at all costs. God hates it.

> "A man's god is that for which he lives."
>
> —*D. Martyn Lloyd-Jones*
> *(1899–1981)*

In 1 Chronicles 5:25 we are told that the members of the half-tribe of Manasseh fell into idolatry: "They broke faith with the God of their fathers, and whored after the gods of the peoples of the land." What a slap to the face of God. They not only turned away from the one true living God, but they turned toward false gods who in reality *have no life in them*. They are "the work of human hands. They have mouths, but do not speak; they have eyes, but do not see; they have ears, but do not hear, nor is there any breath in their mouths" (Psalm 135:15-17; see also 115:4-6). Turning to idols is sheer lunacy.

The New Testament consistently urges Christians to beware of idolatry. Paul instructs, "I am writing to you not to associate with anyone who…is an idolater" (1 Corinthians 5:11). He commands, "Do not be idolaters," and "flee from idolatry" (1 Corinthians 10:7,14). In Galatians 5:20 he affirms that idolatry is among the "works of the flesh." He commands, "Put to death therefore what is earthly in you: sexual immorality, impurity, passion, evil desire, and covetousness, which is idolatry" (Colossians 3:5). John more tenderly exhorts, "Little children, keep yourselves from idols" (1 John 5:21).

God is sovereign over matters of life and death.

First Samuel 31:4-5 tells us, "Saul took his own sword and fell upon it. And when his armor-bearer saw that Saul was dead, he also fell upon his sword and died with him." First Chronicles 10:4-5 likewise affirms, "Saul took his own sword and fell upon it. And when his armor-bearer saw that Saul was dead, he also fell upon his sword and died."

The interesting thing to observe here is that this was done according to God's sovereign will. In 1 Chronicles 10:13-14 we are told, "So Saul died for his breach of faith. He broke faith with the LORD in that he did not keep the command of the LORD, and also consulted a medium, seeking guidance. He did not seek guidance from the LORD. Therefore the LORD put him to death and turned the kingdom over to David the son of Jesse."

Though Saul apparently committed suicide, it was ultimately the Lord who put him to death. This brings to mind God's words in Deuteronomy 32:39: "See now that I, even I, am he, and there is no god beside me; I kill and I make alive; I wound and I heal; and there is none that can deliver out of my hand" (Psalm 139:16).

The secret to success is to have God on your side.

First Chronicles 11:9 tells us, "David became greater and greater, for the LORD of hosts was with him" (2 Samuel 5:10). Here we see an example of *cause and effect*:

Cause: The Lord of hosts was with David.

Effect: David became greater and greater.

We witness this same type of thing all throughout Scripture. Consider Noah as an example. Genesis 6:8 tells us, "Noah found favor in the eyes of the LORD." The Hebrew word for "favor" is typically used in contexts of a superior, stronger person showing favor to a weaker, more inferior person. Noah's favor before God was related to the fact that he was righteous, blameless, and walked with God (verse 9). As a result of God's favor, God rescued Noah and his family from the flood.

We also see from Scripture that "the LORD was with Joseph" and "gave him favor" (Genesis 39:21). Likewise, "the boy Samuel continued to grow both in stature and in favor with the LORD" (1 Samuel 2:26). In the New Testament the angel said to Mary, "Do not be afraid, Mary, for you have found favor with God" (Luke 1:30). All these people became great because the Lord was with them.

My advice: Live righteously and the favor of God will be with you.

It is wise to consult with God about your decisions.

In 1 Chronicles 14:10 we read, "David inquired of God, 'Shall I go up against the Philistines? Will you

---

God Sovereign over Death

Man's "days are determined, and the number of his months is with you, and you have appointed his limits that he cannot pass" (Job 14:5).

"In your book were written, every one of them, the days that were formed for me, when as yet there was none of them" (Psalm 139:16).

"My times are in your hand" (Psalm 31:15).

"The LORD was with Joseph, and he became a successful man."

—*Genesis 39:2*

Cross-References: Seeking God's Guidance

Psalms 5:8 • 25:5 • 27:11 • 31:3 • 43:3 • 61:2 • 139:24 • 143 give them into my hand?' And the LORD said to him, 'Go up, and I will give them into your hand.'" David had learned the importance of not acting impetuously but rather checking things out with God before taking action. This is a lesson we all need to learn. No matter what you are facing in life, go to God in prayer and check things out with Him. After all, Scripture tells us prayer can help us understand God's will (Colossians 1:9-12). Prayer can keep us from harm and pain (1 Chronicles 4:10). And prayer can bring us deliverance from our troubles (Psalm 34:15-22). Sounds good to me!

Always be careful to do things God's way.

First Chronicles 15:11-13 tells us, "David summoned the priests Zadok and Abiathar, and the Levites Uriel, Asaiah, Joel, Shemaiah, Eliel, and Amminadab, and said to them, 'You are the heads of the fathers' houses of the Levites. Consecrate yourselves, you and your brothers, so that you may bring up the ark of the LORD, the God of Israel, to the place that I have prepared for it. Because you did not carry it the first time, the LORD our God broke out against us, because we did not seek him according to the rule.'"

Previously things were done man's way and a disaster ensued. God's anger broke out when the ark had been improperly handled and transported by Uzzah (2 Samuel 6:6-8; 1 Chronicles 13:9-12). Now things would be done God's way, with the ark being handled in a sanctified way. No disaster ensued this time.

A foundational issue we must all deal with is this: will my life be run God's way or my way? The truth is, God knows what He's doing. You don't know what you're doing. For me, it's a no-brainer. God's way it is!

Cross-References: Thanksgiving
1 Chronicles 23:30 • Psalm 30:12 • 35:18 • 69:30 • 95:2 • 100:4 • 116:17 • Daniel 6:10 • Matthew 11:25 • John 6:11 • Ephesians 5:20 • Philippians 4:6 • Colossians 2:7 • 3:15 • 4:2 • 1 Thessalonians 5:18 • 1 Timothy 4:4

Always have a thankful attitude to God.

There is no better person to learn from about thanksgiving than David, for many of the psalms he wrote are brimming with thanksgiving. It is interesting to note how David's song of thanksgiving in 1 Chronicles 16:7-36 is actually a compilation derived from the psalms:

- 1 Chronicles 16:8-22 derives from Psalm 105:1-15.
- 1 Chronicles 16:23-33 derives from Psalm 96:1-13.
- 1 Chronicles 16:34-36 derives from Psalm 106:1-47.

We might consider David's song of thanksgiving to be a medley of thanksgiving psalms. One predominant theme we see in his song is that thanksgiving is intimately connected to worship. My advice: Make sure thanksgiving plays a major role in your worship.

Just because an idea seems good to your thinking does not mean it is God's will for you.

In 1 Chronicles 17:1-2 we read, "Now when David lived in his house, David said to Nathan the prophet, 'Behold, I dwell in a house of cedar, but the ark of the covenant of the LORD is under a tent.' And Nathan said to David, 'Do all that is in your heart, for God is with you.'" It is quite obvious that David wanted to build a house for the Lord—a temple. At first glance it seemed like a good idea. Nathan said go for it. But later that same night, the Lord spoke to Nathan: "Go and tell my servant David, 'Thus says the LORD: It is not you who will build me a house to dwell in...I will raise up your offspring after you, one of your own sons, and I will establish his kingdom. He shall build a house for me, and I will establish his throne forever'" (17:3-4,11-12). Solomon would build the temple.

We learn an important lesson here: just because you have a good idea does not mean it is God's will for you to pursue that idea. As noted previously in the chapter, it is wise to consult with the Lord about all decisions in life (1 Chronicles 14:10; Colossians 1:9-12; Psalm 34:15-22).

Avoid pride. Pursue humility.

In 1 Chronicles 21:1-2 we read, "Satan stood against Israel and incited David to number Israel. So David said to Joab and the commanders of the army, 'Go, number Israel, from Beersheba to Dan, and bring me a report, that I may know their number.'"

The devil was apparently appealing to David's pride. David pridefully wanted to see how many soldiers he had and estimate the collective might of his forces.

The better way is the way of humility, recognizing that it is God who gives the victory, not human might. James 4:10 tells us, "Humble yourselves before the Lord, and he will exalt you." By contrast, "the LORD tears down the house of the proud" (Proverbs 15:25). Christian, beware!

Be strong and courageous.

David gave a great exhortation to his son Solomon in regard to building the temple: "Be strong and courageous and do it. Do not be afraid and do not be dismayed, for the LORD God, even my God, is with you. He will not leave you or forsake you, until all the work for the service of the house of the LORD is finished" (1 Chronicles 28:20). The reason Solomon could be strong and courageous was that the Lord would be with him. The Lord was the source of his strength.

We learn a good lesson here, for the Lord is also the source of our strength. Recall that Jesus affirmed, "Apart from me you can do nothing" (John 15:5). Conversely, the apostle Paul affirmed, "I can do all things through him who strengthens me" (Philippians 4:13). Never forget these two verses!

A Thought to Anchor in Your Heart

Apart from the Lord you can do nothing. But you can do all things through Christ who strengthens you.

2 Chronicles

Instability and apostasy bring a people down.
But reformation lifts them back up.

Second Chronicles picks up where 1 Chronicles left off. The book chronicles the history of Solomon's reign, as well as all of Judah's kings, from Rehoboam through Zedekiah. It covers the kings in the same basic time period as 1 and 2 Kings, but 2 Chronicles omits the kings of Israel, focusing only on those of Judah. Highlights of the book include Solomon's famous prayer for wisdom in ruling as king (1:7-12), Solomon's magnificent temple (5–7), and the queen of Sheba's visit to Solomon (9:1-12). Please consult the previous chapter on 1 Chronicles for background information on both books.

Following are key applicational concepts in 2 Chronicles:

The secret to success is having God on your side.

Recall that in 1 Chronicles 11:9 we were told that "David became greater and greater, for the LORD of hosts was with him" (2 Samuel 5:10). Now, in 2 Chronicles 1:1, we are told, "Solomon the son of David established himself in his kingdom, and the LORD his God was with him and made him exceedingly great." This reminds us of Joseph: "The Lord was with Joseph, and he became a successful man" (Genesis 39:2). My conclusion: Blessing falls upon those who stay close to God.

Timeline

991—Solomon is born.

970—Solomon becomes king.

966—Construction of the temple begins.

959—The temple is completed.

910—Asa becomes king of Judah.

872—Jehoshaphat becomes king of Judah.

792—Uzziah becomes king of Judah.

715—Hezekiah becomes king of Judah.

640—Josiah becomes king of Judah.

450–425—1 and 2 Chronicles are written.

God's Blessing

God seeks to shower blessings on His people (Psalm 144:15). He is "able to do far more abundantly than all that we ask or think" (Ephesians 3:20), and stands ready to do so.

God is ready and willing to give you wisdom whenever you need it.

Solomon was now Israel's king. As a young man, he prayed for God's wisdom: "Give me now wisdom and knowledge to go out and come in before this people, for who can govern this people of yours, which is so great?" (2 Chronicles 1:10). God granted His request.

Cross-References: Praying for Wisdom

2 Chronicles 1:10 • Psalm 90:12 • Proverbs 2:3 • Ephesians 1:17 • Colossians 1:9 • James 1:5

You and I can ask God for wisdom too. James 1:5 says, "If any of you lacks wisdom, let him ask God, who gives generously to all without reproach, and it will be given him." The word "generously" here means "without reserve, liberally, ungrudgingly." Just ask and it will be given!

Obedience to God brings blessing. Disobedience brings chastisement.

The opening chapters of 2 Chronicles focus on the reign of Solomon. We read of the great prosperity of his reign as king (2 Chronicles 1), his building of a magnificent temple (2:1–5:1), and the dedication of the temple (5:2–7:10). We are reminded that great prosperity accompanies obedience to God. Divine discipline, conversely, comes when there is disobedience (7:11-22). This is illustrated in 2 Chronicles 12:2: "In the fifth year of King Rehoboam, because they had been unfaithful to the LORD, Shishak king of Egypt came up against Jerusalem." God disciplined His disobedient people using Egypt as His whipping rod.

God is both right here with us but also high above us.

Scripture affirms that God is both immanent and transcendent—that is, He is both right here with us but also high above us. In 2 Chronicles 6:18 Solomon was speaking of the temple and affirmed, "Will God indeed dwell with man on the earth? Behold, heaven and the highest heaven cannot contain you, how much less this house that I have built!"

God's immanence and transcendence are taught throughout Scripture. Deuteronomy 4:39 says, "Know therefore today, and lay it to your heart, that the LORD is God in heaven above and on the earth beneath; there is no other." Isaiah 57:15 affirms, "For thus says the One who is high and lifted up, who inhabits eternity, whose name is Holy: 'I dwell in the high and holy place, and also with him who is of a contrite and lowly spirit, to revive the spirit of the lowly, and to revive the heart of the contrite.'" In Jeremiah 23:23-24 we read, "Am I a God at hand,

> "Draw near to God, and he will draw near to you."
>
> —James 4:8

declares the LORD, and not a God far away? Can a man hide himself in secret places so that I cannot see him? declares the LORD. Do I not fill heaven and earth? declares the LORD." Here's the good news: there's nowhere I can go where God is not with me!

God desires to be present among His people.

In 2 Chronicles 7:1 we are told that "the glory of the LORD filled the temple." God's glory refers to the luminous manifestation of His person. We are told in Scripture that brilliant light consistently accompanies the divine manifestation in His glory (Matthew 17:2-3; 1 Timothy 6:16; Revelation 1:16). Moreover, the word "glory" is often linked with verbs of seeing (Exodus 16:7; 33:18; Isaiah 40:5) and verbs of appearing (Exodus 16:10; Deuteronomy 5:24), both of which emphasize the visible nature of God's glory. God's glory not only involves brilliant light, but also the presence of smoke (Isaiah 6:4) and a cloud (Numbers 16:42). This visible glory filled the temple in Old Testament times.

The important point to notice is that God within the temple meant God was among His people. God was among His people many ways in Bible times. In the garden of Eden, God walked among Adam and Eve and interacted with them face-to-face (Genesis 1–3). Once sin entered the world, God dwelt among the Israelites via the Jewish tabernacle (Exodus 40:34), and later the temple (2 Samuel 22:7). In New Testament times, God "tabernacled" among us in the person of Jesus (John 1:14). Today Christians are the temple of the Holy Spirit (1 Corinthians 3:16; 6:19). In the New Jerusalem, the heavenly city, God will again dwell with His people face-to-face (Revelation 22:4). I can hardly wait!

> "Our fellowship is with the Father and with his Son Jesus Christ."
> —1 John 1:3

Humility, prayer, seeking God, and turning from wickedness can bring healing to a land.

In 2 Chronicles 7:12 we read, "If my people who are called by my name humble themselves, and pray and seek my face and turn from their wicked ways, then I will hear from heaven and will forgive their sin and heal their land." These are words God spoke specifically to Solomon regarding the Israelites. The verse contains a promise to the Israel of Solomon's time. And yet, we also find in this verse the general principle

A Verse to Remember

"If my people who are called by my name humble themselves, and pray and seek my face and turn from their wicked ways, then I will hear from heaven and will forgive their sin and heal their land."

—2 Chronicles 7:14

that prayer, humility, seeking God, and turning from evil open the door for God to bring healing and revival to a nation (compare with Jeremiah 18:7-9). Oh that America would repent and turn to God!

Our victories come not by human strength but by God's might.

In 2 Chronicles 14:11 we read, "Asa cried to the LORD his God, 'O LORD, there is none like you to help, between the mighty and the weak. Help us, O LORD our God, for we rely on you, and in your name we have come against this multitude. O LORD, you are our God; let not man prevail against you.'" Asa—who recognized that victory comes not by human strength but by God's might—was granted a smashing victory. Burn this truth into your mind!

The Lord shows Himself strong to those whose hearts are committed to Him.

In 2 Chronicles 16:9 we read, "The eyes of the LORD run to and fro throughout the whole earth, to give strong support to those whose heart is blameless toward him." God in His omniscience continually observes everyone's inner thoughts, attitudes, and convictions—including yours and mine. Those with a blameless heart are on the receiving end of God's strong support. My advice: Be wholeheartedly devoted to God.

Seek God above all else.

In 2 Chronicles 16:12-13 we read, "In the thirty-ninth year of his reign Asa was diseased in his feet, and his disease became severe. Yet even in his disease he did not seek the LORD, but sought help from physicians. And Asa slept with his fathers, dying in the forty-first year of his reign."

These verses should not be taken to mean it is wrong to seek the aid of a physician when sick. They simply emphasize that Asa was wrong to seek out a physician while completely excluding the Lord from the picture. God must be put first (Matthew 6:33; Colossians 1:18). As Jeremiah put it, "Cursed is the

---

God All-Powerful

- The Almighty reigns—Revelation 19:6
- Nothing is too difficult—Genesis 18:14
- Abundant in strength—Psalm 147:5
- Surpassingly great power—Ephesians 1:19-21
- No one can thwart—Isaiah 14:27
- No one can reverse—Isaiah 43:13
- Nothing is impossible—Mark 10:27

"Seek first the kingdom of God and his righteousness, and all these things will be added to you."

—Matthew 6:33

man who trusts in man and makes flesh his strength, whose heart turns away from the LORD" (Jeremiah 17:5).

We find balance in our understanding of 2 Chronicles 16:12-13 in recognizing that both the Old and New Testaments recommend the use of medicine (2 Kings 20:7; 1 Timothy 5:23). Moreover, the Bible nowhere condemns going to a physician. Jesus Himself said, "Those who are well have no need of a physician, but those who are sick" (Matthew 9:12). The Bible simply insists that we should seek God first. After all, God is the Great Physician. He is the ultimate Health-Giver.

You cannot be sustained on yesterday's revival. It's better to pursue revival as a continual reality in your life.

In the book of 2 Chronicles we read about Jehoshaphat's revival (17:1-19), Hezekiah's revival (29:1–31:21), as well as Josiah's reforms (34:1-13). God's people were up and down, up and down. There was a revival followed by a period of spiritual decline, then another revival followed by another period of spiritual decline, and so on.

This can be true of us as individuals as well. We can have spiritual good times and spiritual bad times, up and down. While no Christian has a perfect track record of continuous revival, one positive step we can take is to stay rooted in the Word of God. I say this because God's Word can have a reviving effect on our souls. This is what happened when Ezra the priest read the Word of God to the people. We are told that "the ears of all the people were attentive to the Book of the Law" (Nehemiah 8:3). Then "Ezra blessed the LORD, the great God, and all the people answered, 'Amen, Amen,' lifting up their hands. And they bowed their heads and worshiped the LORD with their faces to the ground" (8:6). Amazingly, "all the people wept as they heard the words of the Law" (8:9). They rejoiced that they now understood God's Word (8:12). The Word of God can revive us as well. (You can meditate on Psalm 119 for some encouragement in this regard.)

Parents can influence their children and their children's children for good or bad.

In 2 Chronicles 17:3-4 we read, "The LORD was with Jehoshaphat, because he walked in the earlier ways of his father David. He did not seek the Baals, but sought the God of his father and walked in his

> "A father's holy life is a rich legacy for his sons."
>
> —*Charles Spurgeon (1834–1892)*

commandments, and not according to the practices of Israel." Jehoshaphat was profoundly influenced for good by his great ancestor David.

We see other examples of positive influence in Scripture:

- Uzziah "did what was right in the eyes of the LORD, according to all that his father Amaziah had done" (2 Chronicles 26:4).

- The apostle Paul said to Timothy, "I am reminded of your sincere faith, a faith that dwelt first in your grandmother Lois and your mother Eunice and now, I am sure, dwells in you as well" (1 Timothy 1:15).

This reminds us of Jesus's words in Luke 6:40: "A disciple is not above his teacher, but everyone when he is fully trained will be like his teacher."

Good news: God's angels minister to us in a variety of ways.

Micaiah the prophet said, "I saw the LORD sitting on his throne, and all the host of heaven standing on his right hand and on his left" (2 Chronicles 18:18). Angels are often called God's heavenly host in Scripture. The term "host" has a distinctive military ring to it, referring to God's heavenly army employed as a military force to accomplish His will and engage in His battles.

> "He will command his angels concerning you to guard you in all your ways."
>
> —Psalm 91:11

It should give Christians a supreme sense of security to know that this heavenly army, headed by God Himself, is committed to rendering service to them. This service includes angels being celestial guardians of God's people (Psalm 91:9-11; 2 Kings 6:17); being used by God in answering the prayers of His people (Acts 12:5-10); and escorting believers into heaven following death (Luke 16:22).

The fear of the Lord motivates righteous living.

The judges of the land were warned by Jehoshaphat, "Consider what you do, for you judge not for man but for the LORD. He is with you in giving judgment. Now then, let the fear of the LORD be upon you. Be careful what you do, for there is no injustice with the LORD our God, or partiality or taking bribes" (2 Chronicles 19:6-7). The fear of the Lord motivated their commitment.

The same is true of you and me. We as Christians are called to live in reverent fear of God (1 Peter 1:17; 2:17; 1 Samuel 12:14,24; 2 Chronicles 19:9; Acts 10:35). Fear of the Lord motivates us to be obedient to Him (Deuteronomy 5:29;

Ecclesiastes 12:13) and serve Him (Deuteronomy 6:13). Fear of the Lord motivates us to avoid evil (Proverbs 3:7; 8:13; 16:6). Fear of the Lord is true wisdom (Job 28:28; Psalm 111:10) and the beginning of knowledge (Proverbs 1:7).

Remember: the battle is God's.

The people of Judah were now facing the people of Ammon, Moab, and Mount Seir. They were fearful of this great horde. God assured them, "Thus says the Lord to you, 'Do not be afraid and do not be dismayed at this great horde, for the battle is not yours but God's'" (2 Chronicles 20:15). In modern vernacular, God told Judah, "Don't worry. I've got your back."

> **Cross-References: God Fights Our Battles**
> Genesis 14:20 • Exodus 14:14 • 15:3 • Deuteronomy 1:30 • 3:22 • 2 Samuel 5:24 • Psalm 9:3 • 18:17 • 124:1 • Jeremiah 50:25

Do all your work wholeheartedly.

Hezekiah did his work wholeheartedly: "Every work that he undertook in the service of the house of God and in accordance with the law and the commandments, seeking his God, he did with all his heart, and prospered" (2 Chronicles 31:21). Go thou and do likewise!

A Thought to Anchor in Your Heart

Don't be a lone ranger in dealing with your problems.
Let God fight your battles.

Ezra

God is awesome. He is faithful to His people, keeps His promises to them, sovereignly protects them, and restores them when needed.

The book of Ezra was probably written by Ezra—a scribe-priest (Ezra 7:21)—between 457 and 444 BC. The Hebrew form of Ezra's name means "Yahweh helps." Ezra speaks about the return of the Jewish people from 70 years of captivity in Babylon. This return was permitted by the decree of King Cyrus of Persia. Actually, there were two "returns" from Babylon—one led by Zerubbabel (1–6), and then one under Ezra's leadership nearly six decades later (7–10).

The aim of the first return was rebuilding of the temple (1:1–2:70). The aim of the second return related to Ezra's rebuilding (or reform) of his people's spiritual lives (7:1–8:36). Ezra was instrumental in teaching the Jews about God's law. He sought to revive his people according to this law (9:1–10:44).

Following are key applicational concepts in Ezra:

Count on it: God is always faithful to fulfill His promises.

God Is Faithful

- Keeps His covenant—Deuteronomy 7:9
- Every promise fulfilled—Joshua 23:14
- Faithful in every way—Psalm 89:1-2,8
- Great is His faithfulness—Lamentations 3:22-23
- Faithful even when we are not faithful—2 Timothy 2:13

King Cyrus of Persia, in the first year of his reign (539 BC), issued a decree permitting the Jews of the Babylonian captivity to return to their homeland (Ezra 1). Under Zerubbabel's leadership, the Jewish captives left Babylon for Jerusalem (2). Upon arriving, they built an altar, offered sacrifices, and celebrated the feast of tabernacles. They laid the foundation of the temple and established themselves in the land (3).

The important point to observe is that by returning from Babylon to Israel, the Jewish people were openly demonstrating their faith in God's promises of restoration. This restoration took place "that the word of the LORD by the mouth of Jeremiah might be fulfilled" (Ezra 1:1). The people were seeing a fulfillment of Jeremiah's prophecy before their very eyes.

The Bible often points to God as a promise keeper. Numbers 23:19 (NIV) asserts, "God is not human, that he should lie, not a human being, that he should change his mind. Does he speak and then not act? Does he promise and not fulfill?" Prior to his death, an aged Joshua declared, "Now I am about to go the way of all the earth. You know with all your heart and soul that not one of all the good promises the LORD your God gave you has failed. Every promise has been fulfilled; not one has failed" (Joshua 23:14 (NIV); see also 1 Kings 8:56; Joshua 21:45). God truly is faithful!

My friend, it may be that you are facing deep waters and bitter trials in your own life at present. I urge you to turn to God and trust in His promises. No matter what you are facing, a supernatural tranquility and peace is available to you. It is yours for the taking. Cast yourself on God and His promises—truly trusting in Him—and this peace will be yours (Isaiah 26:3; Philippians 4:6-7). He will sustain you. He is faithful!

Count on it: God's mercy always exceeds His anger.

In Ezra's prayer to God, he said, "After all that has come upon us for our evil deeds and for our great guilt, seeing that you, our God, have punished us *less than our iniquities deserved* and have given us such a remnant as this" (Ezra 9:13, emphasis added). Ezra knew God would have been perfectly just in utterly destroying his people for their great sins. But God's mercy exceeded His anger against them. God was restoring them to their land and temple, just as He promised. What an awesome and merciful God!

God's Word always has a life-changing effect on God's people.

Ezra was "a man learned in matters of the commandments of the LORD and his statutes for Israel" (Ezra 7:11). He "set his heart to study the Law of the LORD, and to do it and to teach his statutes and rules in Israel" (7:10). The Jews were not just returning to their land and their temple; they were also finally returning to the Word of God. Ezra not only preached God's Word to them, but the prophets Haggai and Zechariah encouraged them:

> **A Verse to Remember**
> "Ezra had set his heart to study the Law of the Lord, and to do it and to teach his statutes and rules in Israel."
>
> —*Ezra 7:10*

Ezra

"The Jews built and prospered through the prophesying of Haggai the prophet and Zechariah the son of Iddo" (6:14). This put spiritual wind in their sails.

The times may have changed, but the need for the Word of God has not changed. We need the life-changing influence of God's Word every bit as much as the Jews in Ezra's time. As 2 Timothy 3:15-17 puts it, the Scriptures "are able to make you wise for salvation through faith in Christ Jesus. All Scripture is breathed out by God and profitable for teaching, for reproof, for correction, and for training in righteousness, that the man of God may be complete, equipped for every good work." In all generations, God's Word revives the souls of human beings (Psalm 119:25,37).

God can sovereignly and providentially work through earthly kings to accomplish His will.

God Is Sovereign

- God's purpose will stand—Isaiah 46:10
- His plans alone stand—Psalm 33:8-11
- He rules over all—Psalm 103:19
- He is King of the earth—Psalm 47:2
- He rules all nations—2 Chronicles 20:6
- He is above all rule and authority—Ephesians 1:20-22

"Trust in the LORD with all your heart, and do not lean on your own understanding. In all your ways acknowledge him, and he will make straight your paths."

—*Proverbs 3:5-6*

Scripture reveals that God is sovereign over earthly kings such that He can providentially cause them to show favor toward His people. In Ezra 6:22 we are told "the LORD...had turned the heart of the king of Assyria to them, so that he aided them in the work of the house of God, the God of Israel." This reminds us of Proverbs 21:1: "The king's heart is a stream of water in the hand of the LORD; he turns it wherever he will." We see this illustrated in the cases of Tiglath-Pileser (Isaiah 10:5-7), Cyrus (Isaiah 45:1-4), Nebuchadnezzar (Daniel 4:34), and Belshazzar (Daniel 5:23-25). God is awesome!

Stand strong in the faith—even when opposition rises against you.

The Jews' work of rebuilding the temple was hindered by deceitful enemies who convinced the Persian king to stop reconstruction of the temple (Ezra 4). This greatly tested the returnees' fragile and wavering faith.

Ultimately, however, the Persian king investigated matters, decided in favor of the Jews (under God's providential hand), and allowed the building program to continue (Ezra 5).

Cyrus's decree for rebuilding the temple was re-affirmed. The temple was completed in 516 BC.

We learn an important lesson here. There will always be people who oppose the work of God. There will always be trials and set-backs that crop up. But through it all, we must keep our faith strong, knowing that God can providentially work behind the scenes to open necessary doors for us. As Psalm 37:5 puts it, "Commit your way to the LORD; trust in him, and he will act."

Confession of sin is a necessary component of the spiritual life.

Ezra led his people in the confession of sin before the Lord: "O my God, I am ashamed and blush to lift my face to you, my God, for our iniquities have risen higher than our heads, and our guilt has mounted up to the heavens" (Ezra 9:6). "We have forsaken your commandments, which you commanded by your servants the prophets" (9:10-11). We are then told that "while Ezra prayed and made confession, weeping and casting himself down before the house of God, a very great assembly of men, women, and children, gathered to him out of Israel, for the people wept bitterly" (10:1).

> **Faith in God**
> - Faith is the certainty of what we don't see—Hebrews 11:1-2
> - Live by faith, not by sight—2 Corinthians 5:7
> - Trust in the Lord, not man—Psalm 118:8
> - Trust the Lord with your whole heart—Proverbs 3:5
> - Small faith yields big results—Luke 17:5-6

> "You can pray till doomsday for revival, but you will never get it without repentance and confession of sin in the Christian life."
>
> —Erlo Stegan

The backdrop is that the Jews had returned to their land and would now enjoy their rebuilt temple. But a restoration to the land and the temple was not enough. They also needed restoration to God—and that comes only through repentance and confession. As the psalmist put it, "'I acknowledged my sin to you, and I did not cover my iniquity;' I said, 'I will confess my transgressions to the LORD,' and you forgave the iniquity of my sin" (Psalm 32:5). The people of Ezra's day were in dire need of repentance and confession of their many sins.

When you and I sin, we, too, need to confess to God (1 John 1:9). The Greek word for "confess" literally means "to say the same thing." So when we confess our sin to God, that means we're saying the same thing about our sin that God says about it. We're agreeing with God that we did wrong. No excuses! And following our confession, we can thank God that in His sight our sin is already forgiven, because Jesus paid for it on the cross (Romans 5:10).

Ezra

God's people ought to always be worshipful and joyful.

> "We must rejoice in God when we have nothing else to rejoice in and cleave to him."
>
> —*Matthew Henry (1662–1714)*

Now that the people were back in their land and their temple rebuilt, they could finally resume worship the way God had instructed them to—*full of joy*. We read, for example, that "they kept the Feast of Unleavened Bread seven days with joy, for the LORD had made them joyful" (Ezra 6:22).

All worship of the Lord should be joyful. This is wonderfully reflected in Psalm 95:1-5: "Oh come, let us sing to the LORD; let us make a joyful noise to the rock of our salvation! Let us come into his presence with thanksgiving; let us make a joyful noise to him with songs of praise! For the LORD is a great God, and a great King above all gods." (See also Psalm 100:1-4.)

A Thought to Anchor in Your Heart

Being a joyful Christian is your birthright. Don't let the enemy of your soul, Satan, steal your joy. Starting now, make a joyful noise unto the Lord.

Nehemiah

The combination of prayer and the Word of God can bring great revival that is life-changing and exciting. It can turn around a whole society.

Nehemiah wrote his book between 445 and 425 BC. His name literally means "comfort of Yahweh." Under Nehemiah's leadership, the people would indeed be comforted by Yahweh.

Like the book of Ezra, the book of Nehemiah focuses on the return of the exiles from Babylon. Nehemiah had been a cupbearer for the Persian king Artaxerxes, but moved on to become the governor of Jerusalem in 445 BC. Among his contributions was leading the people in repairing the shattered wall of Jerusalem. The task was completed in a mere 52 days. It would take much longer, however, to rebuild the spiritual lives of the people in Jerusalem. Nevertheless, Nehemiah's work served to raise the morale of the people, who had been utterly demoralized at seeing their beloved city in ruins. He laid the foundation for Josiah's religious reforms.

Following are key applicational concepts in Nehemiah:

Timeline

465— Artaxerxes I becomes king of Persia.

445— Nehemiah goes to Jerusalem; he becomes the governor of Jerusalem; the wall of Jerusalem is rebuilt.

433— Nehemiah returns to Persia.

432— Nehemiah goes back to Jerusalem.

Prayer and decisive action will see you through tough times.

Nehemiah prayed for his people, confessed their sins, and asked God for blessing in exchange for repentance (Nehemiah 1). Nehemiah was then permitted by the Persian king Artaxerxes I to visit Jerusalem to assess the city's condition, and reported back that the city walls needed to be rebuilt (2). Nehemiah promptly headed up a group of people to render repairs (3).

"Do not be anxious about anything, but in everything by prayer and supplication with thanksgiving let your requests be made known to God."

—*Philippians 4:6*

Samaria's king opposed the repairs, but Nehemiah refused to be slowed. He assigned half the people to rebuild, while the others remained on military watch

(Nehemiah 4). Through Nehemiah's prayers and decisive action, the construction work continued (5) and was finally complete in a mere 52 days (6).

This brings to mind James's emphasis that works are the "life signs" that faith is alive (James 2:14-26). That the Jews prayed to God showed their faith in Him, but then they immediately proceeded to take action to bring about what they had requested of God (Nehemiah 4:9). You and I learn a good lesson here. Prayer, faith, and decisive action make a powerful combination.

The object of your prayers is your awesome Father-God in heaven.

Nehemiah addressed his prayer to the "LORD God of heaven, the great and awesome God who keeps covenant and steadfast love with those who love him and keep his commandments" (Nehemiah 1:5). There is no ambiguity here. Nehemiah knew to whom he was praying. In Nehemiah's thinking, God is known not only by *who He is* ("Lord God of heaven, the great and awesome God") but also by *what He has done* (the one who "keeps covenant and steadfast love").

Since New Testament times, you and I are privileged to address our prayers to "our Father in heaven" (Matthew 6:9). We can also address Him as "Abba"—an Aramaic term of great intimacy, loosely meaning "papa" (Romans 8:15). We can go to "papa" with all our needs.

> "You have received the Spirit of adoption as sons, by whom we cry, 'Abba! Father.'"
>
> —Romans 8:15

Jesus often spoke of God as a loving Father (for example, Matthew 6:4-9; 18:19). The apostle Paul affirmed that God is the "Father of mercies and God of all comfort" (2 Corinthians 1:3). God is often portrayed in Scripture as compassionately responding to the personal requests of His people (Psalm 81:10; 91:14-15).

The God of heaven answers the heartfelt prayer of a righteous man.

We learn yet another lesson about prayer in Nehemiah's account. Pay special attention to the words I've italicized in Nehemiah's prayer: "O LORD God of heaven, the great and awesome God who keeps covenant and steadfast love *with those who love him and keep his commandments,* let your ear be attentive and your eyes open, to hear the prayer of your servant that I now pray before you day and

> "The mightier any is in the Word, the more mighty he will be in prayer."
>
> —William Gurnall (1617–1679)

night for the people of Israel your servants, confessing the sins of the people of Israel, which we have sinned against you" (Nehemiah 1:4-6). While Nehemiah's people had fallen in sin, he himself was a righteous man, and God answered his prayer.

This brings to mind James 5:16: "The prayer of a righteous person has great power as it is working." There is a strong connection between righteous living and answered prayer. On the other hand, there is also a strong connection between unrighteous living and unanswered prayer. Proverbs 15:29 says, "The Lord is far from the wicked, but he hears the prayer of the righteous." (See also James 5:16; 1 Peter 3:12.)

God can—as a result of prayer—grant us favor in the eyes of powerful people.

Artaxerxes asked Nehemiah why he was so sad. Nehemiah replied that he was lamenting Jerusalem's destruction. Artaxerxes asked how he could help. Nehemiah instantly and silently prayed to God, and then asked for permission to go to Jerusalem. He wanted Jerusalem to be restored. "The king granted me what I asked, for the good hand of my God was upon me" (Nehemiah 2:8). God gave Nehemiah favor in the eyes of the king.

God often gave His servants favor in the eyes of powerful people in Bible times. Joseph found favor in the eyes of his Egyptian master: "The Lord was with him and...the Lord caused all that he did to succeed in his hands" (Genesis 39:3). When Joseph was wrongfully thrown into prison, "the Lord was with Joseph and showed him steadfast love and gave him favor in the sight of the keeper of the prison" (Genesis 39:21).

Let us not forget what Solomon said in Proverbs 21:1: "The king's heart is a stream of water in the hand of the Lord; he turns it wherever he will." God can give us favor in the eyes of anyone, no matter how powerful their office.

Every believer ought to take a stand for social justice.

Many of the Jews were experiencing economic hardship and had to borrow from wealthy Jews to survive, using their land and even their children as collateral. The children would become slaves of the wealthy Jews if the debts were not paid (Nehemiah 5:1-5). Nehemiah confronted the wealthy Jews and put an end to this exploitation (5:6-13). Nehemiah took a stand for social justice. Jesus, too, took a stand for social justice (Luke 4:18-19). Let us follow their lead!

People desperately need to hear the Word of God, for it can lead to revival.

Nehemiah discovered a genealogical record that enabled his people to be restored to the cities that had been their family inheritance (Nehemiah 7). The people then requested Ezra the priest to read the Law of Moses to them. The Levites helped them all understand it.

We are told that "the ears of all the people were attentive to the Book of the Law" (Nehemiah 8:3). Then "Ezra blessed the LORD, the great God, and all the people answered, 'Amen, Amen,' lifting up their hands. And they bowed their heads and worshiped the LORD with their faces to the ground" (8:6). Amazingly, "all the people wept as they heard the words of the Law" (8:9). They rejoiced that they now understood God's Word (8:12).

The people then "confessed their sins and the iniquities of their fathers" (Nehemiah 9:2). They praised the Lord for how faithfully He had led His people through the years. A revival swept through the nation (9:3-37). The people made a firm covenant with the Lord to obey His commandments (10). Nehemiah then instituted religious reforms (13).

It's quite amazing hearing how the Word of God led to civil, social, and spiritual reforms (Nehemiah 13). Oh that America would have such a revival (2 Chronicles 7:14).

> **Life-Changing Nature of God's Word**
>
> "How can a young man keep his way pure? By guarding it according to your word" (Psalm 119:9).
>
> "I have stored up your word in my heart, that I might not sin against you" (Psalm 119:11).
>
> "Give me life according to your word" (Psalm 119:25).

Be a worshiper of the Lord, for He is worthy.

Nehemiah 8:6 tells us, "Ezra blessed the LORD, the great God, and all the people answered, 'Amen, Amen,' lifting up their hands. And they bowed their heads and worshiped the LORD with their faces to the ground." What a great example of worship. Worship involves reverencing God, adoring Him, praising Him, venerating Him, and paying homage to Him, not just externally (by rituals and singing songs) but in our hearts as well (Isaiah 29:13; see also 1 Samuel 15:22,23).

> "If Christ were standing on this platform, and you saw his pierced hands and the wound in his side, you would be ready to fall down and worship him. You can worship him better still by trusting him in his absence."
>
> —Charles Spurgeon (1834–1892)

Nehemiah

The Hebrew word for worship, *shaha*, means "to bow down" or "to prostrate oneself" (Genesis 22:5; 42:6). Likewise, the New Testament word for worship, *proskuneo*, means "to prostrate oneself" (Matthew 2:2,8,11). Such worship is the proper response of a creature to the divine Creator (Psalm 95:6). Worship can be congregational (1 Corinthians 11–14) or individual (Romans 12:1).

My friend, don't be a spiritual dud. Get into worshiping God—and do it regularly!

You never need to be afraid because the Lord is on your side.

Nehemiah's people were fearful of surrounding peoples who might invade their land (Nehemiah 9). Nehemiah urged, "Do not be afraid of them. Remember the Lord, who is great and awesome" (4:14). This brings to mind Romans 8:31: "If God is for us, who can be against us?"

> "Of whom shall I be afraid? One with God is a majority."
> —*Martin Luther (1483–1546)*

The psalmist boasted, "I will not be afraid of many thousands of people who have set themselves against me all around" (Psalm 3:6). "Though an army encamp against me, my heart shall not fear" (27:3). "In God I trust; I shall not be afraid" (56:4). Nehemiah's people needed to remember this as they resettled in their land (Nehemiah 11–13).

A Thought to Anchor in Your Heart

Your continuous revival hinges on continuous exposure to God's Word.

Esther

God sovereignly and providentially works behind the scenes of human history to accomplish His purposes.

Timeline

486— Xerxes I (Ahasuerus) becomes king of Persia.

479— Esther becomes queen.

474— Haman seeks to destroy the Jews.

473— The first Festival of Purim is celebrated.

465— The book of Esther is written.

Biblical View of Races

God "made from one man every nation of mankind to live on all the face of the earth" (Acts 17:26).

God's redeemed will be from "every tribe and language and people and nation" (Revelation 5:9).

All human beings are equal in terms of their creation (Genesis 1:28), the sin problem (Romans 3:23), God's love for them (John 3:16), and God's provision of salvation (Matthew 28:19).

The book of Esther was written by an unknown author in about 465 BC. Some have suggested that Mordecai, Ezra, or Nehemiah may have written the book, but there is no hard evidence for this. Whoever the author was, he was well aware of Persian culture and had a strong sense of Jewish nationalism.

Esther is distinguished from other Bible books in that God is never mentioned. Yet God is seen sovereignly working behind the scenes throughout the book.

This short book describes how an insidious plot was launched by the evil racist Haman to destroy the Jews. God not only thwarted the plot, but brought the plotter's evil back upon himself—Haman was executed instead of the Jews.

To bring about this end, God had earlier and providentially brought the beautiful (Jewish) Esther to become the Queen of the Persian king, Xerxes I, who ruled Persia from 486 to 465 BC. It would seem that God elevated Esther to this position of authority specifically to save the Jewish race from destruction (Esther 4:14). Her cousin Mordecai was instrumental in helping Esther to understand this fact.

Following are key applicational concepts in Esther:

God has the ability to sovereignly and purposefully place His people in high and strategic positions of authority.

The Persian king Ahasuerus (Xerxes), after some celebratory drinking, demanded that queen Vashti sacrifice her modesty before his court. She refused and the king was outraged. She was promptly deposed (Esther 1).

Mordecai, a gatekeeper for the king, believed his cousin Esther would be the perfect replacement. Esther ultimately became queen and found favor in the eyes of the king (Esther 2).

Meanwhile, Haman—the evil chief officer of King Ahasuerus—hated the Jews and sought to annihilate them. He deviously secured the king's agreement to destroy them by alleging that the Jews cared nothing of the king's laws (Esther 3).

> **Definition: Providence**
>
> Providence refers to God's sovereign governing over all things on earth and in the universe. See Psalm 18:35; 63:8; Acts 17:28; Colossians 1:17; Hebrews 1:3.

Under Mordecai's encouragement, and in God's providence, Esther used her high position to make an appeal on behalf of her people (Esther 4). This appeal thwarted the evil Haman's efforts. All of this called for great faith on the part of Esther.

This reminds us how God also providentially worked behind the scenes to elevate Joseph to a position of great authority. Recall that Joseph was sold into slavery by his own brothers (Genesis 37, 39). While it seemed painful at the time, God was in control all the while. God providentially used these negative circumstances to bring Joseph to Egypt, where He elevated him to a position of great authority (Genesis 41; 50:20). In that position, Joseph was now able to save people from famine.

Dear Christian, such passages provide us with two key lessons. First, if God so chooses, He has the unique ability to put any of us in important and strategic positions. Second, God has a strategic purpose in mind when He does so. My advice: Maintain faith that God knows what He's doing with your life.

God's sovereign hand is always at work in your life, even though you may not be aware of it.

God's hand of providence is evident in many ways in Esther's short book. This includes Mordecai's overhearing of a plot against the king (Esther 2:19-23), Esther's rise to queenship for a specific purpose (4:14), and the king's insomnia on the night before Mordecai's planned execution (6:1-3). God was involved in all of this, though He operated incognito.

> "Faith is to believe what we do not see."
>
> —Augustine (354–430)

This is one reason we need to trust in God. God is working for us in ways our eyes cannot visibly see. That is why we must "walk by faith, not by sight" (2 Corinthians 5:7).

Events you might consider unworthy or insignificant may turn out to be used by God in accomplishing His sovereign will.

All the beautiful young virgins near the king's palace were gathered to participate in a kind of beauty contest, the winners being drafted into King Xerxes' harem. Esther 2:8 tells us, "When the king's order and his edict were proclaimed, and when many young women were gathered in Susa the citadel in custody of Hegai, Esther also was taken into the king's palace and put in custody of Hegai, who had charge of the women." Apparently Esther did not join this beauty contest on her own, as if she were a vain person. Rather, our text tells us she was "*taken* into the king's palace and *put in custody* of Hegai" (2:8, emphasis added). She was taken against her will. In any event, it is clear this was the first step in God providentially elevating Esther to a high position for the specific purpose of frustrating Haman's goal of exterminating the Jews. There is certainly no indication in the text that Esther had to do anything immoral while participating in the contest. The character she evidenced throughout the book was beyond reproach.

God looks not at the externals, but rather cares about the inner beauty of a person.

God Looks at Your Heart

- God "knows the secrets of the heart" (Psalm 44:21).
- "You discern my thoughts from afar" (Psalm 139:2).
- The Lord "sees the heart and the mind" (Jeremiah 20:12).

Esther stood out above the other women, and Hegai "quickly provided her with her cosmetics" (Esther 2:9). The only reason cosmetics were put on her was that she wasn't wearing any, as apparently was her custom.

It is good to be reminded that Scripture consistently emphasizes that God is more interested in what is inside a person than what the person physically looks like. "The LORD sees not as man sees: man looks on the outward appearance, but the LORD looks on the heart" (1 Samuel 16:7). Jesus warned some Jewish leaders, "Woe to you, scribes and Pharisees, hypocrites! For you are like whitewashed tombs, which outwardly appear beautiful, but within are full of dead people's bones and all uncleanness" (Matthew 23:27). It's the inside that's important!

My friend, there's nothing wrong with wearing nice clothes, grooming your hair, and trying to look nice. The more important thing, though, is to ensure you are "wearing" the right virtues: "Clothe yourselves with tenderhearted mercy, kindness, humility, gentleness, and patience" (Colossians 3:12 NLT; see also 1 Peter 3:4; 5:5; Colossians 3:14).

God is sovereign over the actual timing of events.

According to Esther 4:14 (NLT), Mordecai said to Esther, "Who knows if perhaps you were made queen for just such a time as this." As providence had it, Esther indeed was made queen for "such a time as this," thereby rescuing her people just in time.

We see other evidences of God's sovereign control over timing in Scripture. Acts 17:26 tells us God "made from one man every nation of mankind to live on all the face of the earth, *having determined allotted periods* and the boundaries of their dwelling place" (emphasis added). Speaking of Jesus's birth, Galatians 4:4 tells us, "*When the fullness of time had come*, God sent forth his Son, born of woman, born under the law" (emphasis added). Everything is on a divine schedule decreed by God (John 2:4).

> "Never be afraid to entrust an unknown future to an all-knowing God."
>
> *—Anonymous*

You and I, too, have a divine timetable: "In your book were written, every one of them, the days that were formed for me, when as yet there was none of them" (Psalm 139:16).

Don't shy away from speaking up when you really need to speak up.

Esther went to the king, and he asked her, "What is your wish, Queen Esther? It shall be granted you" (Esther 7:2). Esther then boldly interceded before the king on behalf of her people, implicating the wicked Haman as the one seeking the destruction of her people.

It is not always easy for us to speak up when we need to. May the Lord grant us boldness!

Speaking the Truth

- Tell the truth before God— 2 Corinthians 4:2
- Truthful lips endure forever—Proverbs 12:19
- Speak the truth in love— Ephesians 4:15

Those who intend evil for others may find themselves on the receiving end of that same evil.

At a banquet arranged by Esther, the king offered to give her anything up to half his kingdom. She asked only that her people be saved, and that the one behind the plot to attack them be judged. Haman was singled out, and he was promptly hanged on the same gallows he had constructed to hang Mordecai. The king then issued a decree prohibiting the killing of the Jews. As

Do Good, Receive Good

"Let us not grow weary of doing good, for in due season we will reap, if we do not give up" (Galatians 6:9).

"Glory and honor and peace for everyone who does good" (Romans 2:10).

God's providence had it, the enemies of the Jews ended up being destroyed on the very day the Jews were scheduled to be destroyed.

We see, then, that not only did Haman receive the evil he had intended for the righteous Mordecai, but those who had intended to destroy the Jews were themselves destroyed. God often brings about these kinds of reversals in Scripture. "Whoever digs a pit will fall into it, and a stone will come back on him who starts it rolling" (Proverbs 26:27; see also Proverbs 28:10; Ecclesiastes 10:8). The converse is also true. Do good, and good will be returned back upon you.

A Thought to Anchor in Your Heart

Never forget that God is sovereign over your life. He is the Grand Weaver, weaving your life into a tapestry that will bring Him great glory.

Job

Human beings should never doubt God's goodness and sovereign purposes, even in the face of seemingly arbitrary personal suffering.

The book of Job was written by an unknown author, probably prior to 1445 BC. A Jewish tradition ascribes the book to Moses. Other suggestions include Solomon, Elihu, Isaiah, Hezekiah, Jeremiah, and Ezra. Regardless of the author, the book is named after the principal character in the book, Job—whose name apparently derives from a Hebrew word meaning, "persecuted one."

The book has become famous because it deals with a question many human beings have struggled with: if there is a good God, and if God is just, then why do good people suffer? In Job's case, we find an upright man who has done nothing wrong, and yet catastrophe overwhelms him at every side. He loses his possessions as well as his family, and he finds himself engulfed in agonizing physical suffering (Job 1:13-22).

Job's friends visited him and offered him the common wisdom of the day, which said God blesses obedience but brings about calamity for disobedience. The implication is clear: Job's own wickedness must have brought about this calamity. Job knew, however, that he had lived righteously before God, so he knew his friends were misguided in their assessment (Job 3–27). All the while, neither Job nor his friends were aware of what had transpired behind the scenes, with Satan approaching God and requesting permission to bring about these calamities.

Sometime later God finally intervened. While He did not answer all of Job's questions, Job nevertheless seemed satisfied at merely seeing God (Job

Timeline

1526–1406—The life of Moses.

1490–1380—The life of Joshua.

1445—The Ten Commandments are given.

1445—Scholars guesstimate the book of Job was written sometime prior to this year. It is written by an unknown author.

1445–1405—Genesis, Exodus, Leviticus, and Numbers are written within this timeframe.

"God whispers to us in our joys, speaks to us in our difficulties, and shouts to us in our pain."

—C. S. Lewis (1898–1963)

38:1–42:6). In the end, Job was restored in his health and possessions, and all was well. His faith in God, even in the midst of suffering, is the key lesson of the book.

Following are key applicational concepts in Job:

What Satan Can Do to Christians

- Tempt—Ephesians 2:1-3; 1 Thessalonians 3:5
- Tempt to lie—Acts 5:3
- Tempt to immorality—1 Corinthians 7:5
- Hinder their work—1 Thessalonians 2:18
- Wage war against—Ephesians 6:11-12
- Sow tares among—Matthew 13:38-39
- Incite persecutions against—Revelation 2:10
- Oppose with ferocity—1 Peter 5:8
- Plant doubt in minds—Genesis 3:1-5
- Foster spiritual pride in hearts—1 Timothy 3:6

Satan is the accuser of the brethren. Don't let him get you down.

Job 2 portrays Satan before God's throne, bringing accusation against Job, implying that Job would fall if God removed His protective hand. Revelation 12:10 calls Satan the "the accuser of our brothers." The Greek text of this verse indicates that accusing God's people is a continuous, ongoing work of Satan. He never lets up; he accuses God's people "day and night." Satan accuses God's people in two ways. First, he brings charges against believers before God, as he did in Job's case (see also Zechariah 3:1; Romans 8:33). Second, Satan accuses believers to their own conscience. He whispers to them, "You call yourself a Christian? Look at the sin you just committed. God will surely get even with you." My friend, don't listen to the lies of the devil. He is a liar and a murderer who seeks to discourage you and bring you down (John 8:44).

Bad things sometimes happen to good people. Don't be surprised by it.

Job was wealthy, righteous, and respected—"there is none like him on the earth, a blameless and upright man, who fears God and turns away from evil" (Job 2:3). He was not the kind of person one would normally expect to suffer catastrophic adversity. It was only after Satan accused Job before God's throne that God permitted Satan to inflict suffering upon Job. In rapid succession, Job lost his sons and daughters, his sheep and herds, and his servants. He also lost his health (1–2). Yet he maintained his faith in God (1:21).

Job had initially been patient, but he finally broke his silence. He said he wished he had never been born, or that he had succumbed to death immediately after birth. At least that way he would have been spared all this suffering (Job 3).

My friend, bad things do indeed sometimes happen to God's people.

Scripture affirms, "In the world you will have tribulation" (John 16:33). Indeed, "through many tribulations we must enter the kingdom of God" (Acts 14:22).

God in His wisdom does not always provide healing for His children in earthly life.

Notice that when Job was severely afflicted, God did not initially heal him (Job 2–3). Numerous verses in Scripture substantiate that it is not always God's will to heal—whether directly or through one of His servants (such as an apostle). For example, the great apostle Paul could not heal Timothy's stomach problem (1 Timothy 5:23), nor could he heal Trophimus at Miletus (2 Timothy 4:20) or Epaphroditus (Philippians 3:25-27). Paul spoke of "a bodily ailment" he had (Galatians 4:13-15). He also suffered a "thorn...in the flesh" that God allowed him to retain (2 Corinthians 12:7-9). And, as noted previously, God certainly allowed Job to go through an extended time of physical suffering (Job 1–2).

> **God Is All-Wise**
> - God has deep wisdom—Romans 11:33
> - He possesses full understanding—Job 12:13
> - He is the only wise God—Romans 16:27
> - He is full of wisdom and understanding—Proverbs 3:19; James 3:17

Numerous verses in Scripture also reveal that our physical bodies are continuously running down and suffering various ailments. Our present bodies are said to be perishable and weak (1 Corinthians 15:42-44). Paul said "our outer self is wasting away" (2 Corinthians 4:16). Death and disease will be a part of the human condition until that time when we receive resurrection bodies immune to such frailties (1 Corinthians 15:51-55).

Certainly God *can* heal, and often *does* heal. (He healed Job in the end.) But other times God may have sovereign purposes for not healing someone. Ultimate healing comes when we receive our body upgrades—our resurrection bodies. Then our bodies will be glorious!

Life is short and accompanied by many troubles, but you're headed toward a trouble-free afterlife.

Job 14:1-2 affirms, "Man who is born of a woman is few of days and full of trouble. He comes out like a flower and withers; he flees like a shadow and continues not." Job appealed to God, "Remember that my life is a breath" (7:7).

> "The moment you come into this world, you are beginning to go out of it."
>
> —D. Martyn Lloyd-Jones (1899–1981)

Scripture often speaks of the brevity of human life. The psalmist pondered before God, "Behold, you have made my days a few handbreadths, and my lifetime is as nothing before you" (Psalm 39:5). Reflecting back over his life, he said, "My days pass away like smoke" (102:3).

In James 4:14 we are told, "You do not know what tomorrow will bring. What is your life? For you are a mist that appears for a little time and then vanishes." First Peter 1:24 instructs us that "all flesh is like grass and all its glory like the flower of grass. The grass withers, and the flower falls."

It is a sobering exercise to ponder that, should the Lord delay His coming, not only I but my beloved wife and two precious children will one day be lowered into the earth in burial. If that were the end of things, then how despondent life would be. But, praise God, we will all be reunited and live forever in the heavenly country, the eternal city of God, which Christ Himself is constructing (Revelation 21–22; John 14:1-3). What a glorious future we have. In view of that future, it is advantageous to maintain an eternal perspective (Colossians 3:1-2).

God sometimes allows His children to go through periods of suffering so they can condition and strengthen their faith muscles and increase their perseverance.

James 1:2-3 tells us, "Count it all joy, my brothers, when you meet trials of various kinds, for you know that the testing of your faith produces steadfastness." This was certainly true in Job's case (Job 42:7-17). Peter adds, "In this you rejoice, though now for a little while, if necessary, you have been grieved by various trials, so that the tested genuineness of your faith—more precious than gold that perishes though it is tested by fire—may be found to result in praise and glory and honor at the revelation of Jesus Christ" (1 Peter 1:6-7).

> "We learn more in our valley experiences than on our mountaintops."
>
> —Charles Stanley

God has the unique ability to bring long-term good out of short-term suffering. A young child might question why his parent allows him to suffer in going to the dentist, for in his youthful ignorance he has no idea this is for the long-term good of his dental health. Likewise, God may allow us to go through short-term sufferings to bring about long-term benefits. Romans 8:28 tells us, "We know that for those who love God all things work together for good, for those who are called according to his purpose."

Never forget: Satan is on a leash.

God instructed Satan that he could go only so far with Job but no further. In modern vernacular, Satan is "on a leash." He cannot go beyond the parameters set by God. This means we should rest secure in the knowledge that God is in control of the universe and realize that Satan cannot simply do as he pleases in our lives.

> "God never allows pain without a purpose in the lives of His children. He never allows Satan, nor circumstances, nor any ill-intending person to afflict us unless He uses that affliction for our good. God never wastes pain."
>
> —Jerry Bridges

It's also important to realize that God has provided for our defense against Satan and his army of fallen angels (demons). For example, Jesus now lives in heaven to make intercession for us (Romans 8:34; Hebrews 7:25), praying for us on a regular basis (John 17:15). God has provided spiritual armor for our defense (Ephesians 6:11-18). "Wearing" this armor means our lives will be characterized by such things as righteousness, obedience to the will of God, faith in God, and an effective use of the Word of God.

Scripture says each believer must be informed and thereby alert to the attacks of Satan (1 Peter 5:8). Paul warns Christians to "not be outwitted by Satan" (2 Corinthians 2:11). James 4:7 says, "Resist the devil, and he will flee from you." We are to "stand firm" against the devil (Ephesians 6:13-14).

> "Obviously, the greater exposure there is to Scripture the more the Spirit can use this mighty sword in our lives. If you never read or study your Bible, you are terribly exposed to defeat and despair. You have no defense; you have nothing to put up against these forces that are at work. Therefore, learn to read your Bible regularly."
>
> —Ray Stedman (1917–1992)

It is wise to depend upon the Holy Spirit, all the while remembering that "he who is in you is greater than he who is in the world" (1 John 4:4). And let us not forget that God has assigned His angels to watch over us (Psalm 91:9-11).

Dear Christian, here's something to remember: Successfully defeating the powers of darkness ultimately rests not upon what you can do in your own strength but upon what Jesus Christ has already done. You are more than a conqueror through Him who loved us (Romans 8:37).

Be forewarned: friends can have good intentions and yet give bad advice.

Job had to respond to a series of accusations from his friends—Eliphaz, Bildad, and Zophar. Their assessment was that Job was suffering because he must be guilty of committing some sin. There were three rounds of dialogue in the lengthy debate (Job 4–14, 15–21, and 22–26). In each case, Job responded to the accusations of his friends, defending his innocence. Job closed out these three rounds with a lengthy monologue in which he continued to claim innocence (27–31).

Attention then shifted to Elihu, a young person apparently observing the debates (Job 32–37). Elihu suggested Job's suffering was rooted more in the need for purification in his life than for punishment of sins. And perhaps some of his suffering was directed at the self-centeredness into which he had fallen.

I hate to say it, but the mentality of Job's friends is still alive and well in our own day. I've seen it happen. Someone sees a brother or sister in church suffering, and says, "Perhaps there is a hidden sin you need to repent of." This often does much more harm than good. Let's use our mouths to build up, not to tear down (Ephesians 4:29).

You won't always get all the answers you want, but you can take comfort in the fact that you know the good God who does have all the answers.

God Is Good

- God is good—Psalm 106:1; 119:68
- The Lord is good—Psalm 100:5
- Only God is good—Matthew 19:17
- Good to all people—Psalm 145:8-9
- Taste and see—Psalm 34:8

The Lord finally spoke to Job and asked him a series of questions engineered to demonstrate Job's finitude and ignorance (Job 38–41). For example, God asked, "Where were you when I laid the foundation of the earth? Tell me, if you have understanding" (38:4). Job expressed repentance in the face of God's inscrutable sovereignty and wisdom. He did not get all the answers he wanted, but he seemed satisfied to encounter God and rest in His sovereign providence.

Sometimes we wish we knew what God is up to in some of our circumstances. But God tells us, "My thoughts are not your thoughts, neither are your ways my ways, declares the Lord. For as the heavens are higher than the earth, so are my ways higher than your ways and my thoughts than your thoughts" (Isaiah 55:8-9). In Romans 11:33, the apostle Paul declared, "Oh, the depth of the riches and wisdom and knowledge of God! How unsearchable are his judgments and how inscrutable his ways!" My advice: Trust God no matter what.

Rejoice! Your Redeemer lives, and you'll live forever with Him!

In the midst of his suffering, Job affirmed, "I know that my Redeemer lives" (Job 19:25). This was the light that shone so brightly for him. He knew he would yet see his living Redeemer (19:26).

You and I also know our Redeemer lives, for He defeated death and was raised from the dead (Luke 24:1-12,39; John 20:19; 1 Corinthians 15:1-3). We, too, will one day be resurrected. And so "Death is swallowed up in victory. O death, where is your victory? O death, where is your sting?" (1 Corinthians 15:54-55).

You can have an eternal perspective, just as Job did. Colossians 3:2 urges, "Set your minds on things that are above, not on things that are on earth." This will help you to endure whenever life gets hard.

Verses to Remember

"I know that my Redeemer lives, and at the last he will stand upon the earth. And after my skin has been thus destroyed, yet in my flesh I shall see God."

—*Job 19:25-26*

"Anticipating heaven doesn't eliminate pain, but it lessens it and puts it in perspective. Meditating on heaven is a great pain reliever. It reminds us that suffering and death are temporary conditions."

—*Randy Alcorn*

Job

A Thought to Anchor in Your Heart

When you don't understand why certain things have happened to you, that is the most important time to anchor yourself with what you *do* understand. The more you understand Scripture, the better!

Psalms

Life on earth can sometimes be difficult, but God and His Word are our great consolation. We can turn to God with any problem we face, including our deepest personal hurts. God is faithful and He is powerful—worthy of our praise, devotion, and thanksgiving. Through it all, one thing is certain: the righteous are blessed by God, but the wicked suffer many ills.

Timeline

1526—Moses is born. Before he dies in 1406, he writes Psalm 90.

1040—David is born.

1003—David becomes king of all Israel. The 73 psalms of David are written in general proximity to this time.

970—Solomon becomes king. He writes Psalms 72 and 127 in general proximity to this time.

450—By this year, the last of the psalms have been composed—most reflecting Israel's exile and restoration.

A Verse to Remember

"Oh, magnify the LORD with me, and let us exalt his name together!"

—*Psalm 34:3*

The ancient Jews referred to Psalms as "The Book of Praises." The Septuagint—the Greek translation of the Old Testament that predates the time of Christ—titled it "The Book of Psalms."

The book of Psalms seems to be a compilation of five smaller collections or books: 1–41, 42–72, 73–89, 90–106, and 107–150. Each of the five collections closes with an ascription of praise. Book 1 (Psalms 1–41) contains primarily personal psalms relating to David, as well as the doctrines of man and creation. Books 2 and 3 (Psalms 42–72 and 73–89) are primarily national psalms, some of them relating to when the nation was divided into the northern kingdom and the southern kingdom. A heavy emphasis is placed on Israel and redemption, as well as worship and the temple. Books 4 and 5 (Psalms 90–106 and 107–150) are primarily worship psalms. These psalms often focus on man's sojourn on the earth, as well as on praise and the Word of God. The psalms were written from about 1410 to 450 BC.

The many categories of psalms include petition psalms (3, 6, 16, 39, 41, 44); thanksgiving psalms (30, 65); praise psalms (41, 72, 89, 106, 150); penitence psalms (32, 51, 130); psalms of trust in God (for example, 4); psalms of Yahweh's enthronement (for example, 47); psalms of Jerusalem (for example, 48); royal psalms (2, 110); didactic psalms (1, 37, 119); patriotic psalms (44, 46, 126); and imprecatory psalms (7, 35, 55, 58, 59, 69, 79, 109, 137, 139, 140). The psalms are a rich genre of biblical literature.

It seems clear that David was the author of many of the psalms (at least half of them), for many bear his name. Elsewhere we are told David was a talented musician and poet, and so it would have been natural for him to compose such psalms (see, for example, 1 Samuel 16:23). The sons of Korah, Asaph, Solomon, Moses, Heman, and Ethan wrote other psalms (for example, Psalm 82 was written by Asaph).

The psalms were collected for use in temple worship, and were typically set to the accompaniment of stringed instruments. Within Psalms one will find prayers, poetic expressions, liturgies, hymns, and just about every emotion known to man—including happiness, serenity, peace, hatred, vengeance, and bitterness. In Psalms, we find human beings struggling honestly with life and communicating honestly with God, without holding anything back. Because we today struggle with the same kinds of problems and emotions the ancients did, the book of Psalms is one of the most relevant and loved books to modern Christians in the entire Bible. The psalms are indeed timeless.

Following are key applicational concepts in the Psalms:

You can trust in God's Word. Never doubt it.

The psalmist affirms, "The words of the LORD are pure words" (Psalm 12:6). "This God—his way is perfect; the word of the LORD proves true" (18:30). "The law of the LORD is perfect, reviving the soul" (19:7). "The rules of the LORD are true, and righteous altogether" (19:9). "All your commandments are true" (119:151). "The sum of your word is truth, and every one of your righteous rules endures forever" (119:160). My friend, never doubt the truth of God's Word. Let it be the foundation of your life.

> "Disregard the study of God, and you sentence yourself to stumble and blunder through life blindfolded."
>
> —J. I. Packer

Christians ought to always meditate upon the Word of God.

Psalm 1:2 reveals that on God's law the blessed man "meditates day and night." In this type of meditation, the individual believer objectively contemplates and deeply reflects upon God's Word (1:2;

> "Nobody can take away from you those texts from the Bible which you have learned by heart."
>
> —Corrie ten Boom (1892–1983)

Psalms

19:14; Joshua 1:8) as well as His Person and faithfulness (119; see also 19:14; 48:9; 77:12; 104:34; 143:5). There is no subjective emptying of the mind, as is true with modern eastern meditation.

The Hebrew word for "meditate" carries the idea of "murmuring." It pictures an individual reading and concentrating so intently on what he's reading in Scripture that his lips move as he reads. Such Christian meditation fills our minds with godly wisdom and insight.

> "The most important thing I had to do was to give myself to the reading of the Word of God and to meditation on it."
>
> —George Muller (1805–1898)

True hope lies in God and His Word.

The psalmist engages in a bit of inner reflection: "Why are you cast down, O my soul, and why are you in turmoil within me? Hope in God; for I shall again praise him, my salvation and my God" (Psalm 43:5). Elsewhere we find the psalmist praying to God, "Let your steadfast love, O LORD, be upon us, even as we hope in you" (33:22). "And now, O Lord, for what do I wait? My hope is in you" (39:7). "For you, O Lord, are my hope, my trust, O LORD, from my youth" (71:5).

> **God Comforts Us**
>
> "My father and my mother have forsaken me, but the LORD will take me in" (Psalm 27:10).
>
> "This is my comfort in my affliction, that your promise gives me life" (119:50).

As there is hope in God, there is hope in God's Word. The psalmist affirms, "I wait for the LORD, my soul waits, and in his word I hope" (Psalm 130:5). "Those who fear you shall see me and rejoice, because I have hoped in your word" (119:74). "My soul longs for your salvation; I hope in your word" (119:81).

God is an awesome God—worthy of your personal praise and worship.

God is eternal. "From everlasting to everlasting you are God" (Psalm 90:2). "You, O LORD, are enthroned forever" (102:12). "You are the same, and your years have no end" (102:27).

God is infinitely great. "Great is the LORD, and greatly to be praised, and his greatness is unsearchable" (Psalm 145:3). "The LORD is high above all nations, and his glory above the heavens" (113:4).

> "We may ignore, but we can nowhere evade, the presence of God. The world is crowded with Him. He walks everywhere incognito."
>
> —C. S. Lewis (1898–1963)

God is everywhere-present. "Where shall I go from your Spirit? Or where shall I flee from your presence?

Psalms

If I ascend to heaven, you are there! If I make my bed in Sheol, you are there" (Psalm 139:7-8; see also 113:4-6).

God is all-knowing. "O LORD, you have searched me and known me! You know when I sit down and when I rise up; you discern my thoughts from afar. You search out my path and my lying down and are acquainted with all my ways. Even before a word is on my tongue, behold, O LORD, you know it altogether" (Psalm 139:1-4). "The LORD knows people's thoughts" (94:11 NLT). "He knows the secrets of every heart" (44:21 NLT). God "determines the number of the stars; he gives to all of them their names" (147:4). God's "understanding is beyond measure" (147:5).

God is all-powerful. "Great is our Lord, and abundant in power" (Psalm 147:5). The Lord is "strong and mighty" (24:8). He is the "Mighty One" (50:1). "Power belongs to God" (62:11). The psalmist therefore declares, "I will sing of your strength" (59:16). Indeed, "O LORD God of hosts, who is mighty as you are, O LORD" (89:8).

God is sovereign. "The LORD has established his throne in the heavens, and his kingdom rules over all" (Psalm 103:19). The Lord is the "great king over all the earth" (47:2). "The counsel of the LORD stands forever" (33:11).

God is good. "Oh, taste and see that the LORD is good" (Psalm 34:8). "You are good and do good" (119:68). "Oh give thanks to the LORD, for he is good" (106:1). "The LORD is good; his steadfast love endures forever, and his faithfulness to all generations" (100:5). "The LORD is good to all, and his mercy is over all that he has made" (145:9).

> "The sovereignty of God relieves me from anxiety. It doesn't take away my questions. It takes away my anxiety. When I rest in it, I am relieved of the worry."
>
> —*Charles Swindoll*

God is gracious and merciful. "The LORD is merciful and gracious, slow to anger and abounding in steadfast love" (103:8). "Gracious is the LORD, and righteous; our God is merciful" (116:5).

God is righteous and just. "The LORD is righteous in all his ways" (Psalm 145:17). "Righteousness and justice are the foundation of your throne" (89:14). "He will judge the world with righteousness, and the peoples with equity" (98:9).

God is love. God is full of "steadfast love" (Psalm 25:6; 25:7). "The earth is full of the steadfast love of the LORD" (33:5). The Lord is "abounding in steadfast love to all who call upon you" (86:5). "His steadfast love endures forever" (106:1). "With the LORD there is steadfast love" (130:7).

God is so awesome that He merely spoke the words and the universe leapt into existence.

Verses 6 and 9 in Psalm 33 affirm, "By the word of the LORD the heavens were made, and by the breath of his mouth all their host...For he spoke, and it came to be; he commanded, and it stood firm." Such verses indicate that when God engaged in the work of creation, He did so in an instantaneous fashion. Hebrews 11:3 tells us "the universe was created by the word of God." No time interval lapsed between God's commanding words and creation leaping into existence. There was no slow process of evolution involved in any way.

We find more insights on the creation in Genesis. Indeed, three Hebrew words are used in Genesis 1 to describe God's work of creation—*bara* ("to create"), *asah* ("to make"), and *yatsar* ("to form"). God alone was responsible for creating, making, and forming all that is in the universe. And He did so without using preexisting materials. One moment, nothing existed anywhere. The next moment, after God gave the command, the universe leapt into existence. This is known among theologians as *creatio ex nihilo* (creation out of nothing). Our God is an awesome God!

Each one of us is custom-designed by God within our mother's womb.

In Psalm 139:13-14 David affirmed to God, "You formed my inward parts; you knitted me together in my mother's womb. I praise you, for I am fearfully and wonderfully made." My friend, you were no accident. You are a God-designed human being. You are the artwork of God. Rejoice in your special significance before God!

Our Lord is worthy to be praised. Make it a daily habit.

The psalmist affirmed, "I will bless the LORD at all times; his praise shall continually be in my mouth" (Psalm 34:1). "I will sing praises to you" (71:22). "Enter his gates with thanksgiving, and his courts with praise! Give thanks to him; bless his name" (100:4). "Bless the LORD, O my soul, and all that is within me, bless his holy name" (103:1). Praise virtually saturates the psalms (see 106:1; 111:1; 112:1; 113:1; 117:1; 135:1; 146:1; 146:10; 147:1; 148:1).

A Verse to Remember

"He put a new song in my mouth."

—*Psalm 40:3*

Always be ready to testify to others about how great God is.

The psalmist urged, "Tell among the peoples his deeds" (Psalm 9:11). "For this I will praise you, O Lord, among the nations" (18:49). The psalmist wanted to be involved in "proclaiming thanksgiving aloud, and telling all your wondrous deeds" (26:7). "My tongue will sing of your word" (119:172). The psalmist desired to "make known to the children of man your mighty deeds, and the glorious splendor of your kingdom" (145:12). Always be ready to give your testimony.

God's people often yearn for Him and His Word.

Those rightly related to God yearn for His presence. "As a deer pants for flowing streams, so pants my soul for you, O God" (Psalm 42:1). The psalmist affirms, "O God, you are my God; I earnestly search for you. My soul thirsts for you; my whole body longs for you in this parched and weary land where there is no water" (63:1 NLT). The psalmist asks, "Whom have I in heaven but you? And there is nothing on earth that I desire besides you" (73:25).

Such people love and take joy in God's Word. Psalm 19:8 tells us the precepts of the Lord "are right, rejoicing the heart." The psalmist affirms, "Oh how I love your law!...How sweet are your words to my taste, sweeter than honey to my mouth!...My soul keeps your testimonies; I love them exceedingly" (119:97,103,167).

> "God thirsts to be thirsted after."
> —*Augustine (354–430)*

A Verse to Remember
"As a deer pants for flowing streams, so pants my soul for you, O God."
—*Psalm 42:1*

Christians who walk closely with God are full of joy.

Psalm 1:1-2 tells us, "Oh, the joys of those who do not follow the advice of the wicked, or stand around with sinners, or join in with mockers. But they delight in the law of the Lord, meditating on it day and night" (NLT). "Oh, what joy for those whose disobedience is forgiven, whose sin is put out of sight! Yes, what joy for those whose record the Lord has cleared of guilt, whose lives are lived in complete honesty" (32:1-2 NLT). "Oh, the joys of those who take refuge in him" (34:8 NLT). "How joyful are those who fear the Lord—all who follow his ways" (128:1 NLT). "Joyful indeed are those whose God is the Lord" (144:15 NLT).

Don't Forget God
Some people forget all about God (78:11,42; 106:13). *No joy.*
Others choose never to forget Him (103:2; 119:93,153). *Lots of joy.*

Psalms

Great blessing accompanies the life of the person who seeks to walk righteously with God.

The psalmist often speaks of the blessing that accompanies the person who seeks to walk in righteousness before God. The psalmist boasts, "He makes me lie down in green pastures. He leads me beside still waters. He restores my soul. He leads me in paths of righteousness for his name's sake" (23:2-3). We are told "the Lord upholds the righteous" (37:17). Indeed, "the salvation of the righteous is from the Lord; he is their stronghold in the time of trouble" (37:39). "He will never permit the righteous to be moved" (55:22). The psalmist exulted, "My flesh and my heart may fail, but God is the strength of my heart and my portion forever" (73:26). "No good thing does he withhold from those who walk uprightly" (84:11).

God invites you to come to Him in prayer and speak to Him about anything that concerns you.

> "Trouble and perplexity drive us to prayer, and prayer driveth away trouble and perplexity."
>
> —*Philip Melanchton*
> *(1497–1560)*

> "It is when we are out of options that we are most ready for God's surprises."
>
> —*Max Lucado*

The psalmist consistently brought his petitions to God—no matter what the issue. For example, the psalmist consistently prayed for deliverance from his enemies: "Arise, O Lord! Save me, O my God!" (Psalm 3:7). "Save me from all my pursuers and deliver me" (7:1). "Lift yourself up against the fury of my enemies" (7:6). "Deliver my soul from the wicked by your sword" (17:13). "Vindicate me, O God, and defend my cause against an ungodly people" (43:1). "Rescue me, O my God, from the hand of the wicked, from the grasp of the unjust and cruel man" (71:4). "Deliver me, O Lord, from evil men; preserve me from violent men" (140:1). He also prayed for deliverance from the conspiracies of wicked people: "Hide me from the secret plots of the wicked, from the throng of evildoers" (64:2).

The psalmist often prayed for God to lead him and guide him: "Lead me, O Lord, in your righteousness because of my enemies; make your way straight before me" (Psalm 5:8). "Teach me your way, O Lord, and lead me on a level path" (27:11).

He prayed when he felt alone in his problems: "Turn to me and be gracious to me, for I am lonely and afflicted" (Psalm 25:16).

He prayed God would strengthen him from the Word of God: "My soul melts away for sorrow; strengthen me according to your word!" (Psalm 119:28).

"I am severely afflicted; give me life, O LORD, according to your word" (119:107). "Give me life according to your promise" (119:154).

He prayed for God to remove His disciplinary hand: "Remove your stroke from me; I am spent by the hostility of your hand" (Psalm 39:10; see also 32; 51).

It is interesting to observe how often the psalmist urged God to not forget him, and to awake and act on his behalf: "How long, O LORD? Will you forget me forever? How long will you hide your face from me?" (13:1). "How long, O Lord, will you look on?" (35:17). "You have seen, O LORD; be not silent! O Lord, be not far from me!" (35:22). "Awake and rouse yourself for my vindication, for my cause, my God and my Lord!" (35:23). "Be pleased, O LORD, to deliver me! O LORD, make haste to help me!" (40:13). "Awake! Why are you sleeping, O Lord? Rouse yourself! Do not reject us forever!" (44:23). "O God, be not far from me; O my God, make haste to help me" (71:12). "O God, do not keep silence; do not hold your peace or be still, O God!" (83:1; 102:2).

Don't get impatient. Wait on God and He'll come through for you.

God has perfect timing in all things. Like the psalmist of old, you and I must always be willing and ready to wait upon the Lord: "Wait for the LORD; be strong, and let your heart take courage; wait for the LORD" (Psalm 27:14). "Be still before the LORD and wait patiently for him" (37:7). "I waited patiently for the LORD; he inclined to me and heard my cry" (40:1). "For God alone my soul waits in silence; from him comes my salvation" (62:1). "For God alone, O my soul, wait in silence, for my hope is from him" (62:5).

> "Never be afraid to trust an unknown future to a known God."
>
> —Corrie ten Boom (1892–1983)

Commit to regularly expressing your thanks to God for what He has done for you.

Thanksgiving is a common feature in the psalms. We are urged, "Enter his gates with thanksgiving, and his courts with praise! Give thanks to him; bless his name" (Psalm 100:4). "Let us come into his presence with thanksgiving; let us make a joyful noise to him with songs of praise" (95:2). The psalmist affirms, "I will praise the name of God with a song; I will magnify him with thanksgiving" (69:30). The psalmist then affirms directly to God, "I will offer to you the sacrifice of thanksgiving" (116:17). "O LORD my God, I will give thanks to you forever" (30:12).

Psalms

God is willing and ready to give you spiritual wisdom when you need it. Just ask Him.

The psalmist often asked God for wisdom in spiritual matters. "Make me to know your ways, O Lord; teach me your paths" (Psalm 25:4). "Teach me your way, O Lord, and lead me on a level path" (27:11). "Teach us to number our days that we may get a heart of wisdom" (90:12). "Open my eyes, that I may behold wondrous things out of your law" (119:18). "Give me understanding, that I may keep your law and observe it with my whole heart" (119:34). "Give me understanding, that I may know your testimonies" (119:125).

God is an ever-present help in times of affliction and adversity.

> "Bear not a single care thyself,
> One is too much for thee;
> The work is Mine, and Mine alone;
> Thy work—to rest in Me."
>
> —*Anonymous*

A Verse to Remember

"The Lord is my shepherd;
I shall not want."

—*Psalm 23:1*

The psalms consistently emphasize that the Lord is with us in times of affliction and adversity. "The Lord is a stronghold for the oppressed, a stronghold in times of trouble" (Psalm 9:9). "God is our refuge and strength, a very present help in trouble" (46:1). God invites us, "Call upon me in the day of trouble; I will deliver you, and you shall glorify me" (50:15). The psalmist urges, "Cast your burden on the Lord, and he will sustain you" (55:22). "As a father shows compassion to his children, so the Lord shows compassion to those who fear him" (103:13). The psalmist was confident: "Though I walk in the midst of trouble, you preserve my life; you stretch out your hand against the wrath of my enemies, and your right hand delivers me" (138:7). Never forget that God "heals the brokenhearted and binds up their wounds" (147:3). And fear not! As the psalmist put it, "Even though I walk through the valley of the shadow of death, I will fear no evil, for you are with me; your rod and your staff, they comfort me" (23:4).

God is your divine shield. You can find safety in Him.

A Verse to Remember

"He who dwells in the shelter of the Most High will abide in the shadow of the Almighty."

—*Psalm 91:1*

Sometimes the world can seem like a dangerous place. Sometimes we feel just a bit vulnerable. While none of us should purposefully put ourselves in harm's way, we ought to also recognize that God is our helper in times of danger. The psalmist affirmed, "Even though I walk through the valley of the shadow of death, I will fear no evil, for you are with me; your rod and your staff, they comfort me" (Psalm 23:4). He also affirmed to God, "You are a hiding place for me; you preserve me from trouble; you surround me with shouts of deliverance" (32:7). We are promised, "The angel of the Lord encamps around those who fear him, and delivers them" (34:7). "When the righteous cry for help, the Lord hears and delivers them out of all their troubles" (34:17). We are told, "Many are the afflictions of the righteous, but the Lord delivers him out of them all" (34:19). "The Lord will keep your going out and your coming in from this time forth and forevermore" (121:8).

Rejoice! God's angels have been assigned to watch over you.

Angels are a class of beings higher than human beings (Psalm 8:5) and are very powerful (103:20). Psalm 91:11-12 tells us, "He will command his angels concerning you to guard you in all your ways. On their hands they will bear you up, lest you strike your foot against a stone." Angels are also seen as guardians in the New Testament (Matthew 18:10).

> "The angels keep vigil for our safety, take upon themselves our defense, direct our ways, and take care that some harm may not befall us."
>
> —John Calvin (1509–1564)

Keep your faith in God strong. He'll always come through for you.

When you're facing tough circumstances, don't give in to fear or discouragement. Instead, "wait for the Lord; be strong, and let your heart take courage; wait for the Lord!" (Psalm 27:14). "Commit your way to the Lord; trust in him, and he will act" (37:5). "Cast your burden on the Lord, and he will sustain you; he will never permit the righteous to be moved" (55:22). "Trust in him at all times, O people; pour out your heart before him; God is a refuge for us" (62:8).

> **Misplaced Trust**
> - Chariots and horses (Psalm 20:7).
> - Bows and swords (44:6-7).
> - Other human beings (146:3).

Maintain a reverent fear of the Lord.

Psalm 111:10 affirms that "the fear of the Lord is the beginning of wisdom; all those who practice it have a good understanding." We are told, "Blessed is the man who fears the Lord, who greatly delights in his commandments!" (112:1). God "will bless those who fear the Lord, both the small and the great" (115:13). God "fulfills the desire of those who fear him; he also hears their cry and saves

> "He who fears God has nothing else to fear."
>
> —Charles Spurgeon (1834–1892)

Psalms

them" (145:19). "The angel of the LORD encamps around those who fear him, and delivers them" (34:7). We should all therefore "serve the LORD with fear, and rejoice with trembling" (2:11).

Want to please God? Obey Him!

The psalmist affirms his resolve to be obedient to God in all things: "I hasten and do not delay to keep your commandments" (Psalm 119:60). "I will keep your law continually, forever and ever" (119:44).

There is great blessing in obeying God. "Blessed is the man who fears the LORD, who greatly delights in his commandments!" (Psalm 112:1). "Blessed are those who keep his testimonies, who seek him with their whole heart" (119:2). "All the paths of the LORD are steadfast love and faithfulness, for those who keep his covenant and his testimonies" (25:10).

Elsewhere in Scripture we are told that obedience to God brings long life (1 Kings 3:14; John 8:51), happiness (Psalm 112:1; 119:56), peace (Proverbs 1:33), and a state of well-being (Jeremiah 7:23; see also Exodus 19:5; Leviticus 26:3-4; Deuteronomy 4:40; 12:28; 28:1; Joshua 1:8; 1 Chronicles 22:13; Isaiah 1:19).

> ### Verses to Remember
>
> "Blessed is the man who walks not in the counsel of the wicked, nor stands in the way of sinners, nor sits in the seat of scoffers; but his delight is in the law of the LORD, and on his law he meditates day and night."
>
> —Psalm 1:1-2

May your tongue always be used for good.

It is always best for us to use our tongues to speak words of praise to God and build up other people spiritually (Psalm 35:28; 40:3; 71:23). The psalmist was resolved not to use his tongue for evil: "I said, 'I will guard my ways, that I may not sin with my tongue; I will guard my mouth with a muzzle, so long as the wicked are in my presence'" (39:1). He even made it a matter of prayer: "Let the words of my mouth and the meditation of my heart be acceptable in your sight, O LORD, my rock and my redeemer" (19:14). "Set a guard, O LORD, over my mouth; keep watch over the door of my lips" (141:3). Wise. Very wise.

Want to know why you sometimes do bad things? It's the sin nature within.

In Psalm 51:5 David affirmed, "Behold, I was brought forth in iniquity, and in sin did my mother conceive me." This is speaking of original sin—the doctrine that every human being since the time of Adam and Eve has been born into the world with a sin nature. The reality of the sin nature is why Ephesians 2:3 says human beings are "by nature children of wrath."

The universality of sin bears witness to the reality of original sin. In Ecclesiastes 7:20 we read, "Surely there is not a righteous man on earth who does good and never sins." In Isaiah 64:6 we read, "We have all become like one who is unclean, and all our righteous deeds are like a polluted garment. We all fade like a leaf, and our iniquities, like the wind, take us away." In 1 John 1:8 we read, "If we say we have no sin, we deceive ourselves, and the truth is not in us." All of humanity is fallen in sin as a result of the initial sin of our first parents, and it has affected us all in a dreadful, awful way. This was certainly true of the psalmist of old. But there is good news too.

Forgiveness of sin is available from the Lord.

There is no greater feeling of release than that which comes from being forgiven of all sins. The psalmist affirmed, "Blessed is the one whose transgression is forgiven, whose sin is covered" (Psalm 32:1). It is the Lord alone "who forgives all your iniquity" (103:3). "As far as the east is from the west, so far does he remove our transgressions from us" (103:12).

Forgiveness comes through confession of sin: "When I kept silent, my bones wasted away through my groaning all day long...I acknowledged my sin to you, and I did not cover my iniquity; I said, 'I will confess my transgressions to the Lord,' and you forgave the iniquity of my sin" (32:3,5; see also 38:18; 51:4; 1 John 1:9).

Because God loves you, He sometimes allows adversity in your life as a means of discipline— a way of calling you back to His side.

Afflictions and adversities can be used by God as a disciplinary tool for our good. "Blessed is the man whom you discipline, O Lord, and whom you teach out of your law" (Psalm 94:12). The psalmist affirmed, "It is good for me that I was afflicted, that I might learn your statutes" (119:71). God disciplined David when he sinned, and David repented (32; 51). The New Testament teaches us that God brings divine discipline to woo us to repentance and restored fellowship with Him (Hebrews 12:5-11).

> **God Is Slow to Anger**
>
> "His anger is but for a moment, and his favor is for a lifetime" (Psalm 30:5).
>
> "You, O Lord, are a God merciful and gracious, slow to anger" (86:15).

> "We often learn more of God under the rod that strikes us, than under the staff that comforts us."
>
> —*Stephen Charnock*
> *(1628–1680)*

Life on earth is all too short. It is therefore wise to live in light of eternity.

The psalmist affirms, "Surely all mankind is a mere breath" (Psalm 39:11). He is aware: "I wither away like grass" (102:11). "Man is like a breath; his days are like a passing shadow" (144:4). "What man can live and never see death?" (89:48). "The years of our life...they are soon gone, and we fly away" (90:10). The psalmist therefore wisely prayed, "O Lord, make me know my end and what is the measure of my days; let me know how fleeting I am" (39:4). The person who is aware of his mortality—fully cognizant of the uncertainties of life—makes the most of each passing day.

> "Men have been helped to live by remembering that they must die."
>
> —Charles Spurgeon (1834–1892)

The righteous have nothing to fear in death.

Psalm 116:15 affirms, "Precious in the sight of the Lord is the death of his saints." The righteous need not fear death. "Even though I walk through the valley of the shadow of death, I will fear no evil" (23:4). "God will ransom my soul from the power of Sheol, for he will receive me" (49:15). At the moment of death, we can affirm as did the psalmist, "Into your hand I commit my spirit; you have redeemed me, O Lord, faithful God" (31:5).

> "We are immortal till our work is done."
>
> —George Whitefield (1714–1770)

> "Resolved, that I will live so as I shall wish I had done when I come to die."
>
> "Resolved, never to do anything, which I should be afraid to do, if it were the last hour of my life."
>
> —Jonathan Edwards (1703–1758)

Believers look forward to an eternal existence with God.

While believers in Old Testament times did not have a fully developed understanding of the afterlife, they nevertheless spoke in terms indicating a belief in a future life with God. In Psalm 16:9-11, for example, David looked forward to the pleasures of living forever with God: "Therefore my heart is glad, and my whole being rejoices; my flesh also dwells secure. For you will not abandon my soul to Sheol, or let your holy one see corruption. You make known to me the path of life; in your presence there is fullness of joy; at your

> "Heaven must become our first and ultimate point of reference. We are built for it, redeemed for it, and on our way to it. Success demands that we see and respond to now in the light of then."
>
> —Joseph Stowell

right hand are pleasures forevermore." David also affirmed, "Surely goodness and mercy shall follow me all the days of my life, and I shall dwell in the house of the Lord forever" (23:6). He affirms that God is "my portion forever" (73:26).

A Thought to Anchor in Your Heart

Maintain a heavenly perspective. Make every effort to see and respond to *now* in the light of *then*.

Psalms

Proverbs

Wise living enhances our relationship with God and with others, and our overall success in life.

Proverbs

Timeline

991—Solomon is born.

970—David dies and Solomon becomes king.

970–931—Solomon composes his many proverbs over the duration of his kingship.

729–686—King Hezekiah's scribes compile Solomon's proverbs for the book of Proverbs.

The book of Proverbs is a "wisdom book" and contains maxims of moral wisdom—mostly written by Solomon. The maxims were engineered to help the young in ancient Israel acquire mental skills that promote wise living. In Solomon's thinking, wise living was essentially synonymous with godly living, for one who is godly or righteous in his daily behavior is wise in God's eyes. By contrast, a wicked or unrighteous person is foolish.

The word "proverb" literally means "to be like," or "to be compared with." A proverb, then, is a form of communicating truth by using comparisons or figures of speech. The book is titled Proverbs because it is a collection of proverbs.

Solomon, the author of most of the proverbs, was the wisest man who ever lived (1 Kings 3; 4:29-34; see also Proverbs 1:1; 10:1; 25:1; Ecclesiastes 12:9). Other proverbs were written by unnamed wise men (Proverbs 22:17–24:34). The last two chapters were written by the relatively unknown prophets, Agur and Lemuel.

Following are key applicational concepts in Proverbs:

Living according to biblical wisdom leads to the good life.

Living according to biblical wisdom yields peace (Proverbs 3:2), success (3:4), long life and honor (3:16,35; 4:8), pleasantness (3:17), stability (3:23; 4:12), security (3:24), health (4:22), and a straight path to follow throughout life (4:25-27). The more biblical wisdom one gains, the better.

> "The fear of God is both a virtue and a keeper of other virtues."
>
> —*Anonymous*

Fearing the Lord leads to a healthy spirituality.

Fearing the Lord involves showing reverence to Him (Proverbs 2:5; see also Deuteronomy 32:6; Hosea 11:1; Isaiah 1:2; 63:16; 64:8). Such reverence naturally leads to obedience to God. Conversely, the person who feels free to disobey God typically has no fear of God.

Scoffers not only live a downer life; they're also a downer to others. Avoid them.

A scoffer is a mocker. Scoffers are arrogant and haughty (Proverbs 21:24). They have a sinful attitude (24:9) and scorn others (3:34). They breed strife among people (22:10). Unlike wise people, scoffers don't like to be reproved (15:12).

Fools are constantly frustrating. Keep your distance.

Fools lack good sense (Proverbs 12:11; 21:16). They often act without thinking (29:11). They always think they're right, but end up in ruin: "There is a way that seems right to a man, but its end is the way to death" (14:12). They don't like to be instructed (1:7) and don't listen to good advice (23:9). It's not wise to hang around with them (13:20).

Our God is an awesome God. Learn everything you can about Him.

God is holy (Proverbs 9:10) and the Creator of all things (22:2), having made everything for its purpose (16:4). He is omniscient and sees all things (15:3). No one can stand against Him (21:30). He is sovereign over the world of humanity (16:9,33). Indeed, "the king's heart is a stream of water in the hand of the LORD; he turns it wherever he will" (21:1). Despite what human beings plan, it is the purpose of the Lord that will ultimately stand (19:21). Dear Christian, you can trust God with your life!

God probes deeper than your external actions, examining even your motives.

Proverbs 16:2 warns, "All the ways of a man are pure in his own eyes, but the LORD weighs the spirit."

Wisdom

- rebukes sin (1:8-33);
- richly rewards those who seek it (2–3);
- keeps one from dangerous paths (4);
- warns against sensuality (5);
- motivates the slothful (6:1-19);
- represses lustful desires (6:20-35);
- warns against evil women (7);
- rejoices in God (8); and
- contrasts with the ways of folly (9).

Proverbs in the New Testament

Proverbs 25:6-7—Luke 14:10
Proverbs 3:7—Romans 12:16
Proverbs 25:21-22—Romans 12:20
Proverbs 22:9—2 Corinthians 9:7
Proverbs 3:11-12—Hebrews 12:5-6
Proverbs 4:26—Hebrews 12:13
Proverbs 3:34—James 4:6
Proverbs 24:21—1 Peter 2:17
Proverbs 16:7—1 Peter 3:13
Proverbs 10:12—1 Peter 4:8
Proverbs 11:31—1 Peter 4:18
Proverbs 26:11—2 Peter 2:22

Proverbs

Proverbs 17:3 likewise affirms, "The crucible is for silver, and the furnace is for gold, and the LORD tests hearts." Heart motives matter to God.

God is our security blanket. Stay close to Him.

Proverbs 3:25-26 urges, "Do not be afraid of sudden terror or of the ruin of the wicked, when it comes, for the LORD will be your confidence and will keep your foot from being caught." Proverbs 10:29 likewise affirms, "The way of the LORD is a stronghold to the blameless." Don't ever wander away from your security blanket.

God hears the prayers of the righteous.

Solomon tells us "the prayer of the upright is acceptable to him" (Proverbs 15:8). Indeed, "The LORD is far from the wicked, but he hears the prayer of the righteous" (15:29). Cause and effect! Righteous living opens God's ears to your prayers.

> "The prayer of a righteous person has great power as it is working."
>
> —James 5:16

> "Commit your way to the Lord; trust in him, and he will act."
>
> —Psalm 37:5

Trust God moment by moment, 24/7.

One of the most beloved passages in the Bible is Proverbs 3:5-6: "Trust in the LORD with all your heart, and do not lean on your own understanding. In all your ways acknowledge him, and he will make straight your paths." Never forget that "the one who trusts in the LORD will be enriched" (28:25) and "whoever trusts in the LORD is safe" (29:25).

> "I say to you, Love your enemies and pray for those who persecute you."
>
> —Jesus, Matthew 5:44

Be counterintuitive. Treat your enemies well.

Treat your enemies well. "Do not rejoice when your enemy falls, and let not your heart be glad when he stumbles, lest the LORD see it and be displeased, and turn away his anger from him" (Proverbs 24:17-18).

> **A Verse to Remember**
> "An excellent wife who can find? She is far more precious than jewels."
>
> —Proverbs 31:10

Husbands and wives, try to avoid quarrelsomeness.

"As charcoal to hot embers and wood to fire, so is a quarrelsome man for kindling strife" (Proverbs 26:21). Moreover, "a continual dripping on a rainy day and a quarrelsome wife are alike" (27:15). She is as hard to withstand as restraining the wind (verse 16). Husbands and wives should make every effort to avoid quarrelsomeness.

Wives, aspire to make Proverbs 31 a reality in your life.

Proverbs 31 provides a beautiful description of a good and virtuous wife, resourceful and hardworking, taking care of her household. Her inner virtue is far more important than her external beauty.

Parents, train your children to live life rightly.

Proverbs 22:6 says, "Train up a child in the way he should go; even when he is old he will not depart from it." The word "train" comes from a root word that means "palate" or "roof of the mouth." Ancient midwives rubbed the palate of a newborn child with olive oil to give it a desire for food. Christian parents

> **Cross-References: Children**
> Psalm 127:3 • Proverbs 22:6,15 • 29:15 • Mark 10:13-16 • Ephesians 6:1,4 • Colossians 3:20-21

should seek to develop in their child a desire for the things of God. If the child at a young age is given a desire for the Lord and His ways, he will not want to turn aside from it when he reaches adulthood.

Parents who love their children discipline them when they go astray.

A mark of good parents is that they discipline their children when they go astray. "Folly is bound up in the heart of a child, but the rod of discipline drives it far from him" (Proverbs 22:15; see also 13:24; 23:13-14). Of course, disciplinary discomfort can take many forms—including a time out, standing in the corner, being confined to a bedroom, losing privileges, and the like.

> "Bring them up in the discipline and instruction of the Lord."
>
> —*Ephesians 6:4*

Choose your friends carefully.

It is wise to choose friends carefully. Look for a friend who will stay closer to you than a brother (Proverbs 18:24). Beware of superficial friends who buddy up to you because you have money (19:4). Those aren't true friends. Try to avoid making friends with an angry person (22:24; 15:18; 19:11). Also avoid those who are not trustworthy with private matters you share with them (20:19; 16:28; 17:9; 11:13). Don't get close to disingenuous people who are always saying, "I am only joking!" (26:19). A true friend loves you at all times—and *treats* you lovingly—no

Proverbs

matter what (17:17). A good friend offers you good advice because he cares for you (12:26; 27:9).

Make every effort to build a good reputation.

> "A good name is better than precious ointment."
>
> —*Ecclesiastes 7:1*

A good reputation is incredibly important in life. "A good name is to be chosen rather than great riches" (Proverbs 22:1). A good reputation can lead to success in life. "Let not steadfast love and faithfulness forsake you; bind them around your neck; write them on the tablet of your heart. So you will find favor and good success in the sight of God and man" (3:3-4). No kidding, friends. Take this seriously.

Make every effort to avoid being seduced into sexual immorality.

Cross-References: Sexual Immorality
Acts 15:20 • Galatians 5:19 • 1 Corinthians 6:13,18 • 1 Thessalonians 4:3-7

Solomon warns that an immoral woman might try to use seductive words to lure a man into a sexual encounter (Proverbs 7:21; 5:3). If he gives in to the temptation, he will pay an enormous price (7:22-23). Solomon asks, "Can a man carry fire next to his chest and his clothes not be burned? Or can one walk on hot coals and his feet not be scorched? So is he who goes in to his neighbor's wife; none who touches her will go unpunished" (6:27-29). Solomon thus warns, "Let not your heart turn aside to her ways; do not stray into her paths, for many a victim has she laid low" (7:25-26). It is better to "drink water from your own cistern"—that is, limit sexual activities to your spouse alone (5:15).

Righteous living brings many benefits.

Keep God's Commandments and Live
Proverbs 4:4 says, "Keep my commandments, *and live*" (emphasis added). God's commands are intended to help you avoid a hurt-filled life and gain an abundant life.

Righteous living brings God's blessing. God is a "shield to those who walk in integrity" (Proverbs 2:7). God watches over their way (2:8), keeps them on the right path in life (11:5), and makes daily provisions for them (10:3). God makes them flourish in their endeavors (11:28).

Proverbs

Wicked living is accompanied by many hurts.

The way of the wicked brings many hurts in life. Their path is a dangerous one—full of thorns and snares (Proverbs 22:5). They encounter calamity (22:8) and end up in ruin (21:12). They have a guilty conscience that makes them paranoid. "The wicked flee when no one pursues" (28:1). They also experience the boomerang effect: "Whoever digs a pit will fall into it" (26:27).

> "Arrogance has its own built-in misery. The arrogant person may offend others, but he hurts himself more."
>
> —*Billy Graham*

Pride is foolish and injurious. Humility is the better way.

Of the six things God hates, one is "haughty eyes" (Proverbs 6:17). We are told, "Pride goes before destruction, and a haughty spirit before a fall" (16:18). Conversely, "The reward for humility and fear of the LORD is riches and honor and life" (22:4).

Avoid laziness. Be a hard worker.

A lazy person lies around doing nothing, unconcerned with necessary chores (Proverbs 24:30-34; 21:25). He never prepares for the future (20:4). He's always making excuses to avoid work (22:13). He never listens to the advice of others who could put him on the right track (26:16). Such a person is a shame to his parents (10:5). It's better to rise early and take responsibility for providing for yourself and your family (20:13). It's better to work hard like the ants (6:6-8).

Cross-References: Work Hard

Genesis 2:15 • 2 Thessalonians 3:10 • Ecclesiastes 5:18-20 • 1 Thessalonians 4:11-12 • Mark 6:3 • Acts 18:3

Be Wise in Relating to

- the king (25:1-7);
- neighbors (25:8-20);
- enemies (25:21-24);
- fools (26:3-12);
- sluggards (26:13-16); and
- gossips (26:17-28).

Choose your words carefully.

Your words can either bless people or injure them. Words can either build up people or tear them down. "There is one whose rash words are like sword thrusts, but the tongue of the wise brings healing" (Proverbs 12:18). "A soft answer turns away wrath, but a harsh word stirs up anger" (15:1). "A gentle tongue is a tree of life, but perverseness in it breaks the spirit" (15:4; see also 25:11; 16:24).

> "No human being can tame the tongue. It is a restless evil, full of deadly poison."
>
> —*James 3:8*

Proverbs

Don't gossip and keep private matters to yourself.

Proverbs 11:13 instructs, "He who is trustworthy in spirit keeps a thing covered." Proverbs 17:9 likewise tells us, "Whoever covers an offense seeks love, but he who repeats a matter separates close friends." Don't do it!

Be content with what you have.

Avoid envy and be content with what you have. You'll be better off. "A tranquil heart gives life to the flesh, but envy makes the bones rot" (Proverbs 14:30).

> "I have learned in whatever situation I am to be content."
>
> —*Philippians 4:11*

Keep money and wealth in proper perspective.

There's much more to life than the size of your bank account. Don't make an idol out of money and wealth. Other things are much more important. "Better is a little with the fear of the LORD than great treasure and trouble with it" (Proverbs 15:16). "Better is a little with righteousness than great revenues with injustice" (16:8; see also 28:6). Live for the Lord, not for money.

Cross-References: Money
Ecclesiastes 5:10,18 • 1 Timothy 3:3 • 6:9-10,19 • Matthew 19:21 • Romans 12:8 • 1 John 3:17

God loves it when you are kind to the poor.

Proverbs 14:31 tells us that the person who is generous to the needy honors the Lord. Indeed, "Whoever is generous to the poor lends to the LORD, and he will repay him for his deed" (19:17). However, "Whoever closes his ear to the cry of the poor will himself call out and not be answered" (21:13). Don't procrastinate. Help the less fortunate.

It is wise to maintain an eternal perspective.

Death could come at any time. So "do not boast about tomorrow, for you do not know what a day may bring" (Proverbs 27:1; see also Luke 12:16-21). This reminds us of James 4:13-15: "Come now, you who say, 'Today or tomorrow we will go into such and such a town and spend a year there and trade and make a profit'—yet you do not know what tomorrow will bring. What is your life? For you

Cross-References: Eternal Perspective
Hebrews 12:2 • 13:14 • 2 Corinthians 4:17 • Colossians 1:4-5 • 3:1-2 • Revelation 21:1-5

are a mist that appears for a little time and then vanishes. Instead you ought to say, 'If the Lord wills, we will live and do this or that.'" We ought to live with eternity in view.

> ### A Thought to Anchor in Your Heart
>
> It is wise to begin each day with a little prayer:
> *"Lord, please give me the wisdom to handle every circumstance that lies ahead of me today. Please protect my mind and my heart from folly."*

Proverbs

Ecclesiastes

Life apart from God is meaningless. Life only makes sense with God in the picture. One is therefore wisest to pursue a relationship with God early in life.

Ecclesiastes

Futility in the Book of Romans

At the fall, "the creation was subjected to futility" (8:20).

"The whole creation has been groaning together in the pains of childbirth until now" (8:22).

"Not only the creation, but we ourselves...groan inwardly as we wait eagerly for adoption as sons, the redemption of our bodies" (8:23).

The title, Ecclesiastes, is rooted in a Hebrew word (*qoheleth*) meaning, "one who addresses the assembly"—teacher, speaker, or preacher. The author of Ecclesiastes was apparently Solomon, for he is identified as "the son of David, king in Jerusalem" (Ecclesiastes 1:1). The book was probably written about 935 BC.

Most Bible scholars believe Ecclesiastes presents two contrasting ways of looking at man's plight in the world. One is the secular, humanistic, materialistic viewpoint that interprets all things from a limited earthly perspective (a perspective "under the sun")—not recognizing God or His involvement in humankind's affairs (Ecclesiastes 1:14; 2:11,17,26; 4:4,16; 6:9). This earthly perspective is one completely unaided by divine revelation. It sees life as futile and meaningless, with no purpose. There is nothing new under the sun, but rather what is taking place now is what has already taken place many times in the past, and what will take place in the future will simply repeat what is taking place in the present. Truly, there is nothing new. Life is meaningless. There is no ultimate satisfaction in anything we do, because we will end up with the same doomed fate as all the other humans who preceded us.

The other perspective is a godly, spiritual perspective that interprets life and its problems—sometimes very difficult problems—from a God-honoring viewpoint (Ecclesiastes 3:1-15; 5:19; 6:1-2; 9:1). This perspective takes divine revelation into account regarding how life and its problems are to be interpreted. This perspective recognizes God, and is one that finds meaning in and enjoys life. God can be involved in all that we do (2:24-26; 3:13; 5:18-20; 9:7-10). Our ultimate meaning in life is not to be found in the things around us, which pass away, but in God alone (2:25). The conclusion of the writer of Ecclesiastes is that we should remember God while we are still young (12:1).

Following are key applicational concepts in Ecclesiastes:

Our meaning and satisfaction in life are not found in doing the same old things every day.

Solomon asks a pivotal question: "What does man gain by all the toil at which he toils under the sun?" (Ecclesiastes 1:3). From the limited earthly perspective, Solomon observes that everything seems to run in cycles. A generation comes, and then it goes, with another taking its place. The sun rises and the sun sets. The wind blows here and then there. There seems to be no ultimate satisfaction in any of this. Solomon concludes that "all things are full of weariness" (1:8). Indeed, "the eye is not satisfied with seeing, nor the ear filled with hearing" (1:8). He laments, "There is no remembrance of former things, nor will there be any remembrance of later things yet to be among those who come after" (1:11).

> "It is vanity to set your love on that which speedily passes away, and not to hasten to where everlasting joy abides."
>
> —Thomas à Kempis (1380–1471)

From the limited earthly perspective (which leaves God out of the picture), there is no ultimate meaning in engaging in a seemingly endless cycle of doing the same old things day in and day out. One can almost picture people saying, "Been there, done that" on a daily basis. It's all meaningless, Solomon says.

> "If we were given all we wanted here, our hearts would settle for this world rather than the next. God is forever luring us up and away from this one, wooing us to Himself and His still invisible Kingdom, where we will certainly find what we so keenly long for."
>
> —Elisabeth Elliot

Meaning and satisfaction in life are not found in temporal earthly pursuits.

Solomon investigated the possibility of finding meaning in knowledge and wisdom (Ecclesiastes 1:17-18), laughter and pleasure (2:2), wine (2:3), constructing great works (2:4-6), pursuing great wealth (2:7-8), music and women (2:8), worldly recognition (2:9), and worldly pleasures (2:10). He found that all of it was sheer vanity (2:11). Ultimate satisfaction cannot be found in these earthly pursuits (2:18-23). It's all futile.

Solomon then said there is nothing better than to enjoy good meals and try to find some satisfaction in work—for this is from the hand of God. In recognition of God's sovereign providence, he acknowledged, "Apart from him who can eat or who can have enjoyment?" (Ecclesiastes 2:25). But then he added, "If a sinner becomes wealthy, God takes the wealth away and gives it to those who please him. This, too, is meaningless—like chasing the wind" (2:26 NLT). Solomon here hints that even with God in the picture, life has inscrutable challenges that can be difficult to bear.

Even with God in the picture, life can be difficult—and it's hard to figure out why He allows certain things to happen.

God Can Bring Good Out of Evil

"We know that for those who love God all things work together for good, for those who are called according to his purpose" (Romans 8:28). For example, Paul wrote New Testament books while imprisoned. And Joseph was elevated to power in Egypt as a result of his brothers' betrayal of him (Genesis 50:20).

Solomon said everything in the world is foreordained by God (Ecclesiastes 6:10-12). Finite human beings cannot fathom His inscrutable plan (7:1-15). In many cases, life does not seem to add up. The problem of evil is especially difficult to figure out. The best advice Solomon could come up with is to make the volitional choice to enjoy life, despite life's enigmas, difficulties, and mysteries (8). Death awaits us all (9:11-12), so it makes sense to work hard and enjoy life for the limited time we have on earth (9:7-10). Solomon concluded that the path of wisdom is the best game plan (9:15–11:6).

God has put within each of our hearts a yearning for the eternal. We ought therefore to maintain an eternal perspective.

"O God, Thou hast made us for Thyself, and our hearts find no rest until they rest in Thee."

—*Augustine (354–430)*

Solomon affirmed that God "has put eternity into man's heart" (Ecclesiastes 3:11). We all have a sense in our hearts that this life is not all there is—that life continues beyond the grave in the afterlife. It is interesting to observe that from the first book in the Bible to the last, we read of great men and women of God who gave evidence that eternity permeated their hearts. We read of people like Abel, Enoch, Noah, and Abraham—each yearning to live with God in eternity. It is of these blessed saints that New Testament Scripture reveals:

> These all died in faith, not having received the things promised, but having seen them and greeted them from afar, and having acknowledged that they were strangers and exiles on the earth. For people who speak thus make it clear that they are seeking a homeland. If they had been thinking of that land from which they had gone out, they would have had opportunity to return. But as it is, they desire a better country, that is, a heavenly one. Therefore God is not ashamed to be called their God, for he has prepared for them a city (Hebrews 11:13-16).

> "I am going into eternity, and it is sweet for me to think of eternity."
>
> —*David Brainerd (1718–1747)*

All Christians long for heaven. I am reminded of the story of the unbeliever, who, seeking to comfort a dying Christian, said to him, "My poor friend, how sorry I am that you have to leave the land of the living!" The dying Christian, utterly radiant, replied, "You are wrong. I am leaving the land of the dying to go to the country of the living!" Each of us ought to maintain an eternal perspective (Colossians 3:1-2).

Don't fall in love with money. It's a path to heartache.

Solomon said, "He who loves money will not be satisfied with money, nor he who loves wealth with his income; this also is vanity" (Ecclesiastes 5:10). Of course, God does not condemn possessions or riches per se. It is not a sin to be wealthy. (Some godly people in the Bible—Abraham and Job, for example—were quite wealthy.) But God does condemn a love of possessions or riches (Luke 16:13; 1 Timothy 6:10; Hebrews 13:5). A love of material things is a sure sign that a person is living according to a temporal perspective, not an eternal perspective.

Scripture tells us a love of money and riches can lead to sure destruction. The apostle Paul flatly stated that "those who desire to be rich fall into temptation,

The Problem with Money

- There is the trouble in the getting of it.
- There is anxiety in the keeping of it.
- There are temptations in the use of it.
- There is guilt in the abuse of it.
- There is sorrow in the losing of it.
- There is perplexity in the disposing of it.

—*J. C. Ryle (1816–1900)*

Ecclesiastes

into a snare, into many senseless and harmful desires that plunge people into ruin and destruction" (1 Timothy 6:9).

Jesus warned His followers, "Take care, and be on your guard against all covetousness, for one's life does not consist in the abundance of his possessions" (Luke 12:15). He then urged His followers to have an eternal perspective, exhorting, "Do not lay up for yourselves treasures on earth, where moth and rust destroy and where thieves break in and steal, but lay up for yourselves treasures in heaven, where neither moth nor rust destroys and where thieves do not break in and steal" (Matthew 6:19-20; see also John 6:27).

Jesus urged, "Seek first the kingdom of God and his righteousness, and all these things will be added to you" (Matthew 6:33). This means living for God in a righteous way should be our top priority. When we do this, we can rest assured that God will provide us with the necessities of life.

Don't live in the past. Keep your eyes focused on the future.

Solomon said, "Say not, 'Why were the former days better than these?' For it is not from wisdom that you ask this" (Ecclesiastes 7:10). My friend, don't live in the past. Living in the past is like driving a car while looking only in the rearview mirror. The problem is, you don't get very far in life that way. It's better to keep your eyes on what's in front of you. As the apostle Paul put it, "One thing I do: forgetting what lies behind and straining forward to what lies ahead, I press on toward the goal for the prize of the upward call of God in Christ Jesus" (Philippians 3:13-14).

Life on earth is short. Make the best of it by involving God in your life from an early age.

Solomon ultimately concluded that we should live joyfully while we yet have time, for the darkness of death ultimately awaits us all (Ecclesiastes 11:7-8). It is especially important to enjoy life with God in one's youth: "Remember also your Creator in the days of your youth" (12:1).

Solomon gave this good advice: "The end of the matter; all has been heard. Fear God and keep his commandments, for this is the whole duty of man. For God will bring every deed into judgment, with every secret thing, whether good or evil" (Ecclesiastes 12:13-14).

Fear God, Keep Commandments

"Fear God and keep his commandments" (Ecclesiastes 12:13).

"Fear the LORD…keeping all his statutes and his commandments" (Deuteronomy 6:2).

"Fear him and keep his commandments" (Deuteronomy 13:4).

Fearing God has many benefits. All goes well for those who fear God (1 Samuel 12:14). God's mercy goes out to those who fear Him (Luke 1:50). Fear of the Lord leads to riches and honor (Proverbs 22:4). God fulfills the desires of those who fear Him (Psalm 145:19), and God blesses them (Psalm 115:13). Fear of the Lord can lengthen one's life (Proverbs 10:27). Those who fear God are motivated to obey Him (Deuteronomy 5:29) and turn from evil (Proverbs 3:7).

Solomon was also right that we will all face judgment. All believers will one day stand before the judgment seat of Christ (Romans 14:8-10). At that time each believer's life will be examined in regard to deeds done while in the body. Personal motives and intents of the heart will also be weighed. This judgment has nothing to do with whether or not the Christian will remain saved. Those who have placed faith in Christ are saved, and nothing threatens that (Romans 8:30; Ephesians 4:30). This judgment rather has to do with the reception or loss of rewards, based on whether one lived faithfully or unfaithfully after becoming a Christian (1 Corinthians 3:10-15). My advice: Live faithfully!

A Thought to Anchor in Your Heart

Life on earth is short. Life in heaven is long. Live your life on earth faithfully, with a strong eternal perspective.

Ecclesiastes

Song of Solomon

Marital love is one of God's greatest gifts to married men and women.

Marriage

- Rejoice in wife—Proverbs 5:18
- Wife of noble character Proverbs 12:4
- A good wife shows favor from the Lord—Proverbs 18:22
- An ill-tempered wife is troublesome—Proverbs 21:19
- Keep marriage bed pure—Hebrews 13:4
- Jesus on divorce—Matthew 5:31-32

The Song of Solomon, also known as the Song of Songs in ancient Hebrew versions, was written by Solomon shortly after 971 BC. Solomon is said to have written 1005 songs (1 Kings 4:32), and so the ancient Hebrew rendering of the title of this book as Song of Songs indicates this is his best of the bunch.

The Song of Solomon is an extended poem, full of metaphors and imagery, showing the richness of sexual love between husband (lover) and wife (his beloved) (Song of Solomon 1:8–2:7). The backdrop, of course, is that God Himself created male and female (Genesis 1–2), and He created them as sexual beings (Genesis 1:28). Therefore, sex within the boundaries of marriage is God-ordained and is to be enjoyed (Genesis 2:24; Matthew 19:5; 1 Corinthians 6:16; Ephesians 5:31). Of course, in any deep relationship, there is both joy and pain, and the Song of Solomon reflects this, pointing to both the joys and heartaches of wedded love (Song of Solomon 5:2–7:9).

Some Bible expositors through the centuries have interpreted the Song of Solomon allegorically, suggesting that it points to the love relationship between God and Israel. Others suggest it is an allegory pointing to the love relationship between Christ and the church (His bride). However, there is no indication in the text of the book that it is to be taken in any other way than describing an amorous relationship between husband and wife.

Following are key applicational concepts in the Song of Solomon:

God the sovereign Creator ordained that sex is only for a man and woman in marriage.

Sex was a part of God's "good" creation. Indeed, God created sex and "everything created by God is good" (1 Timothy 4:4). But it is good only within the confines of the marriage relationship, which He Himself ordained (Hebrews 13:4).

When God created the first man and woman, He instructed them to "be fruitful and multiply and fill the earth" (Genesis 1:28). God also affirmed, "A man shall leave his father and his mother and hold fast to

> "The Lord God said, 'It is not good that the man should be alone; I will make him a helper fit for him.'"
>
> —*Genesis 2:18*

his wife, and they shall become one flesh" (Genesis 2:24; see also Matthew 19:5; 1 Corinthians 6:16; Ephesians 5:31). The Song of Solomon portrays the beauty of sexual love between a man and woman who are married to each another.

Biblically, a sexual relationship is allowable *only* for a man and a woman in a marriage relationship (1 Corinthians 7:2). It is not intended for a man and another man, or for a woman and another woman, or between a man and woman outside of marriage (Leviticus 18:22; Romans 1:26; 1 Corinthians 6:9-10). The apostles urged all Christians to abstain from all forms of fornication (Acts 15:20). Paul said the body is not for fornication and that a man should flee it (1 Corinthians 6:13,18).

Adultery is condemned in Scripture (Exodus 20:14). In Old Testament times adulterers were to be put to death (Leviticus 20:10). Jesus pronounced adultery wrong even in its basic motives (Matthew 5:27-28). Paul called adultery an evil work of the flesh (Galatians 5:19). John envisioned in the lake of fire some of those who practiced adultery (Revelation 21:8). Hebrews 13:4 exhorts, "Let marriage be held in honor among all, and let the marriage bed be undefiled, for God will judge the sexually immoral and adulterous."

The love between a man and a woman involves the deepest of bonds, just as God intended.

In the Song of Solomon, the young woman—a country girl—had worked for hours in the vineyard under the blazing sun. Yet she was beautiful beyond description (Song of Solomon 1). She felt likewise

Avoiding Adultery

- Adultery starts in the heart—Matthew 15:19
- Make a covenant with your eyes to avoid lustful staring—Job 31:1
- Wisdom will save you—Proverbs 2:16
- Watch out for immoral women—Proverbs 5:3
- Don't give in to flattery—Proverbs 7:5
- Avoid adultery with your eyes—Matthew 5:28
- Sexual immorality brings judgment—1 Corinthians 10:8

Song of Solomon

about her beloved. She dreamed of him coming to be with her (3). She felt desolate apart from him and was intoxicated with love for him (3:1-5). The bond was deep, and her desire for him was indescribably powerful and wonderful. It is as God intended it to be.

A man and woman who develop this deep bond of love marry each other for life.

One day, the young woman's beloved appeared. The wedding procession was grand and splendorous. So wondrous was it that it was fit for King Solomon in all of his glory (Song of Solomon 3:6-11). The ceremony would never be forgotten in the minds of husband and wife. It was the beginning of a lifelong marriage relationship.

Sadly, wedding vows today aren't what they used to be. They used to be *for life*—"till death do us part." Today those words are still often spoken at wedding ceremonies, but the divorce rate has never been higher, even among Christians. Scripture is clear that God Himself created the institution of marriage, and He intended it to be permanent (Matthew 19:4-6). Divorce was never a part of God's original plan. In fact, God hates divorce (Malachi 2:16 NLT). The marriage relationship was intended to be dissolved only when one of the marriage partners dies (Romans 7:1-3; 1 Corinthians 7:8-9; 1 Timothy 5:14).

When sin entered the world, this affected God's ideal for the marriage relationship. Scripture tells us that even though divorce was not God's ideal, He nevertheless permitted it because of human sinfulness (Matthew 19:7-8; Deuteronomy 24:1-4).

Hebrew experts tell us a key meaning of sin in Old Testament times was, "not the way it's supposed to be." God intended marriage to be permanent, but things today are *not the way they are supposed to be.* Human sin has messed things up.

My advice: Make Jesus the heart and center of your marriage. The closer each spouse grows to Jesus, the closer they subsequently grow toward each other. And throughout life, each will be able to exult, "I am my beloved's, and my beloved is mine" (Song of Solomon 6:3).

The marriage relationship is consummated with the act of love.

In the Song of Solomon, the bridegroom gloried in the stunning beauty of his bride. The lovers rejoiced with each other in the sweetness of love as wedding guests dined in the garden. The marriage was consummated as the couple spent the first night together. Joy was abundant (Song of Solomon 4:1–5:1).

God intended for husbands and wives to fulfill each other sexually. This is why the apostle Paul later wrote, "The husband should give to his wife her conjugal rights, and likewise the wife to her husband. For the wife does not have authority over her own body, but the husband does. Likewise the husband does not have authority over his own body, but the wife does. Do not deprive one another, except perhaps by agreement for a limited time, that you may devote yourselves to prayer; but then come together again, so that Satan may not tempt you because of your lack of self-control" (1 Corinthians 7:3-5).

Even the deepest of personal relationships can experience some upsets.

As happens in all marriages, some strife surfaced between the husband and wife in the Song of Solomon. The wife was expressing indifference; the husband withdrew (Song of Solomon 5:2-8). But affection between the two was renewed and they were reconciled (5:9–6:13).

> "A happy marriage is the union of two good forgivers."
>
> —*Ruth Bell Graham (1920–2007)*

Some conflict is inevitable within a marriage relationship. The key thing is what husband and wife choose to do once a conflict emerges. The wrong response is indifference and withdrawal. The correct response is heartfelt communication with each other, mutual repentance before God (if needed), forgiveness, a self-sacrificial attitude that puts the other person first, and a commitment to doing marriage God's way (see, for example, Genesis 2:24-25; Ephesians 5:22-28,33; Hebrews 13:4).

Forgiveness is especially important (see Matthew 6:12,14; Ephesians 4:32; Colossians 3:13). In the New Testament, the Greek term for "forgiveness" (*aphiemi*) comes from a word that means "to let go." Forgiveness is a release, a letting go of self-destructive feelings such as anger and bitterness. Those attitudes poison intimacy with one's spouse. Be a perpetual forgiver!

While husband and wife already have great love for each other at the time of their wedding, that love continues to grow and mature throughout life.

> "A successful marriage requires falling in love many times— always with the same person."
>
> —*Mignon McLaughlin (1913–1983)*

The groom continued to marvel at the incredible beauty of his bride. She loved him utterly and completely. They grew deeper in their understanding of marital love, and their relationship matured (Song of Solomon 7:1–8:4). How wondrous is marital love!

While the Song of Solomon primarily focuses on the physical aspect of marital love, most married couples soon come to realize that marital love involves far more than a sexual relationship. It is a love that involves the whole person—mind, emotions, and will in addition to the physical. It is a love that grows evermore self-sacrificial. It is a love of commitment. It is a love that says, "I'm with you no matter what."

A Thought to Anchor in Your Heart

The more husband and wife draw closer to the Lord, the closer they draw to each other.

Song of Solomon

Isaiah

Our God, our Savior, and our salvation are profoundly awesome!

Isaiah is considered the greatest of the Old Testament prophets. Some have even called him the "prince" of Old Testament prophets. Certainly his book is a prince-sized book, being the third longest in the Bible. Only Jeremiah and Psalms exceed it in length.

The New Testament authors quote from Isaiah quite often—21 times. This shows they thought it was an important book. Jesus thought it was important too. He even inaugurated His public ministry with a quotation from Isaiah (Luke 4:17-21).

Timeline

740—Isaiah's prophetic ministry begins.

740–680—Isaiah writes his book within this time frame.

680—Isaiah's ministry ends.

Post–680—Isaiah is martyred sometime after 680 during the reign of King Manasseh (696–642).

Isaiah's name means "the Lord saves." His name is appropriate, for salvation was an important part of his message to the people of Judah. Of course, salvation and judgment often go together in the Bible. If a person refuses to be saved and turns away from God, then he must suffer the consequences in judgment. Isaiah combines these themes in his book.

Isaiah was born and reared in Jerusalem in days of great prosperity. It would seem his family was an affluent one. He was also apparently highly educated and very intelligent.

According to Jewish tradition, Isaiah's father, Amoz, was a brother of King Amaziah. This would make Isaiah a first cousin to King Uzziah and a grandson of King Joash. Isaiah had many opportunities to fellowship with royalty. He even gave advice on foreign affairs to King Hezekiah.

Isaiah received his call from God in the year of King Uzziah's death (740 BC). His ministry continued through the reign of Hezekiah, who died in 687 BC. This means Isaiah's ministry spanned about half a century. He wrote his book between 740 and 680 BC.

According to tradition, Isaiah was martyred during King Manasseh's reign (696–642 BC) by being sawed in half inside a hollow log. Some believe Hebrews 11:37 may be referring to this event.

Following are key applicational concepts in Isaiah. You will notice that the concepts are loosely grouped topically, beginning with Jesus the Messiah, followed by concepts relating to God, human sin and salvation, angels (both holy and fallen), and exhortations for God's people. This approach helps make the book of Isaiah more assessable for most readers.

Good news: the divine Messiah brings salvation to all humankind.

The book of Isaiah contains more references to the person and work of Jesus Christ than any other book in the Old Testament. Isaiah is often referred to as "the Messianic prophet." He predicted the Messiah's virgin birth (7:14), His deity and kingdom (9:1-7), His righteous reign (11:2-5), His vicarious suffering and death (52:13–53:12), and the wondrous salvation that comes through Christ the Servant-Messiah (49–57). No wonder the great composer Handel based so much of his musical masterpiece, *The Messiah*, on the book of Isaiah. Your Redeemer paid a great price to save you (53:5). He is worthy of praise.

> **A Verse to Remember**
>
> "Behold, the virgin shall conceive and bear a son, and shall call his name Immanuel."
>
> —*Isaiah 7:14*

Don't fall for claims that Jesus was just a good, moral man. Jesus is Yahweh—*absolute deity.*

In Isaiah 40:3 Jesus is prophetically called both Yahweh and Elohim in the same verse: "In the wilderness prepare the way of the Lord [*Yahweh*]; make straight in the desert a highway for our God [*Elohim*]." This verse is a prophecy of John the Baptist preparing for the coming of Jesus Christ (John 1:23) and represents one of the strongest affirmations of Christ's deity in the Old Testament. The term "Yahweh" indicates Jesus is the Eternal One and the sovereign Lord of the universe. The term "Elohim" indicates Jesus is "mighty God." Without Him, there is no Christianity. My advice: follow Him closely.

> **A Verse to Remember**
>
> "With his wounds we are healed."
>
> —*Isaiah 53:5*

Jesus brings us spiritual healing from the infection of sin.

In Isaiah 53:5 we are told Jesus "was pierced for our transgressions; he was crushed for our iniquities; upon him was the chastisement that brought us peace, and with his wounds we are healed." The Hebrew word for healed (*napha*) can refer to either physical healing or to spiritual healing. The context of Isaiah 53:5 indicates that spiritual healing is in view, since "transgressions" and "iniquities" are mentioned. Aren't you thankful to have been "healed" by Jesus? No spiritual disease is terminal when Jesus is in the picture.

Jesus is "God with us"—always present with us.

"Behold, the virgin shall conceive and bear a son, and shall call his name Immanuel" (Isaiah 7:14). The name Immanuel means "God with us" (Matthew 1:22-23). Jesus was "God with us" in the fullest possible sense. He is the everlasting God who stepped out of eternity and into time (as a human) to redeem humanity (see Isaiah 7:1–12:6 for more on the coming of the Messiah). Even today, Jesus is spiritually with us—"to the end of the age" (Matthew 28:20). Rejoice in this fact.

The Lord is our shepherd. The sheep who stay closest to Him are blessed.

In Isaiah 40:11 we read, "He will tend his flock like a shepherd; he will gather the lambs in his arms; he will carry them in his bosom, and gently lead those that are with young." This reminds us of Jesus as the Good Shepherd in John 10: "I am the good shepherd. I know my own and my own know me" (verse 14).

It is interesting to observe that the ancient shepherd in the Near East would often pick a branch off a tree and, as he walked, hold the branch behind him so that the sheep could follow closely and nibble on the morsels. This illustrates a profound truth for us: those who stay nearest the shepherd are the best nourished. The same is true of us. Those of us who stay nearest to our divine Shepherd are the best nourished spiritually.

There is no other God but Yahweh. Trust in Him alone.

God often affirmed in the book of Isaiah that He alone is deity: "Thus says the Lord, the King of Israel and his Redeemer, the Lord of hosts: 'I am the first and I am the last; besides me there is no god'" (Isaiah 44:6). "Is there a God besides me? There is no Rock; I know not any" (44:8). "I am the Lord, and there is no other, besides me there is no God" (45:5). The same thing is emphasized all through the New Testament (Mark 12:29; 1 Corinthians 8:4; Ephesians 4:6; 1 Timothy 2:5; James 2:19; John 5:44; 17:3; Romans

> "As well might a gnat seek to drink in the ocean, as a finite creature to comprehend the Eternal God."
>
> —Charles Spurgeon (1834–1892)

Isaiah

3:29-30; 16:27; Galatians 3:20). We find our greatest fulfillment in a relationship with the one true God (Jeremiah 9:24).

God is both transcendent and immanent. He is both high above us, and right here with us.

> "God has two thrones, one in the highest heavens, the other in the lowliest heart."
>
> —*Dwight L. Moody (1837–1899)*

In Isaiah 57:15 we are told, "For thus says the One who is high and lifted up, who inhabits eternity, whose name is Holy: 'I dwell in the high and holy place, and also with him who is of a contrite and lowly spirit, to revive the spirit of the lowly, and to revive the heart of the contrite.'" God is both *transcendent* ("high and lifted up, who inhabits eternity") and *immanent* (dwelling "with him who is of a contrite and lowly spirit"). This means the high and awesome God of the universe stoops low to help lowly creatures like us in our time of need. Glorious!

God is a God who answers prayers.

Insights on Prayer

- All prayers are subject to God's sovereign will—John 5:14.
- Prayer should be a continual practice—1 Thessalonians 5:17.
- Sin is a hindrance to prayer—Psalm 66:18.
- Righteousness is a benefit to prayer—Proverbs 15:29.
- The Lord's Prayer is a good model prayer—Matthew 6:9-13.
- Be persistent—Matthew 7:7-8.
- Pray in faith—Mark 11:22-24.

Isaiah warned Hezekiah, the Judean king, of a possible Assyrian attack (Isaiah 36). Hezekiah promptly turned to the Lord, pleading for deliverance. The Lord came through and delivered him and his people from the Assyrians (37).

Hezekiah was then told to get his house in order because his life was about to end. He again pled to God: "Please, O LORD, remember how I have walked before you in faithfulness and with a whole heart, and have done what is good in your sight" (Isaiah 38:3). The Lord responded, "I have heard your prayer; I have seen your tears. Behold, I will add fifteen years to your life" (38:5; see chapters 38–39). My friend, never forget that our God answers prayers.

God is holy. He desires *our* holiness.

The seraphim angels proclaimed, "Holy, holy, holy is the Lord of hosts" (Isaiah 6:3). In Isaiah 57:15 God is described as "the One who is high and lifted up, who inhabits eternity, whose name is Holy." God is the absolutely holy One of the universe.

Isaiah

Biblically, God's holiness means not just that He is entirely separate from all evil but also that He is absolutely righteous (Leviticus 19:2). He is pure in every way. God is separate from all that is morally imperfect. The Scriptures lay great stress upon this attribute of God (Exodus 15:11; 1 Samuel 2:2; Psalm 99:9; 111:9).

A key ramification of this is that if we want to fellowship with God, we have to take personal holiness seriously (Hebrews 12:14). Walking daily with God in fellowship necessarily involves living in a way that is pleasing to Him.

Our attempted good deeds are sin-stained. Don't try to earn salvation by works!

Isaiah 64:6 affirms, "We have all become like one who is unclean, and all our righteous deeds are like a polluted garment." Isaiah himself affirmed, "Woe is me! For I am lost; for I am a man of unclean lips, and I dwell in the midst of a people of unclean lips" (6:5). Such verses indicate it's a futile endeavor to seek God's favor by human works. *Everyone* falls short of God's perfection (Romans 3:23). Thankfully, our salvation is not based on works: "By grace you have been saved through faith. And this is not your own doing; it is the gift of God, not a result of works, so that no one may boast" (Ephesians 2:8-9).

God prefers repentance over judgment. Tragically, many humans prefer sin over repentance.

Isaiah prophesied about God's impending judgment against His sinful people of Judah through the whipping rod of the Assyrians (Isaiah 1–5). God was grieved by His people's moral degradation, social injustice, and religious hypocrisy (6). Isaiah warned Judah of swift judgment should they refuse to repent. They indeed did fail to repent and judgment subsequently fell, as promised. We also witness God's judgment falling upon various other nations for their lack of repentance (13:1–23:18). If there's one thing we witness in Isaiah, it's that God blesses obedience but punishes disobedience (28:1–35:10). Why are people so slow to listen? Why do people choose to ignore His warnings? My advice: Repent now!

> **God Is Holy**
> - God is light, no darkness— 1 John 1:5
> - Holy, holy, holy—Isaiah 6:3
> - Cannot be tempted by evil—James 1:13
> - Majestic in holiness— Exodus 15:11
> - None is holy like the Lord—1 Samuel 2:2
> - His name is holy—Isaiah 57:15

> "It is when we notice the dirt that God is most present in us."
> —C. S. Lewis (1898–1963)

Isaiah

Joy awaits God's people on the other side of judgment.

The judgment motif gets especially intense in Isaiah 24. It is not only Israel and her neighbors who were to experience judgment, but the entire world will one day feel the sting of God's judgments.

God, however, is not just a God of judgment. He is also a God who brings redemption. It is noteworthy that the one chapter on judgment in Isaiah (24) is followed by three chapters on God's salvation (25–27). Joy awaits God's people on the other side of judgment (see also 48:1-28). Many believe these chapters refer to the future seven-year tribulation period (judgment) followed by Christ's 1000-year millennial kingdom (joy). What a day that will be! *I can't wait.*

God has the awesome ability to forget your sins.

> **A Verse to Remember**
>
> "I, I am he who blots out your transgressions for my own sake, and I will not remember your sins."
>
> —*Isaiah 43:25*

In Isaiah 43:25 God says, "I, I am he who blots out your transgressions for my own sake, and I will not remember your sins." This reminds us of Hebrews 10:17: "I will remember their sins and their lawless deeds no more." We also recall the affirmation in Psalm 103:12: "As far as the east is from the west, so far does he remove our transgressions from us." To remove sins "as far as the east is from the west" is by definition to put them where no one can ever find them. *That* is the forgiveness God grants believers.

Angels play a significant role in the Bible. Let's be thankful for their various ministries.

> **Angels**
>
> "Are they not all ministering spirits sent out to serve for the sake of those who are to inherit salvation?" (Hebrews 1:14).
>
> "He will command his angels concerning you to guard you in all your ways" (Psalm 91:11).

Isaiah 6:1-5 makes reference to the seraphim angels. The Hebrew term for *seraphim* literally means "burning ones"—speaking of their consuming devotion to God. They are afire with adoration of the holy God, and their constant cry is the holiness of God.

Angels are involved in a variety of important ministries. For example, sometimes they are messengers (Daniel 9). Sometimes they act as guardians of Christians (Psalm 91:9-11). They meet believers at the moment of death (Luke 16:22). They are involved in restraining evil (Genesis 18:22; 19:1,10,11). Sometimes God uses them in answering the prayers of Christians (Acts 12:6-19). We ought to be very thankful for God's provision of angels.

Satan is against Christ and all who follow Him.

Isaiah 14:4-11 reveals that Lucifer became full of pride and sought exaltation and godhood for himself. Lucifer became corrupt, and his name changed to Satan (meaning "adversary"). One third of the angelic realm followed him in rebellion (Revelation 12:4).

> "Everything the devil does, God overreaches to serve His own purpose."
>
> —Oswald Chambers (1874–1917)

Satan and demons stand against Christians in a variety of ways. Satan tempts believers to sin (Ephesians 2:1-3; 1 Thessalonians 3:5), to lie (Acts 5:3), and to commit sexually immoral acts (1 Corinthians 7:5). He hinders the work of believers in any way he can (1 Thessalonians 2:18) and wages war against them (Ephesians 6:11-12). He sows tares among believers (Matthew 13:38-39) and incites persecutions against them (Revelation 2:10). Christian, beware!

No matter what you face in life, fear not. The Lord is with you.

In Isaiah 41:10, God affirms, "Fear not, for I am with you; be not dismayed, for I am your God; I will strengthen you, I will help you, I will uphold you with my righteous right hand." The Hebrew word for "strengthen" in this verse carries the idea of "support," or to "harden against difficulties." The word "uphold" means to "grasp firmly." God's people never need to fear because of God's constant involvement in their lives.

Isaiah 26:3 promises, "You keep him in perfect peace whose mind is stayed on you, because he trusts in you." The word "keep" literally means "guard." "Peace" means "well-being, wholeness, and tranquility."

No Need to Fear

- Don't be afraid of sudden fear—Proverbs 3:25
- Let not your heart be troubled—John 14:27
- If God is for us, who can be against us?—Romans 8:31
- God has not given us a spirit of fear—2 Timothy 1:7

"Perfect" means "complete" or "constant." So God guards our hearts in constant well-being, wholeness, and tranquility—and *this* is a result of trusting in Him.

Good news: there's a new day coming. We're destined for a new heavens and a new earth.

Isaiah 51:6 prophesies that "the heavens vanish like smoke, the earth will wear out like a garment." The "heavens" in this verse refers not to the domain of God, but rather to earth's atmosphere and interstellar space (see Job 35:5; Genesis 1:17; Deuteronomy 17:3).

> "What has happened in the past, what is happening now, and what will happen in the future is all evidence of the unfolding of the purposeful plan devised by the personal God of the Bible."
>
> —Robert Lightner

Isaiah

The earth—along with the first and second heavens (the earth's atmosphere and the stellar universe)—must be renewed. The old must make room for the new. Glorious times are ahead for God's people (Isaiah 58–63).

God in Isaiah 65:17 affirms, "Behold, I create new heavens and a new earth, and the former things shall not be remembered or come into mind." (See also Revelation 21:1-5.) You and I are destined for a new heaven and a new earth. So, like Paul said in Colossians 3:2, "Set your minds on things that are above, not on things that are on earth."

A Thought to Anchor in Your Heart

As Jesus is the heart and center of the book of Isaiah, so Jesus should be the heart and center of your life.

Jeremiah

In the face of judgment, God's people are called to repentance so they can experience spiritual restoration and blessing.

The book of Jeremiah was written by a prophet of the same name between 627 and 570 BC. His name literally means "Yahweh throws," a term referring to the laying of a foundation. Certainly Jeremiah's words, like any prophet's words, were foundational for the people. He was born into a priestly family, and was called from birth to be a spokesman for God (Jeremiah 1:5). He was from the small village of Anathoth (1:1).

Jeremiah began his ministry in Judah during the reign of Josiah (640–609 BC), and continued through the reigns of four other kings: Jehoahaz (609 BC), Jehoiakim (609–598 BC), Jehoiachin (598–597 BC), and Zedekiah (597–586 BC). He prophesied during the same general time as the prophets Habakkuk, Zephaniah, and Ezekiel.

The difficult thing for Jeremiah was that he was given a harsh message to deliver to the people, and he expressed inadequacy in fulfilling the prophetic task to which he was called (Jeremiah 1:6-10). For decades he warned the Israelites of an impending judgment that was coming, but he was virtually ignored (2–35). Nobody would listen. They remained in such horrible sins as flagrant idol worship, adultery, injustice, tyranny against the helpless, and dishonesty. Such sins were causing Jeremiah's people to rush toward painful judgment. And because Jeremiah pointed toward a coming judgment, his life was often endangered by political and religious leaders (36–38).

Babylonian exile was the judgment that finally

Timeline

640–609—The reign of Josiah.

627—Jeremiah's prophetic ministry to Judah begins.

627–570—The book of Jeremiah is written.

609—Jeremiah ministers during the reign of King Jehoahaz.

609–598—Jeremiah ministers during the reign of King Jehoiakim.

598–597—Jeremiah ministers during the reign of King Jehoiachin.

597–586—Jeremiah ministers during the reign of King Zedekiah.

586—Jeremiah's ministry ends.

"Pain is God's megaphone to rouse a deaf world."

—C. S. Lewis (1898–1963)

came upon the people of God (Jeremiah 39–45). Jerusalem and its temple were destroyed in 587 BC, and the Babylonians took all the people captive. Jeremiah mourned for his people.

God calls and commissions people to specific service to Him.

Jeremiah was called and sanctified as God's spokesman even before he was born: "Before I formed you in the womb I knew you, and before you were born I consecrated you; I appointed you a prophet to the nations" (Jeremiah 1:5). God informed him, "Whatever I command you, you shall speak" (1:7). Jeremiah was timid about the assignment—especially since his was to be a message of judgment for unrepentant sin. But God assured him He'd be ever-present with him (1:8).

> ### The Great Commission
>
> "Go therefore and make disciples of all nations, baptizing them in the name of the Father and of the Son and of the Holy Spirit, teaching them to observe all that I have commanded you. And behold, I am with you always, to the end of the age."
>
> —Matthew 28:19-20

We witness divine commissionings throughout Scripture. In Exodus 3:7-8, for example, God commissioned Moses to deliver His people from Egyptian bondage and lead them to the Promised Land. In Judges 6:11-23, God commissioned Gideon to go in His strength against the Midianites. In Judges 13:1-21, He commissioned the mighty Samson through his parents.

Jesus, too, commissioned people to service in New Testament times. For example, He commissioned Simon and Andrew (Matthew 4:18-20), as well as Saul, also known as Paul (Acts 26:14-18).

> ### Fear Not!
>
> "I will not be afraid of many thousands of people who have set themselves against me all around" (Psalm 3:6).
>
> "The LORD is my light and my salvation; whom shall I fear?" (27:1).
>
> "In God I trust; I shall not be afraid. What can man do to me?" (56:11).

You don't have to be eloquent to be a mouthpiece of God. Fear not!

When God called Jeremiah to service, Jeremiah replied, "Ah, Lord GOD! Behold, I do not know how to speak, for I am only a youth" (Jeremiah 1:6). God would not accept excuses. He said to Jeremiah, "Do not say, 'I am only a youth'; for to all to whom I send you, you shall go, and whatever I command you, you shall speak. Do not be afraid of them, for I am with you to deliver you" (1:7-8). God's servants never need to fear other human beings.

A lack of repentance always brings God's disciplinary judgment.

Jeremiah's message of judgment was communicated to the people in a variety of creative ways—sermons, parables, and object lessons. He set forth 12 graphic messages engineered to communicate why judgment would soon fall upon Judah. In irony, Jeremiah indicated that the pagans were more faithful to their false gods than the Judeans were to the one true God. The Judeans fell deeply into idolatry and disobeyed God's covenant.

Jeremiah attempted to confess the people's sins to God. Because their sin was so great and they were unrepentant, it was to no avail. Jeremiah lamented at the sad condition of his people. He prophesied that the people would go into captivity (Jeremiah 2–25).

People sometimes foolishly turn to other religious options instead of turning to the one true God, who alone can bring them true spiritual blessing.

In Jeremiah 2:13 God affirmed, "My people have committed two evils: they have forsaken me, the fountain of living waters, and hewed out cisterns for themselves, broken cisterns that can hold no water." "Living water" here literally means "flowing water." This verse speaks of how Israel had forsaken God, the only true "flowing" source of life-giving nourishment and power. Instead they had sought refuge in idolatrous, pagan (man-made) religions. They had "hewed out cisterns for themselves," which were "broken cisterns that can hold no water." What an utterly foolish trade. My advice: stay solidly grounded in God's Word (see Psalm 119; 2 Timothy 3:15-17).

Avoid Idolatry

God said to Jeremiah's people: "Where are your gods that you made for yourself? Let them arise, if they can save you, in your time of trouble; for as many as your cities are your gods, O Judah" (Jeremiah 2:28).

The New Testament consistently urges Christians to avoid all forms of idolatry (1 Corinthians 5:11; 2 Corinthians 6:16; Galatians 5:20; Colossians 3:5; 1 John 5:21).

Beware of False Prophets

False prophets were predominant in Jeremiah's day (Jeremiah 5:31). This is dangerous, for God's people are vulnerable to deception (Ezekiel 34:1-7; Matthew 7:15-16; Acts 20:28-30; 2 Corinthians 11:2-3; Ephesians 4:14; 2 Timothy 4:3-4).

The person who lacks fear of the Lord is ripe for judgment.

The unrepentant sins of Jeremiah's people proved they lacked fear of God: "Know and see that it is evil and bitter for you to forsake the LORD your God; the fear of me is not in you, declares the Lord GOD of hosts" (Jeremiah 2:19). A lack of fearing God inevitably leads to sin and judgment.

Jeremiah

My friend, never forget that as Christians, we are called to daily live in reverent fear of God (1 Peter 1:17; 2:17; 1 Samuel 12:14,24; 2 Chronicles 19:9; Acts 10:35). Fear of the Lord motivates one to be obedient to Him (Deuteronomy 5:29; Ecclesiastes 12:13) and serve Him (Deuteronomy 6:13). Fear of the Lord motivates one to avoid evil (Proverbs 3:7; 8:13; 16:6). Fear of the Lord is true wisdom (Job 28:28; Psalm 111:10) and the beginning of knowledge (Proverbs 1:7). God blesses those who fear Him (Psalm 115:13). Fear of the Lord leads to riches, honor, and long life (Proverbs 22:4). God shows mercy to those who fear Him (Luke 1:50).

Never forget—God doesn't like it when His people *pretend* to be religious.

Jesus spoke sternly against the religious hypocrisy of His day (Matthew 23:28; Mark 12:15; Luke 12:1).

God affirmed, "Judah did not return to me with her whole heart, but in pretense, declares the LORD" (Jeremiah 3:10). The people of Judah were hypocrites. Hypocrisy involves the pretense of having a virtuous character, or moral/religious beliefs and principles, that one does not really possess (Revelation 3:1). Don't be a faker. Don't be a pretender.

Beware: sin has a way of robbing you of the good things of life.

At the end of your life, it will be bitter to reflect back and ask, "What blessings could have been mine had I lived more faithfully to God?"

God said to the people, "Your sins have kept good from you" (Jeremiah 5:25). Their sins kept God from blessing them—such as bringing them good crops so they could eat well. This reminds us of Jeremiah 2:17, where God says to the people, "Have you not brought this upon yourself by forsaking the LORD your God?" Likewise, in Jeremiah 4:18 God says, "Your ways and your deeds have brought this upon you." Never forget that actions carry consequences.

God prefers authentic spirituality—not empty, religious observances.

God said to Jeremiah's people, "What use to me is frankincense that comes from Sheba, or sweet cane from a distant land? Your burnt offerings are not acceptable, nor your sacrifices pleasing to me" (Jeremiah 6:20). Fancy offerings from a sinful people are sickening to God (Psalm 40:6; 50:7-9; Isaiah 1:11; 43:24;

Jeremiah

66:3; Amos 5:21; Micah 6:6-7). God wants heart-commitment. Don't just go through the motions with God. Be the real thing.

ATTENTION PLEASE: People can "cross the line" so deep into sin that they become irrevocably consigned to judgment. Beware!

God said to Jeremiah, "As for you, do not pray for this people, or lift up a cry or prayer for them, and do not intercede with me, for I will not hear you" (Jeremiah 7:16). God also said, "Even if Moses and Samuel stood before me pleading for these people, I wouldn't help them" (15:1 NLT). Judah's sin was so pervasive that judgment became inevitable. Judah had crossed the line. God gives people time to repent (Revelation 2:21), but if repentance is lacking, judgment falls.

Sinful actions emerge from the fallen human heart. But God can transform the heart.

God affirmed, "This evil people, who refuse to hear my words, who stubbornly follow their own heart and have gone after other gods to serve them and worship them, shall be like this loincloth, which is good for nothing" (Jeremiah 13:10). God also said, "The heart is deceitful above all things, and desperately sick; who can understand it?" (17:9). This is not unlike what Jesus said in the New Testament: "For out of the heart come evil thoughts, murder, adultery, sexual immorality, theft, false witness, slander. These are what defile a person" (Matthew 15:19-20). The glorious good news is that God is in the business of heart transformation. See Romans 12:2; 2 Corinthians 3:18; Psalm 51:10; Galatians 5:22; Philippians 1:6; 2 Timothy 3:15-17.

> "He who doubts human depravity had better study himself."
>
> —Charles Spurgeon (1834–1892)

Always place your trust in the Lord, not in other human beings.

Judah had sought Egypt's help against Babylon's attacks. But God affirmed, "Cursed is the man who trusts in man and makes flesh his strength, whose heart turns away from the LORD. He is like a shrub in the desert, and shall not see any good come. He shall dwell in the parched places of the wilderness, in an uninhabited salt land. Blessed is the man who trusts in the LORD, whose trust is the LORD" (Jeremiah 17:5-7).

Trust God
- Trust God in times of trouble—Psalm 50:15
- Trust in the Lord, not man—Psalm 118:8
- Joy in trusting God—Psalm 40:4 (NLT)
- Blessed are those who trust Him—Jeremiah 17:7
- Trust Him, and He will help you—Psalm 37:5

Jeremiah

This includes not trusting in your own abilities. As Proverbs 3:5-6 puts it, "Trust in the LORD with all your heart, and do not lean on your own understanding. In all your ways acknowledge him, and he will make straight your paths." Put your full trust in God and Him alone.

Faithful servants of God will often meet stiff resistance from other religious leaders.

Judah's false prophets claimed that no judgment was coming. Jeremiah countered, promising that his people would be in captivity in Babylon for 70 years. As a result of his dark prophecies regarding Judah, Jeremiah suffered harsh opposition and persecution (Jeremiah 26–45). The false prophets called for his death. But Judah's leaders spared him this destiny.

Opposition continued to escalate against Jeremiah (Jeremiah 34–35). He was prohibited from entering the temple. His assistant, Baruch, therefore read his proclamations in the temple on his behalf. Jeremiah's prophetic scroll was burned by the king and Jeremiah was imprisoned. After the city fell in judgment, he was taken to Egypt by other Jews. But Jeremiah warned that Egypt, too, would be invaded by the Babylonians. Jeremiah was a bold truth-teller.

> A key lesson: Speaking the truth can sometimes make you unpopular.

While judgment hurts in the present, God yet has a future for His people.

God gave His sinful children a wonderful promise: "For I know the plans I have for you, declares the LORD, plans for welfare and not for evil, to give you a future and a hope" (Jeremiah 29:11). Following a time of discipline, God would bring about wonderful blessing in Israel's future (30–33). Israel will experience the fullness of blessing in the future millennial kingdom, that 1000-year kingdom on earth over which Christ Himself will physically rule.

God also brings us blessing following our times of trial. Recall 1 Peter 5:10: "After you have suffered a little while, the God of all grace, who has called you to his eternal glory in Christ, will himself restore, confirm, strengthen, and establish you."

God showers blessing on those who seek Him wholeheartedly.

Because God's people were now in exile, Jeremiah sought to encourage them. He emphasized that good things happen when God's people seek Him with their

Jeremiah

whole heart: "You will seek me and find me, when you seek me with all your heart. I will be found by you, declares the LORD, and I will restore your fortunes and gather you from all the nations and all the places where I have driven you, declares the LORD, and I will bring you back to the place from which I sent you into exile" (Jeremiah 29:13-14). While there was an initial fulfillment of this during the time of Ezra and Nehemiah, the full blessing will come following the second coming when the Messiah sets up His kingdom on earth (Daniel 2:35,45; 7:13-14,27; 12:1-3,13).

> "You must love the Lord your God with all your heart, all your soul, and all your mind."
>
> —*Jesus (Matthew 22:37)*

Rejoice! The coming Messiah will bring a new day.

Despite the doom of captivity, Jeremiah prophesied that final restoration would come because of the work of the coming divine Messiah. He would institute a new covenant that would bring great blessing to the people—indeed, to *all* people.

The new covenant was an unconditional covenant in which God promised to provide for complete forgiveness of sin (Jeremiah 31:31-34). Under the old covenant worshipers never enjoyed a sense of total forgiveness. Under the new covenant, however, Christ our High Priest made provisions for such forgiveness. When Jesus ate the Passover meal with the disciples in the Upper Room, He spoke of the cup as "the new covenant in my blood" (Luke 22:20; see also 1 Corinthians 11:25). Jesus has done all that is necessary for the forgiveness of sins by His once-for-all sacrifice on the cross. This new covenant is the basis for our relationship with God in the New Testament.

> **A Verse to Remember**
>
> "I will put my law within them, and I will write it on their hearts. And I will be their God, and they shall be my people."
>
> —*Jeremiah 31:33*

Because sin is universal, God's judgment against sin is universal.

Despite the reality of the Messiah's glorious future coming, sin must be dealt with in the present. Jeremiah issued specific prophetic proclamations against Egypt (Jeremiah 46:2-28), Philistia (47:1-7), Moab (48:1-47), Ammon (49:1-6), Edom (49:7-22), Damascus (49:23-27), Kedar and Hazor (49:28-33),

> **The Universality of Sin**
>
> "Surely there is not a righteous man on earth who does good and never sins" (Ecclesiastes 7:20).
>
> "All have sinned and fall short of the glory of God" (Romans 3:23).

Jeremiah

Elam (49:34-39), and Babylon (50:1–51:64). No sinful and unrepentant nation escapes God's judgment. *All* are held accountable.

Jerusalem, of course, was also held accountable. Just as Jeremiah warned, Jerusalem fell (Jeremiah 52:1-34), the city was destroyed (52:1-23), the leaders were killed, and the Jewish common-folk were deported to Babylon (52:24-30). Exile in Babylon lasted 70 years—which was plenty of time for Jerusalem's now-exiled inhabitants to think about what their own sin brought about. But then deliverance came from God. God never fails to deliver His people. Thank You, Lord!

A Thought to Anchor in Your Heart

Praise the Lord for the new covenant! You are forgiven. Totally and completely forgiven. Your slate has been wiped clean by Jesus. Rejoice!

Lamentations

God's discipline falls when His people repeatedly ignore exhortations to repent. Even then, however, new mercies flow from God every day.

The mournful prophet Jeremiah wrote the book of Lamentations in about 586 BC. "Lamentations" means "funeral songs," and is descriptive of its contents. It expresses the anguish of the Israelites over the destruction of Jerusalem by the Babylonians in 587 BC. Jeremiah seems to have witnessed the destruction firsthand. The temple was destroyed, and the people were deported to live in Babylon in exile. This book depicts the funeral of a city.

Worse comes to worse when the Israelites realize the reason this horror has fallen on them is their unfaithfulness to God (Lamentations 1:20-22). Jeremiah, of course, was not surprised at the destruction of Jerusalem, for he had prophesied this judgment for some 40 years (Jeremiah 1–29). But the people had not listened.

In the end, Jeremiah emphasized that God is characterized by love and mercy. And because His compassions never fail (Lamentations 3:23), there is yet hope for the nation (5:19-22).

Following are key applicational concepts in Lamentations:

Timeline

627— Jeremiah's prophetic ministry begins.

627–570— Jeremiah writes the book of Jeremiah within this time frame.

587— The Babylonians overrun and destroy Jerusalem and its temple.

586— Jeremiah writes Lamentations.

> "By chastening, the Lord separates the sin that he hates from the sinner whom he loves."
>
> *—Anonymous*

> "We ought to thank God that he will not let us sin without chastisement."
>
> *—Charles Spurgeon (1834–1892)*

When God's people turn a deaf ear to Him for an extended time, they should not be surprised if He brings discipline.

Jerusalem and its temple had been destroyed. The temple was the heart and center of Jewish religion—the place where God dwelt. Jeremiah compassionately lamented with his people (Lamentations 1:1-22).

Oh, if only the people had listened to his repeated warnings. The people learned the painful lesson that God will do what He says He'll do when repentance is absent.

God has the unique ability to sovereignly use other people in the process of disciplining us.

Lamentations reveals that the Babylonians destroyed Jerusalem and the holy temple. And yet, all the while, God was sovereignly working behind the scenes, using the Babylonians as His whipping rod against His rebellious people, the Jews (Lamentations 2:1-22). Of course, the Babylonians had no idea God was using them in this capacity.

> **God's Sovereignty**
>
> God's sovereignty means He has absolute authority over all things in the universe (Daniel 4:25,35; Romans 9:15-23; 1 Timothy 6:15; Revelation 4:11).

One thing we can surmise from this is that the Lord may use people we know when He disciplines us—perhaps a relative, a boss, a business competitor, or someone who dislikes us. In each case, God always disciplines us for our own good (Hebrews 12:6-9; Psalm 32; 51).

Spiritual leaders often have to wear many hats.

Jeremiah acted as a prophet when warning his people of impending judgment for over four decades. He acted as a fellow brother as he identified with his people and expressed grief over the destruction of Jerusalem and its temple. He took the role of a spiritual father when praying for God's mercy and the restoration of his people (Lamentations 3:1-66).

Even today, church pastors have many roles. Spiritual leadership has its challenges. That's one reason spiritual leaders must meet God-defined qualifications (1 Timothy 3:1-13; Titus 1:6-9).

Your choices always have consequences.

Jeremiah reflected on how severely the city of Jerusalem had been judged by the Lord in His anger. He reflected upon how the sins of the people, prophets, and priests brought all this about (Lamentations 4:1-22). Jeremiah's people had acted unwisely and now suffered the consequences.

> "No marvel that our sorrows are multiplied when our sins are."
>
> —*Matthew Henry (1662–1714)*

My advice: Always repent as soon as you become aware there's a need to repent, thereby averting discipline.

When life throws you a punch, your first best response is to turn to the Lord in prayer.

The Jews in captivity spent time reflecting on their current, horrific state of affairs. They yearned and prayed for deliverance and restoration. These prayers included both confession of sin and an appeal to God's grace (Lamentations 5:1-22). Jeremiah's people would indeed be restored, but not until their present trial yielded its proper fruit—repentance and recommitment to the Lord.

God is always full of mercy, even when He is disciplining us.

Even as Jeremiah's people were in exile, he emphasized that there is a continual flow of mercy from the hand of the Lord (Lamentations 3:22; see also Deuteronomy 30:1-10). As Psalm 103:8 puts it, "The LORD is merciful and gracious, slow to anger and abounding in steadfast love." The reality of God's mercy brings assurance to us that God is not finished with us yet. A new day will come.

Prayer

- Call on the Lord—Psalm 145:18
- Ask, it will be given—Matthew 7:7-8
- Earnest prayer—James 5:17-18
- Believe, receive—Matthew 21:22

Verses to Remember

"The steadfast love of the Lord never ceases; his mercies never come to an end; they are new every morning; great is your faithfulness."

—*Lamentations 3:22-23*

A Thought to Anchor in Your Heart

Early responders—those who repent quickly—will be on the receiving end of a lot less divine discipline than late responders.

Ezekiel

God is faithful even when His own people are
not faithful. Following a time of chastisement,
He brings ultimate restoration and blessing
—just as He promised.

The book of Ezekiel was written by the prophet Ezekiel, the son of Buzi, between 593 and 570 BC. His
messages were for the Jews in exile. God had called
him into service as a prophet when he was about 30
years of age. At the time, he was training to be a priest.
Like all the other Jews, however, he soon found himself living in exile in Babylon, and this captivity would
last 70 years.

Ezekiel's name literally means "God is strong" or
"strengthened by God." To carry on his work of con-
fronting the people regarding their sins, and bringing
comfort to them while in exile, Ezekiel would surely
need God's strength.

As a prophet, Ezekiel was unique. He would often dramatize God's message
by using signs, symbols, and parables. For example, he said the dispersed Jews
were like dry bones in the sun (Ezekiel 37.) By using such techniques, Ezekiel
graphically communicated that God's judgment comes as a result of human sin.
This is the message he proclaimed during the first part of his ministry.

In 597 BC, when he and some 3000 other Jews went into exile in Babylon by
order of Nebuchadnezzar (the uncontested ruler of the world at that time), Ezekiel started to speak a new message. Indeed, he offered words of hope and comfort, teaching that God would re-gather His people from the ends of the earth,
and a new temple would one day be built (Ezekiel 40). He tried to give the people something to look forward to.

Following are key applicational concepts in Ezekiel:

God calls specific individuals to service.

God called and commissioned Ezekiel as His mouthpiece to Judah. Ezekiel witnessed an incredible vision, full of God's glory. It was a vision that stuck with him through his entire ministry. Following this, God gave the prophet instructions and enabled him for his task (Ezekiel 1:1–3:27).

We recall that when the apostle Paul was commissioned for service by the Lord Jesus, he, too, saw a vision. It was a vision of the risen Lord (Acts 9:1-16), and it stuck with him for the duration of his life (22:6-11).

The Lord calls you and me via the Great Commission: "Go therefore and make disciples of all nations, baptizing them in the name of the Father and of the Son and of the Holy Spirit, teaching them to observe all that I have commanded you. And behold, I am with you always, to the end of the age" (Matthew 28:19-20). Let's get to work!

> **Call to Service**
> - "Before you were born I consecrated you"—Jeremiah 1:5
> - "Who will go for us?"—Isaiah 6:8
> - "Follow me"—Matthew 9:9
> - "Set apart for me Barnabas and Saul"—Acts 13:2
> - "Paul…called to be an apostle"—Romans 1:1
> - God gives church apostles, prophets, evangelists, pastors—Ephesians 4:11

Glorious angels serve God and the recipients of His salvation.

Ezekiel 1:5 speaks of "four living creatures," who are apparently the same as the cherubim angels in Ezekiel 10:1-22. They are portrayed as having wings (1:6) and flew in the midst of heaven (10:5). They seem to compare to the "four living creatures" (angels) in Revelation 4:6.

Hebrews 1:14 tells us angels are "ministering spirits sent out to serve for the sake of those who are to inherit salvation." The word "ministering" comes from a Greek word meaning "serve." Angels are spirit-servants who render aid, and this aid is rendered to the heirs of salvation in the outworking of God's purposes on earth.

> **Classes of Angels**
> Archangel—Jude 9
> Seraphim—Isaiah 6:1-3
> Cherubim—Genesis 3:24
> Watchers—Daniel 4:13

What form does this service take? Such ministry can involve protection (Psalm 91:11), guidance (Genesis 19:17), encouragement (Judges 6:12), deliverance (Acts 12:7), supply (Psalm 105:40), empowerment (Luke 22:43), as well as occasional rebuke (Numbers 22:32) and judgment (Acts 12:23). Angelic service is rendered largely unseen and often unrecognized (2 Kings 6:17; Hebrews 13:2).

God's Word comes straight from God, and therefore carries God's authority.

The phrase "Thus says the Lord" is sprinkled all throughout Ezekiel (for example, 2:4; 3:11,27; 5:5,7,8; 6:11; 7:2,5). Ezekiel thereby indicated that the words he spoke were not his own. He passed on to his people what he received directly from God.

Scripture Is Inspired

- "Thus says the Lord"— Ezekiel 2:4
- All Scripture is inspired— 2 Timothy 3:16
- The Holy Spirit moved the biblical writers—2 Peter 1:21

This reminds us of 2 Timothy 3:16-17: "All Scripture is breathed out by God and profitable for teaching, for reproof, for correction, and for training in righteousness, that the man of God may be complete, equipped for every good work." The phrase "all Scripture" includes the book of Ezekiel. That means the book of Ezekiel—like all other Bible books—is "profitable for teaching, for reproof, for correction, and for training in righteousness."

God's people are to proclaim His message regardless of the kind of response expected.

In Ezekiel 2:3-5 God instructs Ezekiel, "Son of man, I send you to the people of Israel, to nations of rebels, who have rebelled against me. They and their fathers have transgressed against me to this very day. The descendants also are impudent and stubborn: I send you to them, and you shall say to them, 'Thus says the Lord GOD.' And whether they hear or refuse to hear (for they are a rebellious house) they will know that a prophet has been among them."

Speak Boldly

- God gives boldness— Psalm 138:3
- Holy Spirit gives boldness— Acts 4:29,31
- Speak boldly for the Lord— Acts 14:3
- Be people of courage— 1 Corinthians 16:13

I've spoken to audiences where I knew there were cultists in attendance. (I've written some books on the cults, so it's not unexpected that cultists show up at my conferences.) Regardless of the reception, I'm resolved to always tell the truth in the name of Jesus Christ. While some will reject you, others will be open to hearing the message of eternal life.

Judgment inevitably falls when people choose rebellion instead of obedience to God.

Ezekiel prophesied a coming judgment on Judah for her unrepentant sins. This judgment was now an absolute certainty (Ezekiel 4–7). Ezekiel spoke much of Judah's sins and abominations, and the subsequent departure of God's glory from the temple. Both the common people and the religious leaders were woefully guilty (8–11).

> **Cross-References: Repentance or Judgment**
> Ezekiel 18:32 • Luke 13:3 • Acts 3:19 • 2 Peter 3:9 • Isaiah 55:6-7

Through a series of signs, sermons, and parables, Ezekiel pointed to how dreadfully Judah had fallen. They were brimming with false prophets who had led the people astray, giving them a false sense of security. He used graphic metaphors to illustrate the dire condition of the people. They were like a vine without fruit, or a wife who had committed adultery. God would therefore sovereignly use the Babylonians as His whipping rod to render judgment against Judah (Ezekiel 12–24).

God also disciplines Christians today if they fall into sin and choose to remain in sin: "My son, do not regard lightly the discipline of the Lord, nor be weary when reproved by him. For the Lord disciplines the one he loves, and chastises every son whom he receives" (Hebrews 12:5-6). God loves His children too much to allow them to remain on a self-destructive path without intervening (Psalm 32; 51).

Make no mistake about it. God sees everything you do.

God said to Ezekiel, "Son of man, have you seen what the elders of the house of Israel are doing in the dark, each in his room of pictures? For they say, 'The Lord does not see us, the Lord has forsaken the land'" (Ezekiel 8:12). Make no mistake about it: God sees everything. He knows all. Nothing is hidden from His omniscient vision (Hebrews 4:13; 1 John 3:20). He knows our words before they are even spoken (Psalm 139:4). He knows the secrets of the heart (Psalm 44:21). He understands every intent of our thoughts (1 Chronicles 28:9). He has unlimited understanding (Isaiah 40:28). Live your life accordingly.

Beware: you don't have as long as you think to repent.

Ezekiel affirmed, "Again a message came to me from the Lord: 'Son of man, you've heard that proverb they quote in Israel: "Time passes, and prophecies come to nothing." Tell the people, "This is what the Sovereign Lord says: I will put an end to this proverb,

> **Cross-References: Time to Repent**
> Genesis 15:16 • Ecclesiastes 8:11 • Isaiah 48:9 • 1 Peter 3:20 • 2 Peter 3:9 • Revelation 2:20

and you will soon stop quoting it." Now give them this new proverb to replace the old one: "The time has come for every prophecy to be fulfilled!""" (Ezekiel 12:21-23 NLT).

This brings to mind how there are mockers today who are unconcerned about the second coming of Jesus Christ. Peter warned, "Scoffers will come in the last days with scoffing, following their own sinful desires. They will say, 'Where is the promise of his coming? For ever since the fathers fell asleep, all things are continuing as they were from the beginning of creation'" (2 Peter 3:3-4).

The day draws near. People ought to repent while there is yet time.

Everyone is personally responsible for his or her own sins.

In Ezekiel 18:20 God affirms, "The soul who sins shall die. The son shall not suffer for the iniquity of the father, nor the father suffer for the iniquity of the son. The righteousness of the righteous shall be upon himself, and the wickedness of the wicked shall be upon himself." God also said, "The soul who sins shall die" (18:4). This brings to mind Jeremiah 31:30: "Everyone shall die for his own iniquity." Romans 14:12 tells us, "Each of us will give an account of himself to God."

> **A Verse to Remember**
>
> "I will judge each of you according to his ways."
>
> —*Ezekiel 33:20*

Dear Christian, this ultimately means I can't blame anyone but myself when I stand before God to give an account of my life. I can't blame my parents. I can't blame the devil. I can't blame anyone. May this be a motivation for us all to take responsibility and live righteously.

God universally judges sin—wherever it is found.

In Ezekiel 25:1–32:32 the prophet warns of God's coming judgment against Ammon (25:1-7); Moab (25:8-11); Edom (25:12-14); the Philistines (25:15-17); Tyre (26:1–28:19); Sidon (28:20-26); and Egypt (29:1–32:32). God shows no partiality with human beings (Deuteronomy 10:17; 2 Chronicles 19:7; Acts 10:34; Romans 2:11). He shows no favoritism (Ephesians 6:9; Colossians 3:25; 1 Peter 1:17). He impartially judges the evil and shows mercy on the repentant. My advice: Live righteously.

Satan is a powerful fallen angel who seeks to do you harm.

Many Bible scholars believe Ezekiel 28:11-19 tells us something of the fall of Lucifer. This being was perfect in his ways until iniquity was found in him (Ezekiel 28:15). What was this iniquity? Verse 17 tells us: "Your heart was proud because of your beauty; you corrupted your wisdom for the sake of your splendor." Lucifer apparently became so impressed with his own beauty, brilliance, intelligence, power, and position that he began to desire for himself the honor and glory that belonged to God alone. The sin that corrupted Lucifer was self-generated pride.

This mighty angelic being was rightfully judged by God: "I cast you to the ground" (Ezekiel 28:17). This doesn't mean Satan had no further access to heaven, for other Scripture verses clearly indicate that Satan maintained this access even after his fall (for example, Job 1:6-12; Zechariah 3:1-2). However, Ezekiel 28:18 indicates Satan was absolutely and completely cast out of God's heavenly government and place of authority (Luke 10:18). His ultimate destiny is the lake of fire (Revelation 20:10).

Christian, be forewarned: Satan seeks to bring you down. He will try to tempt you (Ephesians 2:1-3; 1 Thessalonians 3:5; Acts 5:3; 1 Corinthians 7:5), hinder you in any way he can (1 Thessalonians 2:18), wage war against you (Ephesians 6:11-12), cause division between you and others (Matthew 13:38-39), incite persecutions against you (Revelation 2:10), oppose you with the ferociousness of a hungry lion (1 Peter 5:8), plant doubts in your mind (Genesis 3:1-5), foster spiritual pride in your heart (1 Timothy 3:6), and lead you away "from a sincere and pure devotion to Christ" (2 Corinthians 11:3).

God in His great patience pleads for the wicked to repent. He does not want them to perish.

God affirmed, "As I live, declares the Lord GOD, I have no pleasure in the death of the wicked, but that the wicked turn from his way and live; turn back, turn back from your evil ways" (Ezekiel 33:11). This brings to mind 2 Peter 3:9: "The Lord is not slow to fulfill his promise as some count slowness, but is patient toward you, not wishing that any should perish, but that all should reach repentance." But beware—God's patience will one day run out. Turn to the Lord today.

> "O sinner, the fact that you are alive proves that God is not dealing with you according to strict justice, but in patient forbearance; every moment you live is another instance of omnipotent long-suffering."
>
> —Charles Spurgeon (1834–1892)

God's pattern is to restore His people after chastening them for a time.

God has a future for His people Israel. In this final section of his book, Ezekiel no longer speaks about judgment, but rather focuses on the comfort and consolation of God's people in view of a glorious future (Ezekiel 33–35).

God's people will one day be re-gathered and restored (Ezekiel 36). In the vision of the dry bones in Ezekiel 37, the Lord is miraculously portrayed as bringing the bones back together into a skeleton, and the skeleton becomes wrapped in muscles and tendons and flesh, and God then breathes life into the body. There is no doubt that this chapter in Ezekiel is speaking about Israel, for we read, "Son of man, these bones are the whole house of Israel" (verse 11). This chapter portrays Israel as becoming a living, breathing nation, brought back from the dead, as it were. To be sure, this is portrayed as being a gradual process, but the passage will absolutely be fulfilled.

The year 1948 was pivotal in this regard: In AD 70, Titus and his Roman warriors trampled on and destroyed Jerusalem, definitively ending Israel as a political entity (Luke 21:20). For many centuries since then, the Jews have been dispersed worldwide. In the year 1940, no one could have guessed that within a decade Israel would be a nation again. And yet it happened. Israel achieved statehood in 1948, and the Jews have been returning to their homeland ever since. The vision in Ezekiel 37 is coming to pass just as predicted. And God isn't finished with Israel, for Israel will convert to Christ at the end of the future tribulation period (36:10,24,30,37) and then receive the full blessings of the Abrahamic and Davidic covenants in the millennial kingdom (Genesis 15:12-21; 2 Samuel 7:13). Glorious!

Israel's Rebirth

- Israel will be re-gathered to land—Ezekiel 36:24
- Jews will be re-gathered—Jeremiah 16:15
- Valley of dry bones prophecy—Ezekiel 37

While not on as grand a scale, God likewise restores you and me following our trials. God promises in 1 Peter 5:10, "After you have suffered a little while, the God of all grace, who has called you to his eternal glory in Christ, will himself restore, confirm, strengthen, and establish you." Always be watching for the light at the end of the tunnel.

God can rescue His people from seemingly impossible situations.

Ezekiel 38–39 documents what has come to be called the "Ezekiel invasion" against Israel. This is a future invasion into Israel—either prior to the tribulation period or at the beginning of the tribulation period—by a northern coalition of nations. This coalition includes Russia, Iran, Sudan, Turkey, Libya, Kazakhstan, Kyrgyzstan, Uzbekistan, Turkmenistan, Tajikistan, and Armenia.

The goal of this coalition will be to utterly obliterate the Jews. And with the sheer size of this assault force, Israel will have virtually no chance of defending itself. God, however, will intervene and supernaturally destroy the invaders.

My friend, just as God will rescue Israel in this seemingly impossible situation, so God can rescue us in our seemingly impossible situations. God is "able to do far more abundantly than all that we ask or think" (Ephesians 3:20). God promises, "I will never leave you nor forsake you" (Hebrews 13:5). Trust Him (Proverbs 3:5-6).

Rejoice! A messianic age is on the horizon. Christ will reign among His people.

In Ezekiel 40–48, the prophet provides details about Christ's future millennial kingdom. Worship will be a central feature of this kingdom (43:13–46:24). In this extended section, Ezekiel provides his people a strong prophetic hope. You and I can also have a strong prophetic hope—a hope that motivates righteous living (Titus 2:12-14; 2 Peter 3:11; 1 John 3:2-3).

A Thought to Anchor in Your Heart

The powers of darkness are aligned against all who walk with Christ. Avail yourself of scriptural defenses.

Daniel

God's people are called to reverence Him,
walk humbly before Him, obey Him, and maintain
faith in Him—knowing that He is sovereign and can
bring restoration to them, even after having been
severely disciplined by Him.

Timeline

605—Daniel is taken captive as a youth to Babylon by King Nebuchadnezzar.

600—Daniel becomes an official in Babylon.

562—Nebuchadnezzar dies.

553—Daniel has his first vision.

539—Cyrus overthrows Babylon; Daniel is thrown into the lions' den.

537—Daniel writes his book.

535—Daniel's ministry ends.

Daniel was born into a royal family (Daniel 1:3,6), and was apparently physically attractive (1:4). He became one of the major prophets of the Old Testament. His name means, "God is my judge." He was uncompromising in his faithfulness to God. His contemporaries acknowledged both his righteousness and his wisdom (Ezekiel 14:14,20; 28:3).

Daniel was taken captive as a youth to Babylon by King Nebuchadnezzar in 605 BC. He was likely 15 or 16 years old when this happened. As providence had it, he spent the rest of his life there—perhaps 85 years or more. He was assigned to be a governmental official in charge of assisting with the imported Jews. Daniel authored the biblical book that bears his name (Daniel 8:15,27; 9:2; 10:2,7; 12:4-5).

Following are key applicational concepts in Daniel:

Recognize and respond affirmatively to God's work of discipline in your life.

Daniel 1:1-2 tells us, "In the third year of the reign of Jehoiakim king of Judah, Nebuchadnezzar king of Babylon came to Jerusalem and besieged it. And the Lord gave Jehoiakim king of Judah into his hand." Israel was being severely disciplined by God for its continued disobedience.

One thing we learn from Scripture is that a failure

"Labor to grow better under all your afflictions, lest your afflictions grow worse."

—John Owen (1616–1683)

to repent of sin always brings God's discipline in the life of believers. We recall that following David's sin with Bathsheba, the Lord disciplined David rather severely over an extended time (Psalm 32:3-5; 51). God also disciplines us when we go astray: "My son, do not regard lightly the discipline of the Lord, nor be weary when reproved by him. For the Lord disciplines the one he loves, and chastises every son whom he receives" (Hebrews 12:5-6). Scripture also reminds us that "if we would examine ourselves, we would not be judged by God in this way" (1 Corinthians 11:31 NLT).

Resolve to always be a person of integrity.

Daniel was consistently a man of integrity, and this integrity was evident to all who encountered him (for example, Daniel 1:8-20). Daniel was certainly right in line with Paul's words in 2 Corinthians 8:21: "For we aim at what is honorable not only in the Lord's sight but also in the sight of man."

> **Cross-References: Integrity**
> Psalm 25:21 • 26:1 • Micah 6:8 • Acts 24:16 • Titus 2:1-14 • Hebrews 13:18 • James 1:22-25

The Bible speaks a great deal about what it means to be a person of integrity. For example, "Better is a poor man who walks in his integrity than a rich man who is crooked in his ways" (Proverbs 28:6). "The integrity of the upright guides them" (11:3; see also 20:7).

Make every effort to maintain a good reputation throughout life.

Daniel's stellar reputation began in the first year of his captivity and lasted all the way up until his death. His good reputation not only brought him before kings, but also brought him great honor and exaltation throughout life (Daniel 1:19; 2:46; 5:14). As Christians, we ought always to pursue a good reputation (Proverbs 22:1; Ecclesiastes 7:1).

> **Good and Bad Reputations**
> • *Good reputations*—
>   1 Samuel 2:1-5; Psalm 86:2; Proverbs 22:1
> • *Bad reputations*—
>   2 Samuel 20:1; Proverbs 24:8; Acts 15:37-38

Let us resolve to walk in humility.

Daniel was a humble man who consistently pointed away from his own abilities and pointed rather to God (Daniel 2:27-28). He had the same humble attitude John the Baptist had: "He must increase, but I must decrease" (John 3:30; see also James 4:10; Luke 1:52; 1 Peter 5:5-6; Proverbs 15:33; 22:4; 29:23). Let us seek to daily exalt God in our lives.

Stop sinning and do what is right.

Daniel urged the king, "Break off your sins by practicing righteousness" (Daniel 4:27). Daniel's comment was motivated by two spiritual realities: (1) Sin leads to destruction and death (compare with 1 John 5:16; 1 Corinthians 5:5; 11:29-32; Acts 5:1-11). (2) Righteousness leads to blessing and long life (Proverbs 10:27; Deuteronomy 4:40; 2 Kings 20:1-6; Ephesians 6:2-3). Daniel knew it was in the king's best interest to turn from sin and pursue righteousness. The same thing is true of you and me (Exodus 19:5; Deuteronomy 4:40; Joshua 1:8; 1 Kings 2:3; Matthew 5:2-12).

> "To be sensible of our corruption and abhor our own transgressions is the first symptom of spiritual health."
>
> —J. C. Ryle (1816–1900)

Pray consistently, thankfully, specifically, and urgently.

Daniel 6:10 tells us Daniel "got down on his knees three times a day and prayed and gave thanks before his God, as he had done previously." Notice that Daniel began his prayers with thanksgiving. We are reminded of Psalm 95:2: "Let us come into his presence with thanksgiving." Psalm 100:4 also comes to mind: "Enter his gates with thanksgiving." Following thanksgiving, Daniel brought "petition and plea" before God, making specific requests of Him (Daniel 6:11).

> "Do not be anxious about anything, but in everything by prayer and supplication with thanksgiving let your requests be made known to God. And the peace of God, which surpasses all understanding, will guard your hearts and your minds in Christ Jesus."
>
> —Philippians 4:6-7

Daniel was certainly a believer in intercessory prayer—that is, praying for other people and not just for himself (2:17-18). He was also a believer in the need to make confession of sin during prayer when there was need for it (9:8-15; see also Proverbs 28:13; 1 John 1:9). Still further, we notice that Daniel prayed with a sense of great urgency (Daniel 9:16-19). We are reminded of James 5:16: "The urgent request of a righteous person is very powerful in its effect" (HCSB). The word "urgent" in this verse carries the idea of "earnest" or "heartfelt." Let us resolve to imitate Daniel in how we pray.

Obedience brings
- blessing (Luke 11:28);
- long life (1 Kings 3:14);
- happiness (Psalm 112:1); and
- peace (Proverbs 1:33).

Obey God consistently. Don't give it a second thought. Just do it.

Daniel and his Hebrew friends obeyed God no matter what they faced. The first thing Daniel did after hearing about the king's injunction that no one could pray to any god but Darius for 30 days was to go home and pray to the one true God. Daniel simply would not disobey God. For that he was thrown into the lions' den. God, of course, honored Daniel's obedience by rescuing him from the lions' den (Daniel 6).

Daniel's three Hebrew friends were commanded by Nebuchadnezzar to bow down and worship the golden image. But they simply would not disobey the one true God in this matter. They told the king, "Our God whom we serve is able to deliver us from the burning fiery furnace, and he will deliver us out of your hand, O king. But if not, be it known to you, O king, that we will not serve your gods or worship the golden image that you have set up" (Daniel 3:17-18). God honored their obedience by rescuing them in the fiery furnace (3–4). Daniel and his friends obeyed God no matter what. Let us do the same.

> **Cross-References: God Our Shield**
>
> Genesis 15:1 • Deuteronomy 33:29 • Psalm 33:20 • 84:11 • 115:9 • Proverbs 30:5

Make it your daily goal to maintain a holy fear and reverence for the one true God.

After witnessing God's great power in delivering Daniel from the lions' den, King Darius decreed that "people are to tremble and fear before the God of Daniel" (Daniel 6:26). Of course, no one had to tell Daniel and his Hebrew friends that, for they had consistently lived their lives in the fear of—and reverence for—the one true God. This led to their consistent obedience to God, even in the face of death.

The theme of fearing God or revering God is found not only in Daniel but throughout the whole of Scripture. We learn that God blesses those who fear

> **Fear of the Lord**
>
> - is true wisdom (Job 28:28; Psalm 111:10);
> - motivates obedience to God (Deuteronomy 5:29; Ecclesiastes 12:13); and
> - motivates the avoidance of evil (Proverbs 3:7; 8:13; 16:6).

Him (Psalm 115:13). Fear of the Lord leads to riches, honor, and long life (Proverbs 22:4). God shows mercy to those who fear Him (Luke 1:50). Let us always reverence God not only in what we say, but in how we live our lives.

Walk by faith and not by sight. Do this day by day, moment by moment.

Even when things seem at their most hopeless, the God of miracles can come through in ways we could never have fathomed. Daniel was tossed into a lions'

Daniel

den, which, from a human perspective, is about as bad as things can get. From a "walking by sight" perspective, Daniel knew no one survives a lions' den. But Daniel walked by faith and not by sight. God rewarded that faith by rescuing him from the lions' den (Daniel 6).

Cross-References: Keep Faith Strong

Jeremiah 17:7 • Psalm 40:4 • 118:8 • Proverbs 3:5 • Matthew 15:28 • Romans 10:17 • 2 Corinthians 5:7 • 1 Timothy 1:19 • Hebrews 11:1

The same is true of Daniel's three Hebrew friends. From a human perspective, being thrown into a fiery furnace is about as bad as things can get. From a "walking by sight" perspective, the three knew no one survives a fiery furnace. But they were walking by faith and not by sight. They knew the unseen God could deliver them from the fire (Daniel 3–4).

Regardless of what we encounter in life, let us follow the lead of Daniel and his friends in resolving to *always* walk by faith and not by sight (2 Corinthians 5:7).

Take comfort in God's sovereign control over all things in the universe.

God sovereignly reigns from heaven (Daniel 3 and 6). God is absolutely sovereign in the sense that He rules the universe, controls all things, and is Lord over all (Ephesians 1). He may utilize various means to accomplish His ends, but He is always in control. Nothing can happen in this universe that is beyond the reach of His control. In the book of Daniel, God expressed His sovereignty over the captivity of Israel, the fiery furnace, the lions' den, the rise and fall of kings, the rise and fall of nations, and much more. Rejoice in God's sovereignty!

God's Sovereignty

"My counsel shall stand, and I will accomplish all my purpose" (Isaiah 46:10).

"As I have planned, so shall it be, and as I have purposed, so shall it stand" (Isaiah 14:24).

God can always bring restoration to our lives. Just ask Him!

In Daniel 9, the underlying idea of Daniel's prayer on behalf of Israel was his people's restoration—not only restoration to God but also restoration back to the Promised Land. Daniel sought this with all his heart. In the chapters that follow, God revealed to Daniel that He yet had a future for Israel (compare with Romans 9–11). God would one day restore Israel.

God certainly restores our individual lives as well. *God can restore people spiritually:* "He leads me beside still waters. He restores my soul" (Psalm 23:2-3). *God can restore the joy of salvation:* "Restore to me the joy of your salvation" (51:12). *God can restore us after we've experienced trials:* "After you have suffered a little while, the God of all grace...will himself restore, confirm, strengthen, and establish you" (1 Peter 5:10; see also Psalm 71:20). Let us always remember, as Daniel did, that our God is a God of restoration.

Don't fret if it seems there's a delay in God's answer to your prayer.

Just as angels are sometimes dispatched by God to take care of our prayer requests (Acts 12:6-19), so fallen angels sometimes seek to thwart the angels God uses in the process of answering a particular prayer. This happened when the prophet Daniel prayed. Daniel 10:13 reveals that an angel sent by God to take care of Daniel's prayer request was detained by a more powerful, fallen angel. It was only when the archangel Michael showed up to render aid that the lesser angel was freed to carry out his task. So never fear that God is not listening simply because there seems to be a delay in His answer to your prayer. Keep your faith strong. You are not aware of everything happening in the spiritual world.

> ### A Thought to Anchor in Your Heart
> Daniel was not just a hearer of God's Word;
> he was a doer of God's Word. Go do likewise.

Hosea

God has an everlasting love for His people.
That love motivates not only His redemptive activities
on their behalf, but also His discipline of them—
His "tough love"—when they go astray.

The Price Has Been Paid

Hosea bought Gomer,
redeeming her for 15 shekels (Hosea 3:2). Christians have
been purchased by Christ:
"You were bought with a price"
(1 Corinthians 6:20). The church
was "purchased with his own
blood" (Acts 20:28 NLT).

This touching book, written by the prophet Hosea during the closing days of Jeroboam II in about 710 BC, depicts the heartfelt pain Hosea suffered at the unfaithfulness of his own wife. This, in turn, gave the prophet deep insight into the way God feels when His own people are unfaithful to Him.

Hosea was married to a woman named Gomer (Hosea 1:2), and one day she left him to live with another man. She soon became a prostitute and offered her services to any who were interested. Hosea then found her, and, in compassion, paid for her freedom and took her back to live with him (3).

Just as Gomer had been unfaithful to the marriage covenant, so the Israelites—presently at political peace and enjoying material prosperity—had been unfaithful to the covenant God made with them (Hosea 2:2-5; 6:4-11; 8:1-14). They committed spiritual adultery and turned away from God, just as Gomer had committed physical adultery. In their unfaithfulness, the Israelites engaged in an adulterous relationship with Canaanite deities (such as Baal). Yet just as Hosea loved Gomer, God still loved the Israelites, despite their unfaithfulness (11:1-12).

The Israelites still had time to repent—but time was running out. If they did not repent soon, judgment would fall at the hands of the Assyrians (Hosea 9:1–10:15).

Following are key applicational concepts in Hosea:

Spiritual adultery is grievously offensive to God. Even so, He always seeks the redemption of His people.

Hosea and his wife, Gomer, had three children together, each named by God to communicate something about His impending judgment upon adulterous Israel. Jezreel means "God scatters"; Lo-Ruhamah means "Not pitied"; and Lo-Ammi means "Not my people." God, in severe discipline, intended to scatter His people and show no pity on them because of their relentless unfaithfulness. Just as Gomer ran after other men, so Israel ran after other gods (Hosea 1–3).

Our text tells us Hosea continued to love Gomer. Despite her unfaithfulness, Hosea redeemed her and restored her (Hosea 3:2).

My friend, God has the same kind of love for us, despite the stench of our sin. Romans 5:8 affirms, "God shows his love for us in that while we were still sinners, Christ died for us." Ephesians 2:4-5 affirms, "God, being rich in mercy, because of the great love with which he loved us, even when we were dead in our trespasses, made us alive together with Christ—by grace you have been saved." Even though human beings were unfaithful to God, God sought their redemption, just as Hosea sought the redemption of his wife.

> **Grace and Mercy**
> Hosea had the legal right to have Gomer executed for her crime of adultery. He nevertheless remained faithful to her and redeemed her.
>
> God had the right to obliterate Israel for her adulterous unfaithfulness. But He continued to love her, even though discipline became necessary for a time.

Despite His great love for His people, God disciplines them when they remain in sin and refuse to repent.

Because of the heartbreak Hosea went through regarding his unfaithful wife, Gomer, he was in a better position to understand the heartbreak God felt over His wayward people. The unrelenting love Hosea showed Gomer illustrates the loyal love God has for His people. Yet, despite God's constant appeal to the people to repent, they refused (Hosea 4–9).

As a result God had no choice but to bring discipline upon them. The fruit of their disobedience was dispersion (Hosea 10). They refused repentance, so God necessarily had to refuse further mercy. Chastisement became necessary.

God likewise disciplines us when we remain in sin. He loves us too much not to. As Hebrews 12:5 puts it, "My son, do not regard lightly the discipline of the

> **Cross-References: God's Discipline**
> Proverbs 3:11-12 • 1 Corinthians 11:32 • Revelation 3:19 • Psalm 119:71 • Hebrews 12:5

Lord, nor be weary when reproved by him. For the Lord disciplines the one he loves, and chastises every son whom he receives."

When God's Word is marginalized in a society, sin runs rampant.

Hosea affirmed, "There is no faithfulness or steadfast love, and no knowledge of God in the land" (Hosea 4:1). Because there was no knowledge of God in the land, sin was running rampant and Hosea's people were on the fast-track to judgment. In keeping with this, Hosea proclaimed, "My people are destroyed for lack of knowledge" (4:6). The priests were not ministering God's Word to the people, and so the people experienced a fast slide into the gutter, morally speaking.

This is one thing that causes me concern about America. Presently there are systematic attempts to marginalize God's Word so that it has no influence in politics, in school systems, in the media, and much more. Moreover, even in many churches today the Word of God is mixed in with pop psychology, philosophy, self-help theories, and lots of entertainment. Like the ancient Jews, America seems to be on the fast-track to judgment.

The Bible is like

- *a manufacturer's handbook* that instructs us how to operate our lives;
- *an eyeglass*, helping us to see clearly;
- *a lamp*, shedding light on our path;
- *an anchor* that holds us steady when waves of adversity strike;
- *food* that gives us spiritual nourishment; and
- *a love letter*, expressing God's love for us.

God's "tough love" is ultimately intended to bring restoration.

In Hosea 6:1 we read, "Come, let us return to the LORD; for he has torn us, that he may heal us; he has struck us down, and he will bind us up." God showed Hosea's people tough love so they'd repent and turn back to Him.

Look at it this way. If you have cancer, a surgeon has to put you through painful surgery to remove it. Once it is removed, then you're back on the path to optimal health. Likewise, God sometimes has to do painful surgery on us to remove our spiritual cancer—the cancer of sin. Once removed, we are back on the path to optimal spiritual health.

Observation: It makes good sense to me for Christians to take preventative measures by minimizing sin. The less sin, the less painful surgery is required. "If we judged ourselves truly, we would not be judged" (1 Corinthians 11:31).

Claiming to know God is not enough. If you truly know God, it will be evident in the way you live your life.

Hosea's people, about to experience judgment, claimed, "My God, we—Israel—know you" (Hosea 8:2). The truth is, if a person truly knows God, it will be evident in the way he or she lives.

> "Be doers of the word, and not hearers only, deceiving yourselves."
>
> —James 1:22

This reminds us of Jesus's words in Matthew 7:22-23: "On that day many will say to me, 'Lord, Lord, did we not prophesy in your name, and cast out demons in your name, and do many mighty works in your name?' And then will I declare to them, 'I never knew you; depart from me, you workers of lawlessness.'" Merely claiming to know God is not enough. Don't be deceived.

Mere ritualistic religion is not pleasing to God. Living in harmony with His will is what brings a smile to His face.

The strange thing about Hosea's people is that they continued to go through the motions of offering sacrifices to God. But they mixed these Jewish rituals with paganism, using graven images (Hosea 6:5-7). In so doing, they brought great offense to God.

> **A Verse to Remember**
>
> "I desire steadfast love and not sacrifice, the knowledge of God rather than burnt offerings."
>
> —Hosea 6:6

We must also be cautious not to mix Christianity with worldly influences. The best way to avoid worldly contamination is to stay rooted in God's Word (Psalm 119; 2 Timothy 3:15-17).

Always seek to avoid being molded by this world. Instead, seek to be transformed by God's Word.

The problem for Hosea's people was that they were surrounded by pagan nations, and over time, they allowed some of the pagan practices of those nations to infiltrate their society. They literally became molded by the pagan cultures around them (Hosea 6:4).

> "If the heart be full of sinful thoughts, there is no room for holy and heavenly thoughts. If the heart be full of holy and heavenly thoughts by meditation, there is no room for evil and sinful thoughts."
>
> —William Bridge (1600–1670)

We, today, are in danger of the same thing. So many humanistic, secular, and even pagan influences are around us that we are in great danger of contamination. The remedy is for us to be continually transformed by God's Word. "Do not be conformed to this world, but be transformed by the renewal of your mind" (Romans 12:2).

A divided heart will lead to your downfall.

In Hosea 10:2 we read, "Their heart is false; now they must bear their guilt." The Amplified Bible renders this, "Their heart is divided and deceitful; now shall they be found guilty and suffer punishment." The New Living Translation renders it, "The hearts of the people are fickle; they are guilty and must be punished."

Dear Christian, God is looking for people whose hearts are totally committed to Him. A great psalm to meditate on is Psalm 119, because total commitment is evident throughout (emphases are mine): "Blessed are those whose way *is blameless*" (verse 1). "Blessed are those who...seek him with their *whole heart*" (verse 2). "You have commanded your precepts to be *kept diligently*" (verse 4). "Oh that my ways may be *steadfast* in keeping your statutes" (verse 5). Total commitment, friends!

A Thought to Anchor in Your Heart

Live your life as a Psalm 119 kind of Christian.

Joel

Blessing from God follows obedience to Him.

This book was written by Joel, son of Pethuel, in about 835 BC (Joel 1:1). Joel's name means "the Lord is God."

A devastating swarm of locusts had just ripped through the land of Judah, resulting in famine. This black cloud of devouring insects struck like a firestorm. As these consuming locusts ate up the agricultural produce and caused the light of the sun to be hidden and darkened, Joel saw in this catastrophe a little foretaste of the day of judgment that was surely coming upon God's people (Joel 1:15–2:11). In fact, Joel indicated that as bad as the locust plague was, it would pale by comparison to God's day of judgment. He therefore called the people to repentance (2:12-17). The reality is, Joel said, that God cannot ignore sin. Blessing can only follow obedience.

Following are key applicational concepts in Joel:

Timeline

835— Joel's prophetic ministry begins. The book of Joel is written. Joash becomes king of Judah.

814— Jehoahaz becomes king of Israel.

798— Jehoash becomes king of Israel.

796— Joel's ministry ends.

> "Truth famine is the ultimate and worst of all famines."
>
> —*Carl F. H. Henry (1913–2003)*

When bad things happen, that's a good time to examine your life and purge any known sin.

Joel saw a foretaste of the day of the Lord in the current devastating swarm of locusts that annihilated the land of Judah, resulting in widespread famine and drought (Joel 1:2-12). This resulted in nationwide mourning, and there was a subsequent call to repentance (1:13-20).

Notice four things here: (1) The locust invasion was unexpected. It came out of nowhere. (2) It struck the nation at a point of great vulnerability—the food supply. (3) The result was great mourning. (4) Immediate repentance was the need of the day.

> "A frequent reckoning with ourselves will pluck up sin before it is rooted in the soul."
>
> —*Anonymous*

We, too, sometimes experience unexpected trials that hit us hard at a point of vulnerability—a sudden illness, a sudden financial crisis, a sudden relational crisis, and other types of crises. And—like the ancients—we, too, mourn when such things happen.

Our first response ought to be to seek God's deliverance in the situation. But this is also a healthy time for self-examination—a time to examine our spiritual state and purge anything that needs purging: "Examine yourselves, to see whether you are in the faith" (2 Corinthians 13:5).

Future judgment ought to motivate present repentance for all people.

Joel now switched his perspective to the end-times "day of the Lord." The locust invasion was a graphic metaphor pointing to the more intensive visitation from the Lord in the end times. In that day, the locust invasion will seem mild in comparison to the judgments that will be part of the eschatological day of the Lord (Joel 2:1-11).

As a backdrop, the term "day of the Lord" is used in several senses in Scripture. The Old Testament prophets sometimes used the term for a judgment to be fulfilled in the near future. At other times they used the term as related to the distant eschatological future—the future tribulation period. The immediate context of the term generally indicates which sense is intended.

This future day of the Lord, related to the tribulation period, will be a painful time indeed. This period will be characterized by wrath (Zephaniah 1:15,18), judgment (Revelation 14:7), indignation (Isaiah 26:20-21), trial (Revelation 3:10), trouble (Jeremiah 30:7), destruction (Joel 1:15), darkness (Amos 5:18), desolation (Daniel 9:27), overturning (Isaiah 24:1-4), and punishment (Isaiah 24:20-21). Simply put, no passage of Scripture can be found to alleviate to any degree whatsoever the severity of this time that shall come upon the earth in judgment.

I believe the tribulation judgments are for unbelievers only. I also believe the church will be raptured prior to this time (1 Thessalonians 4:13-17; 1 Corinthians 15:51-52). But you and I as Christians will nevertheless face judgment—that is, the judgment seat of Christ in heaven (Romans 14:8-10; 1 Corinthians 3:11-15; 9:24-27). This judgment doesn't have anything to do with whether or not the Christian will remain saved. Rather, it has to do with the reception or loss of rewards, based on how one lives after becoming a believer. My advice: Let the judgment seat of Christ motivate you to pursue righteousness daily.

> "O spend your time as you would hear of it in the Judgment!"
>
> —Richard Baxter (1615–1691)

Immediate repentance from sin can avert God's judgment.

God's people are called to turn from evil *in the now* and commit to the Lord. Joel indicated it was not too late for his people to avert disaster, if only they would repent: "Return to the LORD your God, for he is gracious and merciful, slow to anger, and abounding in steadfast love; and he relents over disaster" (Joel 2:13). I believe this relates to God's words in Jeremiah 18:7-8: "If at any time I declare concerning a nation or a kingdom, that I will pluck up and break down and destroy it, and if that nation, concerning which I have spoken, turns from its evil, I will relent of the disaster that I intended to do to it." Unfortunately, the Israelites consistently refused to listen.

> "By delay of repentance, sin strengthens, and the heart hardens. The longer ice freezeth, the harder it is to be broken."
>
> —*Thomas Watson (1620–1686)*

You and I learn a good lesson here. Scripture is clear that God disciplines His children when they fall into sin and refuse to repent (Hebrews 12:5-6). So it makes good sense to *preemptively* judge ourselves. "If we judged ourselves truly, we would not be judged" (1 Corinthians 11:31).

> "Sometimes God has to put us flat on our back before we are looking up to Him."
>
> —*Jack Graham*

Despite any disciplinary measures God engages in with His people, He nevertheless has a blessed future awaiting them.

Despite the fact that harsh judgment was coming upon Joel's people, God promised them that their time of suffering would be followed by both material (Joel 2:18-27) and spiritual blessing (2:28-32). God will not forget His people. God will bring restoration in the end. God will finally dwell with His people during the future millennial kingdom—Christ's 1000-year kingdom that follows the second coming of Christ (3:17-21). It is a time to look forward to.

God does much the same with us today. We all go through difficult trials and tribulations, but He always restores us after a time. "After you have suffered a little while, the God of all grace, who has called you to

Prophetic Promises to Israel

- God has a future for Israel—Romans 9–11
- Rebirth of the nation—Ezekiel 36–37
- Israel will be regenerated—Zechariah 12:10; Matthew 23:37-39
- Outpouring of the Holy Spirit—Joel 2:28-29
- Fulfillment of land promises—Genesis 12:1-3; 15:18-21; 17:21
- Fulfillment of the throne promises—2 Samuel 7:16

Joel

his eternal glory in Christ, will himself restore, confirm, strengthen, and establish you" (1 Peter 5:10). My advice: Keep your faith strong in the midst of trials.

Joel

Ministries of the Holy Spirit

- Miraculous human conception of Jesus—Matthew 1:18-20
- Came upon Jesus at baptism—Matthew 3:16
- Inspired Scripture—2 Timothy 3:16; 2 Peter 1:21
- Agent of regeneration—John 3:1-5; Titus 3:5
- Gives spiritual gifts—1 Corinthians 12; 14
- Our divine comforter—John 14; 15:26; 16:7
- Glorifies Jesus—John 15:26
- Guides the church—John 14:25,26
- Convicts people of sin—John 16:7-14
- Produces spiritual fruit—Galatians 5:16-26

There will be a future outpouring of the Holy Spirit on the faithful in Judah.

God affirms, "I will pour out my Spirit on all flesh" (Joel 2:28). In context, "all flesh" refers specifically to the faithful remnant of Judah. This will apparently happen toward the end of the future tribulation period when Israel at last recognizes Jesus Christ as her divine Messiah (Isaiah 44:3-4; Ezekiel 36:27-28; 37:14; 39:29; Zechariah 12:10).

Of course, the Holy Spirit currently has many wonderful ministries to Christians. He gives us spiritual gifts (1 Corinthians 12; 14), is our divine comforter (John 14; 15:26; 16:7), produces spiritual fruit in us (Galatians 5:16-26), and much more. The Holy Spirit's ministry is pivotal to the spiritual life of believers.

A Thought to Anchor in Your Heart

Don't ever attempt to live the Christian life in your own feeble strength. Daily resolve to walk in dependence upon the Holy Spirit.

Amos

God pronounces righteous judgment on unrighteous people.

The book of Amos was written by a prophet of the same name about 755 BC. Amos, whose name means "burden-bearer," was a prophet to the northern kingdom of Israel (Amos 7:14-15). By trade, he was a lowly shepherd and a dresser of fig trees. He lived in Tekoa, south of Jerusalem (1:1). He was a contemporary of Jonah, Hosea, and Isaiah, and prophesied during the reigns of Uzziah and Jeroboam II.

Amos focused heavy attention on the rampant sin and social injustice of his day (Amos 5:24). During his time the land was prosperous and there were many rich people. Yet the rich did not aid those who were disadvantaged. This was not as it should be. Amos, the farmer-turned-prophet, therefore prophesied that a day of judgment was forthcoming when destruction would be inevitable (7:1–9:10).

Ironically, the rich people of Amos's day thought they were bestowed with such great wealth because they were so religious. The falsity of this viewpoint is evident in that they did not use their wealth to do God's work of caring for the poor and disadvantaged. Rather, they exploited the poor to become even richer. From the vantage point of Amos, these rich people were nothing more than hypocrites. It was not long after Amos wrote his book that the Assyrians invaded the land and took the people into captivity. Judgment came just as Amos had prophesied.

Following are key applicational concepts in Amos:

Timeline

793—Jonah's prophetic ministry begins.

792—Uzziah becomes king of Judah.

760—Amos's prophetic ministry begins.

755—Amos writes his short book.

753—Hosea's prophetic ministry begins.

750—Amos's ministry ends.

740—Isaiah's prophetic ministry begins.

God's Lowly Servants

- God often uses lowly people to accomplish His ends (1 Corinthians 1:26-27).
- Amos was a simple herdsman, but was called to be a prophet (Amos 7:14-15).
- David was a simple shepherd boy, but became king (2 Samuel 5).
- Peter was a simple fisherman, but became an apostle (Matthew 4:18-22).

A Verse to Remember

"The Lord GOD does nothing without revealing his secret to his servants the prophets."

—Amos 3:7

Because God cares for the poor, you and I must also care for the poor.

Amos speaks against those "who oppress the poor, who crush the needy" (Amos 4:1). He pronounces woe against those "who drink wine in bowls and anoint themselves with the finest oils, but are not grieved over the ruin of Joseph! Therefore they shall now be the first of those who go into exile" (6:6-7). In other words, those who care nothing for the poor will be the first to receive God's chastisement. God's desire is summarized in Amos 5:24: "Let justice roll down like waters, and righteousness like an ever-flowing stream."

> "Christian life consists of faith and charity."
>
> —*Martin Luther (1483–1546)*

> "You have not lived today until you have done something for someone who cannot pay you back."
>
> —*John Bunyan (1628–1688)*

Take whatever steps you need to avoid spiritual complacency in your life. It's deadly.

The word "complacency" means one feels so satisfied with one's own abilities or situation that he or she feels no need to try any harder. A person feels optimistic because everything seems dandy.

> "Spiritual complacency is more deadly than anything the devil can bring against us in our upward struggle."
>
> —*A. W. Tozer (1897–1963)*

Complacency is never a good thing. But it becomes all the worse when it is realized that the complacency of the rich is rooted in their exploitation of the poor and impoverished. This is what happened in Amos's day.

Amos warned that these individuals had a false sense of security—judgment would soon fall. "Woe to those who are at ease in Zion, and to those who feel secure on the mountain of Samaria" (Amos 6:1). "Woe to those who lie on beds of ivory and stretch themselves out on their couches" (6:4). They thought their great wealth was a sign that God had blessed them. But God warned them, "I will raise up against you a nation, O house of Israel...and they shall oppress you" (6:14). Exile was coming.

> "The one reaction the Christian church ought never to produce in the community is indifference."
>
> —*John Blanchard*

My friend, complacency is a state of being that often develops over an extended time—sometimes so slowly that you're not even aware it's happening. Beware: it is dangerous to the spiritual life. Jesus warned the church in Laodicea, "I know your works: you are neither cold nor hot. Would that you were either cold or hot! So, because you are lukewarm, and neither hot nor cold, I will spit you out of my mouth" (Revelation 3:15-16).

Don't be a faker—going through the motions of being a Christian while your heart is full of compromise.

God said to His people in Amos's time, "I hate, I despise your feasts, and I take no delight in your solemn assemblies. Even though you offer me your burnt offerings and grain offerings, I will not accept them; and the peace offerings of your fattened animals, I will not look upon them. Take away from me the noise of your songs; to the melody of your harps I will not listen" (Amos 5:21-23). The Jews were merely engaging in external rituals with no heartfelt obedience. While they were engaging in religious feasts, they were at the same time trampling on the poor, taking and giving bribes, and depriving people of justice. The religious establishment had become utterly corrupt. God hates such hypocrisy.

> "I desire steadfast love and not sacrifice, the knowledge of God rather than burnt offerings."
>
> —Hosea 6:6

It is all too easy to fall into the rut of spiritual compromise. Someone said (tongue-in-check) that some Christians sow bad seeds all week and then go to church on Sunday to pray for crop failure. Going through the motions of being a Christian is not acceptable to God. God looks at your heart and wants to see consistent faith, obedience, and commitment. Don't be a faker.

Everyone is accountable to God.

Amos pronounced judgment against Syria for its brutal cruelty (Amos 1:3-5), Philistia for engaging in slavery (1:6-8), Phoenicia for breaking a treaty (1:9-10), Edom for its vengeful nature (1:11-12), Ammon for its violent nature (1:13-15), Moab for its unjust practices (2:1-3), and Judah for not honoring the Law (2:4-6). Amos then targeted Israel for not honoring the Law (2:6-16).

Amos set forth three sermons, each beginning with the phrase, "Hear this word" (Amos 3:1; 4:1; 5:1). The first pronounces judgment against Israel because of her iniquities (3). The second delineates Israel's crimes and God's discipline (4). The third specifies Israel's sins and calls the people to repentance (5–6). Israel refused, and would therefore experience the judgment of exile.

Amos then set forth five visions describing the nature of God's judgment. His vision of locusts was an apt metaphor for God's wrath (Amos 7:1-3). His vision of fire pointed to the drought that would follow the locust plague (7:4-6). His vision of the plumb line revealed that God had measured Israel by the rule of His justice and found the nation falling short (7:7-9). His vision of a basket of summer fruit indicated that the people's fruitful years of prosperity had now ended (8:1-14). His vision of the smiting of the temple pointed to a worldwide dispersion of the Jewish people (9:1-10). Bad times were coming. God holds all people accountable.

Restoration

- God restores us—Psalm 71:20
- Restore my life again—Psalm 119:107
- Restore our fortunes—Psalm 126:4

Despite God's judgment in the present, restoration will follow for the faithful remnant.

In the end, God promises restoration. God will bless His faithful remnant in the future (Amos 9:11-15). "In that day I will raise up the booth of David that is fallen and repair its breaches, and raise up its ruins and rebuild it as in the days of old" (verse 11).

A Thought to Anchor in Your Heart

Don't be a faker. Oust any complacency or compromise from your heart. Resolve to be "the real deal" as a Christian from this moment forward.

Amos

Obadiah

The wicked aren't getting away with anything. It's just a matter of time before judgment falls.

Obadiah's name means "servant of the Lord." He wrote his book about 586 BC. He spoke of the coming downfall of Edom, an area directly southeast of the Dead Sea. The Edomites had invaded Judah when Jerusalem was being overrun and destroyed by the Babylonians in 587 BC. The Edomites would thus pay the ultimate price and be destroyed.

The Edomites were descendants of Esau. The biblical record indicates that Esau struggled with his brother Jacob even within their mother's womb (Genesis 25:22), and this struggle continued among their descendants.

Following are key applicational concepts in Obadiah:

Timeline

1900—The Edomites are the descendants of Esau ("brothers of Israel").

1406—The Edomites refuse Israel passage through their land while en route to Canaan.

848–841—Edom rebels against dominion by Judah and sets up an independent state.

587—The Edomites invade Judah as Babylon overruns Jerusalem.

586—Obadiah writes his short book.

The wicked who persecute God's people aren't getting away with anything. They'll face God's judgment for their actions.

Obadiah begins his short book by emphasizing the absolute certainty of the impending overthrow of Edom. The judgment was to be thorough and complete (Obadiah 1:1-9). God's judgment would be just and devastating. Woe to those who persecute God's people!

The failure to help others when one has the ability to do so brings God's displeasure.

The Edomites were being condemned not just for harsh treatment of Judah, but also for not coming to Judah's aid when Babylon attacked. "Do not gloat over the day of your brother in the day of his misfortune; do not rejoice over the

> "Life's most urgent question is: What are you doing for others?"
>
> —Martin Luther King Jr.
> (1929–1968)

people of Judah in the day of their ruin" (Obadiah 1:12). God viewed this attitude as heinous.

Pride goes before destruction.

The people of Edom were characterized by aggression, violence, and self-inflated pride (Obadiah 1:10-14). In the soon-coming judgment, Edom's pride would be debased, its wealth plundered, and its people slaughtered. All who proudly defy God will be brought low and meet their doom as Edom did.

> "The proud man lives halfway down the slope to hell."
>
> —Anonymous

Sinners often experience the "boomerang effect"—they receive what they've dished out to others.

> "Whoever digs a pit will fall into it, and a stone will come back on him who starts it rolling."
>
> —Proverbs 26:27

In the approaching judgment, Edom would be shown the same harsh treatment it had shown to Judah. "As you have done, it shall be done to you; your deeds shall return on your own head" (Obadiah 1:15). This brings to mind the apostle Paul's words in Galatians 6:7: "Do not be deceived: God is not mocked, for whatever one sows, that will he also reap." Conversely, we remember the words of Jesus: "Blessed are the merciful, for they shall receive mercy" (Matthew 5:7).

God restores His people after times of trial.

Whereas Edom would suffer a dark and terrible judgment, Judah would be restored and enjoy a bright and beautiful future (Obadiah 1:17-18). Judah would again possess the land (1:19-20), and God will rule over His kingdom (1:21).

> "Everything that God brings into our life is directed to one purpose: that we might be conformed to the image of Christ."
>
> —Erwin Lutzer

I never get tired of saying it: God also restores you and me after our trials. "After you have suffered a little while, the God of all grace, who has called you to his eternal glory in Christ, will himself restore, confirm, strengthen, and establish you" (1 Peter 5:10).

A Thought to Anchor in Your Heart

Actions always carry consequences. Live your life wisely.

Jonah

Because of God's compassion for all humanity—not wanting any to perish—He is willing to go to extreme measures to reach people with His message.

The book of Jonah was written by Jonah, the son of Amittai, in 760 BC. Some have argued that perhaps Jonah was not the author because he is referred to in the third person (Jonah 1:3,5,9,12; 2:1; 3:4; 4:1,5,8-9). But it was common among Old Testament prophets to speak of their activities in the third person (see Isaiah 37:21; 38:1; 39:3-5; Daniel 1:1–7:1).

Jonah, a prophet of the northern kingdom, was commanded by God to witness to the inhabitants of Nineveh, the capital of Assyria. Since the Assyrians had previously attacked and destroyed Israel, Jonah abhorred the idea of preaching to them, and tried to run from God to get out of this assignment. God providentially manipulated circumstances to bring Jonah to Nineveh. The Ninevites listened to Jonah's message and promptly repented, thereby averting a terrible judgment.

Following are key applicational concepts in Jonah:

It is unwise to resist God's call upon your life.

God commissioned Jonah to proclaim that judgment would fall against the pagan Ninevites unless they repented. Not wanting the Ninevites to repent and turn to God because they had a long track record of cruelty toward God's people, Jonah disobeyed God and took a ship west to Tarshish (Jonah 1:3). He tried to avert any possibility of salvation for the Ninevites. His test of wills with the Almighty would soon prove to be unwise.

Timeline

793— Jonah's prophetic ministry begins.

760— Jonah preaches to Nineveh.

760— Jonah writes his short book.

753— Jonah's ministry ends.

Love Your Enemies

"Love your enemies, do good to those who hate you, bless those who curse you, pray for those who abuse you."

—Jesus (Luke 6:27-28)

"Obey God even when it hurts."

—Anonymous

God's compassion is for all human beings.

God's Compassion

"The LORD, the LORD, a God merciful and gracious, slow to anger, and abounding in steadfast love."

—*Exodus 34:6*

God obviously showed great compassion for the Ninevites in wanting to send Jonah to preach to them. God even asked Jonah, "Should not I pity Nineveh, that great city, in which there are more than 120,000 persons?" (Jonah 4:11).

God also showed great compassion toward the mariners on the ship. He spared them by ending the life-threatening storm as soon as Jonah was thrown overboard (Jonah 1:15).

Still further, God showed great compassion toward Jonah himself—even in the midst of his rebellion. God not only rescued him from drowning (Jonah 1:17), but He was also patient with Jonah in his unrighteous anger (4:4,9) and provided shade from the hot sun for him (4:6).

The disobedience of one person may have adverse consequences for people around him.

To avoid going to Nineveh, Jonah got on a ship headed toward Tarshish. As a consequence, "the LORD hurled a great wind upon the sea, and there was a mighty tempest on the sea, so that the ship threatened to break up" (Jonah 1:4). The innocent mariners were afraid they'd soon sink and drown. The longer Jonah continued his disobedience on the ship, the worst the storm became. "The sea grew more and more tempestuous" (1:11). Still later, the "sea grew more and more tempestuous against them" (1:13). The mariners were forced to make a hard choice: either throw Jonah into the sea and survive or keep Jonah aboard and sink. They finally threw Jonah overboard, and at that moment "the sea ceased from its raging" (1:15).

The point for us to remember is that Jonah endangered everyone onboard the ship by his sinful actions. The lesson we learn from this is that we ought to make every effort to avoid engaging in any action that could potentially bring injury to innocent others.

"This is alone true wisdom, to submit ourselves wholly to the will of God."

—*John Calvin (1509–1564)*

Obedience to the will of God is not a mere option for His children.

When God reveals His will, it is not a mere option as to whether or not we will do as He has willed. It is incumbent upon every believer to obey God's revealed will. This is where Jonah failed. He knew God's will and promptly took actions contrary to His will (Jonah 1:1-3). That is sin (James 4:17). Jonah desperately needed to follow the lead of the psalmist, who said, "I delight to do your will, O my God" (Psalm 40:8).

God sovereignly works in our lives to accomplish His purpose in us.

God providentially controls what He created (Jonah 1:9). Genesis 1 tells us God not only created the seas; He also commanded, "Let the waters swarm with swarms of living creatures" (Genesis 1:20)—which would certainly include fish large enough to swallow human beings. God is sovereign over the creatures of the sea.

> "The sea is his, for he made it, and his hands formed the dry land."
>
> —*Psalm 95:5*

We also notice God's sovereignty in Jonah being thrown overboard. Jonah 1:15 tells us that the mariners threw Jonah into the sea. However, Jonah later acknowledged to God, "*You* cast me into the deep, into the heart of the seas, and the flood surrounded me; all *your waves* and *your billows* passed over me" (2:2, emphasis added).

> "You rule the raging of the sea; when its waves rise, you still them."
>
> —*Psalm 89:9*

God then providentially caused a great fish to swallow Jonah after he was thrown overboard by the sailors, and he spent three restless days and nights within the great fish. As for Jonah *surviving* inside the fish for three days, there is no question that this was a miracle of the Lord. God providentially guided these events from beginning to end.

> "Mightier than the thunders of many waters, mightier than the waves of the sea, the LORD on high is mighty."
>
> —*Psalm 93:4*

Jonah was cognizant that God had sovereignly intervened in his life. He cried out to the Lord from the belly of the fish, giving praise and thanksgiving to God for his deliverance. After the three days, God sovereignly caused the great fish to vomit Jonah out onto dry land so he could then proceed to Nineveh (Jonah 2:10).

The Lord can bring us down; the Lord can lift us up.

On the one hand, God brought Jonah down by having him hurled into the sea. On the other hand, Jonah interpreted God's rescue of him via a fish as a *lifting* up. "You brought up my life from the pit" (Jonah 2:6). (In Hebrew thought, the word "pit" can refer to the grave, or death.) Dear Christian, the Lord can bring us down in discipline, but He can also lift us up when we are down.

God is always willing to show love and mercy to those who repent of their sins.

Once on land again, Jonah was re-commissioned to go to Nineveh and warn the people of impending judgment. He did as instructed, and the entire city repented. Having witnessed their contrition, God held back the judgment He had intended for the city (Jonah 3:10). This is in keeping with God's policy stated in Jeremiah 18:7-8: "If at any time I declare concerning a nation or a kingdom, that I will pluck up and break down and destroy it, and if that nation, concerning which I have spoken, turns from its evil, I will relent of the disaster that I intended to do to it." God is often seen showing mercy where repentance is evident (Exodus 32:14; 2 Samuel 24:16; Amos 7:3,6). As Jonah himself had to admit, "You are a gracious God and merciful, slow to anger and abounding in steadfast love, and relenting from disaster" (Jonah 4:2).

> "To those whom God finds impenitent sinners he will be found to be an implacable judge."
>
> —Matthew Henry (1662–1714)

Even good people can sometimes have a bad attitude.

Jonah was disappointed that the Assyrians were not destroyed, but had instead turned to God and received His mercy. God reminded Jonah that He is gracious and forgiving of all people, even Gentiles, if they repent (Jonah 4:2,11). This brings to mind 2 Peter 3:9, which tells us that God is "not wishing that any should perish, but that all should reach repentance." The Ninevites repented and so were spared judgment. We likewise read in 1 Timothy 2:4 that God "desires all people to be saved and to come to the knowledge of the truth." Jonah was wrong to hold on to ill will.

Repentance
- God commands repentance—Acts 17:30
- Repent and live—Ezekiel 18:32
- Confess and find mercy—Proverbs 28:13
- Unless you repent, you perish—Luke 13:3

God uses imperfect human beings in the work of ministry.

Despite all the failures of Jonah, the city of Nineveh was brought to repentance and turned to the Lord (Jonah 3:6-10). God uses imperfect people to accomplish His purposes. It is a good thing that God does not use only perfect servants, for there are none. "*All* have sinned and fall short of the glory of God" (Romans 3:23, emphasis added). Paul considered himself the chief of sinners (1 Timothy 1:15). This gives us hope that God can use us too.

We all need to hear God's Word and respond to it.

To the Ninevites, God communicated a message of repentance and judgment through Jonah. But God also gave revelation to Jonah about his own deficient character—an unforgiving heart (Jonah 4:4,9-11). My assessment: We all need to hear God's Word and respond to it.

God's children are never alone in their trials.

Being thrown into the sea, being swallowed by a big fish, being vomited up onto dry land by a fish—Jonah was having a tough time. But God was with him through it all (Jonah 1:17; 2:10). This is a pattern we often see in the Bible: God did not keep Joseph from being sold into slavery and taken to Egypt, but He was with Joseph in his unfair circumstances (Genesis 27–50). God did not keep Daniel from the lions' den, but He was with Daniel in the lions' den (Daniel 6). God did not keep the apostle Paul from going to jail, but He was with Paul in his jail experiences (Ephesians 3:1; Philippians 1:7; Colossians 4:10). God is also with us in our trials (1 Peter 1:5-7).

Jonah

> ### A Thought to Anchor in Your Heart
>
> Build this conviction into your heart:
> "I delight to do your will, O my God."

Micah

Idolatry, wickedness, and a lack of social justice
make any society ripe for God's judgment.
And yet there is always hope for the future
because of God's unending mercy.

The book of Micah was written by a prophet of the same name in about 700 BC. The name Micah means "who is like the Lord?" He was a contemporary of fellow prophets Amos, Hosea, and Isaiah in the eighth century BC, and carried on his ministry during the reigns of kings Jotham, Ahaz, and Hezekiah. He preached to Samaria and Jerusalem.

Micah was a simple farmer whose prophetic message was rooted in the injustices and exploitation he had witnessed. His primary message was that those who are rightly related to God should seek social justice and reach out to help the poor and disenfranchised. But instead of this, those who claimed to be right with God in his day continued to ignore social injustices and, indeed, they heinously exploited the poor, thereby actually participating in social injustice. Micah indicted Samaria and Jerusalem, as well as the leaders and people of Israel and Judah. He communicated that God hates injustice. God's desire for people is this: "To do justice, and to love kindness, and to walk humbly with your God" (Micah 6:8).

Cross-References: Social Justice

Deuteronomy 16:20 • 15:7-11 •
Psalm 82:3 • Proverbs 31:8-9 •
22:16 • 14:31 • Isaiah 1:17 • Jeremiah 22:3 • Zechariah 7:9-10 •
Amos 5:11-15 • Micah 6:8 • Matthew 7:12 • Luke 10:30-37 • James 1:27 • 1 John 3:17-18

Micah thundered a stern message that these injustices would not be allowed to continue. Judgment would fall—a judgment so severe, Micah said, that even Jerusalem's temple would be destroyed. Bad times were coming! Following this judgment, however, Micah said God would restore His people and bring about a kingdom of peace through the divine Messiah (Micah 5:2).

Following are key applicational concepts in Micah:

Leaders should never exploit their position in the pursuit of material gain.

When the Jewish nation turned from God in earlier years, it weakened religiously, morally, economically, and politically (1 Kings 12). As the nation strayed further and further from the worship of the one true God, things went from bad to worse. Internal strife weakened the kingdom and it eventually split into two kingdoms—the northern kingdom (retaining the name Israel) and the southern kingdom (called Judah).

Micah focused his primary warnings of God's judgment on the leaders of Judah and Israel for their greed, oppression, and exploitation of the poor, as well as their selfishness and idolatry. These individuals "covet fields and seize them, and houses, and take them away; they oppress a man and his house, a man and his inheritance" (Micah 2:2). These leaders were truly wicked, and they were doing great damage to the common folk.

These leaders would soon learn the direct cause-and-effect relationship between sins of injustice and God's just judgment. None of these leaders would escape the judgment. It would be comprehensive and devastating. "Therefore I strike you with a grievous blow, making you desolate because of your sins" (Micah 6:13).

Personal righteousness must extend beyond one's self to embrace a broader social responsibility.

Social responsibility is a common theme in the book of Micah (1:2-5; 2:3; 6:1-2,9-11). It is also common throughout the rest of Scripture. Isaiah 1:17 tells us, "Learn to do good; seek justice, correct oppression; bring justice to the fatherless, plead the widow's cause." Zechariah 7:9-19 likewise states, "Thus says the LORD of hosts, Render true judgments, show kindness and mercy to one another, do not oppress the widow, the fatherless, the sojourner, or the poor, and let none of you devise evil against another in your heart." Proverbs 31:9 exhorts, "Open your mouth, judge righteously, defend the rights of the poor and needy" (see also Jeremiah 22:3; Proverbs 31:8-9; Luke 10:30-37; Psalm

> "Hospitality is threefold; for one's family, this of necessity; for strangers, this of courtesy; for the poor, this is charity."
>
> —*Thomas Fuller (1608–1661)*

Micah

82:3; 1 John 3:17-18). The fact that this is the focus of so much Scripture shows it is important to the heart of God. God cares about the poor and disenfranchised, and He expects His followers to do something about their needs.

My friend, I have a strong feeling this issue is going to come up at the judgment seat of Christ (2 Corinthians 5:10; Romans 14:10-12). My advice: take the issue of social responsibility seriously.

True religion is not just about ritual. It's also about showing love, justice, mercy, and faithfulness.

The disingenuous religious leaders of Israel and Judah were externally going through the motions with religious rituals, but in reality they were seeking nothing but material gain. They had an outward display of piety, but on the inside had nothing but selfish motives and intents (Micah 6:1-7).

God made the point through the prophet Micah that His great desire was not the mere offering of religious sacrifices at the temple but rather a genuine faith that showed itself in obedience to Him, love for others, compassion for others, kindness toward others, and the pursuit of social justice. "He has told you, O man, what is good; and what does the LORD require of you but to do justice, and to love kindness, and to walk humbly with your God" (Micah 6:8).

One cannot help but recall that Jesus's condemnation of the scribes and Pharisees related to their lack of such virtues. "Woe to you, scribes and Pharisees, hypocrites! For you...have neglected the weightier matters of the law: justice and mercy and faithfulness" (Matthew 23:23; compare with James 1:27). My friend, don't be a faker. Show your commitment to God by how you relate to Him and by how you treat others (James 1:22-25).

> **A Verse to Remember**
>
> "He has told you, O man, what is good; and what does the LORD require of you but to do justice, and to love kindness, and to walk humbly with your God."
>
> —Micah 6:8

Prophecies of the coming divine Messiah give us great hope for the future.

Despite the present evil that existed in Israel and Judah, there was yet hope in view of the reality that the divine Messiah was coming. One day God will reinstitute the kingdom, and God's Ruler—the divine Messiah, Jesus Christ—will rule over the kingdom in

> **A Verse to Remember**
>
> "But you, O Bethlehem...from you shall come forth for me one who is to be ruler in Israel, whose coming forth is from of old, from ancient days."
>
> —Micah 5:2

Micah

perfect peace (Micah 5:2-15). Micah speaks of both a first coming of the Messiah (5:2-3) and a second coming (5:4-15).

Messianic prophecy is a central feature of the Old Testament. Numerous predictions—fulfilled to the "crossing of the *t*" and the "dotting of the *i*" in the New Testament—relate to His birth, life, ministry, death, resurrection, and glory. Hundreds of years before Christ was even born, God prophesied through Micah that Christ the King would be born in Bethlehem (Micah 5:2). We elsewhere learn the Messiah was to be virgin-born (Isaiah 7:14), was to have a ministry of miracles (Isaiah 35:5-6), was to be pierced in His hands and feet (Psalm 22:16) for the sins of humankind (Isaiah 53:5), then resurrect from the dead (Psalm 16:10; 22:22) and ascend into heaven (Psalm 68:18). More than 100 messianic prophecies were fulfilled in the person of Jesus Christ. It is not too much to say that Jesus is the true hope not just for the Jewish people but for the whole world (John 3:16; Ephesians 3:8-10; Colossians 3:11). Praise Jesus!

God's Prophets

The word "prophet"—from the Hebrew word *nabi*—refers to a spokesman for God. In some cases he declared God's message regarding a contemporary situation to humankind. In other cases he foretold God's actions based on divine revelation (2 Samuel 7:27; Jeremiah 23:18).

Many prophecies pointed to the divine Messiah (for example, Micah 5:2).

Micah

A Thought to Anchor in Your Heart

It is always more blessed to give than to receive.

Nahum

No nation is invincible. No nation is invulnerable. Regardless of how powerful a nation may seem to be from a human perspective, unrepentant sin yields divine judgment.

Timeline

663—Nahum's prophetic ministry begins.

650—Nahum writes his short book.

612—Assyria is utterly destroyed, as prophesied by Nahum.

"Pride is a denial of dependence upon God."

—Anonymous

The book of Nahum was written by a prophet of the same name in about 650 BC. Aside from the fact that he was a prophet of God, and that he was a contemporary of Zephaniah, Jeremiah, and Habakkuk, we know little of his life. History is not even clear as to where he came from. What was important was the message he preached.

Nahum's ministry took place toward the end of Josiah's reign. His book describes the fall and destruction of Nineveh—the Assyrian capital—in graphic language. About a hundred years previously, the Ninevites had repented under the preaching of Jonah. But now Nineveh had returned in full force to idolatry, paganism, and brutality (Nahum 3:1-4). Nineveh—brimming with national pride—believed itself invincible and failed to recognize that the only true ultimate power in the universe is the one true God.

Nahum prophesied that even though the Assyrians might seem invincible, their days were numbered; judgment was rapidly approaching. Nineveh is pictured as a prostitute that had brought injury to others, and must now be punished as a prostitute. Just as Nahum prophesied, Assyria was utterly destroyed in 612 BC.

Following are key applicational concepts in Nahum:

A Verse to Remember

"The LORD is a jealous and avenging God."

—Nahum 1:2

God's perfect character demands that He respond to sin.

Nahum begins by describing God's character (Nahum 1:2-6). Understanding God's character

216

helps us better understand why He necessarily had to bring judgment against Nineveh. While God is slow to anger and graceful to those who repent, He is also wrathful—full of vengeance—against those who turn their backs on Him (1:7-8). Because God is holy, He was compelled to respond in judgment against the manifold and ever-worsening sins of the Ninevites (1:9-14).

The good news, Nahum noted, is that this judgment would bring a level of comfort to the people of Judah. After all, the constant threat of potential Assyrian invasion would soon be at a permanent end (Nahum 1:15).

Dear Christian, I am personally thankful that Scripture reveals so many of God's awesome characteristics to us. We call these characteristics the attributes of God. Scripture tells us God is self-existent (Exodus 3:14), eternal (Psalm 90:2), unchanging in His nature (Malachi 3:6), infinite (Psalm 145:3), everywhere-present (Psalm 139:2-12), all-knowing (Psalm 139:4), all-powerful (Genesis 18:14), sovereign (Isaiah 46:10), all-wise (Romans 11:33), all-good (Psalm 34:8), full of love (1 John 4:8), full of grace (Titus 2:11), full of mercy (2 Corinthians 1:3), full of patience (Nahum 1:3), and holy (1 Peter 1:15). God is indeed an awesome God. Praise His name!

> "The knowledge of God is the great hope of sinners. Oh, if you knew Him better, you would fly to Him! If you understood how gracious He is, you would seek Him. If you could have any idea of His holiness, you would loathe your self-righteousness. If you knew anything of His power, you would not venture to contend with Him. If you knew anything of His grace, you would not hesitate to yield yourself to Him."
>
> —Charles Spurgeon (1834–1892)

Our God is a "jealous" God—He desires His people to be utterly faithful and obedient to Him, with not even a hint of infidelity.

Our text tells us God is a jealous God (Nahum 1:2). This is a common theme in Scripture. In Deuteronomy we are told "the LORD your God is a consuming fire, a jealous God" (4:24); "I the LORD your God am a jealous God" (5:9); "the LORD your God in your midst is a jealous God" (6:15); "they stirred him to jealousy with strange gods" (32:16); and "they have made me jealous with what is no god; they have provoked me to anger with their idols" (32:21).

> "God, as a jealous God, is filled with a burning desire for our holiness, for our righteousness, for our goodness."
>
> —Donald Grey Barnhouse (1895–1960)

These verses indicate God is a jealous God not in the sense of having a negative and destructive emotion (like humans often do), but in the sense that He desires His people to be utterly faithful and obedient to Him. It is the unfaithfulness of

Nahum

His people—*infidelity*—that yields a "jealous" reaction. As a jealous God, He will simply not allow another—an idol, for example—to have the honor that is due Him alone (Isaiah 42:8; 48:11). The covenant that God had with Israel demanded fidelity, just as a human covenant of marriage demands fidelity.

Wicked people are often on the receiving end of "the boomerang effect"—they receive what they've dished out to others.

God destroyed Nineveh because the city was brimming with sin, cruelty, rebellion, dishonesty, and corruption (Nahum 3:1-7). Just as the powerful Assyrians had previously crushed other countries without mercy, so now—at the hand of God—Nineveh would be crushed without mercy. I call this the "boomerang effect" because Nineveh would now receive what they had so consistently dealt out to others through the years.

> "Those that will not hear the comfortable voice of God's Word shall be made to hear the dreadful voice of his rod."
>
> —Matthew Henry (1662–1714)

We see numerous references to the boomerang effect in Scripture. For example, Proverbs 26:27 tells us, "Whoever digs a pit will fall into it, and a stone will come back on him who starts it rolling." Psalm 7:15-16 says, "He makes a pit, digging it out, and falls into the hole that he has made. His mischief returns upon his own head, and on his own skull his violence descends." Psalm 9:15 says, "The nations have sunk in the pit that they made; in the net that they hid, their own foot has been caught." Psalm 35:8 says, "Let the net that he hid ensnare him; let him fall into it—to his destruction!"

The wicked should beware!

The same God who judged evil in Bible times will also judge evil in our times.

Sometimes people today seem to rationalize, "Oh, well, that horrible judgment happened in Bible times, but that would never happen today. I believe God is a God of love."

The fallacy in this line of thinking is that God's character has not changed since Bible times. God is still "a jealous and avenging God" who "takes vengeance on his adversaries and keeps wrath for his enemies" (Nahum 1:2). Times may change but God does not change. God will never wink at human sin. Unrepentant sin will always bring eventual judgment from Him.

God Himself affirmed, "I the Lord do not change" (Malachi 3:6; see also Numbers 23:19). Indeed, "He is unchangeable" (Job 23:13). The psalmist said,

"You are the same, and your years have no end" (Psalm 102:27). God is "the Father of lights with whom there is no variation or shadow due to change" (James 1:17). God is always holy and righteous, and He will always be against sin.

My friend, I hate to say it, but such verses cause me concern for America. It seems like America is morally imploding, with ever-escalating moral and spiritual degeneration. Because of the high level of immorality in this country, it is entirely possible that God may bring judgment upon it (see Romans 1:18-32). Christian leaders have been warning about this possibility for decades—and their warnings are typically met with deaf ears, much like prophets were often ignored during Old Testament times. Americans would do well to remember that God "makes nations great, and he destroys them; he enlarges nations, and leads them away" (Job 12:23). Oh, that America would repent.

God Is Sovereign over Nations

- "He makes the nations great, then destroys them; He enlarges the nations, then leads them away" (Job 12:23).

- "From one man he created all the nations throughout the whole earth. He decided beforehand which should rise and fall, and he determined their boundaries" (Acts 17:26 NLT).

- God "removes kings and establishes kings" (Daniel 2:21).

A Thought to Anchor in Your Heart

Be thankful that your God is a jealous God. A god who didn't care if you cheated on him would not be a god worthy of worship.

Nahum

Habakkuk

Don't fret over the seeming inequities of life.
God often uses difficult circumstances—
even painful circumstances—as a means of
disciplining His children. We can trust Him
because He knows what He's doing.

Timeline

612—Habakkuk's prophetic ministry begins.

606—Habakkuk writes his short book.

605—The first deportation from Judah to Babylon occurs.

597—The second deportation from Judah to Babylon occurs.

588—Habakkuk's ministry ends.

586—Judah (the southern kingdom) falls; Jerusalem is destroyed.

God's Patience in the Face of Human Sin

- God's patience in the days of Noah—1 Peter 3:20
- Not willing that any should perish—2 Peter 3:9
- Gives time to repent—Revelation 2:21
- Iniquity not yet complete—Genesis 15:16
- Sentence delayed—Ecclesiastes 8:11

The book of Habakkuk was written by a prophet of the same name in about 606 BC. Aside from the fact that he was a prophet, and a contemporary of Jeremiah, little is known about the man. His Hebrew name, *Habaqquq*, apparently means "one who embraces"—perhaps pointing to how he clings to God regardless of what happens to his nation.

Habakkuk was pained to witness what was going on in Judah. The nation had continuously been called to repentance, but the call had fallen on deaf ears. Judah was stubborn. Sin was predominant. Things were falling apart before Habakkuk's very eyes, going from bad to worse. He was heartbroken over his people.

Perplexed, Habakkuk came to the point where he had to ask God how long this heinous state of affairs could continue. He wondered how long God would be silent in the face of this escalating catastrophe. He wondered why the wicked seemed to prosper without hindrance. Life seemed full of inequities. He wondered if God was even listening. "Where are you God?"

God finally revealed to Habakkuk that though it appeared the wicked were prospering, judgment would come soon enough. And the judgment would be painful.

Following are key applicational concepts in Habakkuk:

God disciplines His children when they go astray and refuse to repent.

Habakkuk had two dialogues with the Lord. In the first (Habakkuk 1:1-11), the prophet pointed to the wickedness of Judah and inquired how long God would be silent about it. God answered that He would use the mighty Babylonians as His whipping rod to discipline the people of Judah. The discipline would be swift and painful. This chastising of Judah was intended to yield repentance. It was intended for Judah's ultimate good.

> "The alternative to discipline is disaster."
>
> —Vance Havner (1901–1986)

God likewise disciplines us today when we go astray and fail to repent. When God disciplines His children, He does not act out of anger or revenge but out of immeasurable love and concern. God loves us far too much to allow us to remain in unrepentant sin. Because He cares for us, He chastens us—and the chastening is often painful.

> "I have never learned anything from God except by the rod."
>
> —Charles Spurgeon (1834–1892)

My friend, are we not much the same way when it comes to our own children? If I saw my son engaging in a sinful lifestyle that was damaging to him, the most unloving thing I could do would be to leave him alone and allow him to continue on that path of destruction. The most loving thing I could do would be to confront him with his sin. If he resisted, then I would have no choice but to discipline him. All the while, my motive would be heartfelt love. I only want what is best for my son. I don't like to do it, but I do it nevertheless because I care for him.

God likewise wants only what is best for us, and for that reason He disciplines us as His own children. His desire is to take away (sin, for example) so He can replace with something better (holiness). Like a gardener prunes a vine so it will be more fruitful, so the Father prunes His children to make them more fruitful (John 15:2). God works in the life of each believer in such a way as to "cut out" all that is bad so he or she will bear more spiritual fruit.

> "Repentance, to be of any avail, must work a change of heart and conduct."
>
> —Theodore L. Cuyler (1822–1909)

At the risk of stating the obvious, here is a basic principle to keep in mind: if we wish to minimize divine discipline due to unrepentant sin on our part, the way to do it is to minimize unrepentant sin. We need to take the initiative to judge our own sin. After all, Scripture teaches that if we would judge ourselves,

Habakkuk

we would not be judged (1 Corinthians 11:31). The people of Judah seemed oblivious to this truth.

God is perfectly wise. He knows just what form of discipline will work best in our lives.

Habakkuk inquired as to why a righteous and holy God would use an incredibly evil nation of people like the Babylonians to bring chastisement upon Judah (Habakkuk 2). God answered that He was fully aware of the transgressions of the Babylonians. However, Judah also stood guilty. Therefore, just as the Babylonians stood under condemnation, so did Judah stand under condemnation. God's intention was to first chastise Judah with the whipping rod of the Babylonians. Then God would deal with the evil of the Babylonians.

God

- is righteous altogether (Psalm 19:9);
- does no wrong (Deuteronomy 32:4); and
- judges in righteousness (Acts 17:31).

We may wonder why God allows certain bad circumstances to emerge in our lives. The truth is, God may use financial problems, an illness, a relational problem, an accident, or a crisis to get our attention and cause us to repent (Hebrews 12:6-9; Psalm 94:12; 1 Corinthians 11:32). He is perfectly wise (Job 12:13; Proverbs 3:19; Romans 11:33; Romans 16:27; James 3:17). Trust Him.

Father knows best! Always trust that God's plan is the best plan for your life.

The Righteous Live by Faith

"The righteous shall live by his faith" (Habakkuk 2:4). This verse is quoted three times in the New Testament—Romans 1:17; Galatians 3:11; and Hebrews 10:38.

An enlightened Habakkuk ends his book with a psalm of praise to God (Habakkuk 3:1-5). He celebrated the power of God (3:6-12) in recognition of the purpose of God (3:13-19). Habakkuk came to see that God's plan is always best. He gained confidence in God's sovereign purposes and expressed joy before the Lord. "Yet I will rejoice in the LORD; I will take joy in the God of my salvation" (3:18).

Never forget: God's ways are not our ways. His actions are beyond our finite understanding.

A key lesson Habakkuk learned was that God's ways are not our ways. His actions are often far beyond what we can possibly understand. Elsewhere in Scripture, God affirmed, "For as the heavens are higher than the earth, so are my ways higher than your ways and my thoughts than your thoughts" (Isaiah 55:9). Later the apostle Paul affirmed, "Oh, the depth of the riches and wisdom and knowledge of God! How unsearchable are his judgments and how inscrutable his ways!" (Romans 11:33). The psalmist affirmed to God, "Your thoughts are very deep!" (Psalm 92:5). He reflected, "How precious to me are your thoughts, O God! How vast is the sum of them!" (Psalm 139:17).

Such words cause me to ponder. Can a *creature* possibly understand all the ways of the divine *Creator*? Can a *finite* being possibly understand all the ways of an *infinite* being? Can a *temporal* being possibly understand all the ways of an *eternal* being? I think not. How awesome is our God!

What all this means, practically speaking, is that even when we don't understand what God is doing in our lives—even when we don't understand why He has allowed something painful to happen—we must trust Him and never waver in our faith. As Solomon once put it, "Trust in the LORD with all your heart, and do not lean on your own understanding. In all your ways acknowledge him, and he will make straight your paths" (Proverbs 3:5-6).

> "Only when God hath brought to light all the hidden things of darkness…will it be seen that wise and good were all His ways, that He…governed all things by the wise counsel of His own will."
>
> —John Wesley (1703–1791)

> "God is to be trusted when His providences seem to run contrary to His promises."
>
> —Thomas Watson (1620–1686)

A Thought to Anchor in Your Heart

When life seems unfair, trust in the Lord with all your heart, and do not lean on your own understanding. God will take care of you.

Habakkuk

Zephaniah

Learn it well: unrepentant sin inevitably brings God's judgment.

Timeline

640—Josiah becomes king of Judah; Zephaniah's prophetic ministry begins.

625—Zephaniah writes his short book.

621—Zephaniah's ministry ends.

Cross-References: God's Judgment

Psalm 94:15 • 96:13 • Ecclesiastes 3:17 • 11:9 • 12:14 • Joel 3:2 • Matthew 25:31-46 • 12:36 • Romans 2:1-3,5 • 14:10,13 • Hebrews 9:27 • 2 Peter 3:7 • Revelation 20:12

The book of Zephaniah was written by a prophet of the same name in about 625 BC. He was the great-great-grandson of the godly King Hezekiah. His ministry took place during the reign of King Josiah of Judah (640-609 BC), and his preaching may have been a factor in some of the reform that took place during Josiah's rule.

Zephaniah's message repeated familiar prophetic themes. God would judge the people for not being faithful to the covenant He had established with them. Instead of living the way He had instructed them, the people picked up the habits of the pagan cultures around them. God would not permit this to continue, so judgment was imminent (Zephaniah 1:2-3; 2:2; 3:6-7). Zephaniah continually hammered home the idea that the day of the Lord was approaching (1:7,14-16; 3:8). He affirmed that the fire of God's judgment would have a purifying effect on the nation, melting away their sinful complacency. Yet he also spoke of the blessing that would eventually come in the person of the divine Messiah (3:14-20).

Following are key applicational concepts in Zephaniah:

Don't misunderstand the nature of God. While He is a God of love, He is also a God of holiness who expresses wrath in the face of unrepentant sin.

People love to talk about the love of God today. They don't like to hear about His wrath. Scripture is clear, however, that while God is a God of love, He is also a holy, righteous, and just God who expresses wrath when circumstances call for it. One would have to be blind not to see the massive evidence for God's judgment in the Bible. The book of Zephaniah records rather severe judgments against the unrepentant: "I will utterly sweep away everything..." (1:2); "I will cut off..." (1:3); "I will stretch out my hand against..." (1:4); "I will punish..." (1:8); "I will bring distress..." (1:17); "Woe to you..." (2:5); "I have laid waste..." (3:6). The Old Testament has numerous other examples. God judged the wicked people of Noah's day, sending a flood to destroy them (Genesis 6–8). He judged Sodom and Gomorrah, sending a volcanic catastrophe upon them (Genesis 18–19). In the New Testament we find that judgment falls on the Jews for rejecting Jesus Christ (Matthew 21:43), on Ananias and Sapphira for lying to God (Acts 5), on Herod for his self-exalting pride (Acts 12:21), and on Christians in Corinth who were afflicted with illness in response to their irreverence in connection with the Lord's Supper (1 Corinthians 11:29-32).

Dear Christian, human beings put themselves in peril to ignore this aspect of God. We are simply not free to redefine God's nature (reducing Him to a mere "God of love") according to our own whims.

Continued unrepentant sin is like a judgment magnet. Repentance, by contrast, averts judgment.

While Zephaniah predicted God's impending judgment on the entire world because of sin (Zephaniah 1:2-3), he concentrated his attention on God's judgment against Judah (1:4-18). Judah's religious leaders were now promoting the worship of false pagan deities, and its government officials were engulfed in dishonesty and corruption. The judgment of the day of the Lord was therefore imminent.

Zephaniah warned that there would be massive desolation, unrelenting distress, and terror at every side. Yet, he said, there was still time for repentance—even if only a remnant repents. This would serve to insulate them from God's hand of judgment (Zephaniah 2:3).

I believe this relates to God's affirmation in Jeremiah 18:7-8. "If at any time I

Attributes of God

- Self-existent—Exodus 3:14
- Spirit—John 4:24
- Eternal—Psalm 90:2
- Does not change—Malachi 3:6
- Infinite—Psalm 145:3
- Everywhere-present—Psalm 139:2-12
- All-knowing—Psalm 147:4-5
- All-powerful—Genesis 18:14
- Sovereign—Isaiah 46:10
- Wise—Romans 11:33
- Good—Psalm 34:8
- Love—1 John 4:8
- Full of grace—1 Peter 5:10
- Merciful—2 Corinthians 1:3
- Patient—Nahum 1:3
- Holy—1 Peter 1:15
- Righteous—Psalm 19:9
- Just—Job 34:12

Agricultural Metaphors in Zephaniah

Those judged by God are like

- chaff that blows away in the wind (2:2);
- a tree uprooted (2:4);
- being overrun with weeds (2:9); and
- a desert (2:13).

Zephaniah

declare concerning a nation or a kingdom, that I will pluck up and break down and destroy it, and if that nation, concerning which I have spoken, turns from its evil, I will relent of the disaster that I intended to do to it." So, Zephaniah warns, if Judah repents now—if even only a remnant of Judah repents—judgment can be averted at least for the remnant. Otherwise, judgment is imminent.

Count on it: God will one day bring justice to the earth.

The term "day of the Lord" is used in several senses in Scripture. Old Testament prophets often used the term of an event to be fulfilled in the near future—an imminent judgment. At other times they used the term of a time of judgment in the distant eschatological future—that is, the future tribulation period. In both cases, the day of the Lord is characterized by God actively intervening supernaturally to bring judgment against sin in the world. The day of the Lord is a time when God actively controls and dominates history in a direct way, instead of working through secondary causes.

> "The Judge is before the door: He that cometh will come, and will not tarry: His reward is with Him."
>
> —*George Whitefield (1714–1770)*

It would seem that Zephaniah has both senses in mind in his prophecy. The imminent fulfillment relates to Babylon's invasion of Judah as a punishment against Judah (Zephaniah 1:4-18; 2:3). The future end-times fulfillment relates to God's judgment of the whole earth (1:18; 3:8-9,11,13-17).

As dark a subject as this is, we can take comfort in a much-needed element of justice. After all, as we observe the world today, tremendous evil is being committed. Many of those committing evil feel immune from accountability. Many are committing great evil against Christians in the name of a false god. But a "day of the Lord" is approaching—it will be a day of accountability, a day of judgment, and a day of devastation. Justice will be done.

The Second Coming of Christ

- Glorious—Revelation 19:11-21
- Visible—Acts 1:9-11
- Every eye will see—Revelation 1:7
- Eagerly awaited—Philippians 3:20
- No one knows the hour—Matthew 24:46-50
- Drawing near—James 5:7-8

Even when things on earth seem at their darkest, the prophetic future can give us hope.

God's wrathful hand will ultimately bring about a cleansing of the nations (Zephaniah 3:8-10)—apparently a reference to the future seven-year tribulation period that precedes the second coming of

Zephaniah

Christ (Revelation 4–18). Israel's restoration will follow, with its inhabitants calling upon the name of the Lord (Zephaniah 3:11-13).

The righteous remnant of Israel will be re-gathered. This relates to the land covenant recorded in Deuteronomy 29:1–30:20, which is unconditional. It was promised that, even though Israel would be dispersed worldwide, the Jews would be re-gathered and restored to the land (Isaiah 43:5-7; Jeremiah 16:14-18). This will take place in Christ's 1000-year millennial kingdom, which follows the second coming (Genesis 12:1-3; 15:18-21; 2 Samuel 7:12-13; 22:51). This will bring joy and jubilation to Israel (Zephaniah 3:14-20).

One thing we can learn from all this is that the prophetic revelations in the Bible regarding our glorious future can encourage us when life gets difficult. Biblical prophecy reminds us that this fallen world is not all there is. There's a new world coming (Revelation 21:1-4).

> "I've read the last page of the Bible. It's all going to turn out all right."
>
> —Billy Graham

A Thought to Anchor in Your Heart

Heaven is your ultimate home. Live your life *now* in view of the glory you will experience *then*.

Zephaniah

Haggai

We must never give up in the face of trials, plummeting into apathy. Instead we must renew our commitment to the Lord.

Haggai was written by a prophet of the same name around 520 BC. Aside from the fact that he was a prophet, we know little of the man. His name literally means "festival," perhaps because he was born on the day of a major festival. His book is the second shortest in the Old Testament, so he was definitely a concise writer. He ministered during the reign of King Darius I (522-486 BC), and was probably about 80 years old when he wrote this book.

In 520 BC Haggai addressed his words to the people in Judah and Jerusalem who had returned from exile. He urged them to get their act together, to set their priorities straight, and to rebuild the temple (Haggai 1:1-11). Only then, he said, would God bring true blessing back upon them.

Cross-References: Indifference

Numbers 32:6 • Joshua 18:3 • Judges 5:17,23 • 2 Chronicles 24:5 • Nehemiah 3:5 • Jeremiah 48:10 • Ezekiel 33:31 • Haggai 1:2 • Luke 10:2

The problem was that when the people first returned from exile in 538 BC as a result of King Cyrus's decree, they made a good start in beginning to rebuild the temple, but now apathy had set in and the whole project had stagnated (Ezra 4:4-5). The people were too busy building their own homes to pay much attention to the temple. Haggai was one of the prophets chosen by God to get the people on their feet again and finish the task. Toward this end, Haggai preached a series of short sermonettes.

Following are key applicational concepts in Haggai:

Everybody gets discouraged. Avail yourself of every opportunity to be a people-encourager.

The returned exiles needed encouragement because they had a defeated state of mind. While they were excited to be home again, they were also despondent over the ruination of their city. They were especially despondent over the fact that it was their own unfaithfulness that had brought about the ruination of the city. Haggai sought to help them overcome this defeated state of mind and move on to obedience and service to God.

> "One of the highest human duties is the duty of encouragement...It is easy to discourage others. The world is full of discouragers. We have a Christian duty to encourage one another."
>
> —*William Barclay (1907–1978)*

The rebuilding of the temple was important not only because it was the religious center of Jewish life, but also because it represented the presence of the one true God among the Israelites before a watching pagan world. For the temple not to be rebuilt might give the impression to pagan nations that the true God was no longer interested in Israel, and no longer paying attention to the covenants He had made with His people. The temple was finally rebuilt by 515 BC.

While Scripture is communicated through men, it has divine authority because it ultimately comes from God.

On the one hand, we note that Haggai's little book came by his own hand (Haggai 1:1,3; 2:1,10). On the other hand, the Lord is the actual source of the words—"Thus says the Lord of hosts" (1:2; see also 1:5,7,9,13; 2:4,8,9,11,14,17,23). Haggai was simply a "messenger of the Lord" who "spoke to the people with the Lord's message" (1:13). This means the Word of God is authoritative. Obey it!

We pay a price when we procrastinate on spiritual matters.

Haggai reprimanded the people for procrastinating in building the temple (Haggai 1:2-6). They had built their own houses, but were indifferent about God's house. They were exhorted to begin rebuilding immediately (1:7-8). Haggai said the reason God had not blessed them was because they had forgotten Him (1:9-11). God rewards those who put Him first and seek to do His will. The people promptly resumed building the temple (1:12-15).

> "Fear God and work hard."
>
> —*David Livingstone (1813–1873)*

Verses to Remember

"Work, for I am with you, declares the Lord of hosts... My Spirit remains in your midst."

—*Haggai 2:4-5*

Haggai

Don't stagnate on past glories. Live with a view to building a great future.

When the older generation of Israelites—well familiar with the former glorious temple built by Solomon—saw this smaller, humbler temple, they were perplexed. It seemed unworthy. Haggai responded with a promise from the Lord that this temple's glory would be greater than the former (Haggai 2:4-5,9).

> **Be Fervent**
>
> "Do not be slothful in zeal, be fervent in spirit, serve the Lord."
>
> —Romans 12:11

Future blessing from God hinges on *present* commitment to God.

Haggai reminded the people how contagious evil is (Haggai 2:10-13), and that the people had indeed become contaminated by it (2:14-17). However, restoring God to first place in their lives would bring blessing from then on (2:18-10). Future blessing hinges on present commitment.

Externally going through the motions is not enough. There must also be heart-change.

It was not enough for the people to engage in the physical effort to finish rebuilding the temple (Haggai 1:7-8; 2:4-5). There must first be heart-change, for it was heart-change that would energize external efforts. The people needed to move from a defeated state of mind to a state of obedience and service to God.

> **Seek First God's Kingdom**
>
> "Seek first the kingdom of God and his righteousness, and all these things will be added to you."
>
> —Jesus, Matthew 6:33

Fear of the Lord provides strong motivation to obey Him.

The people "obeyed the voice of the LORD their God, and the words of Haggai the prophet, as the LORD their God had sent him. And the people feared the LORD" (Haggai 1:12). Fear of the Lord and obedience to Him are often found side by side in Scripture. Deuteronomy 10:12 says, "And now, Israel, what does the LORD your God require of you, but to fear the LORD your God, to walk in all his ways, to love him, to serve the LORD your God with all your heart and with all your soul" (see also Ecclesiastes 12:13; Proverbs 3:7; Acts 10:35). Obedience to God is a natural outgrowth of having a reverent attitude toward Him.

Haggai

Bible prophecy can put wind in your spiritual sails.

To instill a hope in the people, Haggai informed them that one day in the future, the heavens will be shaken (Haggai 2:20-21), evil people will be overthrown (2:22), and the Messiah will be exalted (2:23). Zerubbabel, a leader among the people, was portrayed as a symbol of the Messiah who is coming. This future hope motivated righteousness among Haggai's contemporaries. The same is true of God's people today. Titus 2:12-13 exhorts believers to "renounce ungodliness and worldly passions, and to live self-controlled, upright, and godly lives in the present age, waiting for our blessed hope, the appearing of the glory of our great God and Savior Jesus Christ." The prophetic future gives hope to those living in the present.

> "Live with the realities of the present, anticipate the future with hope, and let go of past disappointments."
>
> —*Charles Swindoll*

It is good to review your priorities from time to time.

Haggai reminded the people that while they busied themselves with their own houses, the house of God—the temple—was lying in ruins. The people cared more about themselves than they cared for God. This showed that their priorities were out of balance. Haggai put the people back on track, keeping God and His temple the top priority (Haggai 1:9-11). Haggai exhorts, "Consider your ways" (1:5,7). Lesson learned! Let us consider *our* ways.

A Thought to Anchor in Your Heart

Make every effort to keep your priorities straight on a daily basis.

Haggai

Zechariah

A lack of hope leads to despair.
With hope, however, hearts can be revived and
restoration to the Lord can take place.

Timeline

538—The people begin returning to their homeland from exile.

536—Construction of the temple begins.

530—Work on the temple halts.

520—Zechariah begins his prophetic ministry.

520—Work on the temple resumes.

520–518—The book of Zechariah is written.

515—The temple is completed.

"Disappointments are inevitable; discouragement is a choice."

—*Charles Stanley*

The book of Zechariah was written by the prophet and priest Zechariah between 520 and 518 BC. His name means "the Lord remembers," and is appropriate because a theme that runs through his message is that God will bring blessing to the people because He remembers the covenant He made with Abraham.

Zechariah was born in Babylon in exile. He and his father, Iddo, were among the first exiles to return to Jerusalem following the exile. Like his contemporary Haggai, Zechariah was a prophet chosen by God to motivate the Jews to finish the task of rebuilding the temple following the exile.

The problem was that when the people first returned from exile in 538 BC, they made a good start in rebuilding the temple, but now apathy had set in and the whole project had stagnated (Ezra 4:4-5). The people were too busy building their own homes to pay much attention to the temple. Zechariah was one of the prophets chosen by God to get the people on their feet again and finish the task.

The people needed encouragement because they had a defeated state of mind. While they were excited to be home again, they were also despondent over the ruination of their city. They were especially despondent over the fact that it was their own unfaithfulness that had brought this ruination. Zechariah, along with Haggai, sought to motivate the people to finish the temple so worship could begin again.

Instead of seeking to motivate the people by rebuking them, Zechariah's approach was to demonstrate the importance of the temple (Zechariah 1–8).

Rebuilding the temple was important not only because it was the religious center of Jewish life, but also because it represented the presence of the one true God among the Israelites before a watching pagan world. For the temple *not* to be rebuilt might give the impression to pagan nations that the true God was no longer interested in Israel, and no longer paying attention to the covenants He had made with His people.

A number of notable messianic prophecies are in the book of Zechariah. For example, Zechariah prophesied that Christ would be betrayed for a mere 30 pieces of silver (Zechariah 11:12-13), that He would be pierced on a cross (12:10), and that He would come again in glory (14:4). As such, Zechariah is an important book for Christological studies in the Old Testament.

> **Cross-References: Key Messianic Prophecies**
> Genesis 12:2 • 2 Samuel 7:12-16 • Isaiah 7:14 • Micah 5:2 • Psalm 22:1 • 16:10 • 110:1 • Zechariah 11:12 • Isaiah 53:5

Following are key applicational concepts in Zechariah:

God has a sovereign plan for His people. We must come to view the unfolding of history as involving providential actions of God on behalf of His people.

In the first part of his book, Zechariah spoke to his people through a series of eight visions—some communicating comfort, others speaking of judgment: (1) God will one day restore and bless His people (Zechariah 1:1-17); (2) The nations that have aligned against Israel will be judged (1:18-21); (3) God will protect Jerusalem (2:1-13); (4) Israel will be restored and redeemed by the coming Messiah (3:1-10); (5) The renewed light of Israel will be rooted in the work of the Holy Spirit (4:1-14); (6) individual sin will be judged (5:1-4); (7) National sin will be removed (5:5-11); and (8) God's judgment will fall upon the nations (6:1-8).

A common emphasis in Scripture is that God is sovereign over the affairs of humanity. So God's sovereign providential actions among His people in Old Testament times should not surprise us. But God is also sovereign over the affairs of earth in our time too. God asserts, "My counsel shall stand, and I will accomplish all my purpose" (Isaiah 46:10). God assures us, "As I have planned, so shall it be, and as I have purposed, so shall it stand" (Isaiah 14:24). Proverbs 16:9 tells us, "The heart of man plans his way, but the LORD establishes his steps." Proverbs 19:21 says, "Many are the plans in the mind of a man, but it is the purpose of the LORD that will stand." Proverbs 21:1 asserts, "The king's heart is a stream of water in the hand of the LORD; he turns it wherever he will." God is the one

Zechariah

"who works all things according to the counsel of his will" (Ephesians 1:11). In short, God providentially controls every particular of the universe. How awesome is our God!

God invites those who are estranged to return to Him.

God affirms, "Return to me, says the LORD of hosts, and I will return to you" (Zechariah 1:3). This word from God is as inviting to us today as it was when God spoke it to Zechariah's people. The verse brings to mind James 4:8: "Draw near to God, and he will draw near to you." My friend, do you feel distant from God? Do you feel that perhaps you've somehow wandered from His side? He invites you to act: *Return to Me. Draw near to Me. All will be well.*

It is good for us to care about Israel—just as God does.

Zechariah warned of those who would turn on Israel, "He who touches you touches the apple of his eye" (Zechariah 2:8). This brings to mind God's words in the Abrahamic covenant: "I will bless those who bless you, and him who dishonors you I will curse" (Genesis 12:3). This is one reason I hope America stays committed to Israel!

God does not like empty ritualism. He wants people to authentically relate to Him and live as He wills them to live.

"He has told you, O man, what is good; and what does the LORD require of you but to do justice, and to love kindness, and to walk humbly with your God."

—*Micah 6:8*

God does not like it when people merely go through the motions with Him, not really pouring their heart into a relationship with Him (Zechariah 7:4-7). Rather, God desires authentic believers who show their commitment to Him not only in how they relate to Him, but in how they relate to others. "Thus says the LORD of hosts, Render true judgments, show kindness and mercy to one another, do not oppress the widow, the fatherless, the sojourner, or the poor, and let none of you devise evil against another in your heart" (7:9-10).

This reminds us of James 1:22: "Be doers of the word, and not hearers only, deceiving yourselves." James goes on to say, "Religion that is pure and undefiled

Zechariah

before God, the Father, is this: to visit orphans and widows in their affliction, and to keep oneself unstained from the world" (1:27). James was strongly rooted in Old Testament Scripture.

As for you and me—let's make sure we are consistent doers of the word!

God's strength more than makes up for human weakness.

God's people were disheartened because their city was a mess and their temple was not yet rebuilt. It all seemed overwhelming to them. They couldn't cope with what faced them in their own strength. But God's word came to them: "Not by might, nor by power, but by my Spirit, says the LORD of hosts" (Zechariah 4:6). God in His unfathomable power helps us! The apostle Paul recognized this, for the Lord said to him, "My grace is sufficient for you, for my power is made perfect in weakness" (2 Corinthians 12:9). Paul could thus boldly say, "I can do all things through him who strengthens me" (Philippians 4:13). So, dear Christian, don't get discouraged. Be empowered by the Lord this minute.

> **A Verse to Remember**
> "Not by might, nor by power, but by my Spirit, says the LORD of hosts."
>
> —*Zechariah 4:6*

Unplug your ears and listen to God's warnings—or else!

Jeremiah's people ignored what God had to say through the prophets. "They refused to pay attention and turned a stubborn shoulder and stopped their ears that they might not hear. They made their hearts diamond-hard lest they should hear the law and the words that the LORD of hosts had sent by his Spirit through the former prophets. Therefore great anger came from the LORD of hosts" (Zechariah 7:11-12).

> "Labor to grow better under all your afflictions, lest your afflictions grow worse."
>
> —*John Owen (1616–1683)*

When will we learn that our God is a God who judges sin—including sin among His own people? When David sinned with Bathsheba, God disciplined him severely (Psalm 32; 51). When the Corinthians partook of the Lord's Supper in an unworthy manner, many of them got sick and some died (1 Corinthians 11:30-31). When Ananias and Sapphira lied to the Holy Spirit by withholding some of the monetary proceeds from a land sale, they lost their lives (Acts 5:1-11). My advice: Make turning from sin an ongoing lifestyle.

Zechariah

Judgment was painful for Israel. But God promised them a re-gathering, restoration, and blessing. You and I will get to see it happen in the prophetic future!

God will yet re-gather, restore, and bless Israel (Zechariah 8:1-7). The complete fulfillment of these verses awaits the establishment of Christ's millennial kingdom following His second coming. Finally the Jewish people will be on the receiving end of all the land promises made to them in the Abrahamic covenant (Genesis 15:12-21; 17:1-14) and the throne promises made in the Davidic covenant (2 Samuel 7:13; 23:5). God promises them, "They shall be my people, and I will be their God, in faithfulness and in righteousness" (Zechariah 8:8). How awesome it will be.

Glorious good news: Jesus was crucified for your sins so you could be saved.

Zechariah 12:10 tells us Jesus was "pierced"—a word that connotes *piercing to death*. Other Bible passages tell us the purpose of that piercing. The New Testament tells us Jesus was crucified on the cross (Matthew 20:19; 21:39; 23:34; 26:2; 27:22,26,35), thereby taking our sins upon Himself so we could be saved.

Paul affirms in 2 Corinthians 5:21, "For our sake he made him to be sin who knew no sin, so that in him we might become the righteousness of God." There has been a great exchange. Jesus took upon Himself what was ours (*our sin*) so that He could give us what was His (*eternal life*). What a Savior we have in Jesus!

We have a wonderful, divine Shepherd who seeks to watch after us as His sheep.

Zechariah 11:1-17 portrays God as bringing judgment upon the wicked shepherds of the people. We are told, "Their own shepherds have no pity on them" (11:5). God then said, "I became the shepherd of the flock doomed to be slaughtered by the sheep traders" (11:7).

The shepherd motif is rich in meaning in Old Testament Scripture (see, especially, Psalm 23). Broadly speaking, Scripture indicates that the shepherd is simultaneously a leader and a companion to his sheep. The shepherd is typically a strong man capable of defending his flock against wild beasts (1 Samuel 17:34-36; Matthew 10:16; Acts 20:29). He is also gentle with his flock, knowing

"The Twenty-third Psalm is the nightingale of the psalms. It is small, of a homely feather, singing shyly out of obscurity; but it has filled the air of the whole world with melodious joy."

—*Henry Ward Beecher (1813–1887)*

Zechariah

their condition (Proverbs 27:23), bearing them in his arms (Isaiah 40:11), adapting himself to their needs (Genesis 33:13-14), cherishing each and every one of them "like a daughter to him" (2 Samuel 12:3). The shepherd was known for seeking out his lost sheep (Ezekiel 34:12) and for rescuing those that were attacked (Amos 3:12). David exulted, "The LORD is my shepherd" (Psalm 23:1).

In view of all this, the shepherd motif became an appropriate way of describing the relationship Jesus Christ has with His people. Indeed, in the New Testament, Jesus is called the Good Shepherd (John 10:1-10), the Great Shepherd (Hebrews 13:20), and the Chief Shepherd (1 Peter 5:4). In contrast to the wicked shepherds of Jeremiah's day, Jesus truly takes care of His sheep.

The Lord Jesus—the divine Messiah—will rescue the Jewish people following their conversion late in the future tribulation period.

Zechariah closes His book with two oracles related to the future Messiah: (1) The Messiah would be rejected in His first coming, being betrayed for a mere 30 pieces of silver (Zechariah 11:13). (2) Just before the second coming, the Jews will be under attack, and they will cry out to the Messiah for deliverance (12). Israel will then be redeemed (13), and the King (Jesus the Messiah) will come to Jerusalem (the Mount of Olives), after which He will judge the nations and reign over the earth (14).

As we compare these verses with other prophetic Bible verses, the scenario appears to be dramatic. It would appear that Armageddon—at the end of the tribulation period—will be the historical context in which Israel will finally become converted (Zechariah 12:2–13:1). The restoration of Israel will include the confession of Israel's national sin (Leviticus 26:40-42; Jeremiah 3:11-18; Hosea 5:15), following which Israel will be saved, thereby fulfilling Paul's prophecy in Romans 11:25-27. In dire threat at Armageddon, with the forces of the antichrist moving against them, Israel will plead for their newly found Messiah to return and deliver them (they will "mourn for him, as one mourns for an only son"—Zechariah 12:10 [NLT]; Matthew 23:37-39; see also Isaiah 53:1-9), at which point their deliverance will surely come (Romans 10:13). Israel's leaders will have finally realized the reason the tribulation has

The Tribulation Period

- There will be a definite period of tribulation at the end of the age—Matthew 24:29-35
- It will be the worst tribulation in history—Matthew 24:21
- Messiah-rejecting Israel will be judged—Jeremiah 30:7; Daniel 12:1-4
- Sinful nations will be judged—Isaiah 26:21
- It will be seven years long—Daniel 9:24,27
- People will prefer death—Revelation 6:16

Zechariah

fallen on them—perhaps due to the Holy Spirit's enlightenment of their under-standing of Scripture, or the testimony of the 144,000 Jewish evangelists, or per-haps the testimony of the two prophetic witnesses.

Is it not awesome to ponder how God can tell us what lies in the future? As God Himself put it in Isaiah 46:9-10, "I am God, and there is no other; I am God, and there is none like me, declaring the end from the beginning and from ancient times things not yet done, saying, 'My counsel shall stand, and I will accomplish all my purpose.'" Glorious!

A Thought to Anchor in Your Heart

Never forget: God's strength is made perfect in human weakness. God calls you to live not by your might but by His Spirit.

Malachi

Spiritual apathy and malaise should not even be named among God's people. We should instead renew commitment to God and be blessed.

The book of Malachi was written by a prophet of the same name between 433 and 400 BC. The word Malachi means "my messenger" or "the Lord's messenger"—a good name for a prophet of God. His is the last book in the Old Testament.

Malachi's ministry took place following the rebuilding of the temple (515 BC). The people had returned to their homeland from exile, but this had not translated into a desire to walk closely with God. They practiced empty rituals without attaching any real meaning to them.

Malachi begins his book by assuring his people of God's constant and unchanging care and compassion for them (Malachi 1:1-5). This was necessary because the people were disillusioned. They were complacent and had lost national pride. Poverty was widespread; there was drought, famine, and ruined crops; and the people had been brutalized by foreign powers. Past promises of restoration had not yet come to pass, and so the people were discouraged. They were even wondering whether the prophets of the past had gotten things right. They were wondering if God cared for them anymore. Spiritual lethargy was at an all-time high. God thus assured them through Malachi that, indeed, He cared about them immensely.

To compound the problem, however, the people in their discouragement were not living as they should before a holy God. They were living in deep sin. There was social corruption, temple worship was a sham, and priests were ignoring their duties (Malachi 1:6–2:16). Malachi therefore uttered not only words of God's love, but words of stern warning. He spoke forceful and indicting words designed to move the people to faithfulness to God. If they continued to live

Timeline

536— Rebuilding of the temple begins.

530— Work on the temple halts.

520— Rebuilding of the temple resumes.

515— Rebuilding of the temple is completed.

Sometime after 515— Malachi's people fall into spiritual apathy and malaise.

433–400— Malachi writes his short book.

like they were, more judgment was surely on the horizon. Repentance is the only remedy that can avert judgment.

Following are key applicational concepts in Malachi:

Never doubt God's love—even when your life seems to be going haywire.

God's Unfathomable Love

Endures forever—
1 Chronicles 16:34
Earth is full of—Psalm 33:5
Abounding—Psalm 86:5
Is unfailing—Isaiah 54:10
Everlasting—Jeremiah 31:3
God so loved the world—John 3:16
Nothing can separate us—Romans 8:38-39
Keep yourself in God's love—Jude 21

The Israelites were so encumbered by difficulties that they were blind to God's love for them. God therefore reminded the people of His special, covenant love for them. "'I have loved you,' says the LORD" (Malachi 1:2, see also verses 3-5). God's love never ends.

God's love for Israel is a common theme in the Old Testament. Recall God's tender words in Hosea 11:1: "When Israel was a child, I loved him." In Isaiah 43:4 God said to Israel, "You are precious in my eyes, and honored, and I love you." God is the one "showing steadfast love to thousands of those who love me and keep my commandments" (Deuteronomy 5:10). In fact, it is because of God's great love for His people that their apathy and malaise were so grievous to Him.

In New Testament times, God's love for *all* people came into view, as is evident in John 3:16: "For God so loved the world, that he gave his only Son, that whoever believes in him should not perish but have eternal life." Romans 5:8 affirms, "God shows his love for us in that while we were still sinners, Christ died for us."

So rejoice that *you are the special object of God's love*. Even when your life seems tough, when things are going wrong, when it seems that no one else even likes you, remember that God loves you and His love will never wane. Say it right now: "God loves me."

God withholds blessing from those living in unrepentant sin.

Despite God's love, the people remained unfaithful to God, engaging in constant sin. The priests showed no respect for God, using diseased animals for sacrifices. The people were indifferent toward God's covenant (Malachi 1:6–2:9). The men of the nation were being faithless and divorcing their wives so they could marry foreign women (2:10-16). Adding insult to injury, the people robbed God by ceasing to bring tithes to Him.

Malachi thus indicated that if the people would only repent, God was ready to pour out showers of blessing upon them (Malachi 3:7-12). In their arrogance, however, the people remained in sin, thereby robbing themselves of His blessing (3:13-15).

One cannot help but notice that the people had apparently not learned any spiritual lessons from their recent exile. They *continued* to ignore God's prophets. They *continued* to callously disobey God's law. God's blessing was therefore withheld.

My friend, I fear that much of the modern church has become insensitive to the things of God and has become complacent, engaging in moral behavior not unlike that of unsaved people. Is it any surprise, then, that so many people today wonder where God's blessing is? Don't miss this fact: there is a cause-and-effect relationship in Scripture between turning from sin and experiencing God's blessing in life. One leads to the other. No repentance. No blessing. My advice: Repent and be blessed!

How you live matters. A judgment is coming.

Malachi prophesied that in a future day of judgment, God would remember the righteous remnant, sparing them just as a father spares his son (Malachi 3:16-18). At the coming of the Messiah, the wicked would be condemned (4:1). This judgment of the wicked will bring consolation to the righteous (4:2).

You and I as Christians will one day stand before the judgment seat of Christ (Romans 14:8-10; 1 Corinthians 3:11-15; 9:24-27). At that time each believer's life will be examined in regard to deeds done while in the body. Personal motives and intents will also be weighed. This judgment doesn't have anything to do with whether you and I as Christians will remain saved. Rather, it relates to the reception or loss of rewards, based on how we lived our lives after we became Christians. Faithful living yields rewards. Unfaithful living leads to a loss of rewards. My advice: Take the long look! Live your life in view of this future judgment.

Blessing and Obedience

Listen carefully—Exodus 15:26
Obey me—Exodus 19:5
Keep my laws—Leviticus 26:3
Obey commands—Deuteronomy 4:40
Careful to obey—Deuteronomy 12:28
Blessing if you obey—Deuteronomy 15:5-6
Only then will you succeed—Joshua 1:8

Significant Judgments

- Judgment of the nations (Matthew 25:31-46)
- Judgment seat of Christ (2 Corinthians 5:10)
- Great white throne judgment (Revelation 20:11-15)

Malachi

Get your act together, for the divine Messiah is coming soon.

Malachi closes his short book with a command for the people to remain obedient to God's law. Connecting the Old Testament to the New Testament, he included a prediction of a forerunner who would prepare the way for the coming Messiah (Malachi 4:5-6). This would be fulfilled in the ministry of John the Baptist preparing the way for the coming of Jesus Christ (Matthew 3:1; 11:14).

At the first coming Jesus came as the Lamb of God (John 1:29), but at the second coming He will come as the King of kings and Lord of lords (Revelation 19:11-21). At the first coming He came in humility, but at the second coming He will come in glory. At the first coming He rode meekly on a donkey, but at the second coming He will ride in exaltation on a white horse. Just as people in Old Testament times looked forward to Christ's first coming, so we today look forward to His second coming. Live your life accordingly!

Significant Messianic Prophecies

- Conceived of a virgin (Isaiah 7:14)
- Born in Bethlehem (Micah 5:2)
- Suffered for our sins (Isaiah 53)
- Pierced in His side (Zechariah 12:10)
- Dying about AD 33 (Daniel 9:24-25)
- Resurrected (Psalm 2; 16)

A Thought to Anchor in Your Heart

Live your life as though the Lord might come today.

Malachi

Matthew, Mark, Luke, and John—
Part 1

Jesus, the messianic King, teaches us what we need to know about rightly relating to God, rightly relating to each other, and how to live a God-honoring life.

The Gospels are selective accounts of the life of Jesus that communicate His identity and His message. That they are selective seems clear from statements we find in the Gospels themselves (Luke 1:1-4; John 20:30; 21:25). One way they are selective is that they focus primarily on Jesus's three-year ministry, with the exception of a short discussion of His birth and infancy (Matthew 1–2; Luke 1–2). Since God the Holy Spirit inspired these Gospels (2 Timothy 3:16; 2 Peter 1:21), we can assume they contain everything God wanted us to know about the words and works of Jesus.

The four Gospel writers were each seeking to reach a different audience. They therefore included different emphases:

Timeline
6 BC—Jesus is born.

6 BC–7 AD—Jesus's infancy through boyhood years.

8–26—Jesus's adolescence and early manhood.

26–27—Jesus is baptized by John the Baptist.

27—Jesus begins His ministry.

30—Jesus is crucified and resurrects from the dead.

50–60—Matthew writes his Gospel.

55—Mark writes his Gospel.

60—Luke writes his Gospel.

85–90—John writes his Gospel.

- Matthew wrote his Gospel between AD 50 and 60 to prove to Jews that Jesus was the promised Jewish Messiah. It contains about 130 Old Testament citations or allusions, more than any other Gospel (for example, 2:17-18; 4:13-15; 13:35; 21:4-5; 27:9-10).

- Mark wrote his Gospel in AD 55, and he had no such Jewish motivation. He sought to portray Jesus in action rather than as a teacher.

He targeted Gentile readers, and therefore went to great lengths in explaining Jewish customs. About one-third of Mark's Gospel focuses on the last week of Jesus's life on earth.

- Luke wrote his Gospel in AD 60, and stressed the wonderful blessings of salvation for all people. He strongly emphasized that God's grace is for the undeserving. Luke—a well-educated and cultured man—wrote his Gospel based upon reliable, firsthand sources (Luke 1:1-4). And even as a medical doctor, he expressed unflinching belief in Jesus's many miracles (4:38-40; 5:15-25; 6:17-19; 7:11-15) as well as His virgin birth (1:35).

- John wrote his Gospel between AD 85 and 90, and focused heavily on the identity of Jesus, thoroughly demonstrating His divine origin and deity. John demonstrated that Jesus has the attributes of deity, including omniscience (John 4:29), omnipresence (14:23), and preexistence (1:1; 8:58; 17:5). This Gospel is evangelistic, seeking to persuade people to trust in Christ for salvation (20:31). The word "believe" occurs almost a hundred times in this Gospel.

In all four Gospels, it is clear that the very heart of Jesus's teaching is the kingdom of God. This refers to God's reign as King over all the earth—even in the hearts of people today. The kingdom of God arrived in New Testament times because the King (Jesus) had arrived. The kingdom was present because the King was present (Matthew 5:3; 8:12; 12:28; 19:24; 21:31; 21:43; 25:34; Luke 12:32; John 3:3,5; 18:36; Romans 14:17; Colossians 1:13; James 2:5; 2 Peter 1:11; Revelation 12:10). There is also a future aspect of the kingdom, involving a 1000-year reign of Christ on earth following His second coming (Revelation 20:1-6).

> **Cross-References:**
> **Life Is in Jesus**
> John 3:15-16 • 4:10-14 • 5:21-26,39-40 • 6:27-58 • 7:37-38 • 8:12 • 10:10,27-28 • 14:6

> **Cross-References:**
> **Jesus Is the Light**
> John 1:4,9 • 8:12 • 9:5 • 12:35,46 • 1 John 1:5 • 2:8 • Revelation 1:16

Following are key applicational concepts in the four Gospels.

Jesus—the object of our faith—is eternal deity. You can therefore trust Him with everything.

Jesus is God. He is the Creator. He is the light of all humanity. And in Him is life. These are themes we see repeated throughout John's Gospel. Jesus, as the object of our faith, is truly worthy of our trust and allegiance (John 1:1-5).

Jesus's name means "Yahweh saves." He came into the world to save you.

The name Jesus means "Yahweh saves" or "Yahweh is salvation" (Matthew 1:21). This name is the counterpart of the Old Testament name, "Joshua." Just as Joshua in the Old Testament led Israel out of the wilderness experience into a new land and a new life, so Jesus leads people out of the wilderness experience of sin into a new sphere of salvation and the abundant life. He came into the world to save you. Rejoice!

Jesus is Immanuel—meaning "God with us." Jesus is with us no matter where we go.

Jesus is Immanuel, which means "God with us" (Matthew 1:23). Truly, Jesus was "God with us" in the fullest possible sense. He is the everlasting God who stepped out of eternity and into time (through the incarnation) to redeem humanity. Even today, Jesus is "God with us," for He is always spiritually present with us and among us (28:20).

> **Cross-References: Jesus Is God**
> John 8:58 • 20:28 • Revelation 1:8 • 22:13,16 • Isaiah 9:6 • Hebrews 1:8 • Mark 2:5-12 • Colossians 2:9 • Titus 2:13 • Philippians 2:6 • Matthew 1:23

Don't be surprised if you encounter people with opposite views of Jesus. Some love Him; others hate Him.

In Nazareth, the babe Jesus was visited by magi from the east. They followed a "star" to His house. When they beheld Jesus, they worshiped Him, presenting Him with gifts of gold, frankincense, and myrrh. These were gifts typically given to a king in biblical times (Matthew 2:1-12).

Herod, meanwhile, was threatened with the possible prospect of a challenging king. He engaged in a failed plot to murder Jesus (Matthew 2:13-23). There were many collateral casualties in this Satan-driven plot (Revelation 12:4).

Today it is much the same. Some people love Jesus and worship Him. Others abhor Him. Some people are simply indifferent to Him. How sad!

Repentance isn't an act of mere lip service. It needs to be proven by actions.

John the Baptist warned the Pharisees and Sadducees, "Bear fruit in keeping with repentance" (Matthew 3:8). This reminds us of how the apostle Paul urged that people "should repent and turn to God,

> "To do so no more is the truest repentance."
>
> —Martin Luther (1483–1546)

performing deeds in keeping with their repentance" (Acts 26:20). My friend, repentance is not an act of mere lip service. It requires real action!

Beware: the devil will seek to tempt you and bring you down.

Jesus Himself experienced Satan's temptations. The devil waited 40 days, until Jesus was at His weakest from hunger. But Jesus defeated the devil via the Word of God (Matthew 4:1-17; Luke 4:1-15). Because Jesus went through temptation, He is able to help us in our temptations (Hebrews 2:17-18; 4:15). We must also beware of the devil's schemes (2 Corinthians 2:11), resist his efforts (James 4:7; 1 Peter 5:8), and keep on the armor of God (Ephesians 6:10-20).

> "Lies and false reports are among Satan's choicest weapons."
>
> —J. C. Ryle (1816–1900)

Resisting Temptation

- Don't let evil overcome you (Romans 12:21).
- Don't let sin control you (Romans 6:12).
- Don't lose your secure footing (2 Peter 3:17).
- God will help you (1 Corinthians 10:13).

Cross-References: Signs

Matthew 12:38 • 16:1 • 24:3 • 27:42 • Mark 8:11 • 15:32,36 • Luke 11:16,29 • 21:7 • 23:8 • John 2:18 • 6:30 • 20:25

Don't limit the Lord by your human expectations about what He can or cannot do. He is a miracle-worker.

Scripture often refers to the miracles of Jesus as "signs" (John 4:54; 6:14; 9:16). These signs were strategically performed by Jesus to signify His true identity and glory as the divine Messiah.

Thirty-five separate miracles performed by Christ are recorded in the Gospels. Of these, Matthew mentioned 20; Mark, 18; Luke, 20; and John, 7. But these are only a selection from among many miracles He did (Matthew 4:23-24; 11:4-5; 21:14). Dear Christian, don't limit the Lord by your human expectations about what He can or cannot do. He's God. He can do anything. Trust Him with your problems.

God loves you so much it hurts Him. Don't ever doubt it.

Cross-References: God's Love

Romans 5:5,8 • 8:32,39 • 2 Corinthians 13:14 • Ephesians 2:4-5 • 2 Thessalonians 2:16 • Titus 3:4 • Hebrews 12:6 • 1 John 3:1 • 4:9,16,19

Salvation is a free gift from God. But it cost God everything to pay for that free gift—the death of His own beloved Son. God loves you so much it literally hurts Him: "God so loved the world, that he gave his only Son, that whoever believes in him should not perish but have eternal life" (John 3:16). "God shows his love for us in that while we were still sinners, Christ died for us" (Romans 5:8).

Jesus—and not your ego—needs to reign on the throne of your heart. He must increase. You must decrease.

John the Baptist was a humble man. His humility caused him to see that he had no intrinsic greatness, but rather his ministry was given to him by heaven. John's entire purpose was to point people to Jesus, which necessitated pointing away from himself. He even verbalized that Jesus must *increase* while he must *decrease* (John 3:22-36). My friend, like John the Baptist, you and I ought to be clothed with humility (Colossians 3:12; 1 Peter 5:5-6).

> **A Verse to Remember**
> "Seek first the kingdom of God and his righteousness, and all these things will be added to you."
>
> *—Matthew 6:33*

Demons will seek to attack you. Fear not— Jesus has authority over them.

Jesus did not teach like the teachers the people were accustomed to—the Jewish leaders. He taught as one who had intrinsic authority. He promptly proved His authority by commanding a spirit to come out of a man (Mark 1:21-28; Luke 4:31-37). Do you want to make the demons wary of getting too close to you? Stay close to Jesus!

> **Cross-References: Jesus's Authority**
> Mark 1:27 • 5:20 • 6:2 • 7:37 • 10:24-32 • 11:18 • 15:5

Jesus invites you to follow Him day by day, moment by moment.

Jesus did not call the religious elite to follow Him. Rather, He called people like fishermen and a tax collector to follow Him.

As Jesus sat at a table with tax collectors and sinners, the religious elite—the Pharisees—snubbed their noses at Him. Jesus was fellowshipping with what they considered to be the "lower class," the dregs of society (Matthew 9:9-13; Mark 2:13-17; Luke 5:27-32).

My friend, I don't ever want to be a part of the "religious elite." I just want to follow Jesus. Staying close to Jesus is where all the blessing is.

If you're down on yourself because of sin, you need a spiritual physician named Jesus.

> "The recognition of sin is the beginning of salvation."
>
> *—Martin Luther (1483–1546)*

Jesus said, "Those who are well have no need of a physician, but those who are sick...I came not to call the righteous, but sinners" (Matthew 9:12-13). By using the word "righteous," Jesus was not referring to those who were actually righteous in God's sight, but rather to those who were righteous in their own esteem, such as the scribes and Pharisees (Luke 16:14-15). Jesus came to minister to people who humbly acknowledged that they were sinners and needed a Savior. Jesus had no ministry to the self-righteous except to announce their condemnation before God.

I don't know about you, but I'd rather admit I'm an ailing patient (diseased by sin) in need of the divine doctor (Jesus) than pretend that I have no debilitating sin disease (as did the Pharisees). There is spiritual healing in Jesus, our Great Physician!

Jesus teaches the path to true happiness and blessing. The question is, will you follow this path?

> "God has charged himself with full responsibility for our eternal happiness and stands ready to take over the management of our lives."
>
> —A. W. Tozer (1897–1963)

The word "beatitudes" comes from the Latin word, *beatus*, meaning "blessed." The word is an appropriate one to describe the eight blessings Jesus pronounces at the beginning of the Sermon on the Mount in Matthew 5:1-12, each beginning with "Blessed are..."

The word "blessed" literally means "happy," "fortunate," or "blissful." Blessing involves a divinely bestowed sense of well-being, which constitutes a little foretaste of heaven itself. In the beatitudes, Jesus depicts the means of a person attaining a divinely bestowed sense of well-being in daily life. True happiness is found in following Jesus's wise words.

> "We were made to be prisms refracting the light of God's glory into all of life."
>
> —John Piper

Don't isolate yourself from the society around you. Influence it for Christ!

Christians are called to be the salt and the light of the world (Matthew 5:13-16). Though it may be politically incorrect, Christians must openly and proactively stand for Christ and Christian values in a secularized society.

> "Any unmortified desire which a man allows in will effectually drive and keep Christ out of the heart."
>
> —Charles Wesley (1707–1788)

Do whatever you need to do to stop lust from intruding upon your mind.

In Matthew 5:29 Jesus said, "If your right eye causes you to sin, tear it out and throw it away. For it is better that you lose one of your members than that your whole body be thrown into hell" (see also Matthew 18:8-9 and Mark 9:43-48). I do not think Jesus is actually teaching self-mutilation, for even a blind man can lust, and someone with no hands can yearn to steal. (Remember, sin begins in the heart—Jeremiah 17:9.)

Many scholars believe Jesus is using a hyperbole in this verse. A hyperbole is a figure of speech that purposefully exaggerates to make a powerful point. In the present case, the hyperbole is used to emphasize the need for drastic action in dealing with sin. To keep from offending God by sin, radical changes are often necessary.

Christians should so consistently tell the truth that no one ever doubts their word.

In Bible times oaths were so common that people assumed when one did not take an oath that he or she might be lying. To counter this, Jesus said Christians should have absolutely no duplicity in their words. Let your yes be yes and your no be no (Matthew 5:33-37).

As hard as it is to do, we are called to love those who are unlovable in our midst.

The Jewish leaders taught that we should love those near and dear to us (Leviticus 19:18), but hate our enemies. Jesus refuted this idea, instructing His followers to love even their enemies (Matthew 5:43-48; Luke 6:27-36; see also Luke 23:34; Acts 7:60; Galatians 5:22-23). After all, God the Father loves all people, and we as Christians are to take on the family likeness, imitating God in our love for all people (Matthew 5:48). This means you and I are called to love the unlovable. It might not be easy, but we imitate Christ when we do it.

Don't be earth-focused. Be heaven-focused.

We ought to have a "top-down" perspective, seeking to earn heavenly rewards instead of earthly rewards that are temporal and will pass away. We must live with eternity's values in mind (Matthew 6:19-21).

> "I value all things only by the price they shall gain in eternity."
> —John Wesley (1703–1791)

Life is fragile. Handle with prayer.

The Greek tenses in Matthew 7:7-8 communicate the idea, "*Keep on* asking and it will be given; *keep on* seeking and you will find; *keep on* knocking and the door will be opened." Don't give up on prayer! Keep at it, 24/7. Your life will be much better for it.

> "Prayer will make a man cease from sin, or sin will entice a man to cease from prayer."
> —John Bunyan (1628–1688)

Treat others with the same respect and consideration you appreciate receiving.

Jesus provides a guiding principle of life: do unto others as you would have them do unto you (Matthew 7:12). No matter where you are, no matter the time of day, no matter your circumstances—follow this Golden Rule.

Your wisest course of action is to build your life on Christ's words.

Building our lives on Christ's words (Matthew 7:24-27; Luke 6:46-49) means we *hear* His words, *understand* His words, and then choose to *obey* His words (James 1:22-25). We render complete obedience, not partial obedience.

A Thought to Anchor in Your Heart

Never forget: a life built upon the words of Jesus Christ is a life of blessing, peace, and spiritual vitality.

Matthew, Mark, Luke, and John—
Part 2

Jesus, the messianic King, teaches us what we need to know about rightly relating to God, rightly relating to each other, and how to live a God-honoring life.

In the previous chapter we explored some of the initial teachings of Jesus in His early ministry. As His ministry broadened, He provided many more important teachings.

Following are key applicational concepts in the four Gospels:

People will either respond to God's *light* or His *heat*. A lack of repentance brings judgment.

Jesus pronounced woes against unrepentant cities where He had performed mighty miracles (Matthew 11:20-24). When people are given good reason to believe, and yet remain in unbelief, judgment becomes imminent. The wisest policy is to respond immediately to God's light.

Jesus is our one and only true source of spiritual rest. Go to Him now.

Jesus urged, "Come to me, all who labor and are heavy laden, and I will give you rest. Take my yoke upon you, and learn from me, for I am gentle and lowly in heart, and you will find rest for your souls. For my yoke is easy, and my burden is light" (Matthew

Timeline

27— Jesus begins His ministry.

28— A sinful woman anoints Jesus with expensive perfume.

28— Jesus teaches some parables of the kingdom.

29— Jesus commissions 12 apostles to spread His message.

29— John the Baptist is executed.

29— Jesus miraculously feeds more than 5000.

29— Jesus urges Christians to take up their crosses to follow Him.

"Jesus began His ministry by being hungry, yet He is the Bread of Life. Jesus ended His earthly ministry by being thirsty, yet He is the Living Water. Jesus was weary, yet He is our rest."

—*Gregory of Nazianzus (329–390)*

11:28-30). Jesus invites all who are burdened by religious legalism to go to Him for rest.

Notice that this verse does not say "come to church" or "come to a Bible study" to obtain rest. Certainly going to church and Bible studies are important. But Jesus is the heart and center of Christianity. We are to go *to Him* for rest.

The word *rest* in our passage carries the idea of "refreshment" and "relief." My friend, do you need refreshment and relief? What are you waiting for?

> "We must of necessity be servant to someone, either to God or to sin…The man who surrenders to Christ exchanges a cruel slave driver for a kind and gentle Master whose yoke is easy and whose burden is light."
>
> —A. W. Tozer (1897–1963)

A person shows his or her true colors by the things he or she does in life.

Jesus reveals that a person's true nature is revealed by the fruit he or she bears in life (Matthew 12:33-37). A person who consistently helps the poor, for example, shows a compassionate heart. A worthy question to ponder is this: what fruit do others behold in my life?

The person with the most sins forgiven by God loves God the most.

A sinful woman—perhaps a prostitute—anointed Jesus's head with an expensive perfume while He was a dinner guest in the home of Simon the Pharisee. Her weeping pointed to her repentance before the Lord. Simon said Jesus would have sent her away had He known her true character. But Jesus defended her and pointed to her salvation. Jesus indicated that the person with many sins forgiven by God loves God the most. That was the case with this woman (Luke 7:47-48).

> "I remember two things: that I am a great sinner and that Christ is a great Savior."
>
> —John Newton (1725–1807)

Those who do the Father's will have the closest relationships with Jesus.

Jesus said His true family members are those who do the will of the Father (Matthew 12:48-50; Mark 3:31-35). Such people are His true brothers and sisters. Such people have the most intimate relationships with Him.

Don't expect everyone to have the same response to the preaching of God's Word. They won't!

Jesus taught a parable in which a sower threw seed on four different types of soil: wayside soil, rocky soil, thorn-ridden soil, and good soil (Matthew

13:1-23; Mark 4:1-20; Luke 8:4-15). The parable portrays different responses to the preaching of God's Word. In some cases, God's Word takes root and bears fruit. In other cases, the seed of God's Word does not take root for one reason or another. Has God's Word taken root in your heart?

Don't underestimate the Lord. He can do things you never could have imagined. As the Creator of the universe, He can exercise power over the natural realm.

Jesus is not simply the sovereign Lord over humanity. He is also the sovereign Lord over the created universe—including the stormy sea the disciples and Jesus found themselves on (Matthew 8:23-27; Mark 4:35-41; Luke 8:22-25). Jesus, of course, calmed the storm, thereby calming the nerves of the frightened disciples.

Let us never forget that it is no more difficult for Jesus to calm the storms of our lives than it was for Him to calm the storm on the lake with His disciples. Turn to Him today!

> ### Cross-References: Storm Calmed
> Psalm 65:7 • 89:9 • 93:4 • 107:29 • Jonah 1:15 • Matthew 14:32
>
> ### Jesus Calms Storms
> Jesus is the Creator: "All things were made through him, and without him was not any thing made that was made" (John 1:3).
>
> He exercises providential control over that which He created (Colossians 1:17; see also Hebrews 1:3). Jesus reigns!

Don't fear demonic spirits. Jesus has authority over them all.

Jesus is not simply the sovereign Lord over humanity and the sovereign Lord over the created universe. He is also the sovereign Lord over the demonic realm. The demons recognized this, for they addressed Jesus as "Son of the Most High God." Jesus cast countless demons out of a man and into pigs, who then ran into a lake and drowned (Matthew 8:28-34; Mark 5:1-20; Luke 8:26-39). If you ever feel you're being harassed by demons, turn to the Lord in prayer and ask for His sovereign intervention. He reigns!

Jesus is a divine healer—but faith is a prerequisite.

Jesus engaged in two rapid-fire miracles, both of which were "signs" of His identity as the divine Messiah—His divine "ID Card" (Matthew 9:18-26; Mark

> "Faith does not operate in the realm of the possible. There is no glory for God in that which is humanly possible. Faith begins where man's power ends."
>
> —*George Muller (1805–1898)*

5:21-43; Luke 8:40-56). He healed a woman with a hemorrhage and raised the daughter of a synagogue ruler from the dead.

One must not forget the biblical teaching that Jesus Himself is the Creator of the universe (John 1:3; Colossians 1:16). Healings and resurrections are therefore in perfect keeping with His role as Creator. He who is the Creator exercises authority over what He created.

One must also not miss the important role of faith in these miracles. To the woman with a hemorrhage, Jesus said, "Take heart, daughter; your faith has made you well" (Matthew 9:22). Regarding the synagogue ruler's daughter, Jesus instructed, "Do not fear, only believe" (Mark 5:36). Dear Christian, when you have a serious prayer request—such as a request for healing—go to the Lord in faith.

> **Faith in God**
>
> "Without faith it is impossible to please him, for whoever would draw near to God must believe that he exists and that he rewards those who seek him" (Hebrews 11:6).
>
> Keep your faith in God strong.

Some know-it-alls dismiss Jesus without even considering the evidence for His identity. All you can do is move on.

When Jesus came to Nazareth, where He grew up, some of the locals spoke of Him with a contempt born of familiarity (Matthew 13:53-58; Mark 6:1-6; Luke 4:16-30). To them, Jesus was nothing special. It is as if they were thinking, "We've known Jesus since he was a child, and now he's standing before us claiming to be the Messiah. What nerve and audacity he has!" The people of Nazareth had plummeted into deep unbelief. Jesus moved on to other cities, where people with faith received mighty miracles.

There's more kingdom work to do than there are kingdom workers to do it. Why not play a part?

Jesus lamented the pastoral negligence of the Jewish leaders. He therefore encouraged prayer for raising up laborers to participate in the evangelistic harvest (Matthew 9:35-38). How about it? Do you want to play a role? Count me in!

You as a Christian are a part of the kingdom of God. Your calling as a Christian is to submit to the messianic King.

> "If you love me, you will keep my commandments."
>
> —Jesus Christ (John 14:15)

Jesus commissioned His 12 apostles to spread His message about the kingdom of God (Matthew 10:1-15; Mark 6:6-13; Luke 9:1-6). The term "kingdom of

God" is used in Scripture in two primary senses—a present sense and a future sense. The present sense involves the idea that God spiritually rules over His people who have been delivered from the kingdom of darkness and transferred to the kingdom of Jesus Christ (Colossians 1:13). The kingdom exists wherever Christians are submitting to the kingship and rule of Christ (1 Corinthians 4:20).

> "If anyone loves me, he will keep my word."
>
> —Jesus Christ (John 14:23)

The future aspect of the kingdom relates to the future millennial reign of Christ on earth. Following the second coming, Christ will institute a kingdom of perfect peace and righteousness on earth that will last for 1000 years. After this reign of true peace, eternity begins (Revelation 21–22). This kingdom is prophesied multiple times in the Old Testament (for example, Isaiah 65:17–66:24; Jeremiah 25:30-31; Zechariah 14:9-17).

Jesus was persecuted. Don't be surprised that His followers are also persecuted.

Jesus informed His disciples that they'd experience persecution as they spread the news about the kingdom of God (Matthew 10:16-33). Scripture elsewhere reveals that all those who serve Christ will experience some level of persecution (Matthew 5:10-11; 2 Timothy 3:12). There is no need to fear, however. God sovereignly helps us through all of it (Mark 13:11-13).

It's possible your family might turn on you because of your allegiance to Jesus.

Jesus said, "Do not think that I have come to bring peace to the earth. I have not come to bring peace, but a sword" (Matthew 10:34). In other words, as evangelism takes place some will accept Christ and others will reject Him— even within the same family. The work of evangelism is like a spiritual sword that divides people—even within families. Of course, Jesus urged unqualified allegiance to Him, no matter what.

Even good people suffer and die unjustly on earth. Don't worry! Justice will prevail in the end.

John the Baptist had been imprisoned by Herod because he condemned Herod's adulterous marriage to his brother Philip's wife, Herodias. At an opportune moment, she imposed upon Herod to have John

> "Each of us will give an account of himself to God."
>
> —Romans 14:12

executed by beheading (Matthew 14:3-12; Mark 6:17-29). John is one of many examples of God's good people suffering and dying unjustly. God's justice will prevail in the end (Revelation 20:11-15).

Jesus is your source of spiritual nourishment.

A Verse to Remember

"I am the bread of life; whoever comes to me shall not hunger, and whoever believes in me shall never thirst."

—*John 6:35*

In the broader context of John 6, Jesus had just performed a tremendous miracle in feeding more than 5000 people with five barley loaves and two fishes. The crowd had eaten a meal that satisfied their physical hunger. Christ now wanted to give them something to satisfy their spiritual hunger and give them eternal life. It comes by partaking of the bread of life, Jesus Himself. Our passage informs us that just as one must consume or partake of physical food to sustain physical life, so one must spiritually appropriate Christ to have spiritual life. Just as the ancient Jews were dependent on manna (bread) to sustain physical life, so we are dependent on Jesus (the bread of life) for our spiritual life (John 6:22-59). My friend, Jesus is your spiritual nourishment. Feast upon His spiritual nourishment daily.

Be on guard against unbelief and hypocrisy, both of which are injurious to the spiritual life.

Cross-References: Hypocrisy

Matthew 6:5,16 • 7:5 • Luke 6:46 • 11:39 • 16:15 • James 4:8 • 1 Peter 2:1

Jesus warned His disciples that the Jewish leaders were corrupting the entire nation. These leaders were full of unbelief and hypocrisy—both of which are spiritually cancerous to Christians (Matthew 16:5-12; Mark 8:14-21). That's why we today need to guard against unbelief and hypocrisy. The best way to fight these is to pursue daily intimacy with Jesus and stay firmly planted in God's Word.

Jesus calls for a radical commitment from His followers—a commitment that requires obedience to the point of death.

"To take up the cross means that you take your stand for the Lord Jesus no matter what it costs."

—*Billy Graham*

Jesus urged, "If anyone would come after me, let him deny himself and take up his cross and follow me. For whoever would save his life will lose it, but whoever loses his life for my sake will find it" (Matthew 16:24-25; see also Mark 8:34-38; Luke 9:23-27). Jesus is calling for a total commitment. The idea is this: "If you really want to follow Me, do not do so in word only, but put your life on the line and follow Me on the path of the cross—a path that will involve sacrifice, self-denial, and possibly even suffering and death for My sake."

Note that there is a distinction in Scripture between salvation and discipleship. All Christians are saved, but not all Christians choose the path of discipleship. While salvation is free, discipleship can be costly. In salvation, it is Christ who pays the price (on the cross); in discipleship, it is the believer who pays the price (by taking up his cross and following Jesus). Salvation involves a new birth; discipleship involves a lifetime of growth following the new birth.

My friend, join me. Let's be Christ's disciples!

The one who humbles himself like a child is the greatest person in the kingdom of heaven.

Jesus went against traditional wisdom in saying that the path to greatness in the kingdom of God is becoming like a little child (Matthew 18:1-5; Mark 9:33-37; Luke 9:46-48). The way up is down. One must be humble, dependent, and trusting.

Christians engaged in unrepentant sin must be confronted.

Jesus taught there are progressive steps to be taken in the event of known sin in a Christian's life (Matthew 18:15-20). One must first speak privately with the person. If he does not listen, take two or three witnesses (Deuteronomy 19:15). If he still does not listen, take it before the church. If he still does not listen, he is to be treated as an outsider. Hopefully, such treatment will lead to repentance and restoration.

> **Cross-References: If Your Brother Sins**
> Leviticus 19:17 • Luke 17:3 • Galatians 6:1 • James 5:19-20

Dear Christian, sin is too serious to ignore. It's like a cancer that grows if left unchecked. The church must excise it when necessary.

Christ calls us to forgive others without limit.

Christians have been forgiven an incalculably large debt of sin by God. Every Christian is thus called to forgive the wrongdoings of others (Matthew 18:21-35).

> "There is no torment like the inner torment of an unforgiving spirit. It refuses to be soothed, it refuses to be healed, it refuses to forget."
>
> —*Charles Swindoll*

True enlightenment comes by following He who is the light of the world.

A Verse to Remember

"I am the light of the world. Whoever follows me will not walk in darkness, but will have the light of life."

—John 8:12

The Messiah and Light

- Psalm 27:1 affirms, "The LORD is my light and my salvation."
- Isaiah 60:19 promises, "The LORD will be your everlasting light."

Jesus affirmed He is the light of the world who delivers people from darkness (John 8:12-20; see 1 John 1:7). The prophet Isaiah had described the future coming of salvation in terms of people living in darkness seeing a great light (Isaiah 9:2; see also Matthew 4:16). This was fulfilled in Jesus. He is the true light in the sense that He is God's complete and full revelation of God to humanity. Christ banishes the spiritual darkness by the light He shines in the world.

A Thought to Anchor in Your Heart

Jesus is your daily source of rest, refreshment, and relief. Release your burdens into His sovereign hands.

Matthew, Mark, Luke, and John— Part 3

Jesus, the messianic King, teaches us what we need to know about rightly relating to God, rightly relating to each other, and how to live a God-honoring life.

Following are yet further key applicational concepts derived from the teachings of Jesus in the four Gospels:

Do you feel like you're living in bondage? Take heart. The truth will set you free.

Jesus encouraged His followers, "You will know the truth, and the truth will set you free" (John 8:32). Those who trust in Jesus and abide in His word—not just hearing it, but obeying it—are set free from the shackles of sin and experience the grace-filled life of spiritual liberty.

Beware: Satan is a liar and a murderer. Deception and destruction are his goals for you.

Jesus said the devil "was a murderer from the beginning, and does not stand in the truth, because there is no truth in him. When he lies, he speaks out of his own character, for he is a liar and the father of lies" (John 8:44). The word "murderer" literally means "man killer" (1 John 3:12,15). Hatred is the

Timeline

29— Jesus heals a man born blind; miraculously feeds more than 5000; defends a woman caught in adultery; sends out 70 followers to spread His message; teaches the parable of the good Samaritan; and reveals He is the Good Shepherd.

30— Jesus warns about the danger of wealth; teaches a parable on prayer; teaches the parable of the prodigal son; teaches the parable of the rich man and Lazarus; encounters an unfruitful fig tree; and pronounces woes on the scribes and Pharisees.

Cross-References: Set Free

• Romans 8:2 • 2 Corinthians 3:17
• Galatians 5:1,13

motive that leads a person to commit murder. Satan hates both God and His children, so he has a genuine motive for murder.

> "Whom the devil cannot deceive, he tries to destroy, and whom he cannot destroy, he attempts to deceive."
>
> —Ray Stedman (1917–1992)

The word "father" in the phrase "father of lies" is used metaphorically of the originator of a family or company of persons animated by a deceitful character. Satan was the first and greatest liar. Beware, Christian—Satan seeks to deceive you and bring you down!

Be a people-helper every chance you get.

> "We hurt people by being too busy. Too busy to notice their needs. Too busy to drop that note of comfort or encouragement or assurance of love. Too busy to listen when someone needs to talk. Too busy to care."
>
> —Billy Graham

A lawyer asked Jesus how to inherit eternal life. Jesus affirmed the lawyer's summary of the law: Love God supremely (Deuteronomy 6:4-5) and love your neighbor (Leviticus 19:18). But the lawyer asked, "Who is my neighbor?"

Jesus told the parable of the good Samaritan to demonstrate the meaning of showing compassion to a neighbor. Ironically, the people in the parable, who one would naturally expect to show compassion—the priest and the Levite—showed no compassion. The one not expected to show compassion—the Samaritan—showed compassion (Luke 10:25-37).

> "A man can be so busy making a living that he forgets to make a life."
>
> —William Barclay (1907–1978)

The big idea: be a people-helper every chance you get, even to perfect strangers!

Don't be anxious and troubled by the tyranny of the urgent.

Jesus visited Mary and Martha. While with them, He taught that one should not let the tyranny of the urgent take a higher priority than spiritual matters—such as commitment to the Lord (Luke 10:38-42). Dear Christian, the tyranny of the urgent will enslave you if you let it. Make Jesus your top priority!

Two Attitudes in Praying

The wrong attitude is to pray pridefully, arrogantly, and self-righteously—like the Pharisees in New Testament times.

The right attitude is to pray humbly, recognizing that you are a fallen and wounded sinner (Luke 18:9-14).

God looks mercifully upon repentant sinners (Proverbs 28:13).

Pray daily about all the important matters in your life.

Jesus modeled how to pray in the Lord's Prayer (Luke 11:1-13). In this one prayer we find praise (verse 2), a personal petition (verse 3), a request for forgiveness (verse 4), and a request for deliverance from temptation (verse 5).

My friend, if you don't pray, you rob yourself of the blessing of witnessing God answer your prayers. It is good to recall the words of James: "You do not have, because you do not ask" (James 4:2).

Don't be hypocritical, judgmental, and prideful. Those traits don't sit well with Jesus.

Jesus pronounced woes upon the Pharisees and scribes because of their hypocrisy, their preoccupation with external matters in religion, their dishonesty, their judgmentalism, their pride, and their spiritual blindness. These people were all show with no substance. They preached, but did not practice. They talked the talk, but did not walk the walk. They also inflicted heavy spiritual burdens on the common people. And they were Jesus's most forceful critics (Luke 11:37-54). Take a good look at the scribes and Pharisees and do all you can to never be like them.

> "God sends no one away empty except those who are full of themselves."
>
> —Dwight Moody (1837–1899)

Covetousness is injurious to the soul. Avoid it. It will warp your perspective on life.

Jesus warned, "Be on your guard against all covetousness, for one's life does not consist in the abundance of his possessions" (Luke 12:15). We are reminded of the apostle Paul's words to young Timothy: "Godliness with contentment is great gain, for we brought nothing into the world, and we cannot take anything out of the world. But if we have food and clothing, with these we will be content. But those who desire to be rich fall into temptation, into a snare, into many senseless and harmful desires that plunge people into ruin and destruction. For the love of money is a root of all kinds of evils. It is through this craving that some have wandered away from the faith and pierced themselves with many pangs" (1 Timothy 6:6-10). Do whatever you have to do to avoid enslavement to materialism.

> **A Verse to Remember**
>
> "Be on your guard against all covetousness, for one's life does not consist in the abundance of his possessions."
>
> —Luke 12:15

Matthew, Mark, Luke, John

Don't worry about things. Entrust all concerns into God's sovereign hands.

For the one who focuses only on earthly values, anxiety is the natural result. But for the one who focuses on eternity's values, anxiety is banished, for the Lord oversees everything. Don't worry about things. The sovereignty of God relieves us of worry (Luke 12:22-34). Rest secure in the Lord.

> "Half our miseries are caused by things that we think are coming upon us."
>
> —J. C. Ryle (1816–1900)

Because we don't know precisely when the Lord will come for us, we need to be ready by living righteously at all times.

Those who profess to serve Christ must make a pivotal choice: be faithful servants, doing the Lord's will at all times, or be unfaithful servants, neglecting God's will and living self-indulgently. The faithful will be rewarded at the Lord's return; the unfaithful will be punished (Luke 12:35-48). Since we don't know when the Lord is returning, it makes sense to pursue righteous living perpetually, so we'll be ready for Him at all times.

> It is wise to live as if Jesus were coming today, and yet prepare for the future as if He were not coming for a long time. Then you are prepared for both time and eternity.

Be forewarned—it's possible your family might turn on you because of your allegiance to Jesus.

As evangelism takes place, some will accept Christ and others will reject Him, even within the same family. Christ is much like a spiritual sword that divides people (Luke 12:49-53). If it happens to you, fear not. Now you're in a new family—the family of God (Mark 3:31-35).

Seek reconciliation with your accuser before legal action is taken. You'll be glad you did.

Sometimes people seem blind to common sense. They ought to make peace with their accusers before they go to trial in court and end up in prison (Luke 12:57-59). A little reconciliatory effort now can save you from a big headache later. Be wise!

A failure to repent can bring dire consequences.

Some Galileans were slain by Pilate's soldiers while offering sacrifices at the temple so that their blood was mixed with that of the sacrifices. Christ indicated that this horrible thing did not happen to them because they were worse sinners than others. All people need to repent. "Unless you repent, you will all likewise perish" (Luke 13:1-5). Learn the lesson well: a failure to repent can bring dire consequences.

> Cross-References: Repentance
>
> 2 Chronicles 7:14 • Psalm 51:17 • Proverbs 28:13 • Ezekiel 18:30-32 • Matthew 3:2 • Acts 3:19 • 2 Corinthians 7:10 • 1 John 1:9

God judges those who appear fruitful on the outside but are not truly fruitful.

Jesus and the disciples came upon a fig tree. Since the fig tree had leaves on it (Matthew 21:19), from a distance it gave the appearance of being fruitful. Upon closer examination, they could see there was no fruit at all. Jesus's cursing of the fig tree was an acted-out parable that taught that God will judge those who give an outer appearance of fruitfulness but in fact are not fruitful at all (like the Pharisees) (Matthew 21:18-22; Mark 11:12-14,20-25).

Jesus is the Good Shepherd. His love for His sheep is boundless.

Jesus is our Good Shepherd. He has an intimate relationship with His sheep, calling them by name. They listen to His voice, and follow and obey Him. He liberates His sheep so they are truly free and unfettered with the chains of any kind of bondage. So much does the Good Shepherd love His sheep that He lays His life down for them (John 10:1-21).

Here's something to remember: the sheep who are healthiest are those who stay closest to the shepherd.

> Jesus's Sheep
>
> In the West, shepherds typically drive the sheep from behind.
>
> Near Eastern shepherds lead the sheep from the front, using their voices to call them.
>
> Jesus, the Good Shepherd, leads us and calls us to follow Him (John 10:4).

Everyone who exalts himself will be humbled. He who humbles himself will be exalted. Live your life accordingly!

Jesus told a parable that emphasized one of His most common themes—the way of humility leads to real advancement (Luke 14:7-14). In the Beatitudes

> Cross-References: Humility
>
> Luke 14:7-11 • Romans 12:3 • Ephesians 4:2 • Philippians 2:3-4

Jesus taught that it is the meek who will inherit the earth (Matthew 5:5). Scripture consistently teaches that God shows grace to humble sinners instead of proud people like the Pharisees (Luke 18:9-14). The way up is down!

There is great joy in heaven when a single sinner repents.

Using an illustration of a shepherd with a single lost sheep, Jesus emphasized how much heaven rejoices when a single sinner repents (Luke 15:1-7). Let's keep those angels rejoicing!

God welcomes repentant sinners into His arms.

The parable of the prodigal son reveals God's boundless love toward those who are lost and turn to Him for forgiveness. This parable gives hope to every sinner (Luke 15:11-32).

It may be that even now you feel far from God. Perhaps you have stumbled off the path. Perhaps you feel alienated from Him. Turn to Him immediately, for His arms are open wide. Do it now. He yearns to embrace you with His love.

It is always wise to plan for the future.

Jesus tells a parable depicting a business manager who was commended for using his ingenuity in taking advantage of present opportunities and relationships to prepare for the future. We learn a good lesson here. Make a habit of using your ingenuity in the present in preparing for the future (Luke 16:1-13).

A life devoted solely to earthly pleasures comes to sudden ruin in the afterlife.

Jesus told a parable about a rich man who had everything in earthly life but gave no thought to God or eternal matters. Lazarus, by contrast, was a poor man who had little in earthly life, but depended upon God. Once they died, the rich man's money was no help in averting his eternal suffering. Lazarus, by contrast, enjoyed paradise (Luke 16:19-31). My friend, remember that life on earth is so short that it's like a dot. Life in heaven is long, like a line. So doesn't it make good sense to live for the line and not for the dot?

> "He is no fool who gives what he cannot keep to gain what he cannot lose."
>
> —Jim Elliot (1927–1956)

Jesus is the resurrection and the life. Because of Jesus, you and I will be resurrected.

Jesus was alerted that Lazarus, whom He loved deeply, was ill. He affirmed that Lazarus's situation would ultimately bring much glory to God. Notice He didn't say Lazarus would not die, but only that the final outcome would not be death. Jesus ended up raising Lazarus from the dead, thereby validating His claim to be "the resurrection and the life."

It is particularly relevant that Jesus didn't head toward Lazarus's home as soon as He heard of the illness. By the time Jesus arrived, Lazarus had been dead four days. This made Christ's miracle of resurrection all the more impressive. Christ issued the command, and life emerged out of death. Lazarus was alive again (John 11:1-44).

One thing is certain. Because Christ is "the resurrection and the life," He will one day resurrect us just as effortlessly as He resurrected Lazarus. I can't wait to get my body upgrade!

Be persistent in your prayer requests to God.

Jesus told a parable that emphasized the need to be persistent in prayer (Luke 18:1-8). This is in keeping with Jesus's teaching in Matthew 7:7, "Ask, and it will be given to you." The literal Greek says, "*Keep on* asking, and it will be given you." Be persistent! Don't give up. Pray, pray, pray!

> ### A Verse to Remember
> "Whatever you ask in prayer, believe that you have received it, and it will be yours."
>
> —*Mark 11:24*

There is a danger to great wealth. It can distract you from your need for the Savior.

A rich young ruler asked Jesus how to inherit eternal life. Jesus said to follow the commandments of God. The ruler responded that he had kept the commandments. Jesus said he must do one thing more—sell all that he had and give it to the poor. The man became sad, for he had great wealth. Jesus wasn't teaching salvation by works. He was simply trying to help the man see that his unwillingness to give money to the poor indicated he had not even kept the first great commandment to love God more than anything

> "Materialism may be called 'affluenza.'"
>
> —*Mrs. Ray Stedman*

> ### Cross-References: Wealth
> Matthew 6:24 • 1 Peter 5:2 • 1 Timothy 3:2-3 • 6:9-10 • Hebrews 13:5 • Ecclesiastes 5:10 • Jeremiah 49:4

else, such as money (Matthew 19:16-30; Mark 10:17-31). Don't let money side-track you! Remember—you can't take money with you into the afterlife!

The believer must be willing to freely serve Christ without seeking exaltation or sticking up for personal rights.

> "He is genuinely great who considers himself small and cares nothing about high honors."
>
> —Thomas à Kempis (1380–1471)

Jesus told a parable in which the workers labored for different lengths of time—some long, some short—and yet all were paid the same at the end of the day. Jesus's purpose was not to teach economics. His main point was that every believer ought to be willing to continually serve the Lord, knowing that the Lord will abundantly take care of them. Our main goal is to serve, not to see how much reward we can get out of it (Matthew 20:1-16).

Whoever wants to be great in the kingdom of heaven must become a servant.

The mother of James and John—two of Jesus's disciples—wanted Jesus to give her sons prominent places in His kingdom. Jesus said such matters are in the Father's hands. Besides, He said, the one who wants to be great must become a humble servant (Matthew 20:20-28; Mark 10:35-45).

A Thought to Anchor in Your Heart

It is all too easy to play the role of Christian without really being fully committed. Don't be a faker. Be authentic. Be the real thing!

Matthew, Mark, Luke, and John—

Part 4

Jesus, the messianic King, teaches us what we need to know about rightly relating to God, rightly relating to each other, and how to live a God-honoring life.

Following are yet further key applicational concepts derived from the teachings of Jesus in the four Gospels:

The gist of God's law comes down to this: we must love the Lord with all our being—and love our neighbors as ourselves.

A Pharisee asked Jesus about the greatest commandment. Jesus said the first is to love God supremely with one's whole being (Deuteronomy 6:4-5). The second is to love one's neighbor (Leviticus 19:18). These two commands constitute a summary—the bottom line—of God's law (Matthew 22:34-40; Mark 12:28-34). So, my friend, love God and love others. That's the heart of the matter.

Take comfort in Jesus's foreknowledge and sovereignty over human history. He is Lord over all!

The Olivet Discourse is so named because Jesus delivered this message "as he sat on the Mount of Olives" (Matthew 24:3). The disciples had asked, "What will be the sign of your coming and of the end of the age?" (verse 3). The Olivet Discourse is Jesus's

Timeline

30— Jesus speaks about signs of the end times, among other important matters.

30 (Passion Week, Thursday, April 2)—Jesus celebrates His final Passover with the disciples, institutes the Lord's Supper, teaches on the coming of the Holy Spirit, predicts Peter's denial, and prays in Gethsemane.

30 (Passion Week, Friday, April 3)—Jesus is crucified and buried.

30 (Sunday, April 5–May 14)— Jesus resurrects from the dead and makes many appearances.

30 (May 14)—Christ ascends into heaven.

Cross-References: Love God/Others

Leviticus 19:18 • Matthew 5:43 • 19:19 • Mark 12:31 • Luke 10:27 • Romans 13:9 • Galatians 5:14 • James 2:8

response. Highlights include His prediction of the appearance of false Christs, wars, earthquakes, famines, and cosmic disturbances (Matthew 24:1-29; Mark 13:1-23; Luke 21:5-24).

Gloriously, however, Jesus will come again following this time of distress: People "will see the Son of Man coming on the clouds of heaven with power and great glory" (Matthew 24:30). Jesus will judge the wicked, set up His righteous kingdom, and blessing will prevail. A big change is coming. A new day is on the horizon. Let us rejoice at what lies in store for us.

The Second Coming

- Jesus will come again just as He left—physically and visibly (Acts 1:9-11).
- Jesus will come as the King of kings and Lord of lords (Revelation 19:11-16).
- Every eye will see Him (Revelation 1:7).

Human blindness to sin and the need for repentance is itself a manifestation of sin (1 John 2:11; Revelation 3:17).

Don't be surprised if it seems as though people are living it up in these last days, unconcerned and oblivious to spiritual matters. Our Lord warned us it would be this way.

Our Lord warned us about what the world would be like in the days prior to His second coming. "As were the days of Noah, so will be the coming of the Son of Man. For as in those days before the flood they were eating and drinking, marrying and giving in marriage, until the day when Noah entered the ark, and they were unaware until the flood came and swept them all away, so will be the coming of the Son of Man" (Matthew 24:37-39). Many today are oblivious to spiritual things and care only about the here and now. My goal is to reach as many of them for Christ as possible. Will you join me?

All people will be held accountable for how they lived their lives. God is a just Judge.

Following His second coming, Jesus will judge the nations that survive the tribulation period (Matthew 25:31-46). The nations are metaphorically composed of the "sheep" and the "goats," representing the saved and the lost among the Gentiles in the tribulation period. They are intermingled and require separation by a special judgment. The basis of the judgment is how Christ's "brothers"—apparently the 144,000 Jewish evangelists of Revelation 7 and 14—were treated. (Only believers would dare feed them and make provisions for them during the tribulation period, for

"There are only two kinds of people in the end: those who say to God, 'Thy will be done,' and those to whom God says in the end, 'Thy will be done.'"

—C. S. Lewis (1898–1963)

the antichrist will be against them.) The result of the judgment is twofold: the righteous (sheep) enter into Christ's 1000-year millennial kingdom; the unrighteous (goats) are cast into the lake of fire. The rest of the wicked dead will face the great white throne judgment following the millennial kingdom (Revelation 20:11-15).

It is important for us not to forget that our holy and righteous God is also a God of judgment. All people will be held accountable for how they lived during their earthly years. Earthly choices have eternal consequences.

Even Christians will be judged at the judgment seat of Christ (Romans 14:10; 1 Corinthians 3:10-15). At that time each believer's life will be examined with regard to deeds done while in the body, and personal motives and intents will be weighed. Now, those who have placed faith in Christ are saved, and nothing threatens that. Rather, this judgment has to do with the reception or loss of rewards, based on how Christians lived following their spiritual conversion.

> "It ought to be the business of every day to prepare for our last day."
>
> —Matthew Henry (1662–1714)

Jesus set a great example for us regarding humility and self-denial.

Normally it was the job of a household servant to wash a guest's feet, not the master of the household. By washing the disciples' feet, Jesus placed Himself in the role of a servant. This was a living parable of humility and self-denial— something the disciples would need to have in the days ahead after His death and resurrection (John 13:1-20). We learn a good lesson here. Humility and self-denial must characterize all Jesus-followers.

> "Walk humbly with your God."
>
> —Micah 6:8

Celebrate the Lord's Supper often, always remembering the sacrifice Jesus made for you.

Jesus instituted the Lord's Supper at the last Passover meal He celebrated with the disciples (Matthew 26:26-29; Mark 14:22-25; Luke 22:14-23). The bread represented His body and the cup represented His blood.

The apostle Paul later revealed that the bread and wine are symbols and reminders of Jesus in His death and resurrection (1 Corinthians 11:24-25). The elements also remind us of the basic facts of the gospel (11:26), our anticipation of the second coming (11:26), and our oneness as the body of Christ (10:17).

Dear Christian, when you celebrate the Lord's Supper, make sure you've repented of all known sin and that your heart is prepared for this sacred ordinance (1 Corinthians 11:27-29).

Jesus knows we're going to sin even before we commit the act. And yet He still has compassion for us.

At the Last Supper, Jesus told the disciples what they surely did not want to hear: "You will all fall away because of me this night." Peter said *no way*. But the Lord informed Peter that he would deny Him three times before the cock crowed twice (Matthew 26:30-35; Mark 14:26-31; Luke 22:31-34; John 13:36-38). One thing we learn from this is that Jesus foreknows when we're going to sin. Despite that foreknowledge, He still has compassion for us. He even seeks our restoration after we fall into sin, just as He restored Peter (John 21:15-16). What an awesome Savior we have.

> **Foreknowledge Defined**
>
> Foreknowledge is the attribute of God (Jesus) that involves God's complete knowledge of all that will transpire in the future (Acts 2:23; Romans 8:29; 11:2; and 1 Peter 1:2).

The path to greatness in Christ's kingdom is to become a servant of all.

Knowing that Jesus would soon die, the disciples began to argue about who among them was greatest. Jesus said the humble servant is greatest in God's kingdom (Luke 22:24-30). How easy it is to get sidetracked by our own personal, self-seeking agendas. Jesus says the way up is down. Be a servant. Choose humility.

Don't listen to apostate preachers who say there are many paths to God. Heeding their words is a path to hell.

> "A man who was merely a man and said the sort of things Jesus said would not be a great moral teacher. He would either be a lunatic—on the level with the man who says he is a poached egg—or else he would be the Devil of Hell. You must make your choice. Either this man was, and is, the Son of God: or else a madman or something worse."
>
> —C. S. Lewis (1898-1963)

Jesus affirmed in no uncertain terms, "I am the way, and the truth, and the life. No one comes to the Father except through me" (John 14:6). Jesus is the only way to salvation. This same thing was emphasized by Peter: "There is salvation in no one else, for there is no other name under heaven given among men by which we must be saved" (Acts 4:12). Paul likewise said, "There is one God, and there is one mediator between God and men, the man Christ Jesus" (1 Timothy 2:5). Those who preach that salvation can also be found in other religions are preaching falsehood. Don't listen to them.

Rejoice! The Holy Spirit was sent by Jesus to be our Helper, our Advocate, our Comforter.

Knowing that He would soon be crucified, resurrected, and ascended into heaven, Jesus promised His followers some wonderful blessings they would soon experience: (1) the Holy Spirit will be their Helper, Comforter, and Advocate; (2) they will enjoy union with Christ; (3) the Holy Spirit will teach them; and (4) they will enjoy supernatural peace (John 14:15-31).

> **Cross-References: Our Helper**
> John 14:16,26 • 15:26 • 16:7

Regarding the Holy Spirit, Jesus said, "I will ask the Father, and he will give you another Helper, to be with you forever" (John 14:16). The word *Helper* is a rich one—carrying the meaning of comforter, advocate, one who strengthens. The thoughts of encouragement, support, assistance, care, and the shouldering of responsibility for another's welfare are all conveyed by this one word.

Notice also that Jesus said the Holy Spirit would be "*another* Helper." It is interesting that two New Testament Greek words can be translated by the English word "another." The first one means "another of a different kind." The second means "another of the same kind." This second word is the one used in John 14:16.

Jesus is saying He will ask the Father to send another Helper of the same kind as He Himself—that is, a personal, ever-present helper. Just as Jesus was a personal comforter who helped the disciples for three years during His earthly ministry, so now Christ's followers would have another personal comforter—the Holy Spirit—who would be with them throughout their lives. Rejoice in this truth!

Jesus is the Vine. You and I are "branches." We draw our spiritual vitality from Him.

The Father's purpose is that every Christian consistently bear fruit. Jesus said the Father works in each believer's life to bring about maximum fruit. But this can't take place without the Christian (the "branch") remaining in constant union with—abiding in—Jesus Christ (the "Vine"). We draw our spiritual vitality from Christ. We are spiritually nourished as we stay "plugged in" to Him. Spiritual famine is the result of the "branch" breaking union with the "Vine" (John 15:1-11).

> **Cross-References: Bearing Fruit**
> Psalm 1:2-3 • Micah 3:8 • Zechariah 4:6 • Matthew 13:23 • 2 Corinthians 3:18 • Galatians 5:22-23 • Ephesians 3:16-17 • Philippians 1:6 • 2 Peter 1:5-8 • 1 John 3:6

We will all encounter tribulation in the world. But rejoice! Christ has overcome the world.

Jesus affirmed, "In the world you will have tribulation. But take heart; I have overcome the world" (John 16:33). Jesus earlier revealed that the world system was hostile to His message and ministry (1:5,10; 7:7). But that doesn't matter, for Jesus has overcome the world. He is the Victor. And because He is the Victor, He tells His followers to "take heart"— literally, "be courageous" or "cheer up." The reality is that because Jesus has overcome the world, Christ's followers—in union with Him—can also overcome the world. As the apostle Paul would later put it, "In all these things we are more than conquerors through him who loved us" (Romans 8:37).

When someone you know is facing dark circumstances, become an intercessory prayer warrior on their behalf.

Jesus and His disciples entered Gethsemane to pray. On this occasion—the crucifixion imminent—Jesus apparently experienced distress such as He had never experienced before in His short earthly life. In His hour of greatest need, the Lord wanted those dearest to Him to be there for Him in prayer (Matthew 26:36-46; Mark 14:32-42; Luke 22:39-46).

Jesus preferred to not have to drink this "cup." He was no doubt looking in His mind's eye toward the separation from the Father He would experience when the sins of humanity would be poured upon Him (Matthew 27:46). Yet He willingly submitted His will to that of the Father (26:39). Instead of offering up prayer support, however, the disciples fell asleep. In Jesus's hour of greatest need, He ended up "going it alone."

Don't fall asleep when you become aware of a friend facing dark circumstances. Be there for them in intercessory prayer.

Jesus was crucified on the cross of Calvary for your sins. Such was His awesome love for you.

Jesus was now to be crucified. He was forced to carry the crossbeam of His cross by Himself (John 19:17). Even for a healthy young man in good shape, this would have been difficult. Jesus, who had just been severely scourged, quickly became too weak and needed assistance. So Simon was drafted into service. We know little of the man. He was probably in Jerusalem to celebrate the Passover, and had no idea that he would play this role in aiding Jesus to the place of execution (Matthew 27:32; Mark 15:21).

Once Jesus arrived at Golgotha (the "place of the skull"), He was offered wine mixed with gall, a first-century, pain-killing narcotic. Jesus refused it. He then suffered Roman crucifixion, a slow and torturous form of death, generally reserved for criminals, slaves, and non-Romans. Such crucifixion was not only painful, but also caused the victim to slowly suffocate.

> ### Jesus Saves
> Some at the cross mocked Jesus: "He saved others; he cannot save himself" (Mark 15:31).
> The truth is, Jesus loved us so much that He dared not save Himself, choosing instead to save us (John 15:13).

In crucifixions, it was common to post a sign stating the crime of the victim. In Jesus's case, the sign read, "This is Jesus, the King of the Jews." Jesus was mocked and taunted by people who were passing by as well as the Jewish leaders (Matthew 27:33-44; Mark 15:22-32; Luke 23:33-43; John 19:17-30). Oh, the utter blindness of such individuals!

Why did Jesus suffer such a tortuous death? Jesus once said, "Greater love has no one than this, that someone lay down his life for his friends" (John 15:13). Jesus laid down His life *for you* because of His great love *for you*. Never forget it.

Rejoice! Jesus resurrected from the dead. He defeated death! Because He resurrected, you and I will be resurrected as well.

> ### Cross-References: Resurrection
> Matthew 22:31-32 • John 11:25 • Acts 1:21-22 • 4:2,33 • Romans 1:3-4 • 6:5 • 1 Peter 1:3 • 3:21

Following Jesus's crucifixion and burial, Mary Magdalene and Salome decided to visit His tomb with the intention of anointing His body with spices. Upon their arrival, they were surprised by an angel who informed them that Jesus had resurrected from the dead. The angel instructed them to go tell the disciples the good news.

The good news for you and me is not simply that Jesus is risen; it's also good news that you and I will be risen just as He has risen (1 John 3:2; 1 Corinthians 15).

Jesus made many convincing appearances to His followers. You can trust that the resurrection really happened as reported in the New Testament.

For 40 days, the resurrected Jesus appeared to reliable witnesses on 12 different occasions. He was witnessed by Mary (John 20:10-18), Peter (1 Corinthians 15:5), John (John 20:1-10), Paul (Acts 9:1-9), the disciples on many occasions (Luke 24:13-35; 24:36-49; John 20:24-31; 21; Matthew 28:16-20), and 500 brethren at the same time (1 Corinthians 15:6). Jesus "showed himself to these men and gave many convincing proofs that he was alive. He appeared to them over a period of forty days and spoke about the kingdom of God" (Acts 1:3).

The resurrection of Christ was thoroughly attested in the book of Acts. "This Jesus God raised up, and of that we all are witnesses" (Acts 2:32). "You killed the Author of life, whom God raised from the dead. To this we are witnesses" (Acts 3:15).

There is no question that Jesus resurrected from the dead. Don't doubt it for a second.

Let's share the good news of the gospel with all the people of the earth.

"Oh Lord, give me souls, or take my soul!"

—*George Whitefield (1714–1770)*

Cross-References: The Great Commission

Matthew 28:19-20 • Mark 1:17 • 16:15-20 • Acts 1:8 • 14:21-22 • Colossians 1:28-29

The resurrected Jesus met with His followers in Galilee and charged them with the Great Commission. They were to make disciples of all nations, and baptize them in the name of the Father, the Son, and the Holy Spirit. Jesus—who, as God, is eternal and omnipresent—promised to be with His followers until the end of the age (Matthew 28:16-20; Mark 16:14-18; Luke 24:36-49; John 20:19-23). The Great Commission is just as applicable to you and me today as it was when it was first given. So engage!

Jesus ascended into heaven. But rejoice! He's coming back.

After Jesus appeared to many people over a 40-day period, he "parted from them and was carried up into heaven" (Luke 24:51). As Acts 1:9 puts it, "He was lifted up, and a cloud took him out of their sight." One day, however, He will come again (Titus 2:13; 1 Timothy 6:13-15; 2 Timothy 4:8; Revelation 19:11-21). I can't wait!

A Thought to Anchor in Your Heart

He is risen; He is risen indeed.

Acts

Christians are empowered by the Holy Spirit to spread the gospel worldwide. People of all nationalities are privileged to become a part of the church.

Acts was written by Luke in AD 61, about a year after he wrote his Gospel. While the book is titled after the acts of the apostles, it actually focuses more predominantly on the acts of the Holy Spirit *through* the apostles.

There is a close connection between the Gospel of Luke and Acts. Luke's Gospel contains an orderly account of the accomplishments of Jesus during His earthly life. Acts contains an orderly account of the accomplishments of Jesus, through the Holy Spirit, in the 30 years following His resurrection and ascension. As such, Acts serves as a link between the four Gospels and the epistles.

Here are three noteworthy facts about Acts:

1. Acts chronicles how Christianity miraculously spread among both Jews and Gentiles around the northern Mediterranean, including Samaria (Acts 8:5-25); Phoenicia, Cyprus, and Antioch (9:32–12:25); Phrygia and Galatia (13:1–15:35); Macedonia (15:36–21:16); and Rome (21:17–22:29).

2. Acts is a book of transitions—from Judaism to Christianity, from law to grace, and from Jews alone as the people of God to Jews and Gentiles as the people of God.

3. The events in the book of Acts are thoroughly attested by eyewitnesses (Acts 1:8,22; 2:32,40; 3:15; 5:32; 6:13; 7:44,58; 10:39,41,43; 13:31; 14:3,17; 15:8; 22:5,15,20; 26:16).

Following are key applicational concepts in Acts:

Timeline

47–49—Paul, Barnabas, and John Mark go on their first missionary journey.

49–52—Paul and Silas go on their second missionary journey.

53–57—Paul goes on his third missionary journey.

60—Luke writes his Gospel.

61—Luke writes Acts.

The Apostles

- The apostles were hand-picked by the Lord (Matthew 10:1-4; Acts 1:26).
- They were the special recipients of God's self-revelation (1 Corinthians 2:13).
- They were authenticated by miracles (Acts 2:43; 3:3-11; 5:12; 9:32-42).

Acts

The evidence that Jesus resurrected from the dead is weighty and extensive. Rejoice! This gives us confidence that we, too, shall be resurrected.

Acts picks up where the Gospels left off. Just as the Gospel accounts portray Jesus as appearing to His followers to prove His resurrection from the dead, so the book of Acts portrays Jesus as continuing to appear to His followers for 40 days (Acts 1:3). After providing proof of His resurrection over this extended time, Jesus ascended into heaven (1:6-11) and is now exalted at the right hand of God (2:33). Peter's sermon at Pentecost focused heavily on Jesus's resurrection (2:24-32).

> "Taking all the evidence together, it is not too much to say that there is no historic incident better or more variously supported than the resurrection of Christ."
>
> —*Canon Brooke Westcott (1825–1901)*

The good news is that because Jesus resurrected, we have assurance that we'll also be resurrected (1 Corinthians 15; 1 John 3:2). One day we'll all get body upgrades.

The Holy Spirit is an ever-present source of spiritual power and blessing for the believer.

The risen Lord instructed His followers to stay in Jerusalem so the promise concerning the Holy Spirit would be fulfilled (Acts 1:5,8; 2:1-13). It occurred a week and a half later, and the disciples became supernaturally empowered by the Holy Spirit. This empowerment filled them with new courage, and they boldly proclaimed the message of the resurrected Lord.

Filled with the Spirit

Ephesians 5:18 says we are to be *filled* with the Holy Spirit. This means we are to be *controlled* by the Holy Spirit. In the Greek, it's a present tense, indicating we are to be *perpetually* filled.

Scripture reveals that the Holy Spirit is involved in many wonderful ministries. He is the agent of regeneration and brings about the new birth (John 3:1-5; Titus 3:5). He gives Christians spiritual gifts (1 Corinthians 12; 14). He empowers us for service (Ephesians 4:12). He is our divine comforter or helper (John 14; 15:26; 16:7). He bears witness to and glorifies Jesus Christ (John 15:26). He guides the church (John 14:25-26). He convicts people of sin (John 16:7-14). And He produces wonderful spiritual fruit in believers (Galatians 5:16-26). The Holy Spirit's ministry is pivotal to the spiritual life of all believers.

Some people reject Jesus even in the face of convincing evidence that He is the divine Savior. But don't let that ever dissuade you from sharing the gospel.

A lame man was instantly healed at Peter's command (Acts 3:1-10). This added further credence to the truth that the divine Messiah, Jesus Christ, was now risen and exercised His omnipotence in mighty miracles through the apostles.

> "I look upon all the world as my parish."
> —John Wesley (1703–1791)

Peter then delivered a sermon to some of the inhabitants of Israel—Jews who had just witnessed the miracle (Acts 3:11-26). Peter called on them to repent of their rejection of Jesus. Had they repented, times of restoration and renewal would have fallen upon them. But Peter's words fell on deaf ears. They rejected Jesus despite the evidence. As we will see, however, Peter continued speaking the truth about Jesus throughout the rest of the book of Acts.

Trust in Jesus *and nothing else* for your salvation.

Peter asserted in no uncertain terms that there are not many paths to salvation. Speaking of Jesus, he said, "There is salvation in no one else, for there is no other name under heaven given among men by which we must be saved" (Acts 4:12). Salvation in Jesus alone

> "Heaven is large, but the way to heaven must be narrow."
> —Henry Smith (1560–1591)

is preached throughout the rest of the book of Acts (for example, 5:42; 8:12,35; 16:31). You might want to meditate on John 14:6 and 1 Timothy 2:5. Jesus alone saves!

We must always obey God, even if it conflicts with the commands of human authorities.

The Jewish Sanhedrin interrogated Peter and John regarding a man's healing. Peter and John affirmed the resurrected Christ healed the man, but this aggravated the Sadducees because they denied the doctrine of the resurrection. There was great concern that this

> "To be right with God has often meant to be in trouble with men."
> —A. W. Tozer (1897–1963)

man's healing would draw even more people to Jesus Christ, giving the Christian movement further momentum. The Sanhedrin therefore warned them to speak no further in Jesus's name. They replied that they were compelled to obey God rather than men (Acts 4:20). After their release, the believers prayed for continued boldness. My friend, follow their example!

Beware: sin among Christians can bring temporal judgment from God.

Ananias and Sapphira sold some land and feigned giving all the money to help meet needs in the church, but they secretly kept some of it. They lied to the Holy Spirit and deceived the church community. For this they forfeited their lives—a temporal judgment that caused the church to fear God (Acts 5:1-11). Apparently, at this early stage in the church, such fear of God was necessary to ensure the church's survival.

> ### Fearing God
>
> - Christians are to live in reverent fear of the Lord (1 Peter 1:17; 2:17).
> - Fear of the Lord motivates obedience (Deuteronomy 5:29; Ecclesiastes 12:13).
> - It also motivates the avoidance of evil (Proverbs 3:7; 8:13; 16:6).

> "You are a Christian because somebody cared. Now it's your turn."
>
> —Warren Wiersbe

We are God's witnesses, not just when it's comfortable, but also when it's uncomfortable.

More and more signs and wonders were performed by the apostles, and the church continued to expand. The apostles were rearrested and re-interrogated by Jewish authorities. Again, they boldly asserted that they must obey God rather than men (Acts 5:12-42). Today we need a baptism of boldness to fall upon the church. Far too many Christians have succumbed to the disease known by its Latin term, *non-rock-a-boatus*. Be courageous in the name of Jesus!

Part of being a Christian is helping others.

Not all the needs were being met within the church, particularly among widows, so deacons were appointed to watch over them (Acts 6:1-7). This reminds us of James 1:27: "Religion that is pure and undefiled before God, the Father, is this: to visit orphans and widows in their affliction, and to keep oneself unstained from the world." Let's be Spirit-filled people-helpers!

> "One of the old martyrs said to his persecutors as they were leading him to his death, 'You take a life from me that I cannot keep, and bestow a life upon me that I cannot lose.'"
>
> —Dwight L. Moody (1837–1899)

Sometimes standing for Christ can involve the ultimate sacrifice.

Stephen was a powerful preacher, an able debater, and performed convincing signs and wonders among

Acts

the people. But he was framed for blasphemy and arrested by the Jewish authorities. He ably defended himself before the Sanhedrin with a lengthy speech that exalted Jesus as the true Messiah. He was subsequently stoned to death (Acts 6:8–7:60).

Even so, God brought good out of evil (Romans 8:28). The biblical record of Stephen's commitment to Christ has inspired Christians to faithfulness since the first century.

God's glorious good news is for all people, with no exclusions. Ethnicity doesn't matter!

The good news of the gospel was preached to the Samaritans, people hated by the Jews. Many of them became believers. The Holy Spirit was imparted to these new members of the body of Christ just as the Spirit had earlier been imparted to Jewish believers in Christ on the day of Pentecost (Acts 8:1-40). All are one in Christ, regardless of ethnicity (see also 10:1–11:18). Jesus welcomes all!

God can redeem and transform even those who may appear unredeemable.

God brought Saul to faith in Christ. Saul had formally persecuted the church. He sought to imprison Christians. Amazingly, after his conversion, he became an incredibly powerful and bold witness to Jesus Christ (Acts 9:1-31). What a miracle!

God sends increased revelation to those who respond to the little revelation they have.

Cornelius was obedient to the limited amount of "light" he had received—that is, he had been obedient to Old Testament revelation (Acts 10:2). But he did not have enough "light" to believe in Jesus as Savior. God promptly sent Peter to Cornelius's house to explain the gospel, after which Cornelius believed in Jesus and was saved (10:44-48).

All Races Are Equal

All humans are equal in terms of

- their creation (Genesis 1:28);
- the sin problem (Romans 3:23);
- God's love for them (John 3:16); and
- God's provision of salvation for them (Matthew 28:19).

"I remember two things very clearly: I am a great sinner and Christ is a great Savior."

—John Newton (1725–1807)

Acts

Persecution cannot stop the growth of the church of Jesus Christ.

Acts records how the persecution against the church progressively worsened. There was no sign of it letting up. Things were getting intense. And yet the church also continued to grow. Despite the Roman sword against the church's throat, the church grew exponentially (Acts 11:19-30).

My friend, there is persecution of the church today in various parts of the world. Some Christians are even being killed for their faith in Christ. But rejoice! The church continues to grow. Bless the Lord!

Angels are among us, and they're active on our behalf.

Herod Agrippa I sought to destroy the infant church. Toward that end, Peter was thrown in jail. The church immediately prayed for Peter's deliverance, and God broke Peter out of jail via an angel. Peter then went to the house of John Mark's mother and knocked on the door. Disbelief eventually gave way to relief as those within the house realized Peter really was safe and back with them (Acts 12).

Angels are "ministering spirits sent out to serve for the sake of those who are to inherit salvation" (Hebrews 1:14). You don't see them, but they're there!

Christianity involves not rules and rituals, but a living relationship with Jesus Christ.

The Jerusalem Council was convened to consider whether Gentile converts should be required to adopt the ceremonial requirements of Judaism to become Christians. As president of the council, James said he did not want to burden the Gentile converts—especially in regard to the ritual of circumcision (Acts 15:1-21). This reminds us that Christianity is not about law but about grace. It is not about rituals but about a relationship with Christ (Philippians 3:8).

Biblical Insights on Persecution

- The godly will suffer persecution (2 Timothy 3:12).
- We should not be surprised if the world hates us (1 John 3:13).
- Those persecuted for righteousness are blessed (Matthew 5:10-11).
- We ought to rejoice in being counted worthy to suffer (Acts 5:41).

Guardian Angels for Christians

"Because you have made the Lord your dwelling place...he will command his angels concerning you to guard you in all your ways" (Psalm 91:9,11).

Meditate on 2 Kings 6:17; Luke 16:22; and Matthew 26:53.

"Christianity isn't only going to church on Sunday. It is living twenty-four hours of every day with Jesus Christ."

—Billy Graham

No matter who claims what, it is wise to test all doctrinal claims against Scripture.

Paul preached in Berea, and his listeners "received the word with all eagerness, examining the Scriptures daily to see if these things were so" (Acts 17:11). In other words, the Bereans tested everything Paul said against the Scriptures to make sure he was telling it straight. Notice that Paul was not angry with the Bereans, but rather he commended them. The Scriptures are our supreme authority (2 Timothy 3:15-17).

God is sovereignly and providentially with us in our work of ministry.

When Paul was evangelizing in Corinth, the Lord spoke to him in a vision. "Do not be afraid, but go on speaking and do not be silent, for I am with you, and no one will attack you to harm you, for I have many in this city who are my people" (Acts 18:9-10). Dear Christian, God has not changed. He still providentially watches over His children.

> "We can confidently say, 'The Lord is my helper; I will not fear; what can man do to me?'"
>
> —*Hebrews 13:6*

Beware of deceptions from false teachers.

While en route to Jerusalem, Paul stopped at Miletus to visit with elders of the church at Ephesus. While there he urged them to stand for the truth of the gospel and resist the advances of false teachers. He warned, "I know that after my departure fierce wolves will come in among you, not sparing the flock; and from among your own selves will arise men speaking twisted things, to draw away the disciples after them" (Acts 20:29-30). False teachers preach a counterfeit Jesus and a counterfeit gospel, which yields a counterfeit salvation. Beware!

Satan and Falsehood

- Satan inspires *false Christs* (Matthew 24:4-5).
- He employs *false teachers* who bring in "destructive heresies" (2 Peter 2:1).
- He sends out *false prophets* (Matthew 24:11).
- He sponsors *false apostles* who imitate the true apostles of Christ (2 Corinthians 11:13).

Paul shows us what it means to take up our crosses to follow Jesus.

Paul told some fellow believers, "I am ready not only to be imprisoned but even to die in Jerusalem for the name of the Lord Jesus" (Acts 21:13). This brings to mind Jesus's earlier words: "If anyone would come after me, let him deny

> "To take up the cross means that you take your stand for the Lord Jesus no matter what it costs."
>
> —*Billy Graham*

Acts

himself and take up his cross and follow me. For whoever would save his life will lose it, but whoever loses his life for my sake will find it" (Matthew 16:24-25).

The Lord is sovereign over life and death. We need not fret over human mortality.

Jesus Sovereign over Death

Jesus said, "I have the keys of Death and Hades" (Revelation 1:18).

Jesus decides who lives, who dies, and when.

Paul set sail for Rome as a prisoner. While en route, the ship encountered a violent storm with threatening waves. The crew feared the ship might sink. Paul then received a vision from the Lord. He promptly assured the ship's crew—based on the vision—that everyone would survive. As it happened, the ship was torn apart by violent waves, but the entire crew survived, as the Lord promised (Acts 27). Never forget that the Lord alone is in charge of when people die (Job 14:5; Psalm 31:15; 139:16; Acts 17:26).

A Thought to Anchor in Your Heart

The Holy Spirit baptizes believers (1 Corinthians 12:13), indwells believers (1 Corinthians 6:19), fills believers (Ephesians 5:18), gives spiritual gifts to believers (1 Corinthians 12:11), produces fruit in believers (Galatians 5:22-23), guides believers (Romans 8:14), and intercedes for believers (Romans 8:26). Stay close to Him!

Romans

Unrighteousness alienates us from God. God therefore devised a plan of salvation—centered on the atonement of Jesus Christ—whereby He imputes righteousness to believers through faith in Christ, and then progressively brings about personal righteousness (sanctification).

The apostle Paul wrote this epistle to the church at Rome in AD 57 (Romans 1:8,10-15; 15:14-17). Rome was a hub-city connected by road to numerous other cities in the ancient world. It was thus a strategic city in the spread of the gospel.

The church at Rome was predominantly made up of Gentile believers (Romans 1:5,13; 11:13; 15:15-16). But there was also a strong minority of Jewish believers (2:17; 9–11; 14).

Paul had a strong desire to visit the church of Rome (Romans 1:10-15). He apparently wrote this letter to prepare the way for his eventual visit to the city (15:14-17). Romans is the most theological of all of Paul's letters.

Following are key applicational concepts in Romans:

Don't ever be ashamed of the gospel.

Paul affirmed, "I am not ashamed of the gospel, for it is the power of God for salvation to everyone who believes" (Romans 1:16). Paul always boldly told the truth about Jesus, for he knew that eternal souls were at stake. Dear Christian, when eternal souls are at stake, there's no room for shame. The gospel is a matter of life and death.

Timeline

54–68—Nero reigns in Rome.

57—The apostle Paul writes the epistle to the Romans.

60–61—Paul travels to Rome.

61–62—Paul is imprisoned in Rome.

62–63—Paul is released from prison.

63–67—Paul is taken to Rome and imprisoned again.

64—Nero blames Christians for the great fire in Rome and persecutes them.

67—Paul is martyred.

> "I reckon him a Christian indeed that is neither ashamed of the gospel nor a shame to it."
>
> —Matthew Henry (1662–1714)

Romans

All people—Jews and Gentiles—are guilty before God. No person should ever pretend he or she is any better than anyone else. *Everyone* needs to be saved.

> "Abounding sin is the terror of the world, but abounding grace is the hope of mankind."
>
> —A. W. Tozer (1897–1963)

The Gentiles stand condemned because they have suppressed the knowledge of God they have gained from "general revelation"—that is, revelation in the world of nature (the starry universe—see Psalm 19) and their inner conscience (Romans 1:18-32). They turned to idolatry and paganism instead of turning to God.

All Have Sinned

- "All we like sheep have gone astray; we have turned—every one—to his own way" (Isaiah 53:6).
- "Surely there is not a righteous man on earth who does good and never sins" (Ecclesiastes 7:20).
- "If we say we have no sin, we deceive ourselves" (1 John 1:8).

The Jews likewise stand condemned by God because they have failed to live up to God's infinitely righteous standards. Paul, himself a Jew, provided a "reality check" for his fellow Jews by reminding them that they had consistently failed to obey God's law (Romans 2:17-29) and had failed to believe God's Word (3:1-8).

The conclusion is obvious: *All* stand guilty before God (Romans 3:9-20). That includes you and me, my friend. That's bad news. But Paul doesn't leave it there. He next shares the good news—salvation in Jesus Christ. We should never forget the depth of depravity Jesus rescued us from.

Sin: Missing the Target

- The word *sin* means "to miss the target."
- Sin is failure to live up to God's standards.
- All of us miss the target.

God shows no partiality, and neither should we.

Paul affirmed, "God shows no partiality" (Romans 2:11). God carries out His righteous standards justly and with equity. There is never any partiality or unfairness in God's dealings with people (Zephaniah 3:5; Romans 3:26). We, too, should show no partiality (James 2:4; 3:17).

Cross-References: No Partiality

Ephesians 6:9 • Acts 10:34 • Galatians 2:6 • Colossians 3:25 • 1 Peter 1:17

We are justified not by works but by faith alone. No one can earn God's salvation, so don't even try.

Since no one—Jew or Gentile (including you and me)—has it within them to attain the righteousness that leads to salvation, God's solution is to impute righteousness to those who believe in Christ. This is the doctrine of justification (Romans 3:21-31; 4:25). Justification involves not just acquitting the believing sinner of all sin, but also assigning the very righteousness of Christ to his or her account. This justification cannot be earned, but rather is given entirely by God's grace (3:21-24), based on the blood sacrifice of Jesus (3:25-26). It is a gift received by faith alone (3:27-31). How great a salvation this is!

> "I felt my heart strangely warmed, I feel I did trust in Christ, Christ alone, for salvation; an assurance was given me that he had taken away my sins, even mine, and saved me from the law of sin and death."
>
> —*John Wesley (1703–1791)*

God's wondrous plan of salvation centers entirely on the atoning death of Jesus Christ.

Without Jesus, there is no salvation. Paul summed things up by saying that we are "justified by his grace as a gift, through the redemption that is in Christ Jesus, whom God put forward as a propitiation by his blood, to be received by faith" (Romans 3:24-25; see also 4:23-25; 5:6-11,15-19; 6:1-10; 7:4-6; 8:1-4). Propitiation means Jesus's sacrificial death on the cross provided full satisfaction of God's holy demands against a sinful people, thereby averting His just wrath against them (1:18; 2:5,8; 3:5). Because of this propitiation, we can freely and justly be "declared righteous" or saved (3:4,20,24,28).

> **Cross-References: The Blood of the Lamb**
> Matthew 26:28 • Mark 14:24 • John 6:53 • Acts 20:28 • 1 Corinthians 11:25 • Colossians 1:14 • 1 John 1:7 • Revelation 1:5 • 5:9

Good news: we have *peace with God* through faith in Jesus Christ. Live daily with that wondrous reality.

Because we are declared righteous, we now have peace with God (Romans 5:1). The Father sees believers through the "lens" of Jesus Christ. And because there is peace between the Father and Jesus Christ, there is also peace between the Father and believers, since believers are "in Christ."

> **Looking Through the Lens**
> If one were to look through a piece of red glass, everything would appear red. Similarly, when we believe in Jesus Christ as our Savior, God looks at us through the lens of our Lord Jesus Christ. He sees us in all the white holiness of His Son.

As Christians, we are now dead to sin but alive unto God. We've got new spiritual life!

Paul speaks not only about the *imputation* of righteousness, but also the *impartation* of righteousness—all based on our union with

Christ. That is, in union with Christ, our old sinful selves were crucified with Christ. We "died to sin" (Romans 6:2). Moreover, in union with Christ, we were resurrected and brought to life. We have "newness of life" in Christ (6:4).

Paul therefore instructed, "Consider yourselves dead to sin and alive to God in Christ Jesus" (Romans 6:11). He urged, "Let not sin therefore reign in your mortal body, to make you obey its passions. Do not present your members to sin as instruments for unrighteousness, but present yourselves to God as those who have been brought from death to life, and your members to God as instruments for righteousness" (6:12-13).

As Christians, we've died to the law through Christ. The weight of the law is no longer on our shoulders.

Because of what Christ has accomplished, the Christian has been set free from the penalties of the law (Romans 7:1-6). Paul said, "Now we are released from the law, having died to that which held us captive, so that we serve in the new way of the Spirit and not in the old way of the written code" (7:6). In place of the sense of condemnation brought about by a failure to obey the Law, the Christian now enjoys a sense of freshness and vitality in relating to God, through the directing and empowering ministry of the Holy Spirit (8:4). Rejoice!

Even people we think of as holy Christians are acutely aware of their woeful sinfulness.

> "It is not the absence of sin but the grieving over it which distinguishes the child of God from empty professors."
>
> —A. W. Pink (1886–1952)

> "I am persuaded the more light we have, the more we see our own sinfulness."
>
> —J. C. Ryle (1816–1900)

Paul, whose commitment to Christ is unparalleled, said, "I do not do what I want, but I do the very thing I hate...I know that nothing good dwells in me, that is, in my flesh. For I have the desire to do what is right, but not the ability to carry it out" (Romans 7:15-18). My friend, it seems that the closer we draw to God, the more we are aware of our sin and our need for God's grace.

Rejoice! Christians have no further condemnation!

Paul provides us with this glorious good news: "There is therefore now no condemnation for those who are in Christ Jesus. For the law of the Spirit of life has set you free in Christ Jesus from the law of sin and death" (Romans 8:1-2).

This passage indicates there is literally "no punishment" for those who are in Christ Jesus. There has been a great exchange (8:3-5). As the Reformer Martin Luther once put it, Christ took upon Himself what was ours (sin) so that He could give us what was His (righteousness). Because of this great exchange, we have been removed from a state of condemnation before God. Indeed, we are now at peace with God. Glorious!

> **A Verse to Remember**
>
> "There is therefore now no condemnation for those who are in Christ Jesus."
>
> —*Romans 8:1*

Romans

Rejoice again—we are adopted into God's eternal family, and God is our Papa.

Paul affirmed, "You have received the Spirit of adoption as sons, by whom we cry, 'Abba! Father!'" (Romans 8:15). "Abba" is an Aramaic term of great intimacy, loosely meaning "daddy" or "papa." Paul elsewhere reminds us that God is the "father of compassion" of all believers (2 Corinthians 1:3 NIV).

Paul also affirmed, "The Spirit himself bears witness with our spirit that we are children of God, and if children, then heirs—heirs of God and fellow heirs with Christ" (Romans 8:16-17). As members of God's family, we have an inheritance awaiting us in heaven. I can't wait!

In all things God works for the good of those who love Him.

Paul affirms, "We know that for those who love God all things work together for good, for those who are called according to his purpose" (Romans 8:28). A good example is Joseph, who was sold into slavery by his own brothers (Genesis 37). While it was painful at the time, God was still in control. God ended up using these negative circumstances to bring Joseph to Egypt, where He elevated him to a position of great authority so he could save many people from famine (Genesis 41).

> "As children of a sovereign God, we are never victims of our circumstances."
>
> —*Charles Stanley*

We are often unaware of why God allows certain circumstances to fall upon us. But one thing we can rest upon for sure is that God can bring good out of any such circumstances. This means you and I must trust Him in the midst of those circumstances. Never let go of your trust in God (Proverbs 3:5-6).

We are more than conquerors through Him who loved us. So live like a conqueror!

"I am sure that neither death nor life, nor angels nor rulers, nor things present nor things to come, nor powers, nor height nor depth, nor anything else in all creation, will be able to separate us from the love of God in Christ Jesus our Lord."

—*Romans 8:38-39*

Our salvation in Jesus Christ is secure. Nothing can threaten it. Paul asks, "If God is for us, who can be against us?" (Romans 8:31). He also asks, "Who shall separate us from the love of Christ?" (8:35). The implied answer is *no one*. "We are more than conquerors through him who loved us" (8:37).

Faith comes by hearing the Word of God.

If someone should ask, "How can I increase my faith?" the answer is, saturate your mind with God's Word.

Paul affirmed that "faith comes from hearing, and hearing through the word of Christ" (Romans 10:17). Faith comes from hearing the Word of God. This reminds us of John's Gospel, "written so that you may believe that Jesus is the Christ, the Son of God, and that by believing you may have life in his name" (John 20:31).

God ultimately fulfills His promises to people even when they reject Him.

Jewish guilt is rooted in their attempt to accomplish their own righteousness (at which they failed) instead of God's plan of righteousness by faith (Romans 9:30–10:4). All the Jews had to do in New Testament times was turn to Christ the Savior in faith, but most refused, and hardened themselves against Christ (10:9-10). The Jewish people heard the gospel (10:18), they understood the gospel (10:19-20), but by their own choice, they rejected it. God is therefore justified in condemning them. Yet God still has a future for Israel (9–11).

There is yet a future salvation for Israel. God *always* fulfills His promises.

The good news is that God is not yet finished with the Jews. Israel's current rejection by God is neither complete nor is it final (Romans 11:1-10). It is not complete because there has always been a believing remnant (of which Paul was a part). It is not final because Israel will one day gloriously turn to the true Messiah and blessing will be restored to the nation (11:25-27). Meanwhile, God is bringing good out of Israel's hardness of heart, for it opens the door for Him to pour out salvation and blessings upon the Gentiles (11:11-15).

Spend regular time in God's Word, for it can transform your mind.

Paul urges, "Do not be conformed to this world, but be transformed by the renewal of your mind" (Romans 12:2). Our minds are transformed via the ministry of the Holy Spirit as we spend time reading and meditating upon God's Word (Psalm 119:11; Colossians 1:28; 3:10,16; Philippians 4:8).

> "I have stored up your word in my heart, that I might not sin against you."
>
> —Psalm 119:11

Your inner spiritual transformation always shows itself in outward fruit.

Romans closes with an extended exhortation for believers to live out their salvation. Paul speaks of the Christian's duty to God (Romans 12), to the governmental authorities (13), and to other people (14–16). Inner transformation always shows itself in outward fruit.

> "Be doers of the word, and not hearers only."
>
> —James 1:22

God wants us all to submit to authority.

The apostle Paul commanded believers to be submissive to the government because authority is ordained of God (Romans 13:1-7). Paul said resistance to government is, in the final analysis, resistance against God (13:2). Government, Paul says, resists evil (13:4).

It is noteworthy that some eight years later, after having been imprisoned a number of times by the Roman government, Paul had not changed his mind. He still taught that Christians should obey the government (1 Peter 2:13-17).

God wants us to show love and respect to each other.

Believers must show love to their neighbors, for love comes from God. Such love fulfills the requirements of the law. Further, as we walk with Christ, our daily conduct ought to conform to the conduct of Christ (Romans 13:8-14). We should begin to "take on the family likeness."

In keeping with this, Paul said strong Christians need to give consideration to their weaker brothers and sisters so they do not offend or injure them. The strong and the weak should be accepting of each other, and not judge each other (Romans 14:1-23; 15:7-13).

Romans

Christians will one day stand before the judgment seat of Christ.

Paul said, "We will all stand before the judgment seat of God." "Each of us will give an account of himself to God" (Romans 14:10,12). Each believer's life will be examined in regard to the things done while in the body. Personal motives and intents of the heart will be weighed.

Live for the Line

Life on earth is brief—it is like a dot. Life in heaven is long—it is like a line. Live for the line, not the dot.

Now, those who have placed faith in Christ are saved, and nothing threatens that. Believers are eternally secure in their salvation (John 5:24; 10:29; Ephesians 4:30; 1 John 5:10-13). This judgment has to do with the reception or loss of rewards based on the believer's personal stewardship of the gifts, talents, opportunities, and responsibilities given to him in this life.

A Thought to Anchor in Your Heart

You have been acquitted of all sin and declared righteous by God, all because of Jesus. Your slate has been wiped clean. Condemnation is gone forever!

1 Corinthians

The church is too important to ignore injurious problems that need fixing.

Paul wrote this epistle to "the church of God that is in Corinth" in AD 55 (1 Corinthians 1:2). Corinth was a strategic center in Greece—a hub of commerce from north to south, from east to west. The city had a mixed population—Roman, Egyptian, Latin, Greek, and Oriental. A gospel message proclaimed in Corinth might find its way to the distant regions of the inhabited earth.

Corinth's moral character also made it a fertile field for the gospel. The city contained the Temple of Aphrodite, the Greek goddess of love where 1000 sacred prostitutes (priestesses) were made available to its cultists. This led to sexual debauchery all over the city. The Greek word *korinthiazomai*, meaning literally "to act the Corinthian," came to mean "to practice fornication."

Paul had done missionary work in Corinth. After he moved on to Ephesus, he received notice that there were problems in Corinth. He wrote this epistle to address these problems.

Following are key applicational concepts in 1 Corinthians:

Timeline

50–51— Paul travels to Corinth and spends 18 months planting a church there.

51— Paul has a hearing before the proconsul Gallio in Corinth.

55— Paul writes his first epistle to the Corinthians from Ephesus.

56— Paul writes his second epistle to the Corinthians from Ephesus.

57— Paul writes Romans while in Corinth.

Christians are called to maintain unity in the church. No divisions. No contentions.

The church at Corinth was lacking in unity. It was divided into four basic factions, each having its own leader and particular emphasis—Paul (the Corinthians' father in Christ), Apollos (a powerful preacher), Cephas (leader of the Twelve), and Christ Himself (1 Corinthians 1:12-13). Apparently, each respective faction was acting in an antagonistic way toward the other three.

"Be united with other Christians. A wall with loose bricks is not good. The bricks must be cemented together."

—*Corrie ten Boom (1892–1983)*

Cross-References: Unity

2 Corinthians 13:11 • Ephesians 4:3 • Philippians 1:27 • 4:2 • Colossians 2:2 • 1 Peter 3:8

Seeking to do away with such divisiveness, Paul emphasized that we are all "one" in Christ (1 Corinthians 1:13). He teaches this pivotal idea by asking, "Is Christ divided?"—more literally, "Is Christ parceled out among you?"

Paul wanted the Corinthian Christians to be "united in the same mind" (1 Corinthians 1:10). The word "united" comes from a Greek word used for setting bones by a physician, and of mending broken nets. The idea is that Paul wanted the church to be without hurtful fractures, divisions, and strife—the kind of strife that causes individual believers to separate from another.

My friend, if this was a problem in Corinth, it is a much bigger problem in churches today. We so need to heed Paul's words. Let's all pursue unity!

Baptism is important, but it is not a part of the gospel that saves.

In 1 Corinthians 1:17 Paul said, "Christ did not send me to baptize but to preach the gospel." Paul here draws a clear distinction between baptism and the gospel. And since it is the gospel that saves (15:1-2), baptism is clearly not necessary to attain salvation. Rather, baptism should be the first act of obedience to God *following* a person's conversion to Christ.

Get excited—heaven is an unimaginably awesome place.

> "This is glorious! Earth recedes, Heaven is opening, God is calling me."
>
> —Dwight L. Moody, upon his deathbed (1837–1899)

Speaking of heaven, the apostle Paul affirmed, "What no eye has seen, nor ear heard, nor the heart of man imagined, what God has prepared for those who love him—these things God has revealed to us through the Spirit" (1 Corinthians 2:9-10). This means death is not a *terminus*, but a *transition* into great glory (Romans 8:18). My friend, heaven will be splendorous—more so than we can possibly imagine. God desires that we be heaven-focused Christians (Colossians 3:1-2). The earthly-focused Corinthians really needed to hear this.

The Holy Spirit helps us to understand God's Word.

> "If the Holy Spirit guides us at all, he will do it according to the Scriptures, and never contrary to them."
>
> —George Muller (1805–1898)

The Corinthian believers were ill equipped to discover God's wisdom on their own. They needed help in understanding God's Word. Paul said the Holy Spirit is our divine Teacher (1 Corinthians 2:2-16). The Holy Spirit guides us through God's Word (2 Timothy 3:15-17).

1 Corinthians

Believers will one day face Christ at His judgment seat.

All believers will one day stand before the judgment seat of Christ (1 Corinthians 3:11-15; 9:24-27; Romans 14:8-10). At that time each believer's life will be examined in regard to deeds done while in the body. Personal motives and intents of the heart will also be weighed.

Paul used a building metaphor to emphasize his point. He affirmed, "If anyone builds on the foundation with gold, silver, precious stones, wood, hay, straw—each one's work will become manifest, for the Day will disclose it, because it will be revealed by fire, and the fire will test what sort of work each one has done" (1 Corinthians 3:12-13). Notice that the materials Paul mentions in this passage are combustible in increasing degrees. Obviously the hay and straw are the most combustible. Then comes wood. Precious metals and stones are not combustible.

> **A Verse to Remember**
>
> "No one can lay a foundation other than that which is laid, which is Jesus Christ."
>
> —1 Corinthians 3:11

Bible expositors have debated what these materials represent. Perhaps the gold, silver, and costly stones represent Christ-honoring motives. Perhaps wood, hay, and straw represent carnal attitudes, sinful motives, pride-filled actions, and selfish ambition. Paul wanted the Corinthians to "build" their lives wisely.

What kind of materials are you building your life on?

Your body is a temple of the Holy Spirit, so don't commit sexual immorality.

Paul said, "The body is not meant for sexual immorality, but for the Lord, and the Lord for the body" (1 Corinthians 6:13). He urged, "Flee from sexual immorality...The sexually immoral person sins against his own body. Or do you not know that your body is a temple of the Holy Spirit within you, whom you have from God? You are not your own, for you were bought with a price. So glorify God in your body" (6:18-20).

> **Sexual Immorality**
>
> - Avoid it (1 Corinthians 6:13,18).
> - Avoid even the suspicion of it (Ephesians 5:3).
> - Flee it like Joseph did (Genesis 39:12).

Dear Christian, this is a powerful motivation to avoid sexual sin. It boils down to this: your body is a temple of God. God paid a *huge* price for it (the blood of Christ). That means God owns it. So don't even think about using your body for sin, for that defiles God's temple (Acts 15:20; 1 Thessalonians 4:3-7).

Unrepentant sexually immoral believers must be put out of the church as a disciplinary measure to motivate repentance.

A case of incest erupted within the Corinthian church—a man was having relations with his father's wife, perhaps a stepmother. Paul chastised the church for its failure to take disciplinary action. He ordered the church to oust the unrepentant sexual offender from fellowship until he repented and could be restored to fellowship.

Paul then made an important qualification. He drew a distinction between how we relate to unbelievers outside of the church and believers within the church. Paul was not telling the Corinthians to avoid all fellowship with unbelievers, for we need to evangelize them. But Christians must separate from believers who engage in willful unrepentant sin. Separation is a form of discipline intended to bring the sinning believer to repentance (1 Corinthians 5).

Believers should not file lawsuits against each other.

Paul urged church members in Corinth to stop taking legal action against each other in secular civil courts. It is better to settle differences within the Christian community—for example, by consulting one or more respected Christians (1 Corinthians 6:1-11).

Christians must make efforts to avoid offending the consciences of weaker brothers and sisters.

Some believers in Corinth thought it was no problem to eat meat that had been sacrificed to idols. Others were offended by the idea, considering it as participating in idolatry. Though Paul agreed in principle that it was fine to eat such meat, he urged believers to avoid doing so if it would injure the conscience of another. He indicated it is sometimes best to limit liberty to avoid conflict over a minor matter (1 Corinthians 8).

Evangelism is more effective when carried out with cultural sensitivity.

Paul accommodated himself to the needs and characteristics of others to evangelize among them more effectively. To the Jew, he became as a Jew to win the Jew for Christ. To the weak, he became as weak that he might win the weak for Christ. He sums it up this way: "I have become all things to all people, that by all means I might save some" (1 Corinthians 9:22).

Believers must avoid all forms of idolatry.

Paul warned that Christians must stay away from the worship of idols (1 Corinthians 10:1-22). Spiritual compromise had taken place among God's people in the past. During the wilderness experience, the Israelites succumbed to worshiping pagan gods (Numbers 25:1-18). Corinth was brimming with idols. Today the temptations are different. Idolatry might take the form of loving money, or fame, or prestige, or even immorality. We must always be on guard against idolatry.

> "A man's god is that for which he lives, for which he is prepared to give his time, his energy, his money."
>
> —D. Martyn Lloyd-Jones (1899–1981)

God always provides a way of escape when we are tempted.

Paul affirmed to the Corinthians, "No temptation has overtaken you that is not common to man. God is faithful, and he will not let you be tempted beyond your ability, but with the temptation he will also provide the way of escape, that you may be able to endure it" (1 Corinthians 10:13). My friend, we are tempted to do wrong every single day. The question is, will we avail ourselves of the way of escape God provides, or will we ignore it and succumb to sin?

A Verse to Remember

"God is faithful, and he will not let you be tempted beyond your ability, but with the temptation he will also provide the way of escape."

—1 Corinthians 10:13

Christians must celebrate the Lord's Supper in a respectful and honorable way.

First Corinthians 11:29-32 speaks of Christians in Corinth who were afflicted with illness—and even premature death—in response to their irreverence in connection with the Lord's Supper. Apparently some of the carnal Christians at Corinth were celebrating the Lord's Supper as a gluttonous, drunken feast. They were profaning what was sacred. Paul said, "That is why many of you are weak and ill, and some have died" (11:30). Paul urged, "If we judged ourselves truly, we would not be judged" (11:31).

Death as a Judgment

Unrepentant sinful living can lead to premature death (1 Corinthians 11:30; 1 John 5:16).

Righteous living leads to long life (Proverbs 10:27; Deuteronomy 4:40; 2 Kings 20:1-6).

1 Corinthians

Use your spiritual gift(s) to bless and build up others in the body of Christ.

Spiritual gifts are special abilities bestowed sovereignly by the Holy Spirit upon individual believers for the purpose of edifying the church (1 Corinthians 12:11). These gifts include teaching, pastoring, evangelizing, the message of wisdom, the message of knowledge, faith, healing, miraculous powers, prophecy, distinguishing between spirits, speaking in different tongues, and the interpretation of tongues (1 Corinthians 12:8-10; see also Ephesians 4:7-13 and Romans 12:3-8). Each of us has one or more spiritual gifts, and they are not all the same. But each gift is to be used for the mutual benefit and blessing of the body of Christ.

A hallmark of the Christian life is love.

> "The cure of boasting is to boast in the Lord all the day long."
>
> —*Charles Spurgeon (1834–1892)*

All the spiritual gifts must be exercised according to love. Regardless of how gifted a person may be, he is nothing but a "noisy gong" or a "clanging cymbal" if he does not have love (1 Corinthians 13). This instruction was needed, for some of the Corinthians were displaying pride, boasting, and one-upmanship in connection with their spiritual gifts. Let's try to avoid being a gong or cymbal.

Church services must be orderly so they won't scare away visiting unbelievers.

A Verse to Remember

"Whether you eat or drink, or whatever you do, do all to the glory of God."

—*1 Corinthians 10:31*

Paul said to the Corinthians, "What then, brothers? When you come together, each one has a hymn, a lesson, a revelation, a tongue, or an interpretation. Let all things be done for building up" (1 Corinthians 14:26). Paul then laid down guidelines on the exercise of spiritual gifts in the church so there would be no disorder in the church. After all, Paul said, "God is not a God of confusion but of peace" (14:33). This instruction was necessary because apparently too many people were speaking in tongues and giving prophecies all at the same time. This led to disarray in the church.

Cross-References: Resurrection

John 5:25,28,29 • 6:39,40,44,54 • 11:24-25 • 2 Corinthians 5:1 • Philippians 3:21 • Acts 24:15

Rejoice! Just as Christ was resurrected, so you and I will be resurrected.

The resurrection of Christ is the cornerstone of Christianity. Paul not only provided evidence that the event occurred, but also spoke of the nature of the resurrection body. Because Christ resurrected, we, too, shall be resurrected. Death will finally be defeated (1 Corinthians 15).

The rapture could take place at any moment. Be ready!

In 1 Corinthians 15:51-52 Paul describes the rapture as occurring "in the twinkling of an eye." The bodily transformation believers will experience will be near instantaneous. One moment they will be on earth in mortal bodies, the next moment they will be instantly transformed into their glorified resurrection bodies. Let's all be ready!

The Imminent Rapture

- The term *imminent* literally means "ready to take place" or "impending."
- The rapture is imminent (1 Thessalonians 1:9-10; Titus 2:13).
- This ought to motivate us to live in purity (2 Peter 3:10-14; 1 John 3:2-3).

1 Corinthians

A Thought to Anchor in Your Heart

Don't go to church just to soak up blessing. Use your spiritual gift(s) there to bless others!

2 Corinthians

Church life can sometimes be difficult. The intrusion of false doctrine can cause contention and division. Confrontations can be painful. But a commitment to sound doctrine helps restore stability.

Timeline

50–51— Paul travels to Corinth and spends 18 months planting a church there.

55— Paul writes his first epistle to the Corinthians from Ephesus.

56— Paul writes his second epistle to the Corinthians from Ephesus.

The apostle Paul wrote his second epistle to the Corinthians in AD 56. The occasion was that false prophets had penetrated the Corinthian church and had assaulted Paul's character and authority. Unfortunately, some of the Corinthians apparently believed the lies of these false prophets and rebelled against Paul.

These false teachers were leading the people astray, and unless Paul acted decisively, the entire church might become engulfed in false doctrine. Paul intervened and made a "painful visit" to them (2 Corinthians 2:1). He followed up this visit with a "severe letter" (no longer in our possession—2:4).

Later, Titus passed on news to Paul that the majority of Corinthian believers had repented of their rebellion against him (2 Corinthians 7:7). Grieved at past strained relations, Paul wrote this letter with a view to clarifying his ministry, his calling, his God-given authority as an apostle, and to soothe the wounds of the recent conflict.

Following are key applicational concepts in 2 Corinthians:

"God does not comfort us to make us comfortable but to make us comforters."

—*John Henry Jowett (1864–1923)*

God comforts us in our afflictions so that we may in turn comfort others.

Paul revealed that God comforted him in his afflictions, which thereby enabled him to be a channel of comfort to the Corinthians in their afflictions. Likewise, God's comfort to the Corinthians through Paul could then enable them to become channels of comfort to others who were suffering (2 Corinthians 1:3-11). My friend, God's comfort has a ripple effect!

God has put the Holy Spirit within our hearts as a guarantee of what is yet to come.

Life on earth can be hard. But the Holy Spirit in our lives is "a guarantee" of what is to come (2 Corinthians 1:22). The word "guarantee" was used among the Greeks to refer to a pledge that guaranteed final possession of an item. It was sometimes used of an engagement ring that acted as a guarantee that a marriage would take place. The Holy Spirit is a "guarantee" in the sense that His presence in our lives guarantees our eventual total transformation and glorification into the likeness of Christ's glorified resurrection body (Philippians 3:21).

Church members guilty of gross sin should be forgiven and restored to church fellowship following true repentance.

Paul instructed the Corinthians to forgive a man who had engaged in incest but who had now repented (2 Corinthians 2:5-13; see 1 Corinthians 5:1-13). He said they should "forgive and comfort him, or he may be overwhelmed by excessive sorrow" (verse 7). The purpose of church discipline is not to perpetually punish a person but rather to restore the person upon repentance.

> "The voice of sin is loud, but the voice of forgiveness is louder."
>
> —Dwight L. Moody (1837–1899)

Beware of peddlers of God's Word. They are plentiful and they are dangerous.

Paul said the false teachers who penetrated the Corinthian church were "peddlers of God's word" (2 Corinthians 2:17). The word "peddler" literally means "to corrupt," and was sometimes used in contexts of con men who sought to sell as genuine an inferior product that was only a cheap imitation. The false teachers in Corinth peddled inferior ideas.

We are sufficient in God alone.

Paul affirmed, "Not that we are sufficient in ourselves to claim anything as coming from us, but our sufficiency is from God" (2 Corinthians 3:5-6). He recognized that in himself he was inadequate to do God's work, and therefore depended on God. This reminds us of 2 Corinthians 9:8: "God is able to make all grace abound to you, so that having all sufficiency in all things at all times, you may abound in every good work." God is sufficient!

> "Jesus Christ is for all the New Testament writers the living and only panacea for all illness, weakness, and distress."
>
> —Erich Sauer (1898–1959)

2 Corinthians

Take comfort. Our afflictions are light and momentary. They're preparing us for heavenly glory.

Paul said of his trials, "This light momentary affliction is preparing for us an eternal weight of glory beyond all comparison" (2 Corinthians 4:17). For Paul, the future glory he would experience with the Lord in heaven far outweighed any affliction he experienced in this world (Romans 8:17-18; 1 Peter 1:6-7).

An eternal perspective that looks to "the things that are unseen" strengthens us as we face trials.

Paul affirmed, "We look not to the things that are seen but to the things that are unseen. For the things that are seen are transient, but the things that are unseen are eternal" (2 Corinthians 4:18). Paul's ability to patiently endure through his afflictions depended on looking beyond the temporal to the eternal. This reminds us of Moses. "By faith Moses, when he was grown up, refused to be called the son of Pharaoh's daughter, choosing rather to be mistreated with the people of God than to enjoy the fleeting pleasures of sin. He considered the reproach of Christ greater wealth than the treasures of Egypt, for he was looking to the reward" (Hebrews 11:24-26).

Good news: our resurrection bodies will be powerful and they will be permanent.

The apostle Paul graphically described death as being like an earthly tent being torn down. "We know that if the tent that is our earthly home is destroyed, we have a building from God, a house not made with hands, eternal in the heavens" (2 Corinthians 5:1).

Our present bodies, Paul said, are but temporary and flimsy abodes. They are weak, frail, and vulnerable. We "camp" in these "tents" during our journey toward heaven.

Our earthly bodies are not designed to be lasting

> "The Lord gets His best soldiers out of the highlands of affliction."
>
> —Charles Spurgeon (1834–1892)

> "A spiritual kingdom lies all about us, enclosing us, embracing us, altogether within reach of our inner selves, waiting for us to recognize it. God Himself is here waiting our response to His Presence. This eternal world will come alive to us the moment we begin to reckon upon its reality."
>
> —A. W. Tozer (1897–1963)

A Bible Promise

"We do not lose heart. Though outwardly we are wasting away, yet inwardly we are being renewed day by day."

—2 Corinthians 4:16 NIV

> "Anticipating heaven doesn't eliminate pain, but it lessens it and puts it in perspective. Meditating on heaven is a great pain reliever. It reminds us that suffering and death are temporary conditions."
>
> —Randy Alcorn

2 Corinthians

habitations. But a time is coming when these "habitations" will be resurrected, and our resurrection bodies will be permanent and indestructible—like a building. That is a day to look forward to.

Recipe for spiritual blessing: walk by faith and not by sight.

While speaking of dying and going to be with the Lord, Paul affirmed, "We walk by faith, not by sight" (2 Corinthians 5:7). We are reminded of Hebrews 11:1: "Faith is the assurance of things hoped for, the conviction of things not seen." The believer's faith in his future reality with the Lord gives him or her strength to endure present trials.

> "Trusting God means looking beyond what we can see to what God sees."
>
> —Charles Stanley

Don't fear death. To be absent from the body is to be at home with the Lord.

Paul affirms, "We would rather be away from the body and at home with the Lord" (2 Corinthians 5:8). The Greek word for "with" in the phrase "home *with* the Lord" suggests face-to-face fellowship. It is a word used of intimate relationships. Paul thereby indicated that the fellowship he expects to have with Christ immediately following his physical death will be one of great intimacy.

Live your life with the daily expectancy that you will face the judgment seat of Christ.

All believers will one day stand before the judgment seat of Christ (*Bema*) (2 Corinthians 5:9-10). Each believer's life will be examined in regard to deeds done while in the body. Personal motives and intents of the heart will also be weighed. In view of that reality, Paul affirmed, "We make it our aim to please him" (5:9).

Possible Forfeiture of Rewards

Some may lose rewards at the judgment seat of Christ (1 Corinthians 3:15). They may experience a sense of shame (2 John 1:8).

Jonathan Edwards (1703-1758) therefore urged, "Resolved, never to do anything, which I should be afraid to do, if it were the last hour of my life."

Rejoice! You are a new creature in Christ.

Paul said, "If anyone is in Christ, he is a new creation" (2 Corinthians 5:17). At the moment of conversion, the believing sinner is made spiritually alive. He is regenerated (John 3:3; Titus 3:5; 1 Peter 1:23). Paul then affirmed, "The old has passed away; behold, the new has come" (2 Corinthians 5:17). The person's

A Verse to Remember

"If anyone is in Christ, he is a new creation."

—2 Corinthians 5:17

2 Corinthians

old value systems, priorities, and beliefs give way to a new nature that focuses on God and His Word.

We are all ambassadors for Christ. Represent Him well.

Perhaps one of the best pictures of a person who communicates with gentleness and respect is an ambassador. The apostle Paul says, "We are ambassadors for Christ, God making his appeal through us" (2 Corinthians 5:20). For an ambassador, it is not just *what* you say that is important, it is also *how* you say it. Let's not just be *effective* communicators of God's truth; let's also be *gracious* communicators of God's truth.

Rejoice! Jesus took what was ours so He could give us what is His.

Paul affirms, "For our sake he made him to be sin who knew no sin, so that in him we might become the righteousness of God" (2 Corinthians 5:21). While Jesus was always without sin *actually*, He was made to be sin for us *judicially*. That is, by His death on the cross, He paid the penalty for our sins and canceled the debt of sin against us. So while Jesus never committed a sin *personally*, He was made to be sin for us *substitutionally*.

> "Lord Jesus, you are my righteousness, I am your sin. You have taken upon yourself what is mine and given me what is yours. You have become what you were not so that I might become what I was not."
>
> —Martin Luther (1483–1546)

Believers should not be unequally yoked with unbelievers.

Paul urged, "Do not be unequally yoked with unbelievers" (2 Corinthians 6:14). This verse does not prohibit the inevitable interactions with unbelievers that are a part of everyday life (1 Corinthians 5:9-10). Rather, Paul was calling the Corinthians to separate from false teachers. After all, such false teachers would do nothing but lead the Corinthian believers astray (2 Corinthians 11:3). The best option is to always be yoked with Christ (Matthew 11:29-30).

Unequally Yoked

Christians are not to be unequally yoked with unbelievers (2 Corinthians 6:14).

"Do not...take part in the sins of others; keep yourself pure" (1 Timothy 5:22).

"Take no part in the unfruitful works of darkness" (Ephesians 5:11).

Make every effort to help your brothers and sisters who are in financial need.

The Macedonian Christians had been liberal in their giving to the needy brethren in Jerusalem, who were experiencing something of a famine (2 Corinthians 8:1-6). Paul desired that the Corinthian believers do the same (8:7–9:15). He let them know their generosity would be rewarded by God. As a motivation for giving, Paul reminded them how Jesus gave Himself on their behalf. He also reminded them that God loves a cheerful giver.

Beware of those who teach a different Jesus, a different spirit, or a different gospel.

False prophets are dangerous because, among other things, they teach a different Jesus who preaches a different gospel (2 Corinthians 11:4)—and that combination yields a "different" salvation (which is no salvation at all). Salvation is found only in the true Jesus and the true gospel (John 14:6; Acts 4:12). This is why Paul constantly urged his followers to beware of false prophets.

Beware: Satan can mimic an angel of light.

Paul tells us, "Satan disguises himself as an angel of light" (2 Corinthians 11:14). Scripture reveals that Satan has his own church—the "synagogue of Satan" (Revelation 2:9); his own ministers—ministers of darkness that bring false sermons (2 Corinthians 11:4-5); his own system of theology—"teachings of demons" (1 Timothy 4:1; Revelation 2:24); ministers that proclaim a counterfeit gospel (Galatians 1:7-8); false teachers who bring in "destructive heresies" (2 Peter 2:1); false prophets (Matthew 24:11); and false apostles who imitate the true apostles (2 Corinthians 11:13). Satan is a master deceiver. Beware!

> **Satan the Arch-Deceiver**
> - Satan distorts Scripture (Matthew 4:6).
> - Satan outwits humans (2 Corinthians 2:11).
> - Satan masks himself (2 Corinthians 11:14).
> - Satan is a master deceiver (Revelation 12:9).

God's strength is made perfect in human weakness.

As a true apostle, Paul received exceedingly great revelations in a vision. To keep him humble, God allowed him to suffer a thorn in the flesh (2 Corinthians 12:7). The Greek word for "flesh" indicates a bodily ailment of some sort. And it hurt.

Paul prayed to the Lord three times that this thorn might be taken away. God said no. Paul's affliction was not for *punishment* but for *protection*—that is,

> **A Verse to Remember**
> "My grace is sufficient for you, for my power is made perfect in weakness."
>
> —2 Corinthians 12:9

protection from a self-inflated attitude. So we find Paul boasting in his weakness, for when he is weak, Christ's power is all the more present.

It is wise for Christians to periodically examine themselves to ensure they are in the faith.

Paul urged, "Examine yourselves, to see whether you are in the faith" (2 Corinthians 13:5). The Amplified Bible renders it well: "Examine and test and evaluate your own selves to see whether you are holding to your faith and showing the proper fruits of it."

A Thought to Anchor in Your Heart

Christ is fully sufficient to meet your every need. When you are weak, God's strength is abundantly available.

Galatians

Our salvation is a free grace-gift received by faith alone—with no works involved.

Paul wrote this epistle "to the churches of Galatia" in AD 50 (Galatians 1:2). The backdrop is that Judaizers had infiltrated some of Paul's congregations, claiming he made the gospel more appealing to Gentiles by removing Jewish legal requirements. They taught that after believing in Christ, the Gentile must take an additional step and become a Jew through circumcision, eat only the right kinds of foods, and participate in certain Jewish feast days (Acts 15:24; 20:29-30). This effectively added works to grace.

Paul taught that salvation is a gift that is received solely by faith in Christ (Galatians 3:24-26). He warned that if anyone delivered to the church any other gospel than the one previously handed down—including this legalistic gospel from Judaizers—they were *accursed before God* (1:8). He strongly affirmed that salvation is through *faith alone* by *grace alone*, and there is no requirement for Gentiles to "become Jews" to be true Christians.

Following are key applicational concepts in Galatians:

The gospel is not a man-made idea but rather comes straight from God through an apostle of God. You can therefore trust it with no doubts whatsoever. Believe it and rejoice!

Paul affirmed to the Galatians that he was "an apostle—not from men nor through men, but through Jesus Christ and God the Father" (Galatians 1:1; see also verses 15-20). The false teachers tried to

Timeline

47–49— Paul, Barnabas, and John Mark set out on their first missionary tour.

49–50— Paul wrote his epistle to the Galatians to rescue them from a false gospel of legalism.

49–50— Paul and Silas visit south Galatia.

49–50— Timothy joins Paul and Silas as they journey through north Galatia to Troas.

Grace and Peace (Galatians 1:3)

- Paul said, "Grace to you and peace from God our Father and the Lord Jesus Christ."

- These are important words for people engulfed in legalism (like the Galatians).

- The word "grace" means "unmerited favor."

- Because of God's unmerited favor, humans can have peace with God (Romans 5:1-2).

Galatians

undermine Paul's gospel by first undermining his authority. They claimed he was not a true apostle of God. Paul therefore established his apostleship in no uncertain terms. He was made an apostle not by men, but by God Himself. Case closed!

Paul then affirmed, "The gospel that was preached by me is not man's gospel. For I did not receive it from any man, nor was I taught it, but I received it through a revelation of Jesus Christ" (Galatians 1:11-12). Paul's gospel message was backed by the other apostles in Jerusalem (2:1-10). Since the true gospel came from God, the Galatians were to reject all other gospels—that is, *man-made* gospels—including the one taught by the false teachers who had infiltrated the churches in Galatia.

Don't ever fall for a gospel of works. It is a hellish false doctrine.

Paul expressed dismay at the Galatians' departure from a grace-gospel (Galatians 1:6-10). They had apparently given some credence to the false teachings of the Judaizers.

Paul affirmed that those who bring a different gospel are "accursed." This comes from the Greek word *anathema*, which refers to consigning the offending person to eternal hell (Romans 9:3; 1 Corinthians 12:3; 16:22).

My friend, let Paul's strong words be a lesson to us. Any gospel that conflicts with the gospel of grace taught by Paul is to be outright rejected.

Because of Christ's work on the cross, we enjoy true freedom and newness of life.

The law brought condemnation. But Jesus Christ—through His work of salvation on the cross—delivered us from the law and brought us freedom and newness of life. Jesus "gave himself for our sins to deliver us from the present evil age" (Galatians 1:4).

A Verse to Remember

"Even if we or an angel from heaven should preach to you a gospel contrary to the one we preached to you, let him be accursed."

—*Galatians 1:8*

Cross-References: Paul's Apostleship

Romans 1:1 • 11:13 • 1 Corinthians 9:1 • 15:9 • 2 Corinthians 1:1 • 11:5 • Ephesians 1:1 • Colossians 1:1 • 1 Timothy 1:1 • 2 Timothy 1:1

"Whitefield and Wesley might preach the gospel better than I do, but they cannot preach a better gospel."

—*Charles Spurgeon (1834–1892)*

The Gospel

The word "gospel" means "good news." By trusting in Christ, we are

- justified (Romans 3:24);
- reconciled (2 Corinthians 5:19);
- forgiven (Colossians 2:14); and
- adopted (Romans 8:14).
- That's very good news indeed!

Galatians

"Christ redeemed us from the curse of the law...so that we might receive the promised Spirit through faith" (3:13-14).

Paul indicated that just as we are identified with Christ in His death, so we are identified with Christ in His resurrection life. Paul affirmed, "I have been crucified with Christ. It is no longer I who live, but Christ who lives in me. And the life I now live in the flesh I live by faith in the Son of God, who loved me and gave himself for me" (Galatians 2:20). Glorious!

> "'Christ liveth in me.' And how great the difference!—instead of bondage, liberty; instead of failure, quiet victories within; instead of fear and weakness, a restful sense of sufficiency in Another."
>
> —Hudson Taylor (1832–1905)

Rejoice! You and I are made right with God by faith alone in Christ alone.

Paul affirmed that "a person is not justified by works of the law but through faith in Jesus Christ." He said, "By works of the law no one will be justified" (Galatians 2:16).

The word "justified" is a legal term. Negatively, the word means one is once-for-all pronounced not guilty before God. Positively, the word means one is once-for-all pronounced righteous. When a person trusts in Christ for salvation, he is pronounced "not guilty" and once-for-all righteous (Galatians 2:15-17; 3:11,24; 5:4).

> ### Cross-References: Justification
>
> Genesis 15:6 • Acts 13:39 • Romans 3:20-28 • 5:1 • 1 Corinthians 6:11 • Galatians 3:6 • Philippians 3:9 • Hebrews 10:38 • 11:4

Though the Jews previously tried to earn right standing with God by works, Paul indicated that God's declaration of righteousness (justification) is provided "by his grace as a gift" (Romans 3:24). The word "grace" means "unmerited favor." It is because of God's unmerited favor that human beings can freely be "declared righteous" before God.

This does not mean God's declaration of righteousness has no objective basis, because it does. The word "redemption" literally means "ransom payment." This is a word adapted from the slave market. We were formerly enslaved to sin and Satan, but Jesus ransomed us by His death on the cross. His shed blood was the ransom payment (Romans 3:25). This makes justification possible. Thank You, thank You, thank You, Lord Jesus!

Galatians

We began our walk with Christ through faith. We also experience our growth in Christ through faith.

> "The most damnable and pernicious heresy that has ever plagued the mind of man was the idea that somehow he could make himself good enough to deserve to live with an all-holy God."
>
> —Martin Luther (1483–1546)

Paul asked the Galatians, "Did you receive the Spirit by works of the law or by hearing with faith? Are you so foolish? Having begun by the Spirit, are you now being perfected by the flesh?" (Galatians 3:2-3).

Dear Christian, Paul's point was that the Galatians became Christians in the first place *by faith, and not by works.* Now they were to experience spiritual growth *by faith, and not by works.* The same is true of you and me.

Abraham was justified by faith alone, and that same principle applies today.

Paul, a Hebrew of Hebrews, knew the Old Testament well. To make his case about justification, Paul affirmed that Abraham "believed God, and it was counted to him as righteousness" (Galatians 3:6). He says the same thing in Romans 4:3: "Abraham believed God, and it was counted to him as righteousness."

Paul indicated there has never been any other means of salvation than by grace through faith. Even the Old Testament teaches justification by faith. That being so, the Galatians should not listen to the claims of the false teachers.

Listen, my fellow believer. Some today are setting forth a false gospel—a gospel tainted by requiring you to "do this" or "do that." These are days for discernment. Don't be deceived. Test all gospel claims against the Scriptures (see Acts 17:11).

While the law can't save anyone, the law is good because it acts like a tutor that leads people straight to Jesus for salvation.

A very important function of the law is that it is like a tutor that leads us to Christ for salvation (Galatians 3:24-25). Among the ancient Romans, it was the job of a tutor to lead a child to school. Just as an ancient tutor would lead a child to school, so the law is our tutor in leading us straight to Jesus Christ, the Savior. The law does this by showing us our sin and then pointing to the marvelous grace of Christ.

Once we have "arrived" to Christ—trusting in Him as our Savior, and being justified by faith—the law has done its job and it no longer holds sway over us.

As Paul put it in Romans 10:4, "Christ is the end of the law for righteousness to everyone who believes."

Don't ever slip from grace into legalism. That amounts to trading freedom for slavery.

Paul informs the Galatians that he is "perplexed"—literally, "at his wits' end"—over them, for they have essentially traded freedom for slavery by shifting from a grace-gospel to a works-gospel (Galatians 4:8-20). My friend, we might rephrase Paul's thought this way: "You guys absolutely boggle my mind. What on earth were you thinking, trading in your freedom for a life of oppressive bondage? Have you lost your minds?"

> **A Verse to Remember**
>
> "For freedom Christ has set us free; stand firm therefore, and do not submit again to a yoke of slavery."
>
> —*Galatians 5:1*

Our freedom in Christ does not mean freedom to sin. Rather, it means freedom to love and serve Christ without fear of condemnation by the law.

Believers who have been delivered from the law must be cautious not to fall into lawlessness (Galatians 5:13-15). We are set free not only from bondage to the law, but also bondage to sin. Our liberty in Christ should therefore never be used as an excuse to engage in easy sin. Rather, our freedom ought to motivate us to love and serve Christ.

Walking in dependence on the Holy Spirit leads to victory over the flesh and the manifestation of the fruit of the Spirit in our lives.

Paul says, "Walk by the Spirit, and you will not gratify the desires of the flesh" (Galatians 5:16). The word "walk" in this verse is a present tense verb, indicating continuing action. We are to persistently and continually walk in dependence upon the Spirit. As we do this, we will live in a way that is pleasing to God.

Paul also indicated that as we walk in the Spirit, the fruit of the Spirit grows in our lives. "The fruit of the Spirit is love, joy, peace, patience, kindness, goodness, faithfulness, gentleness, self-control" (Galatians 5:22-23). Notice that the qualities listed in Galatians

> "You might as well try to hear without ears, or breathe without lungs, as try to live a Christian life without the Spirit of God in your heart."
>
> —*Dwight Moody (1837–1899)*

> **A Verse to Remember**
>
> "Walk by the Spirit, and you will not gratify the desires of the flesh."
>
> —*Galatians 5:16*

Galatians

5:22-23 present an accurate profile of Jesus Christ Himself. The character of our Lord is reproduced in our lives as we walk in dependence upon the Spirit. As we walk in the Spirit, we progressively take on the family likeness (as members of God's forever family).

Bear One Another's Burdens (Galatians 6:2)

We not only need God, we need each other. Here's a strategy: "Whatever you wish that others would do to you, do also to them" (Matthew 7:12).

Never get weary in doing good.

Paul urges us to bear each other's burdens and never get weary in doing good (Galatians 6). He says this right after urging us to walk in the Spirit. The one who walks in the Spirit is empowered and motivated to help his brothers and sisters and seek to do good! Let it be so in each of our lives.

A Thought to Anchor in Your Heart

Because you are justified by faith alone, you can do nothing to add to the salvation already provided for you in Christ. Jesus has done it all. Rejoice!

Galatians

Ephesians

We are blessed to have incredible spiritual riches in Jesus Christ.

Paul wrote this epistle "to the saints who are in Ephesus" in AD 61. Ephesus was a city characterized by luxurious homes, elegant buildings, and wide avenues. It was a leading commercial and trade center of the ancient world, and was understandably one of the more prominent cities in the province of Asia.

Ephesus was well known for its temple of the Roman goddess Diana, a building considered one of the seven wonders of the world. The city was brimming with pagans.

During his third missionary tour, Paul spent three years in Ephesus building up the church (Acts 19). When he left, his young associate Timothy pastored there for another year, seeking to establish the church in sound doctrine (1 Timothy 1:3,20).

Paul later wrote Ephesians while a prisoner in Rome in AD 61. He intended it to be a circular letter to be read not just at the church at Ephesus but at other churches as well.

You will notice there are no commands in chapters 1–3, but over 30 commands in chapters 4–6. Paul provides the doctrinal basis for living in chapters 1–3 (focusing on the believer's riches and blessings in Jesus Christ), and then draws the practical application of that doctrine in chapters 4–6. More specifically, in view of the reality that we are positionally "in Christ," we are now to walk for Christ as we continue to live on earth. We must walk in unity (Ephesians 4:1-16), in holiness (4:17-32), in love (5:1-6), in the light (5:7-14), in wisdom (5:15-6:9), and in victory (6:10-20). Paul thoroughly demonstrates how doctrine affects duty.

Timeline

52—Paul travels through Ephesus on his second missionary tour.

52—Apollos is mentored by Aquila and Priscilla in Ephesus.

54—Paul returns to Ephesus and ministers there for a few years.

56—Paul writes 1 Corinthians from Ephesus.

60–61—Paul travels to Rome.

61—Paul is imprisoned in Rome.

61—Paul writes his epistle to the Ephesians from prison.

> "God is more anxious to bestow his blessings on us than we are to receive them."
>
> —Augustine (354–430)

Ephesians

Following are key applicational concepts in Ephesians:

We are all born into the world spiritually dead, separated from God because of our sin. Praise the Lord, we are brought near to God in Christ, our sin-bearer.

> **Sin in the Heart**
>
> "The heart of the human problem is the problem of the human heart."
>
> —*Adrian Rogers (1931–2005)*

Human beings are born into the world in a state of sin. The sin nature—rooted in Adam and Eve's sin—is passed on from the moment of conception. That is why Ephesians 2:3 says we are "*by nature* the children of wrath" (emphasis added). Other Bible passages make this same point. In Psalm 51:5 David lamented, "Behold, I was brought forth in iniquity, and in sin did my mother conceive me."

This sin has alienated human beings from God (Romans 3:9-20). However, Jesus—by His work on the cross—has shattered that alienation and brought us near to God. "Now in Christ Jesus you who once were far off have been brought near by the blood of Christ" (Ephesians 2:13).

No more alienation. Praise Jesus!

> **Cross-References: Adoption into God's Family**
>
> Romans 8:14,29 • Galatians 3:26 • 4:5 • Philippians 2:15 • Hebrews 12:6-9 • 1 John 3:1

You have incredibly rich spiritual blessings in Jesus Christ. Don't live like a spiritual pauper.

God's eternal purposes include the redemption, adoption, forgiveness, and sealing of a special people—*Christians*—who will forever live with God. Incredibly rich blessings are ours because of Jesus Christ. "Blessed be the God and Father of our Lord Jesus Christ, who has blessed us in Christ with every spiritual blessing in the heavenly places" (Ephesians 1:3).

> **Verses to Remember**
>
> "Now to him who is able to do far more abundantly than all that we ask or think, according to the power at work within us, to him be glory in the church and in Christ Jesus throughout all generations, forever and ever."
>
> —*Ephesians 3:20-21*

My friend, the Ephesian believers lived like spiritual paupers, perhaps unaware that such rich blessings were theirs in Jesus Christ. That's why Paul reminded them of this. Paul knew they could not possibly live as vibrant Christians unless they were aware of their spiritual riches.

I wonder if the same is sometimes true of us? Do we live day to day with the awareness of how rich we are in Christ? We cannot be reminded of this pivotal truth often enough.

Ephesians

Rejoice! All three persons in the triune God play a role in our salvation: the Father, the Son, and the Holy Spirit. God must really love us!

A careful reading of Scripture reveals that it was the Father who planned and ordained salvation (Ephesians 1:3-6,13-14; 2:4,8-9; see also John 3:16; Isaiah 53:6,10). This plan was not an emergency response conceived as a plan of rescue after humankind fell, but rather was the Father's sovereign choice in eternity past.

Jesus's role was that of Redeemer. "In him we have redemption through his blood" (Ephesians 1:7). Our various spiritual blessings are all rooted in Him—"in Christ" (1:3), "through Jesus Christ" (1:5), "in Christ" (1:9), "in him" (1:10), "in him" (1:11), "in Christ" (1:12). How awesome is our beloved Savior.

Ephesians 4:30 indicates that believers are sealed unto the day of redemption by the Holy Spirit (see also Ephesians 1:13-14). This seal, which indicates ownership, authority, and security, cannot be broken. The seal guarantees our entry into heaven.

Our salvation rests on God's amazing grace. Works play no role, so don't even try.

Our salvation, from beginning to end, is a result of God's amazing grace. "By grace you have been saved through faith. And this is not your own doing; it is the gift of God, not a result of works, so that no one may boast" (Ephesians 2:8-9). "In him we have redemption through his blood, the forgiveness of our trespasses, according to the riches of his grace, which he lavished upon us" (1:7-8). The word "grace" means "undeserved favor." Because salvation is a grace-gift, it can't be earned. It's free! We can't attain it by a good performance.

Grace is necessary because any attempt to save ourselves by good deeds is futile. It cannot be done. No matter how hard we try, it is no use. The source

---

Cross-References: God's Sovereignty

Exodus 15:18 • Deuteronomy 4:39 • 10:14 • 2 Chronicles 20:6 • Psalm 33:8-11 • Isaiah 40:21-26 • 46:10 • Romans 14:11

A Bible Promise

"When you believed, you were marked in him with a seal, the promised Holy Spirit, who is a deposit guaranteeing our inheritance until the redemption of those who are God's possession—to the praise of his glory."

—*Ephesians 1:13-14 NIV*

God's Eternal Purpose (Ephesians 3:11)

What has happened in the past, what is happening today, and what will happen in the prophetic future is all evidence of the unfolding of the eternal purposes of God.

"God loves each one of us as if there were only one of us to love."

—*Augustine (354–430)*

Ephesians

of salvation lies in God's grace, not in our personal exertions of willpower, or in efforts of discipline, or any other self-effort. Salvation is free!

Christians have spiritual unity in Jesus Christ—we are all "one body." It therefore makes good sense to seek to live in day-to-day unity.

In God's wondrous salvation both Jews and Gentiles become one in the body of Christ. People from every tribe and nation are a collective unity in the body of Christ (Ephesians 2:11-22). The church is a single organism composed of many parts (that is, many Christians)—with each "part" having a specific and important function. Our working together in perfect harmony hinges on such virtues as humility, gentleness, and mutual support. Christ is the head of this organism (4:1-16).

> In essentials, *unity*; in non-essentials, *liberty*; and in all things, *charity*.

What all this means is that since we are spiritually one in Christ, we should seek unity with our brothers and sisters in Christ. Let's do it.

No people groups are excluded from invitation into God's eternal family. Let's therefore tell everyone about Jesus.

Paul speaks of a glorious mystery in Ephesians 3. In the Bible, a "mystery" is a truth that cannot be discerned simply by human investigation, but requires special revelation from God. Generally, this word refers to a truth that was unknown to people living in Old Testament times, but is now revealed to humankind by God (Matthew 13:17; Colossians 1:26).

What was *known* in Old Testament times was that God was bringing salvation to the Jewish people. What was *unknown*—but was now being revealed through Paul—is that the Gentiles would also be recipients of God's salvation and blessings. "This mystery is that the Gentiles are fellow heirs, members of the same body, and partakers of the promise in Christ Jesus through the gospel" (Ephesians 3:6). This means the good news of salvation in Jesus Christ is for all people everywhere.

Since this is the case, doesn't it make good sense for us to share the good news of the gospel with all people everywhere? Jesus, the Lamb of God, is said to have "ransomed people for God from every tribe and language and people and nation," and "made them a kingdom and priests to our God" (Revelation 5:9-10). Let's do our part.

> "Go therefore and make disciples of all nations."
>
> —*Jesus Christ (Matthew 28:19)*

Daily transformation is a key component of the Christian life. Let's continually put away the old (sin) and bring on the new (right living).

Paul emphasized that because the church is made up of many individual members, each member must be considerate of each other. Toward that end, they must "put off" the old sinful self, and "put on" the new self—the Christ-submitting self (Ephesians 4:17-32). The goal: daily transformation!

We ought to walk in love 24/7, just as Jesus did.

Paul calls us to love others as Christ loved us. This type of love means treating our brothers and sisters with integrity. More specifically, believers—motivated by love—must seek to avoid the sins that characterize their sinful natures, such as sexual immorality, impurity, and crude speech (Ephesians 5:1-21).

"To love means loving the unlovable."

—G. K. Chesterton (1874–1936)

Resisting such sins becomes possible by yielding to the Holy Spirit. Paul exhorts, "Be filled with the Spirit" (Ephesians 5:18). To be filled with the Holy Spirit means one's life will be controlled or governed no longer by self but by the Holy Spirit. It is not a matter of acquiring more of the Spirit, but rather of the Spirit of God acquiring all of the individual. The filling of the Spirit is accomplished in the life of a believer when he or she is fully yielded to the indwelling Holy Spirit. A person "full of the Holy Spirit" behaves in a way fitting with that filling. That is, the person acts in a way pleasing to God, avoiding sin and loving others.

Our walk with Christ ought to affect our family relationships.

Husbands are to love their wives as Christ loved the church; wives are to submit to their husbands (Ephesians 5:22-33); and children must obey their parents (6:1-3). God invented the family unit in the first place (Genesis 1:26-27; 2:18). It therefore makes good sense to operate the family unit according to His instructions.

Ephesians

The devil aims to bring you down. Don't neglect to put on God's armor.

"There are two equal and opposite errors into which our race can fall about the devils. One is to disbelieve in their existence. The other is to believe, and to feel an excessive and unhealthy interest in them."

—C. S. Lewis (1898–1963)

God provides us with armor to protect us against the devil. "Put on the whole armor of God, that you may be able to stand against the schemes of the devil" (Ephesians 6:11). "Wearing" this armor means our lives will be characterized by righteousness, obedience to God, faith in God, and an effective use of God's Word.

A Thought to Anchor in Your Heart

The devil seeks to make you feel like a worm and a pauper before God. Don't listen to him. You are loved by God and are incredibly rich in Jesus Christ.

Ephesians

Philippians

The Christian life is characterized by joy,
a heavenly perspective, confident living in Christ,
righteous living, peace, and contentment.

Paul wrote this letter to the believers "at Philippi" in AD 63. The Philippian church began small. Because Philippi was a Roman colony, there were too few Jews to warrant the establishment of a synagogue, which required a minimum of ten adult Jewish men. The Jews therefore met for prayer by the river Gangites on the Sabbath. It was at this location that Paul addressed the first converts of Philippi during his second missionary tour.

The Philippian church eventually experienced some problems. There were intense rivalries (Philippians 2:3-4), legalistic disturbances caused by Judaizers (3:2-3), and some who were flirting with worldliness (3:18-19). Because of these internal problems, Paul wrote this letter as a corrective measure.

Following are key applicational concepts in Philippians:

Timeline

50—Paul and his companions visit Philippi during their second missionary tour and plant a church.

57—Paul revisits Philippi to collect funds for the church at Jerusalem.

61—Paul is imprisoned in Rome.

63—Paul writes his epistle to the Philippians while imprisoned.

You can have joy even in the midst of life's most difficult circumstances.

Christians can experience joy even during life's roughest moments. Paul is a perfect example of this. He was full of joy even in the face of persecution, imprisonment, and the threat of death. Not only did Paul experience joy while he was in prison (Philippians 1:18; see also 2:17-18); he also urged the Philippians, "Rejoice in the Lord always; again I will say, rejoice" (4:4; see also 3:1). Notice that Paul was not talking about a happiness dependent on one's external

> "Disappointments are inevitable; discouragement is a choice."
>
> —*Charles Stanley*

Cross-References: Joy
Nehemiah 8:10 • Psalm 16:11 • 30:5 • 89:16 • 126:5 • 132:16 • Isaiah 12:3 • 35:10 • Luke 2:10 • John 15:11 • 16:24 • 17:13 • Romans 14:17

Philippians

circumstances. Paul said to rejoice "in the Lord." The Lord is the fount of joy from which we drink. While our circumstances may change, the Lord does not change. He is always there as our source of joy. So, dear Christian, drink of Him richly, today and forevermore.

God will never give up on you. He will complete His work of salvation in you—all the way into heaven.

Paul told the Philippians, "He who began a good work in you will bring it to completion at the day of Jesus Christ" (Philippians 1:6). Paul is apparently here referring to the third stage of salvation, which is glorification. As a backdrop, the salvation we have in Christ is threefold, involving the past, present, and future. In terms of the past, God has delivered us from the penalty of sin and wiped our slate clean. This happens the moment we trust in Christ for salvation (Acts 16:31). The present aspect of salvation involves deliverance from the power of sin in our daily lives (Romans 8:13; Philippians 2:12). In the future, when we enter into glory (in heaven), we will be finally delivered from the very presence of sin (Romans 13:11; Titus 2:12-13). In this third stage, we will have glorified resurrection bodies in heaven, and sin will be a thing of the past. God will thus bring salvation "to completion." Rejoice!

Sometimes difficult circumstances in life can serve to help spread the gospel.

Paul was being persecuted, was now in prison, and faced the possibility of death. Yet even in these dire circumstances he could inform the Philippians that what had happened to him actually furthered the cause of Christ (Philippians 1:12). As a result of Paul's imprisonment, the gospel had become known throughout the entire imperial guard (1:13). As well, Paul's imprisonment served to embolden other brothers in Christ to speak the truth of the gospel without fear (1:14). God is a master at bringing good out of evil (Romans 8:28).

Whether we live or die, all is ultimately good. To live is Christ but to die is gain.

Paul affirmed, "For to me to live is Christ, and to die is gain" (Philippians 1:21). For Paul to live would mean more fruitful service for Christ, including service among the Philippians (verse 22). However, being with Christ is far better than remaining in the physical body. Paul knew that the very moment after physical death occurred, he would be with Christ.

Paul then said, "I am hard pressed between the two. My desire is to depart and be with Christ, for that is far better" (Philippians 1:23). The word for "depart" was used in biblical times in reference to a ship being loosed from its moorings to sail away from the dock. The "mooring" that kept Paul from departing to heaven was his commitment to work among believers on earth until his work was complete. His ultimate desire, however, was to "sail" directly into God's presence.

> "The best moment of a Christian's life is his last one, because it is the one that is nearest heaven."
>
> —*Anonymous*

Blessed Either Way

Whether we live or die, *all is good*. If we live, we serve Christ on earth. If we die, we go to be with Christ in heaven.

The word "depart" was also used in biblical times for freeing someone from chains. Here on earth we are anchored to the hardships and heartaches of this life. In death these chains are broken. We are set free for entry into heaven.

This reminds us of 2 Corinthians 5:8, where Paul said he preferred to be "away from the body and at home with the Lord." The Greek word for "with" in the phrase "home with the Lord" suggests close, face-to-face fellowship. Paul indicated the fellowship he expects to have with Christ immediately following his physical death will be one of great intimacy.

We should all live in a manner worthy of the gospel.

Paul urged the Philippian believers, "Let your manner of life be worthy of the gospel of Christ" (Philippians 1:27). Paul often made this point to his readers (Ephesians 4:1; Colossians 1:10; 1 Thessalonians 2:11-12). His primary idea was that a Christian's manner of living needed to be consistent with what he or she believed. This reminds us of what James said: "Be doers of the word, and not hearers only, deceiving yourselves" (James 1:22).

Putting others above ourselves helps us to maintain unity in the church.

Paul urged, "Do nothing from selfish ambition or conceit, but in humility count others more significant than yourselves. Let each of you look not only to his

Cross-References: Humility

Micah 6:8 • Luke 14:10 • 22:26 • Romans 11:20 • 12:3 • James 4:10 • 1 Peter 5:5

Philippians

own interests, but also to the interests of others" (Philippians 2:3-4). Paul's underlying emphasis was that there needed to be church unity. One means of attaining that unity was for church members to be humble, putting each other first.

> "You can have no greater sign of a confirmed pride than when you think you are humble enough."
>
> —William Law (1686–1761)

> "Humility is a self-forgetfulness."
>
> —C. S. Lewis (1898–1963)

Christ is our greatest example of humility. Paul therefore instructed, "Have this mind among yourselves, which is yours in Christ Jesus, who, though he was in the form of God, did not count equality with God a thing to be grasped, but emptied himself, by taking the form of a servant, being born in the likeness of men" (Philippians 2:5-7). My friend, Paul's main idea is this: be humble like Jesus was.

Christians ought to make every effort to remedy internal problems in the church.

Paul instructed the Philippians, "Work out your own salvation with fear and trembling" (Philippians 2:12). This verse has nothing to do with assurance of final salvation for individual believers. Contextually, the Philippian church was plagued by (1) rivalries (2:3-4; 4:2); (2) the influence of legalistic Judaizers (3:2-3); and (3) some in the church who were living in worldliness (3:18-19). This church as a unit was in need of "salvation."

> "Behold, how good and pleasant it is when brothers dwell in unity."
>
> —Psalm 133:1

The Greek word for "work out" refers to bringing something to a conclusion. Paul was calling the Philippians to solve all the church's problems and "work them out to the finish." Like the Philippians, Christians today should make every effort to remedy internal problems in their churches. After all, a strong church breeds strong Christians.

Philippians

> "If you feel that you can follow a few little rules to make you a mature Christian, then you have fallen into a subtle trap of legalism."
>
> —J. Vernon McGee (1904–1988)

Our righteousness is not self-manufactured but rather comes through faith in Christ.

Judaizers infiltrated the Philippian church and taught that a person needed to be circumcised and then follow various Jewish laws to be right with God. Interestingly, though Jewish leaders often called Gentiles "dogs," Paul here calls the Judaizers "dogs." And even though Judaizers prided themselves as representatives of righteousness, Paul calls them evil (Philippians 3:2). Paul turned the tables. He wouldn't allow legalism!

Nothing compares with knowing Jesus!

The apostle Paul, before his conversion to Christ, was committed to a life of Jewish legalism. How misguided! "Whatever gain I had, I counted as loss for the sake of Christ. Indeed, I count everything as loss because of the surpassing worth of knowing Christ Jesus my Lord" (Philippians 3:7-8). At his conversion, Paul came to the sudden and devastating realization that all his impressive Jewish credentials counted for nothing in terms of knowing Christ.

Don't make your Christianity about obeying rules. Make it all about knowing Jesus—and knowing Him intimately.

Our daily mind-set should always be to press toward the goal that lies ahead.

Paul said something highly motivating in Philippians 3:13-14: "One thing I do: forgetting what lies behind and straining forward to what lies ahead, I press on toward the goal for the prize of the upward call of God in Christ Jesus." People ponder two things when they look at their past—their *past glories* and their *past failures*. Our pasts can distract us from what is really important—loving and fellowshipping with Christ now and in the future. Press on!

Your true citizenship is in heaven. Choose to live *now* in view of *then*.

Paul reminded the Philippians, "Our citizenship is in heaven, and from it we await a Savior, the Lord Jesus Christ, who will transform our lowly body to be like his glorious body" (Philippians 3:20-21). We may be earthly citizens, too, but in terms of our ultimate destiny, we are citizens of heaven. We are pilgrims passing through, on our way to another country, another land, another city (Hebrews 11:16). And we behave ourselves on earth in view of our glorious future in heaven.

> "Take courage. We walk in the wilderness today and in the Promised Land tomorrow."
>
> —*Dwight L. Moody (1837–1899)*

Philippians

Don't worry. Pray about your needs and be at peace.

Five Components of Prayer

- Thanksgiving (Psalm 95:2; 100:4)
- Praise (Psalm 34:1; 103:1-5,20-22)
- Worship (Exodus 20:3-5; Hebrews 12:28)
- Confession (Proverbs 28:13; 1 John 1:9)
- Specific requests to God (Philippians 4:6-7)

Paul urges, "Do not be anxious about anything, but in everything by prayer and supplication with thanksgiving let your requests be made known to God. And the peace of God, which surpasses all understanding, will guard your hearts and your minds in Christ Jesus" (Philippians 4:6-7).

My friend, whatever you're struggling with—personal relationships, finances, an illness, the workplace—bring it before God in prayer. If you're anxious about *anything*, pray immediately. Cast your anxieties on God, for He cares for you (1 Peter 5:7).

"The whole secret of abundant living can be summed up in this sentence: 'Not your responsibility but your response to God's ability.'"

—*Carl F. H. Henry (1913–2003)*

The Christian's contentment is rooted in the full sufficiency of Jesus Christ.

Paul affirmed, "I have learned in whatever situation I am to be content...I can do all things through him who strengthens me" (Philippians 4:11-13). We can be content no matter our external circumstances because of the full sufficiency of Jesus Christ (2 Corinthians 9:8).

A Thought to Anchor in Your Heart

Remember the Three *B*s: be content, be at peace, and be full of joy.

Colossians

**Make Christ supreme in your life.
He is sufficient for your every need.**

Paul wrote this epistle "to the saints and faithful brothers in Christ at Colossae" (Colossians 1:2), hence the title Colossians. He wrote the epistle in about AD 61.

Colossae was about 100 miles east of Ephesus. While Paul had never been to the city, he had heard about the church from his associate Epaphras (Colossians 1:7-8). Some of the news he heard bothered him—aberrant doctrines had penetrated the church. So Paul wrote this epistle while in prison to correct these errors, but he also gave great spiritual encouragement.

Following are key applicational concepts in Colossians:

God's Word is not just to provide us with information, but to bring about personal transformation.

Paul affirms that the word of truth bears fruit (Colossians 1:5-6). Indeed, being "filled with the knowledge of his will" enables us to "to walk in a manner worthy of the Lord, fully pleasing to him, bearing fruit in every good work and increasing in the knowledge of God" (1:9-10). My friend, the Word of God is not just intended to fill your mind with more knowledge. It is intended to transform you from the inside out. God's Word is life-changing (Romans 12:2).

Our hope of heaven motivates us to live God's way.

Every Christian has a "hope laid up" in heaven (Colossians 1:5). We will one day receive "the

Timeline
- 17— Colossae experiences a powerful earthquake.
- 61— Paul is imprisoned in Rome.
- 61— Paul writes an epistle to the Colossians while in prison in Rome.
- 64— Colossae experiences another powerful earthquake.

"All Scripture is breathed out by God and profitable for teaching, for reproof, for correction, and for training in righteousness."

—2 Timothy 3:16

"A heart in heaven will be a most excellent preservative against temptations, a powerful means to kill thy corruptions."

—Richard Baxter (1615–1691)

Colossians

inheritance of the saints in light" (1:12). This hope is a powerful motivator to live God's way. We live *now* in view of *then*.

We derive strength to patiently endure directly from God.

Paul exhorts us, "May you be strengthened with all power, according to his glorious might, for all endurance and patience with joy" (Colossians 1:11). This means our patient endurance of the trials is rooted not in our strength—which, in reality, is weakness—but rather in God's almighty strength. He is our divine enabler.

Because Christ is supreme in reality, He must be supreme experientially in our lives.

Supremacy of Christ
Matthew 3:11 • John 3:31 • 13:13 • Acts 2:36 • Romans 14:9 • Hebrews 1:4 • 3:3 • 8:6 • Revelation 1:4-5

Paul affirms that Christ is preeminent over all things in the universe (Colossians 1:15-19). He must also be supreme in our lives. He and He alone should be ruling on the throne of our hearts. Dear Christian, is something else now supreme in your heart, distracting you from Christ? Oust it immediately. Make Christ supreme in your life!

Rejoice! In Christ you are holy, blameless, and above reproach. Anchor yourself on this truth.

Because of Jesus's work on the cross, you and I are "holy and blameless and above reproach before him" (Colossians 1:22). Can there be any better news for the Christian? I do not have the capability of making myself holy and blameless. But in Christ I am holy and blameless. What a wondrous gift is God's grace-salvation!

The true secret of the Christian life is "Christ in you."

In Colossians 1:27 Paul speaks of "Christ in you, the hope of glory." This is an amazing truth. Believers are in Christ (2 Corinthians 5:17; Ephesians 1:4) and Christ is in believers (Romans 8:10; 2 Corinthians 13:5). Believers can therefore look forward to sharing in Christ's glory when He comes for us (Colossians 3:4; Romans 5:2; 8:18, 30; 2 Corinthians 4:17; Galatians 5:5; 1 Peter 5:10).

"Apart from me you can do nothing" (John 15:5).

"I can do all things through him who strengthens me" (Philippians 4:13).

Colossians

Don't let anyone talk you out of your faith by human reasoning.

It is important for you to become knowledgeable of the spiritual truths of the Bible so "no one may delude you with plausible arguments" (Colossians 2:4). Indeed, Paul says, "See to it that no one takes you captive by philosophy and empty deceit, according to human tradition" (2:8). Humanists, atheists, cultists, and advocates of false religions present many arguments against Christianity. Don't buy it. Don't listen. Hold fast to the Scriptures!

Christ is fully sufficient for your needs. Christians are rooted and built up in Him alone.

Paul urges, "As you received Christ Jesus the Lord, so walk in him, rooted and built up in him and established in the faith" (Colossians 2:6-7). Don't be rooted and built up in self-help books. Don't be rooted and built up in religious rules and rituals. Be rooted and built up in Christ alone. He is all you need.

Rest secure, for Jesus reigns over all.

Jesus Christ is the "head of all rule and authority" (Colossians 2:10). Because He is the head of all rule and authority, we listen to Him alone, and not to those who offer other religious ideas—such as the false teachers who sought to deceive the Colossian believers. Christ is also the head over all angels, whom the false teachers in Colossae were seeking to exalt. Jesus reigns over all!

Don't fall into legalism. Your relationship with God is not based on obeying rules.

Christians should be cautious against falling into legalism. Christianity is not based on rules like "Do not handle, do not taste, do not touch" (Colossians 2:21). Christianity is not founded upon "asceticism and severity to the body" (2:23). In Christ we have died to such things (2:20). Focus your attention on your personal relationship with Christ, not on legalistic practices.

Total Sufficiency of Christ

- False teachers in Colossae claimed legalistic religious traditions had to be followed.
- Paul countered that Christ is totally sufficient for salvation and the Christian life.
- We submit to Christ alone (Colossians 2:8-23).

Verses to Remember

"As you received Christ Jesus the Lord, so walk in him, rooted and built up in him and established in the faith, just as you were taught, abounding in thanksgiving."

—*Colossians 2:6-7*

Colossians

An eternal perspective motivates us to live God's way.

The apostle Paul tells us to maintain an eternal perspective: "Seek the things that are above, where Christ is." Indeed, "Set your minds on things that are above, not on things that are on earth" (Colossians 3:2). The original Greek of this passage communicates the idea "*Keep on* seeking the things above, 24/7." As we do this, we are motivated to dump all the sinful baggage of our former lifestyles (3:5-11).

> "Resolved, to endeavor to my utmost to act as I can think I should do, if I had already seen the happiness of heaven, and hell torments."
>
> —*Jonathan Edwards*
> *(1703–1758)*

Christ is all that matters, and He lives in you.

Paul says "Christ is all, and in all" (Colossians 3:11). We have an intimate union with Christ, and all Christians are bound together in Christ. Because of that union, we can draw on His strength for the victorious life. As John 15:1-10 puts it, we are "branches" plugged into the "vine" (Jesus), thereby producing fruit.

> **A Verse to Remember**
>
> "Set your minds on things that are above, not on things that are on earth."
>
> —*Colossians 3:2*

God forgave you. You must forgive others.

We are instructed, "As the Lord has forgiven you, so you also must forgive" (Colossians 3:13). There is no place for holding a grudge in the Christian life. In fact, Jesus told us we should forgive others *without limit* (Matthew 18:21-22). Are you holding any grudges? Let go of them today!

> "Every man should keep a fair-sized cemetery in which to bury the faults of his friends."
>
> —*Henry Ward Beecher*
> *(1813–1887)*

Don't worry. Let Christ's peace rule in your heart.

Worry and anxiety are plagues among human beings today. Anxiety is an epidemic in Western society. Paul, however, instructs, "Let the peace of Christ rule in your hearts" (Colossians 3:15). The word "peace" refers to God-given tranquility. The tranquility of Christ can rule in our hearts if we allow it. This brings to mind what Jesus said earlier: "Peace I leave with you; my peace I give to you. Not as the world gives do I give to you. Let not your hearts be troubled, neither let them be afraid" (John 14:27).

> "The beginning of anxiety is the end of faith, and the beginning of faith is the end of anxiety."
>
> —*George Muller (1805–1898)*

Colossians

Let Christ's words dwell in your heart. They will make you wise.

Paul urged the Colossian believers to "let the word of Christ dwell in you richly" (Colossians 3:16). The words of Christ are recorded in Scripture. This means we must let the words of Scripture dwell in us richly. The word "dwell" carries the idea of God's Word making its home in our hearts. As we daily study and meditate upon Scripture, rich spiritual fruit emerges in our lives.

Do everything as a representative of Jesus Christ, ultimately serving the Lord, not people.

We are instructed, "Whatever you do, in word or deed, do everything in the name of the Lord Jesus" (Colossians 3:17). Indeed, "Whatever you do, work heartily, as for the Lord and not for men" (3:23). This makes sense because our ultimate payday involves not earthly wages but heavenly riches (Matthew 6:19-21).

Family relations are a huge blessing when done God's way.

God is the one who invented the human family in the first place (Genesis 1:26-27; 2:18). It therefore makes good sense to operate the family unit according to His instructions. God has instructions for husbands, wives, and children (Colossians 3:18-21).

Live right. A judgment is coming.

Paul says, "From the Lord you will receive the inheritance as your reward...the wrongdoer will be paid back for the wrong he has done" (Colossians 3:24-25). Believers will one day face the judgment seat of Christ, where they'll either receive rewards or lose rewards, depending upon how they lived as Christians (Romans 14:10; 2 Corinthians 5:10).

> **A Heavenly Perspective**
> Psalm 16:11 • 2 Corinthians 5:1-8 • 1 Corinthians 15:50-55 • Philippians 1:21-23 • Colossians 3:1-2 • 1 Peter 1:4

Pray a lot. It makes all the difference.

Christians are urged, "Continue steadfastly in prayer" (Colossians 4:2). We see this same admonition in the teachings of Jesus. "Ask, and it will be given to you" (Matthew 7:7). This is a present tense in the Greek. It carries the idea "*Keep on* asking and it will be

> "Prayer is not overcoming God's reluctance, but laying hold of His willingness."
>
> —*Martin Luther (1483–1546)*

Colossians

given to you." We ought to all be persistent in prayer (Psalm 116:2; Daniel 6:10; Romans 12:12; 1 Thessalonians 5:17).

Live wisely among unbelievers.

Christians are exhorted, "Walk in wisdom toward outsiders" (Colossians 4:5). First Thessalonians 4:12 likewise instructs, "Walk properly before outsiders." We "must be well thought of by outsiders" (1 Timothy 3:7).

Dear Christian, people are always more open to hear what you have to say about Christ if they witness the change He has made in your life.

A Thought to Anchor in Your Heart

Make this your prayer today: *Jesus, You will be my all in all. You alone will reign in my heart. I will enjoy Your spiritual presence from morning to night.*

---

1 Thessalonians

The prophetic future has profound implications for all people. It means ultimate deliverance for Christians. It means judgment for unbelievers.

Thessalonica was a capital of the Roman province of Macedonia in northern Greece. It was a prosperous port. The church of Thessalonica was founded around AD 50. The apostle Paul wrote 1 Thessalonians in early AD 51 (1 Thessalonians 1:1).

Paul had earlier visited Thessalonica for a short time. He would have stayed longer, but Jewish resistance shortened his stay. The Jews did not like it when Paul won converts to Christianity from among their own. For Paul's safety, the Christians in Thessalonica sent him to Berea (Acts 17:1-10). Paul wrote this epistle to instruct the church on God-honoring living in light of the prophetic future (including the rapture).

Following are key applicational concepts in 1 Thessalonians:

Timeline

- 15—Tiberius Caesar removes Thessalonica's status as a free city when the locals protest increased taxation.
- 44—Claudius Caesar restores Thessalonica's status as a free city.
- 50—Paul, Silas, and Timothy preach in Thessalonica.
- 50—The church at Thessalonica is founded.
- 51—Paul writes his first and second epistles to the Thessalonians a number of months after his ministry among them.

Keep yourself anchored on faith, hope, and love.

The apostle Paul commended the Thessalonians for maintaining faith, hope, and love (1 Thessalonians 1:2-3). You and I are to follow their example: "Since we belong to the day, let us be sober, having put on the breastplate of faith and love, and for a helmet the hope of salvation" (5:8). Faith, hope, and love will keep you grounded in your walk with Christ. Never let go of these three.

> "Hope is never ill when faith is well."
>
> —John Bunyan (1628–1688)

Don't allow anything to become an idol in your life. Serve only the living and true God.

Paul was so very pleased at how the Thessalonians had turned from idolatry in their lives. "You turned to God from idols to serve the living and true God" (1 Thessalonians 1:9). God consistently condemns idolatry in all its forms (Exodus 20:4; Leviticus 26:1; 2 Kings 9:22)—not only idols like golden calves. Anything that takes His place in one's life can function as an idol—including money and wealth. It's helpful to occasionally conduct a self-inventory of your life to oust any idols that have wormed their way in (2 Corinthians 13:5).

> "A man's god is that for which he lives, for which he is prepared to give his time, his energy, his money, that which stimulates him and rouses him, excites, and enthuses him."
>
> —D. Martyn Lloyd-Jones (1899–1981)

Rejoice! Christians are destined not for wrath but for deliverance.

Scripture assures us the church is not appointed to wrath (1 Thessalonians 1:9-10; 5:9). This means the church cannot go through the "great day of wrath"—that is, the future seven-year tribulation period (Revelation 6:17; 14:10,19; 15:1,7; 16:1).

Cross-References: The Rapture
John 14:1-3 • 1 Corinthians 15:51-53 • Philippians 3:20-21 • 4:5 • Colossians 3:4 • 1 Thessalonians 1:10 • 2:19 • 5:9,23 • Titus 2:13

First Thessalonians 1:10 explicitly states that Jesus "delivers us from the wrath to come." The word "delivers" in the original Greek means "to draw or snatch out to oneself, to rescue, to save, to preserve." This seems to be referring to the rapture of the church prior to the beginning of the tribulation period. In fact, the "snatching up" in 1 Thessalonians 1:10 sounds notably similar to the description of the rapture in 1 Thessalonians 4:16-17: "We who are alive, who are left, will be caught up together with them in the clouds to meet the Lord in the air..." The phrase "caught up" here literally means "snatch up" or "take away."

Your ultimate goal must always be to please God, not other human beings.

The apostle Paul affirmed, "We speak, not to please man, but to please God who tests our hearts" (1 Thessalonians 2:4). This is a common emphasis in Scripture. Paul elsewhere affirmed, "If I were still trying to please man, I would not be a servant of Christ" (Galatians 1:10). Paul urged, "Whatever you do, work heartily, as for the Lord and not for men" (Colossians 3:23). We must keep our priorities straight. It is all too easy to fall into the rut of being a people-pleaser. Our top priority ought to be to live as a God-pleaser.

Beware that Satan seeks to thwart Christian ministry.

Paul affirmed to the Thessalonians, "We wanted to come to you—I, Paul, again and again—but Satan hindered us" (1 Thessalonians 2:18). Satan hinders in many different ways. Satan opposes Christians with the ferociousness of a hungry lion (1 Peter 5:8). Satan and his demons seek to wage war against and defeat believers (Ephesians 6:11-12). Satan incites persecutions against believers (Revelation 2:10). Demons seek to hinder answers to the prayers of believers (Daniel 10:12-20). Any Christian who seeks to serve Christ in ministry will be hindered in one way or another by Satan and his demons. Keep on your spiritual armor (Ephesians 6:10-20)!

> "I know well that when Christ is nearest, Satan is also busiest."
>
> —*Robert Murray M'Cheyne (1813–1843)*

The attacks of Satan can weaken the faith and endurance of believers.

Paul wrote to the Thessalonians, "When I could bear it no longer, I sent to learn about your faith, for fear that somehow the tempter had tempted you and our labor would be in vain" (1 Thessalonians 3:5). Satan tempts Christians to bring them down. We are therefore best served to not be ignorant of his schemes (2 Corinthians 2:11; 11:14). And allow me to repeat: keep your spiritual armor on (Ephesians 6:10-20)!

> "Temptation is to see the tempter standing outside the back door of your heart. Sin is to unlock that door so that he may have his desire. Victory is to open wide the front door of your heart, inviting the Savior to enter and give you strength to bar tight the back door."
>
> —*E. Schuyler English (1900–1981)*

Avoid lustful passion and steer clear of all forms of sexual sin.

Paul strongly urged the Thessalonian Christians to avoid all forms of sexual immorality: "This is the will of God, your sanctification: that you abstain from sexual immorality; that each one of you know how to control his own body in holiness and honor, not in the passion of lust" (1 Thessalonians 4:3-5). Paul reminded them that "the Lord is an avenger in all these things" (4:6). Paul elsewhere affirmed that the body is not made for

Three Aspects of Sanctification

- *positional sanctification*—being "positionally set apart" from sin (1 Corinthians 6:11)
- *progressive sanctification*—growing daily in holiness (1 Peter 1:16)
- *ultimate sanctification*—once we're in heaven (1 John 3:2)

fornication and that a man should flee it (1 Corinthians 6:13,18). Be cautious, dear Christian. Sexual sin is an epidemic today.

Do your fair share of the work.

The apostle Paul urged that there should be no idlers in the church, sitting around, awaiting the Lord's coming. Everyone should do their fair share of the work instead of sponging on the generosity of fellow Christians (1 Thessalonians 4:9-12). Do your part!

Always seek to live a quiet life and mind your own business.

Paul urged the Thessalonians, "Aspire to live quietly, and to mind your own affairs, and to work with your hands" (1 Thessalonians 4:11). What a contrast this is to many modern people who live loudly, mind everyone else's business, and avoid as much work as they can get away with. Paul's words are worthy of reflection.

You can look forward to a glorious reunion with all your Christian loved ones.

One day you and I will enjoy a grand and glorious reunion with all our Christian loved ones. Paul, speaking of the future rapture of the church, writes, "The dead in Christ will rise first. Then we who are alive, who are left, will be caught up together with them in the clouds to meet the Lord in the air, and so we will always be with the Lord" (1 Thessalonians 4:16-17). Scripture reveals that we'll all be resurrected and then live in each other's company with the Lord forever. Never again will death separate us from Christian loved ones—for all of us will be perpetually basking in the glory of eternal life. Awesome!

> "No two Christians will ever meet for the last time."
>
> —Anonymous

> "When we get to Heaven, the joy of seeing our loved ones once again is immeasurably increased when we realize that all of us will indeed be perfect! There will be no more disagreements or cross words, hurt feelings, or misunderstandings."
>
> —Anne Graham Lotz

If you're worried that the wicked are getting away with committing great evil, realize that *they're not*. A day of judgment is coming.

When we look around at the world today, it often seems that the wicked are getting away with all kinds of sinful acts—many of them horrific in nature. But Scripture reveals they're not getting away with anything. "Destruction will come upon them" and "they will not escape" (1 Thessalonians 5:3). A day of judgment is coming. God will bring about complete justice in the end.

The wicked will face judgment at the great white throne judgment (Revelation 20:12-13). The purpose of this judgment is to populate the lake of fire. Scripture reveals there will be degrees of punishment in the lake of fire (Matthew 10:15; 16:27; Luke 12:47-48; Revelation 22:12). They will be commensurate with the degree of evil committed by each respective person. Woe to all who face Christ at the great white throne judgment.

> "Every man shall give an account of his own works, a full and true account of all that he ever did while alive, whether it was good or evil."
>
> —John Wesley (1703–1791)

Always be on guard in your spiritual life. Live as one of the "children of the day."

The apostle Paul urged, "You are all children of light, children of the day. We are not of the night or of the darkness. So then let us not sleep, as others do, but let us keep awake and be sober" (1 Thessalonians 5:5-6). My friend, the children of light are careful to walk in the light (1 John 1:5-7). They are cautious not to "sleep" in spiritual indifference. They are "awake" to matters of spiritual importance. They are "sober" in the way they live.

Prophecy and Purity

The imminence of the rapture should motivate us to live in purity and righteousness. Meditate on Romans 13:11-14; 2 Peter 3:10-14; and Titus 2:13-14.

Never pay back evil for evil.

Paul instructs, "See that no one repays anyone evil for evil, but always seek to do good to one another and to everyone" (1 Thessalonians 5:15). Paul elsewhere wrote, "Bless those who persecute you; bless and do not curse them" (Romans 12:14). Peter said, "Do not repay evil for evil or reviling for reviling, but on the contrary, bless" (1 Peter 3:9).

Jesus much earlier urged His followers to turn the other cheek (Matthew 5:39). He also said, "Love your enemies and pray for those who persecute you" (Matthew 5:44).

Sometimes there's nothing harder to do than loving your "enemies"—whoever they may be. Just remember—you are like Christ when you choose not to pay back evil for evil. Ask for God's help in this. He'll come through for you.

1 Thessalonians

Always be joyful, no matter what.

> "A heavenly mind is a joyful mind; this is the nearest and truest way to live a life of comfort."
>
> —Richard Baxter (1615–1691)

The apostle Paul taught that we should be joyful in our Christian lives no matter what comes our way. He instructed the Thessalonians, "Rejoice always" (1 Thessalonians 5:16). He told the Philippian believers, "Rejoice in the Lord always; again I will say, rejoice" (Philippians 4:4).

Christians can experience "the joy of the Holy Spirit" (1 Thessalonians 1:6). Joy is a *fruit* of the Holy Spirit (Galatians 5:22). Walking in the Spirit naturally produces joy. Romans 14:17 therefore affirms, "The kingdom of God is not a matter of eating and drinking but of righteousness and peace and joy in the Holy Spirit."

A Thought to Anchor in Your Heart

In death, communion with Christian loved ones is broken only for a short time. Your eyes will once again see them. Your ears will once again hear them. Your arms will once again embrace them. Rejoice in this reality!

2 Thessalonians

It is best for Christians to maintain a balanced and discerning perspective on life as they await the coming of the Lord.

Paul wrote this second epistle to the Thessalonians during the summer of AD 51. Several months had passed since he wrote 1 Thessalonians. His purpose for this second epistle was to further explain and clarify God's program of events relating to the day of the Lord—including Christ's second coming. He also wanted to encourage the brethren to correct the disorders that remained among them.

Following are key applicational concepts in 2 Thessalonians:

As a Christian, maintain a thankful attitude before God.

Paul begins with thanks to God for the faith and love of the Thessalonians, as well as their firm stand for Christ in the face of persecution (2 Thessalonians 1:1-4). They were setting a great example for other Christians.

Thankfulness is a common theme in Scripture. The Psalms—familiar to Paul, a Jew—often speak of thankfulness to God (Psalm 30:12; 35:18; 69:30). Famous verses on thanksgiving include Psalm 95:2, "Let us come into his presence with thanksgiving," and Psalm 100:4, "Enter his gates with thanksgiving." Daniel gave thanks three times a day (Daniel 6:10). Jesus also gave thanks (Matthew 11:25). Ephesians 5:20 instructs us to give thanks "always and for everything to God the Father in the name of our Lord Jesus Christ." We ought to thank God for all He has done (Philippians 4:6) and even *overflow* with thanksgiving (Colossians 2:7; see also 3:15).

Timeline

50— Paul, Silas, and Timothy preach in Thessalonica.

50— The church at Thessalonica is founded.

51— Paul writes his first and second epistles to the Thessalonians a number of months after his ministry among them.

56— Paul revisits the Thessalonian church.

"When it comes to life, the critical thing is whether you take things for granted or take them with gratitude."

—*G. K. Chesterton (1874–1936)*

Fear not—the wicked aren't getting away with anything. Judgment awaits them.

> "God will bring to light every circumstance that accompanied each word and action. He will judge whether they lessened or increased the goodness or badness of them."
>
> —*John Wesley (1703–1791)*

Paul assured the Thessalonians that the wicked people who were presently causing them suffering would one day be irrevocably punished following the second coming of Christ (2 Thessalonians 1:5-12). Paul assured them that the wicked weren't getting away with anything. While they may seem to flourish at the present moment, the clock is ticking, and their time is running out.

The wicked will be judged at the great white throne judgment (Revelation 20:11-15). Christ is the divine Judge, and those who are judged are the unsaved dead of all time. The judgment takes place at the end of the millennial kingdom, Christ's 1000-year reign on planet Earth. Those who face Christ at this judgment will be judged on the basis of their works (Revelation 20:12-13). They are judged according to their works not only to justify their condemnation but to determine the degree to which each person should be punished throughout eternity (Matthew 10:15; 16:27; Luke 12:47-48; Revelation 20:12-13; 22;12).

Get motivated—Christians will one day share in Christ's glory!

> "The lack of long, strong thinking about our promised hope of glory is a major cause of our plodding, lack-luster lifestyle... It is the heavenly Christian that is the lively Christian."
>
> —*J. I. Packer*

Paul informed the Thessalonians, "To this he called you through our gospel, so that you may obtain the glory of our Lord Jesus Christ" (2 Thessalonians 2:14; see also 1:10,12). The glory of believers is a common theme in Scripture, especially as contrasted to our present sufferings on earth. Paul said, "This light momentary affliction is preparing for us an eternal weight of glory beyond all comparison" (2 Corinthians 4:17). Likewise, he said, "I consider that the sufferings of this present time are not worth comparing with the glory that is to be revealed to us" (Romans 8:18). Are you presently enduring suffering? Take heart, for glory awaits you! It's just a matter of time.

> **Cross-References: The Day of the Lord**
> Isaiah 65:17-19 • 66:22 • Amos 5:18-20 • Obadiah 15 • 2 Peter 3:10-13 • Revelation 4–18

Don't get upset about claims regarding the timing of end time events.

Some of the Thessalonian brethren were concerned that the day of the Lord (the future tribulation period and beyond) had already come. Some phony epistles had apparently surfaced teaching this idea. Paul responded that there were certain noticeable events that would take place before this eschatological day comes—including the emergence of the antichrist and various social upheavals during the tribulation period (2 Thessalonians 2:1-12). Since those things have not happened yet, the day of the Lord has clearly not come. My advice: Stay focused on the Word of God, and this will keep you on track regarding prophetic events.

> **Cross-References: The Antichrist**
> 1 John 2:18 • 4:3 • 2 John 1:7 • Revelation 13:1-10 • 19:20

Always beware of counterfeit signs and wonders.

The apostle Paul tells us "the coming of the lawless one is by the activity of Satan with all power and false signs and wonders" (2 Thessalonians 2:9). Many ask if Satan can really perform miracles.

> **Cross-References: Satanic Power**
> Job 1:12 • Luke 4:6 • Acts 26:18 • Ephesians 6:12

Although Satan has great spiritual powers, there is a gigantic difference between the power of the devil and the power of God. God is infinite in power (omnipotent); the devil is finite and limited.

Satan can do what we might call Grade-B supernormal "signs." But he cannot perform Grade-A supernatural miracles, which only God can do (see, for example, Exodus 8:19). Keep in mind that the devil is a master magician and a super scientist. With his vast knowledge of God, man, and the universe, he is able to perform "false signs and wonders."

One recalls that Simon the sorcerer in the city of Samaria amazed people with his Satan-inspired magic (Acts 8:9-11), but the miracles accomplished through Philip were much greater (8:13). The devil's counterfeit miracles do not compete with God's true miracles.

Stand firm on the Word of God, no matter what emerges in your life.

Paul instructed the Thessalonians, "Stand firm and hold to the traditions that you were taught by us, either by our spoken word or by our letter" (2 Thessalonians 2:15). Paul had earlier passed down some apostolic teachings about the second coming of Christ to the Thessalonian Christians via oral tradition. (That

> "If you wish to know God, you must know His Word. If you wish to perceive His power, you must see how He works by His Word. If you wish to know His purpose before it comes to pass, you can only discover it by His Word."
>
> —Charles Spurgeon (1834–1892)

is, Paul *verbally communicated* authoritative teachings.) Once Paul and the other apostles committed their teachings to written form and then died (so that they could no longer exercise their living authority as apostles), the written Scriptures alone became the final authority for matters of faith and practice (2 Timothy 3:15-17). What that means for Christians is that we stand firm on the teachings of the apostles *as recorded in the Word of God*.

The Lord protects you from the evil one—Satan.

Paul informs the Thessalonians, "The Lord is faithful. He will establish you and guard you against the evil one" (2 Thessalonians 3:3). This is important, for no human being has the strength in him- or herself to stand against the devil. It is our Lord who protects us.

This protection ultimately comes in several forms. First, the Lord Jesus is prayerfully interceding for us, and His prayers are always answered (Romans 8:34; Hebrews 7:25)! Second, remember that "he who is in you is greater than he who is in the world" (1 John 4:4). Further, we are provided the armor of God against the devil (Ephesians 6:10-20). Without wearing this spiritual armor, you and I don't stand a chance against the forces of darkness. But with the armor on, victory is ours. "Wearing" this armor means our lives will be characterized by such things as righteousness, obedience to the will of God, faith in God, and an effective use of the Word of God.

> "Obviously, the greater exposure there is to Scripture the more the Spirit can use this mighty sword in our lives."
>
> —Ray Stedman (1917–1992)

Effective use of the Word of God is especially important for spiritual victory. Jesus used the Word to defeat the devil during His wilderness temptations (Matthew 4:1-10). We must learn to do the same.

No Christian should be idle—exploiting the charity of other Christians—as they await the coming of the Lord.

Apparently some among the Thessalonians got so caught up in prophetic excitement that they stopped working, and they lived off the charity of others. Paul said such individuals were to be rebuked. He urged, "Keep away from any brother who is walking

Avoiding Idleness

- Believers are exhorted to avoid idleness and be committed to work as they await the Lord's coming (2 Thessalonians 3:6-13).
- Hebrews 6:12 urges believers not to be sluggish.
- Romans 12:11 urges believers not to be "slothful in zeal."
- Proverbs 18:9 speaks lowly of the person who is "slack in his work."

The Pauline Epistles ‖ 339

in idleness…You yourselves know how you ought to imitate us, because we were not idle when we were with you…If anyone is not willing to work, let him not eat" (2 Thessalonians 3:6-7,10).

> ### A Thought to Anchor in Your Heart
>
> Use your time wisely, making the most of every single day. Let it never be said that you wasted your time!

1 Timothy

We "fight the good fight" not only for personal spiritual well-being, but also for the benefit of the Christian church.

Paul wrote this epistle between AD 62 and 64 and addressed it "to Timothy, my true child in the faith" (1 Timothy 1:2). Timothy was a young and trusted colleague of Paul. He became a convert of Paul's in Lystra and grew quickly in his spiritual life. He became a leader in the church and even represented Paul to others in various churches (Acts 17:4,15; 1 Corinthians 4:17).

Paul in this epistle speaks as a more mature, experienced pastor to a younger, inexperienced pastor (Timothy). He provided advice to Timothy regarding situations that might be encountered in the process of leading a church, including how to deal with false doctrine (1 Timothy 1:3-7; 4:1-3) and disorder in worship (2:1-15). Paul also discussed the qualifications for church leaders (3:1-14) and encouraged Timothy to stay focused on the work of ministry and not get sidetracked.

Following are key applicational concepts in 1 Timothy:

Shepherds (church pastors) must always be ready to fight off the wolves (false teachers), for they can injure the sheep (church members).

"If God consistently sent lightning bolts in response to bad doctrine, our planet would sparkle nightly like a Christmas tree."

—*Philip Yancey*

Seven years earlier, Paul warned the Ephesian elders that "fierce wolves" (false teachers) would seek to ravage the church (Acts 20:29-30). These false teachers were now in full force. Timothy, as a shepherd of the church, was to defend biblical doctrine at all costs (1 Timothy 1:3-11).

Good news: Christ can save even the worst of sinners.

Paul thought of his own conversion as an example of God's amazing grace in saving the worst of sinners. "Christ Jesus came into the world to save sinners, of whom I am the foremost" (1 Timothy 1:15). The word "foremost" means "first in rank." Paul considered himself as having been the worst of the worst (compare with Romans 7:7-12). This gives you and me hope! If God in His grace saved Paul—a former persecutor of the church—then He can save anyone through His grace. Rejoice in this fact!

Never give up. Fight the good fight.

Christ not only saved Paul, but called him to ministry. Paul was now passing the mantle of ministry to Timothy. Just as Paul fought the good fight of faith, so now Timothy was to fight the good fight (1 Timothy 1:12-20; see also 6:11-21). You and I are to do the same. We must never give up, no matter what trials we may encounter. Fight the good fight. Endure!

Very important: always keep your conscience clear.

Paul pointed to the importance of Christians keeping a good conscience (1 Timothy 1:19; compare with 4:2). God has written His law on the human heart (Romans 2:15), and when we violate what we know to be right, our conscience passes judgment on our action and we feel guilty. A person with a wounded conscience finds it difficult to live a vibrant Christian life. We can keep a clear conscience by (1) avoiding unrepentant sin, and (2) confessing to God whenever we do fall into sin (1 John 1:9).

> **Cross-References: The Fight of Faith**
>
> 1 Kings 2:2 • 2 Chronicles 15:7 • Isaiah 35:4 • Haggai 2:4 • Zechariah 8:9 • 1 Corinthians 16:13 • Ephesians 6:10

> "Faith helps us when we are down; but unbelief throws us down when we are up."
>
> —*John Bunyan (1628–1688)*

> "A good conscience is a mine of wealth. And in truth, of what greater riches can there be, what thing more sweet than a good conscience?"
>
> —*Bernard of Clairvaux (1090–1153)*

Pray for others. It changes things!

Paul said, "I urge that supplications, prayers, intercessions, and thanksgivings be made for all people, for kings and all who are in high positions, that we may lead a peaceful and quiet life" (1 Timothy 2:1-2). We pray for each other because we all have needs and hurts in life. We pray for rulers because they can throw Christians into jail, as had happened with Paul. Prayer changes things. Remember what James said: "You do not have, because you do not ask" (James 4:2).

Elders and deacons in the church must *believe right* and *act right* so they can properly engage in their respective ministries.

> "The preacher's sharpest and strongest preaching should be to himself."
>
> —E. M. Bounds (1835–1913)

Paul speaks of the spiritual qualifications of elders (1 Timothy 3:1-7) and deacons (3:8-13). His essential instruction is that leaders in the church must hold to *sound doctrine* and have *good character*. This ensures not only healthy spiritual growth among church members, but also serves to insulate the church from false teachers.

Beware: the devil can use pride to make you fall.

Paul said it is possible for a person to be "puffed up with conceit and fall into the condemnation of the devil" (1 Timothy 3:6). Pride was at the heart of Lucifer's fall (Isaiah 14:12-15; Ezekiel 28:13-18). Just as Lucifer fell from a position of honor and authority because of pride, so a Christian can fall because of pride. Beware! Pursue humility.

Beware of false teachers and apostasy.

The Danger of Deception

- Beware of false prophets (Matthew 7:15-16).
- Beware of "fierce wolves" (Acts 20:28-30).
- Christians can be "led astray" (2 Corinthians 11:2-3).
- A word to the wise: stay anchored in the Word of God (2 Timothy 3:15-17).

Paul warned of false teachers and apostasy. He urged Timothy to watch his doctrine closely. Just as good doctrine leads to a healthy spirituality, so bad doctrine can be spiritually injurious. The best way to combat error is the constant exposition of God's Word (1 Timothy 4).

Spend plenty of time in staying spiritually fit.

Paul often used sports metaphors to make his points. He urged, "Train yourself for godliness" (1 Timothy 4:7). The word "train" was used in New Testament times to refer to the rigorous training an athlete undergoes. Just as an athlete works hard to stay in good physical shape, so we as Christians must work hard to stay in good spiritual shape.

Elsewhere, Paul made reference to running a race with a view to winning, keeping one's eye on the finish line (1 Corinthians 9:24). Paul also referred to boxing, using it as a metaphor to buffeting his body (9:26).

Winners of these contests in Greece would receive a crown of laurel, pine, or olive leaves. Likewise, the Christian who "runs the race well" can look forward to receiving a crown as a reward from God (1 Corinthians 9:25). In the case of Greek athletics, it was often a government official or even an emperor who bestowed the crown to the winning athlete. But for the Christian, Christ Himself will hand out these crowns at the judgment seat of Christ (2 Corinthians 5:10).

Both the church and family members are called to care for widows.

Scripture often speaks of God's compassion toward widows (Psalm 68:5; 146:9; Mark 12:41-44; Luke 7:11-17). Paul clarifies what type of "widow" should be cared for in the church. She must be a Christian, have no family to take care of her, and be at least 60 years old. Widows who have family members should be cared for by them. In 1 Timothy 5:3-16, the apostle Paul instructs that young women (who should marry), idle women, gossipers, and busybodies are ineligible for church "handouts."

Pursue godliness and be content with your life. You will be blessed.

Paul warned about the unbiblical idea that godliness results in material blessing. The pastor ought to focus on godliness while being content with what he has (1 Timothy 6:3-16). The man of God specifically— *and all Christians generally*—ought to crave godliness, not money.

You can't take money with you into the afterlife.

Paul said, "We brought nothing into the world, and we cannot take anything out of the world" (1 Timothy 6:7). He warned, "Those who desire to be rich fall into temptation, into a snare, into many senseless and harmful desires that plunge people into ruin and destruction" (6:9).

> "I have learned in whatever situation I am to be content. I know how to be brought low, and I know how to abound. In any and every circumstance, I have learned the secret of facing plenty and hunger, abundance and need. I can do all things through him who strengthens me."
>
> —*Philippians 4:11-13*

Paul's comments reflect those of Jesus: "Take care, and be on your guard against all covetousness, for one's life does not consist in the abundance of his possessions" (Luke 12:15). Jesus then urged His followers to have an eternal perspective, exhorting, "Do not lay up for yourselves treasures on earth, where moth and rust destroy and where thieves break in and steal, but lay up for yourselves treasures in heaven, where neither moth nor rust destroys and where thieves do not break in and steal. For where your treasure is, there your heart will be also" (Matthew 6:19-21; see also John 6:27).

My friend, let me emphasize that God does not condemn possessions or riches per se. It is not a sin to be wealthy! (Some godly people in the Bible—Abraham and Job, for example—were quite wealthy.) But God does condemn a love of possessions or riches (Luke 16:13; 1 Timothy 6:10; Hebrews 13:5). A love of material things is a sure sign that a person is living according to a temporal perspective, not an eternal perspective.

A Thought to Anchor in Your Heart

Fight the good fight of faith. Never give up. Never retreat. Never fall back. Stay strong in the Lord and move forward toward the finish line.

2 Timothy

Here's how to survive and thrive
in the face of life's difficulties:
stay rooted in God's Word,
stay single-minded, patiently endure,
and fight the good fight of faith.

Paul wrote this epistle between AD 66 and 67, and addressed it to "Timothy, my beloved child" (2 Timothy 1:2). When Paul wrote the epistle, he was in prison and expected to be executed shortly (1:16; 2:9). The letter contains Paul's last words to Timothy (4:6-8).

Paul encouraged Timothy to maintain the faith, hold on to sound doctrine, be faithful in ministry, and preach the gospel relentlessly (2 Timothy 1:6,13,14; 3:15–4:5). He was essentially passing the baton to young Timothy, encouraging him to stay true to his calling.

Following are key applicational concepts in 2 Timothy:

Stand firm in the power of the gospel—and don't give way to fear, intimidation, or shame. Be a bold witness for Christ.

Paul reminds young Timothy that "God gave us a spirit not of fear but of power and love and self-control" (2 Timothy 1:7). Therefore, Paul says, don't back off sharing the gospel with people (2:8). Be bold (compare with Acts 4:13,29,31; 14:3). Don't give way to fear or intimidation. These are words we very much need to hear in the modern church. Bold Christians, arise! Fear not!

Timeline

62–64—Paul writes his first epistle to his young apprentice Timothy.

64–67—Rome burns. Nero blames and persecutes Christians.

67—Paul is arrested in Rome and writes 2 Timothy from prison.

67—Paul is martyred.

> "Of whom shall I be afraid? One with God is a majority."
>
> —Martin Luther (1483–1546)

Don't be surprised if you experience suffering. It's a common part of the Christian life.

Paul exhorts Timothy to courageously share in the suffering that afflicts all who are committed to the gospel of Jesus Christ. "Share in suffering for the gospel by the power of God" (2 Timothy 1:8). "Share in suffering as a good soldier of Christ Jesus" (2:3). This counters TV preachers who claim that suffering is always a result of sin in the Christian's life. Don't fall for this idea. Godly Christians suffer. Expect it. Learn to patiently endure it (4:5).

Be single-minded in your service to the Lord.

> "I have one passion only: It is he! It is he!"
>
> —Nicolas von Zinzendorf (1700–1760)

The Christian who has one foot in the kingdom and one foot in the world has divided interests. Double-mindedness is not good for the Christian life. Paul uses a military metaphor to make his point: "No soldier gets entangled in civilian pursuits, since his aim is to please the one who enlisted him" (2 Timothy 2:4). Our goal is to please the one who enlisted us—Jesus Christ. Don't be double-minded.

God's Word is like

- an *eyeglass* that helps us see spiritual realities;
- a *lamp* to light our path (Psalm 119:105);
- an *anchor* that sturdies us in adversity;
- spiritual *food* to nourish us (Hebrews 5:12); and
- a *love letter* from God (John 3:16-17).

Seek always to rightly interpret God's Word.

Paul said, "Do your best to present yourself to God as one approved, a worker who has no need to be ashamed, rightly handling the word of truth" (2 Timothy 2:15). The phrase "do your best" means "be persistent and make a maximum effort." The phrase "rightly handling" means "cutting it straight"—that is, we are to be precise and accurate in Bible interpretation. Don't forget that errant interpretations lead to errant doctrines!

Flee Youthful Passions

"Flee youthful passions and pursue righteousness" (2 Timothy 2:22).

"Flee from sexual immorality" (1 Corinthians 6:18).

This is illustrated in the life of Joseph (Genesis 39:12).

Make it your daily goal to pursue righteousness and avoid youthful lusts.

We are not only to seek a right interpretation of God's Word; we are also to live it out in our lives. Paul thus instructs young Timothy, "Flee youthful passions and pursue righteousness" (2 Timothy 2:22). Paul also instructed him to avoid quarrelsomeness and correct opponents with gentleness (2:24-25). By this gentle approach, some might come to a knowledge of the truth and repent of their wrongdoing (2:26).

False teaching and godlessness will surge in the end times. Let this motivate you to remain a faithful witness of the truth.

Paul warned Timothy of an impending time of apostasy. People will increasingly fall prey to empty religiosity and false teaching (2 Timothy 3:1-9). This is all the more reason for Christians to stand strong as faithful witnesses of Christ.

Word Study: Apostasy
The word "apostasy" comes from the Greek word *apostasia*, meaning "falling away." It refers to a willful defection from the faith.

Don't be surprised if you're persecuted. It happens often to faithful Christians.

Paul tells Timothy that "all who desire to live a godly life in Christ Jesus will be persecuted" (2 Timothy 3:12). Paul had already faced much persecution (Acts 9:23-25; 13:50; 14:5-6; 17:10). The wonderful thing, though, is that the Lord is in the rescuing business (2 Timothy 4:17-18; Psalm 34:4,6,19; Isaiah 41:10; Daniel 3:17; Acts 26:16-17). So, dear Christian, don't sweat persecution!

Cross-References: Evil Times
Genesis 6:12 • 1 Kings 19:10 • Psalm 12:1 • Isaiah 59:14 • Jeremiah 5:1 • Micah 7:2 • Ephesians 5:16

Anchor yourself in the Word of God, which has the power to transform your life.

In view of the coming apostasy and persecution of Christians, Paul instructs Timothy to stand strong in defending the Word of God (2 Timothy 3:15-17). Scripture is inspired by God and is transformational—"profitable for teaching, for reproof, for correction, and for training in righteousness" (3:16). What a tragedy so many Christians today spend so little time reading it.

"The vigor of our spiritual life will be in exact proportion to the place held by the Bible in our life and thoughts."
—*George Muller (1805–1898)*

Always be ready to preach the word in season and out of season.

Paul exhorted Timothy to be ready to preach the word in season and out of season—that is, anytime an opportunity arises (2 Timothy 4:1-5). Timothy was to

"You are a Christian because somebody cared. Now it's your turn."
—*Warren Wiersbe*

be on call 24/7—always ready to speak a word of truth from Scripture. Timothy is a good model for us.

Seek to keep the faith and fight the good fight.

> "A good conscience will be found a pleasant visitor at our bedside in a dying hour."
>
> —J. C. Ryle (1816–1900)

Paul affirmed to Timothy, "I have fought the good fight, I have finished the race, I have kept the faith" (2 Timothy 4:7). Mission accomplished! Oh that you and I would be able to quote Paul's words at the end of our lives.

Be encouraged: faithful service will yield rewards at the judgment seat of Christ.

Paul affirmed, "There is laid up for me the crown of righteousness, which the Lord, the righteous judge, will award to me on that Day" (2 Timothy 4:8). "That Day" refers to the future judgment seat of Christ, where Christ will hand out rewards to Christians (or withhold them) in the form of crowns. Faithful Christians will be rewarded. Unfaithful Christians may have rewards withheld (Romans 14:10; 2 Corinthians 5:10). Ponder this, and act accordingly!

A Thought to Anchor in Your Heart

Stay rooted in God's Word and fight the good fight of faith.

Titus

There is an unbreakable link between our faith in Christ and the way we behave in the world.

The apostle Paul wrote this epistle between AD 62 and 64 and addressed it to "Titus, my true child in a common faith" (Titus 1:4). Titus was a young pastor and leader of the church in Crete. He was one of Paul's trusted inner circle of friends and ministry associates (2 Corinthians 8:23).

Titus was an uncircumcised Gentile. He was a living illustration of one of Paul's teachings: Gentiles need not be circumcised to be saved.

Following are key applicational concepts in Titus:

Christians, as bondservants of the Lord, are called to fully obey their Master.

Paul refers to himself as "a servant of God" (Titus 1:1). This can also be translated "bondservant of God" or "slave of God." Elsewhere Paul refers to himself as "a servant of Christ" (Romans 1:1; Galatians 1:10).

You and I are to be servants of God and Christ as well. Peter exhorts us, "Live as people who are free, not using your freedom as a cover-up for evil, but living as servants of God" (1 Peter 2:16). This is in keeping with the fact that we have been "bought with a price" (1 Corinthians 6:20; 1 Peter 1:18-19). My friend, there is joy in serving God. May your joy be full.

We learn how to live godly lives from the truths found in Scripture.

Paul said, "I have been sent to proclaim faith to those God has chosen and to teach them to know the truth that shows them how to live godly lives" (Titus

Timeline

49—Paul, Titus, and Barnabas arrive in Jerusalem to attend the Jerusalem Council.

56—Paul, while in Ephesus, sends Titus to mediate a conflict between Paul and the Corinthian church.

62–64—Paul writes his epistle to Titus; Paul commissions Titus to train elders for churches in Crete.

Cross-References: Obedience to God

1 Samuel 15:22 • Psalm 119:2 • Matthew 6:24 • John 14:15,21 • 1 John 3:22

"Urgently we do need a revival of personal godliness. This is, indeed, the secret of church prosperity."

—*Charles Spurgeon (1834–1892)*

1:1b NLT). The more we know about Scripture, the more we are able to grow in godliness. Conversely, the more ignorant we are of Scripture, the less we grow in godliness.

> "Godliness is the child of truth, and it must be nursed by its own mother."
>
> —William Gurnall (1617–1679)

You can be confident in your salvation because God is a promise keeper.

Titus 1:2 makes reference to "eternal life, which God, who never lies, promised before the ages began." Some Christians—particularly Christians with a sensitive conscience—have struggled with the possibility that maybe they're not really saved. Paul says we can be confident in our salvation because God is a promise keeper, and He never breaks His promises. "Does he speak and then not act? Does he promise and not fulfill?" (Numbers 23:19 NIV). Joshua told his people, "Not one of all the good promises the Lord your God gave you has failed" (Joshua 23:14 [NIV]; see also 1 Kings 8:56; Hebrews 6:18). So, drive the stake into the ground today. Resolve to never doubt your salvation again, for God has promised, and He will deliver what He has promised.

Eternal Life and God's Grace

Eternal life is a *grace gift* from God. "Grace" literally means "unmerited favor." It refers to the undeserved, unearned favor of God, with no good works involved.

We receive salvation freely by God's grace (Titus 2:13-14).

Elders in the church must *believe right* and *act right* so they can teach and protect others.

Titus, as a pastor in Crete, was charged by Paul to organize the churches there by appointing elders. These elders were to meet certain spiritual qualifications. In a nutshell, they must hold to correct doctrine and they must manifest evidence of godliness in the way they live (Titus 1:5-9; see also Acts 20:17-28; Ephesians 4:11; Philippians 1:1; 1 Thessalonians 5:12). Only then would they be able to teach others about doctrine and Christian living. Only then could they help protect against false teachers.

Take a stand against anyone who tries to spiritually enslave other Christians by legalism.

False teachers had emerged—members of "the circumcision party"—who were teaching that men had to be circumcised and adhere to Mosaic ceremonies to be in a right relationship with God (Titus 1:10-14).

Cross-References: Deceivers

Romans 16:18 • 2 Corinthians 11:13 • Ephesians 4:14 • 2 Timothy 3:13 • 2 John 1:7 • Revelation 18:23

Paul urged, "Rebuke them sharply, that they may be sound in the faith, not devoting themselves to Jewish myths and the commands of people who turn away from the truth" (1:13-14). What this means for you and me is that we should not allow ourselves to be negatively influenced by legalists. Our salvation is entirely by grace (2:11-14).

We are not saved by good works. But good works naturally surface in the life of a believer who has been saved by grace.

The apostle Paul reveals that holiness *follows* the salvation that is by grace alone, not causes it. That is, works are not the *condition* of our salvation, but a *consequence* of it. Works are not the *root* of our salvation, but rather the *fruit* of our salvation. While we are saved by grace through faith, we are saved for good works (Titus 1:16; 2:7,14; 3:1,8,14).

All people—both young and old—must be taught sound scriptural truths that transform their lives.

Sound doctrine is for everyone (Titus 2:1-8). "Sound doctrine" carries the idea of "healthy doctrine." It produces a sense of spiritual well-being, whereas unsound doctrine (such as that taught by false teachers) is spiritually injurious.

> **Cross-References: Doctrine**
> Proverbs 4:2 • Matthew 24:5 • Mark 16:15-16 • 1 Corinthians 1:10-17 • 2 Corinthians 4:2 • 1 Timothy 4:1-3,6,13 • 2 Timothy 2:15 • Hebrews 13:9 • 2 John 10

If sound doctrine leads to a sense of spiritual well-being, don't you think it is wise to expose ourselves to as much sound doctrine as possible?

Your good behavior as a Christian can make the gospel attractive to unbelievers.

Paul says believers, by engaging in bad behavior, can cause unbelievers to revile the Word of God (Titus 2:5). Good behavior, by contrast, will ensure that opponents of the gospel won't be able to say anything bad about us (2:8). How you behave matters. Is this not a powerful motivation to live righteously?

Biblical prophecy can motivate us to live righteously.

God doesn't tell us the future just to show off. He doesn't give us prophecy to teach us mere intellectual facts about "eschatology." It is highly revealing that

> "Live as if Christ died yesterday, rose this morning, and is coming back again tomorrow."
>
> —*Martin Luther (1483–1546)*

Titus

many verses in the Bible that deal with prophecy follow with an exhortation to personal purity in the way we live our lives. This means studying Bible prophecy ought to change the way we live. It ought to have an effect on our behavior.

A great passage that illustrates this is Titus 2:12-13, for it instructs us to "renounce ungodliness and worldly passions, and to live self-controlled, upright, and godly lives in the present age, waiting for our blessed hope, the appearing of the glory of our great God and Savior Jesus Christ." In other words, we live righteously as we await Christ's coming.

Make every effort to maintain unity with your brothers and sisters in Christ.

Paul instructs believers to avoid such things as controversies, dissensions, quarrels, and division (Titus 3:9-11). Such things disrupt the body of Christ, the church. How much better it is to maintain unity in the church (Romans 12:16; Ephesians 4:3; Philippians 1:27; 2:2; 1 Peter 3:8).

A Thought to Anchor in Your Heart

Plan your life according to your full lifetime expectancy, but live your life as though Christ could come today.

Philemon

Our faith in Christ shows itself in the love and forgiveness we show to others.

Philemon was written in AD 63 by the apostle Paul. It was addressed to "Philemon our beloved fellow worker" (Philemon 1:1). He was a friend of Paul's and a leader of the Colossian church.

Onesimus, a slave, had escaped from Philemon's household and probably went to Rome. Perhaps Onesimus reasoned that in the booming population of Rome, no one would notice him. He ended up meeting Paul in prison. Under Paul's leading, Onesimus became a Christian.

Paul was aware Onesimus could be executed as a runaway slave. Paul sent Onesimus back to Philemon with a letter urging him to set Onesimus free as a brother in Christ so he could assist Paul in ministry. Paul urged Philemon to forgive Onesimus, just as Christ had forgiven Philemon.

Following are key applicational concepts in Philemon:

Timeline
60—Paul arrives in Rome.
63—While in prison in Rome, Paul encounters Onesimus, a runaway slave.
63—Paul writes his short epistle to Philemon.

Philemon

Slavery in Bible Times
Slaves had rights under the Mosaic Law. Harsh treatment was prohibited (Leviticus 25:39), and slaves were eventually to be set free (Exodus 21:2).

Faith in Christ shows itself in how one lives—particularly in showing love to others.

Paul knew two things about Philemon: (1) He was a man with a strong faith in Jesus Christ. (2) He was a man who showed loved to others. Paul affirmed to Philemon, "I hear of your love and of the faith that you have toward the Lord Jesus and for all the saints" (Philemon 1:5; see also 1:7). Philemon is a man worthy of imitation.

"To love means loving the unlovable. To forgive means pardoning the unpardonable."

—G. K. Chesterton (1874–1936)

Those who follow Jesus can become useful for the kingdom of God.

Onesimus had apparently informed Paul that, as a slave, the service he had rendered to Philemon was

Cross-References: Forgiveness
Matthew 6:12-15 • 18:21-22 • Mark 11:25 • Luke 6:37 • Romans 12:17,19 • Ephesians 4:32

less than full-hearted. Paul said to Philemon, "Formerly he was useless to you, but now he is indeed useful to you and to me" (Philemon 1:11). Onesimus, by becoming a believer and becoming obedient to Christ, was now useful for the kingdom of God. This shows the transformative power of the gospel of grace.

This is an encouragement to us. If Onesimus can be transformed, then so can you and I.

> "The voice of sin is loud, but the voice of forgiveness is louder."
>
> —Dwight L. Moody (1837–1899)

The goodness in your heart will surface when you voluntarily choose to do good, without compulsion.

Paul knew that he—as an apostle—could have "lorded it over" Philemon and commanded him to set Onesimus free. Instead he showed the grace to let Philemon make that choice. Paul said, "I preferred to do nothing without your consent in order that your goodness might not be by compulsion but of your own accord" (Philemon 1:14). Goodness is a fruit of the Holy Spirit (Galatians 5:22). The person who walks with God overflows with goodness toward others.

One way your faith in Christ shows itself is in engaging in self-sacrificial actions toward others.

> "Forgiveness is not an occasional act, it is a permanent attitude."
>
> —Martin Luther King Jr. (1929–1968)

Paul urged Philemon to receive Onesimus "as you would receive me." Paul then placed any debt Onesimus might have to his own account (Philemon 1:17-19). Paul was showing self-sacrificial love on Onesimus's behalf, knowing that his friend Philemon would reciprocate with self-sacrificial love.

A Thought to Anchor in Your Heart

Christ showed self-sacrificial love in dying for you on the cross. You imitate Him when you show self-sacrificial love to others.

Hebrews

Christ is a superior revealer of God; a superior redeemer of humans, who offered a superior sacrifice on the cross; a superior High Priest, who enacted a superior covenant; and a superior object of faith. Let us therefore resolve to never fall away from Him in the face of trials, but rather endure in our faith.

Hebrews was written about AD 68, though scholars are unsure who wrote it—perhaps the apostle Paul, Apollos, or Barnabas. The epistle refers to itself as a "word of exhortation" (Hebrews 13:22).

The exhortation draws heavily on the Old Testament and urges Hebrew Christians to remain steadfast in their commitment to Christ and His cause. These Jewish believers were going through a severe period of persecution (Hebrews 10:32-34).

For a Jew to become a believer in Christ in the first century required sacrifice. Such a believer was immediately branded as an apostate and a blemish to the Jewish nation. He was considered "unclean." He was expelled from the synagogue; his children were denied attending school at the synagogue; and he lost his job. Furthermore, the Jewish high priest had the authority to throw him into jail (Hebrews 10:33-34). Such circumstances apparently caused many of these Jewish believers to wane in their commitment to Christ.

At first, these Jewish Christians joyfully accepted persecution (Hebrews 10:34). After a while, it became too much for them to bear and their endurance weakened (10:35-36). While they never entertained thoughts of renouncing Jesus, they nevertheless

Timeline

68—Hebrews is written by an anonymous writer.

70—Jerusalem and its temple are destroyed by Titus and his Roman warriors.

95—Clement of Rome quotes the book of Hebrews in his letter to the Corinthians.

Cross-References: Spiritual Maturity

1 Corinthians 13:11 • 14:20 • Ephesians 4:13,15 • Philippians 1:27-30 • 4:12 • 2 Thessalonians 1:3 • 2 Timothy 2:22 • 3:16-17 • 1 Peter 5:10 • 2 Peter 3:18 • 1 John 2:14

Warnings in Hebrews

- Don't drift from what you've heard (2:1-4).
- Don't disbelieve God's voice (3:7-14).
- Don't drift from God's Word (5:11–6:20).
- Don't despise truth (10:26-39).
- Don't devalue God's grace (12:15-17).

expressed the desire to drift back into the outward observances of Judaism— rituals, ceremonies, and sacrifices (6:1-2). They reasoned that if they externally took part in such Jewish rituals, the Jewish high priest might be satisfied and leave them alone.

This "word of exhortation" teaches that Jesus is the ultimate fulfillment of the Old Testament, and that He is greater than all Old Testament institutions (Hebrews 1:5–7:28). So to step back into Judaism is unacceptable. The author of Hebrews called his readers to move on to maturity in the Christian faith (6:1).

Following are key applicational concepts in Hebrews:

If you want to know what God is like, then look at Jesus.

The ultimate revelation of God was Jesus Himself. Jesus—as eternal God— took on human flesh so He could be God's fullest revelation to humankind (Hebrews 1:2-3). Jesus was a revelation of God not just in His person (as God) but in His life and teachings as well. By observing the things Jesus did and the things Jesus said, we learn a great deal about God. This is why Jesus said, "Whoever believes in me, believes not in me but in him who sent me. And whoever sees me sees him who sent me" (John 12:44-45).

Jesus revealed

- God's awesome power (John 3:2);
- God's incredible wisdom (1 Corinthians 1:24);
- God's boundless love (1 John 3:16); and
- God's unfathomable grace (2 Thessalonians 1:12).

Jesus is superior to

- prophets (1:1-3);
- angels (1:4-14; 2:5);
- Moses (3:1-6);
- Joshua (4:6-11); and
- human priests (6–7).

Because Jesus is supreme over all things in the universe, He must also take the supreme place in your heart and life.

In making the case to these Jewish believers not to retrogress into the external practices of Judaism, but instead move on to Christian maturity, the author laid out convincing evidences that Christ is superior to the old Jewish system in every way. For example, Jesus is superior to the prophets (Hebrews 1:1-3) and to the angels, through whom revelations were delivered (1:4-14).

A prime reason Jesus is superior is that He is God. Jesus "is the radiance of the glory of God and the exact imprint of his nature" (Hebrews 1:3; see also 2:5-18). The word "radiance" is literally "effulgence" or "shining forth." The word indicates not a reflection but an outshining of resplendent light. It indicates a shining forth to the world of the very character, attributes, and essence of God in Jesus

Christ (John 1:14). Jesus is not just a reflection of the Father's glory; Jesus's glory is radiating from within His very being.

Interestingly, the phrase "exact imprint" was used among the ancients of an engraving tool or a stamp, often in reference to the minting of coins. So the word indicates an "exact expression." In the present context, Jesus is portrayed as the absolute authentic representation of God's being (John 14:9). The writer of Hebrews could not have affirmed Christ's deity in any stronger terms.

So, my friend, don't forget or ignore the superiority and supremacy of Jesus as God. It is a no-brainer that He must take the supreme place in your heart and life.

Never take God's grace-gift of salvation lightly, for Christ paid the ultimate price at the cross for this gift.

Because Jesus is superior, we ought not neglect the salvation message we have been taught from Him. We must not drift away from His grace-teachings in favor of the legalistic teachings of old Judaism (Hebrews 2). The author of Hebrews indicates that if ignoring the law in Old Testament times was a serious matter, it is much more serious to ignore Christ and His work of salvation. Dear Christian, Christ gave His life to save you. Never take it lightly!

> "We are called to an everlasting preoccupation with God."
>
> —A. W. Tozer (1897–1963)

Cross-References: Redemption Through the Blood of Christ

Acts 20:28 • Romans 5:9 • Colossians 1:14,20 • 1 John 1:7 • Revelation 1:5 • 5:9

Unbelief, sin, and a hardened heart can rob you of spiritual rest.

Those who followed Moses in the wilderness had unbelieving and hardened hearts and sinned against God. As a result, they did not enter rest in the Promised Land (Psalm 95:7-11). The writer of Hebrews therefore urged his readers not to let their hearts get hardened in sin and unbelief—like those in Moses's time—and fail to enter God's spiritual rest (Hebrews 3:1–4:13).

Remedy for Hardened Hearts

- Regular exposure to God's Word (Psalm 119)
- Obedience to God (John 14:21; 1 John 5:3)
- Immediate repentance upon falling into sin (Acts 3:19)

Jesus is your faithful High Priest, ready to meet your every need.

Just as Jesus was shown to be superior to the Old Testament prophets, the angels, and Moses in

Jesus Our High Priest

- Jesus represents God the Father to us.
- Jesus represents us to God the Father.
- Jesus is our go-between (1 Timothy 2:5).

Hebrews

Hebrews 1–3, so now Christ's priesthood is shown to be superior to the Levitical priesthood (Hebrews 4:14–5:10; 7). Notice the contrast: The Levitical priesthood involved many priests; Christ is our single High Priest. Levitical priests were tainted by sin; Christ was without sin. Levitical priests offered animal sacrifices; Christ offered Himself as a once-for-all sacrifice. Levitical priests died; Christ lives on forever. Christ—your eternal High Priest—is ready to meet all your spiritual needs. "Let us then with confidence draw near to the throne of grace, that we may receive mercy and find grace to help in time of need" (4:16).

Don't allow tough circumstances to cause you to spiritually stagnate. Keep moving on to spiritual maturity in Jesus Christ.

> "We must accept finite disappointment, but we must never lose infinite hope."
>
> —*Martin Luther King Jr. (1929–1968)*

These Jewish believers had it tough. As noted previously, when Jews became Christians in the first century, the high priest put heavy-duty pressure on them. This caused some of the Jewish Christians to become gun-shy in their Christian lives. They weren't as open about their Christian faith. They thought if they kept a low profile, the high priest would lighten up on them. The author of Hebrews countered by instructing them not to stagnate, but to "go on to maturity" and render absolute commitment to the faithful High Priest, Jesus Christ (Hebrews 5:11–6:12).

Life can be hard. But the worst thing you can do when life gets hard is to spiritually stagnate. Don't let it happen. Keep growing in Christ. That will make all the difference!

Your salvation is rock-solid secure because God's promises are trustworthy and Christ is our eternal King-Priest.

> "God's promises are like the stars; the darker the night the brighter they shine."
>
> —*David Nicholas*

Eternal Security

Ephesians 4:30 promises that believers are permanently sealed by the Holy Spirit, guaranteeing full redemption. Meditate on John 10:28-30 and Romans 8:29-39.

God's promises are trustworthy, and so the salvation of the Jewish believers is sure and steadfast. After all, Christ's priesthood is eternal, and He removed sin forever by His one sacrifice at Calvary (Hebrews 6:13-20).

Christ is a priest after the order of Melchizedek, whose name is made up of two words meaning "king" and "righteous." Melchizedek foreshadows Christ as a righteous King/Priest. We are also told that Melchizedek was the king of Salem, a word that means "peace."

Hebrews

This points forward to Christ as a righteous King-Priest of peace (Hebrews 7:1-28).

Think about it. Because Christ is your King, He reigns over your life. Your role is to submit in all things. Because Christ is the righteous King-Priest *of peace*, He is not only your source of peace with God (Ephesians 2:14); He is also your source of personal peace. "Peace I leave with you; my peace I give to you" (John 14:27). Trust Him in all things!

The new covenant enacted by and through Jesus Christ enables God to actually forget your sins. This makes possible a genuine and intimate personal relationship with God.

Jesus Christ—with His superior priesthood (Hebrews 8:1-5)—has brought about a new covenant of grace, which is clearly superior to the old covenant of law (8:6-13). This superior covenant is based on a single, final sacrifice for sin, with a High Priest who is enthroned at the right hand of God, and who ministers in a true heavenly sanctuary on our behalf. This High Priest is Jesus.

Best of all, dear Christian, the new covenant does what the old covenant could not do. It brings about the true forgiveness of sins and yields a personal relationship with God. God promises, "I will be merciful toward their iniquities, and I will remember their sins no more" (Hebrews 8:12). Glorious!

Jesus's once-for-all sacrifice took care of your sin forever. Jesus has done it all. Good-bye legalism!

Christ's superior covenant is based on His superior sacrifice (Hebrews 9:1–10:18). The theological backdrop is that the earthly tabernacle provided only limited access to God. Moreover, the earthly tabernacle necessitated the continual offering of sacrifices, year after year. Since the continual sacrifice of animals could not truly take away sin, a worshiper in the old system could not be fully restored to God. The old system was inadequate.

How much better is Christ's once-for-all sacrifice, which enabled Him to completely remove sin and attain eternal redemption for all of God's people? Because He has brought about the forgiveness of sins once-for-all, there is no longer any need for an offering for sin (Jeremiah 31).

Hebrews

The Superiority of the New Covenant

The Old Covenant	The New Covenant
brought death	brings life
was impossible for humans to fulfill	is fulfilled by Christ
required annual atonement for sin	is satisfied by Christ's once-for-all atonement
restricted access to God	provides open access to God

All this was highly significant for the Jewish Christians to whom this epistle was addressed. Because Christ is superior—that is, superior in His person (God), superior in His priesthood, and brought about a superior covenant—it would be sheer folly for these Jewish believers to stagnate as Christians, choosing instead to continue flirting with the external observances of Judaism in a misguided effort to placate the Jewish high priest, who was persecuting them. It is wiser to resolve to move on to maturity as Christians.

The lesson for you and me is simply this: Jesus has done it all. Trust no one else and nothing else for your salvation. Good-bye legalism. Forever!

We can now confidently draw near to God, our sin problem having been forever eradicated through Jesus.

The Throne of Grace (Hebrews 4:16)

You and I are privileged to approach God's throne of grace, where we receive grace and mercy in time of need.

Are you in need of timely help? What are you waiting for?

Christ alone is our hope and our Savior. We need nothing more. Jesus has completed the work of salvation on our behalf, and it remains for us only to trust in Him. We can now draw near to God's throne of grace with a full assurance of faith (Hebrews 10:19-39).

This was especially important for the Jewish readers of this epistle. Despite persecutions from the high priest, they were to live with no further doubt or wavering. They were instructed to hold fast to their Christian confession, despite external Jewish threats. They were to encourage each other as the "day" (of judgment) for the Jews and their temple drew near. (Jerusalem and the temple were destroyed in AD 70, two years after Hebrews was written in AD 68.)

A strong faith—involving a strong assurance of things hoped for, the conviction of things not seen—will help you endure through trials.

The author of Hebrews not only defines the nature of faith (Hebrews 11:1-3), but also provides many real-life examples of faith (11:4-40). These examples were a strong encouragement to these discouraged Jewish Christians. They encourage us as well.

> "Endurance is the queen of all virtues."
>
> —Chrysostom (347–407)

Run the Christian race that is set before you, always keeping your eyes on Jesus.

These Jewish believers needed to fix their eyes not on the Jewish high priest but on Jesus Himself. They needed to keep their gaze on Jesus, just as a runner fixes his gaze on the finish line.

My friend, just as a runner runs with endurance, letting go of all that weighs him down, so you and I ought to run with endurance to the finish line of heaven, letting go of all sin (Hebrews 12).

> "If you wish to be disappointed, look to others. If you wish to be downhearted, look to yourself. If you wish to be encouraged…look upon Jesus Christ."
>
> —Erich Sauer (1898–1959)

We all die once—and then face the judgment.

Hebrews 9:27 tells us, "It is appointed for man to die once, and after that comes judgment." This short life on earth is the only time we have to decide for or against Christ. Once we die, there is no further opportunity—no second chance—to believe in Jesus for salvation. No wonder Paul said, "Behold, now is the day of salvation" (2 Corinthians 6:2).

Let your faith in God show itself in the way you live.

Faith in God is not a mere mental exercise. Rather, it should show itself in daily life—by loving others, being hospitable, visiting those in prison, being sexually pure, having a right perspective on money, and more (Hebrews 13:1-5,7,9,16,17,21). Faith also remembers, "The Lord is my helper; I will not fear; what can man do to me?" (13:6).

Examples of Walking by Faith (Hebrews 11)

- Daniel's rescue in the lions' den (Daniel 6).
- David's victory over Goliath (1 Samuel 17).

God loves you too much to allow you to remain in unrepentant sin.

God disciplines us not to *punish* us for sin but rather to *rescue* us from sin. (Christ has already taken our punishment for sin.) When God disciplines His children, that in itself is a sign of His love and compassion, for God loves His children too much to let them harm themselves by remaining in sin (Hebrews 12:6). How awesome is our God! How awesome is His love!

A Thought to Anchor in Your Heart

Faith is "the assurance of things hoped for, the conviction of things not seen" (Hebrews 11:1). Faith grows through exposure to God's Word (Romans 10:17).

Hebrews

James

True faith manifests itself in all areas of life—
including the fair treatment of others, how one
speaks to others, one's attitude toward money,
patience in the midst of suffering, and more.

James, the oldest half-brother of Jesus, wrote this letter between AD 44 and 49. He was writing to Jewish Christians—"to the twelve tribes"—who were in danger of giving nothing but lip service to Jesus (James 1:1). This situation may have arisen as a result of the severe persecution of Herod Agrippa I (Acts 12). Perhaps some of these Jewish Christians had become a little "gun-shy" about openly living the Christian life. James's intent, therefore, is to distinguish true faith from false faith. He shows that true faith results in outward works, which become visible evidences of faith's invisible presence.

Following are key applicational concepts in James:

Timeline

33—Jesus appears to James after resurrecting from the dead.

37—The apostle Paul meets with James and Peter on his first visit to Jerusalem after his conversion.

44—James becomes the leader of the church at Jerusalem.

44–49—James writes his epistle to Jewish Christians.

62—James is stoned to death.

We can retain joy in our hearts when trials emerge, knowing that they refine our faith.

Everyone has trials and temptations. James says these constitute tests of our faith. He tells us God allows us to encounter these trials because they mature our faith and increase our patient endurance as we continue to depend upon Him. Trials, then, can serve a good purpose in our lives. Even in the midst of such trials, God can give us wisdom so we understand what He is doing in our lives through such trials (James 1:1-12). Through it all, we have joy (1:2).

> "Each problem is a God-appointed instructor."
>
> —*Charles Swindoll*

363

Faith recognizes that our temptations come not from God but from our own inner sinful natures.

Apparently some of the Jewish believers to whom James was writing found an excuse for sinning by claiming "I am being tempted by God." James responded that God does not tempt, nor can He be tempted. Our temptations emerge not from God but from the sinful natures we all have within us (James 1:13-18).

I want to draw your attention to a contrast in James 1. Just as a proper response to sin (repentance and confession) can restore a person spiritually, so a wrong response to sin results not only in spiritual poverty but can ultimately—if repentance is lacking—lead to death (James 1:15). This is a sobering reality. Let us act accordingly!

Faith shows itself in the avoidance of angry reactions.

> "Christian life consists of faith and charity."
>
> —Martin Luther (1483–1546)

James is famous for emphasizing the practical outworking of faith in the Christian life. A key point he makes in this regard is that one who has faith in God will seek to avoid angry reactions toward others (James 1:19-21). An angry mind-set is incompatible with faith in God.

This brings to my mind the importance of walking in the Spirit. As we daily walk in dependence upon the Holy Spirit, the fruit of the Spirit emerges in our lives—including "love, joy, and peace" (Galatians 5:22). Love, joy, and peace "crowd out" anger in one's life.

Faith shows itself in being a "doer of the Word."

> "A doctrine has practical value only as far as it is prominent in our thoughts and makes a difference in our lives."
>
> —A. W. Tozer (1897–1963)

> "More depends on my walk than talk."
>
> —Dwight L. Moody (1837–1899)

James stressed the importance of righteous conduct that grows out of a living faith. He says it is not enough to be a *hearer* of God's Word; one must be a *doer* of God's Word (James 1:22-25). He stressed that faith without works is dead (2:14-26), meaning that our faith in Christ must show itself in the way we live. Anyone who merely claims to have faith, but does not show that faith in the way he or she lives, has a spurious faith.

Faith shows itself in the avoidance of prejudice.

True faith also shows itself in the way we treat other people. More specifically, a person of faith does not discriminate against others (James 2:1-13). Faith in God is incompatible with favoritism toward the wealthy and discrimination against the poor. The biblical pattern is that we must love *all* people for the sake of Christ.

The absence of benevolent actions reveals a "dead faith."

James indicates that merely claiming to have faith is not enough. Genuine faith is evidenced by works. James gives a powerful analogy to illustrate his point. Apart from the spirit, the body is dead; it's a lifeless corpse. Similarly, apart from the evidence of good works, faith is dead. It is lifeless and nonproductive (James 2:14-26). My advice: periodically examine your life to ensure that your faith is alive and well.

> **Cross-References: Faith**
> Luke 17:5 • 18:8 • Romans 10:17 • 14:23 • 2 Corinthians 5:7 • Galatians 5:6 • 1 Timothy 1:5 • Hebrews 11:1,39 • 1 John 5:4

Faith shows itself in the taming of the tongue.

James says a believer's faith in God shows itself in how he or she speaks to other people (James 3:1-12). The person of faith does not misuse the tongue in dialoguing with others, for harsh words can do great injury (see, for example, Psalm 141:1-4). Be cautious in your words!

> "An unbridled tongue is the chariot of the devil, wherein he rides in triumph."
>
> —*Edward Reyner (1600–1660)*

Faith in God yields fruitful wisdom from God.

Fruitful wisdom is an *action-oriented* kind of wisdom. It is a wisdom that shows itself in one's deeds (James 3:13-18). It has to do not so much with a continual acquiring of more truth, but rather the application of truth one already has. My friend, never forget that wisdom from God is intended to be a fruit-bearing wisdom.

> "The tongue is but three inches long, yet it can kill a man six feet high."
>
> —*Anonymous*

> **Cross-References: Good Works**
> Matthew 5:16 • Colossians 1:10 • 1 Timothy 6:18 • Titus 2:7,14 • 3:8 • Hebrews 10:24 • James 2:17-18 • 1 Peter 2:12

James

A worldly attitude can distract you away from faith in God.

James warns, "If you want to be a friend of the world, you make yourself an enemy of God" (James 4:4 NLT). The idea here is, "If you want to be a worldly person—focusing on the prideful and selfish pursuit of earthly pleasures—you are no true friend of God" (see 4:1-12).

> "This world and that to come are two enemies. We cannot therefore be friends to both; but we must resolve which we would forsake and which we would enjoy."
>
> —*Clement of Alexandria*
> *(150–215)*

We've all learned by hard experience that the world offers many lures that can distract us from faith in God. Let us therefore daily resolve to turn from a worldly focus to a godly focus, from self-serving pride to God-exalting humility.

Self-confidence and self-reliance can hinder your faith in God.

Human beings are not in ultimate control of their lives, even though they live under the illusion that they are. God alone is the true Sovereign of the universe (Acts 18:21; 1 Corinthians 4:19; 16:7; Philippians 2:19,24). Instead of trusting in our finite and temporal selves, it is much wiser to trust in the infinite and eternal God who reigns from heaven (James 4:13-17).

The love of money can distract you from faith in God.

James Draws from Jesus

- Love of money (James 5:1-6; Luke 12:15)
- Humility (James 4:10; Matthew 5:5)
- Judging (James 4:11-12; Matthew 7:1)
- Swearing (James 5:12; Matthew 5:34-37)

James indicates that money and wealth can be a big distraction from faith and commitment to God (James 5:1-6). This is a common emphasis in Scripture. The apostle Paul warned that "those who desire to be rich fall into temptation, into a snare, into many senseless and harmful desires that plunge people into ruin and destruction" (1 Timothy 6:9). Jesus understandably warned His followers, "Take care, and be on your guard against all covetousness, for one's life does not consist in the abundance of his possessions" (Luke 12:15). Your first priority ought to always be to "lay up for yourselves treasures in heaven, where neither moth nor rust destroys and where thieves do not break in and steal" (Matthew 6:19-20; see also John 6:27).

The faith-life is a life of patient endurance.

James closes his epistle by encouraging his readers to patiently endure their sufferings in view of their faith in the future prospect of the coming of the Lord

James

(James 5:7-12). He indicates that regardless of the trials that inevitably surface in life, believers can rest assured that God has a purpose in allowing His children to encounter such trials. Faith helps us to patiently endure.

The faith-life is a life of prayer.

James says instead of "going it alone" through trials and tribulations, it is better to turn to God in prayer with the faith that God answers prayer (James 5:13-15). Such prayer can bring healing—both spiritual and physical. We rob ourselves of blessing when we neglect prayer. "You do not have, because you do not ask" (4:2).

A Bible Promise

"Draw near to God, and he will draw near to you."

—*James 4:8*

"We stand tallest and strongest on our knees."

—*Charles Stanley*

A Thought to Anchor in Your Heart

Don't be a faker. Make sure your faith in God shows itself in the way you live.

James

1 Peter

While trials and suffering are hard to swallow, the right perspective makes all the difference.

Peter, a fisherman who became one of the 12 disciples, wrote his first epistle around AD 63 or 64. It was intended for scattered groups of Christians in the five Roman provinces that covered the greater part of modern Turkey. Peter probably wrote from Rome at the outbreak of Emperor Nero's persecution. Having already endured a beating at Herod's hands, Peter probably wrote his brethren in Asia to encourage and strengthen them in facing the Neronian persecution. It may well be that Peter recalled his Lord's injunctions, "Strengthen your brothers" (Luke 22:32), and "Feed my lambs" (John 21:15-17). At the end of his life, Peter was crucified upside-down in Rome during Nero's persecution.

Following are key applicational concepts in 1 Peter:

Our living hope of the afterlife sustains us as we encounter trials on earth.

Christians enjoy a living hope through the resurrection of Christ from the dead. A wondrous inheritance awaits each of us in heaven (1 Peter 1:1-4). This future hope gives us strength as we encounter trials on earth (1:5-12). The apostle Paul was very much in agreement with Peter. He said, "Set your minds on things that are above, not on things that are on earth" (Colossians 3:2).

1 Peter

Because of the salvation we have in our soon-coming Savior, we ought to live in reverence of God and pursue holiness in daily life.

The proper response of the Christian to the wonderful salvation we have in Christ is a life of holiness (1 Peter 1:13-21). This is especially so since Christ is coming again.

Because of the common grace-salvation we have in Jesus, let's resolve to love each other as brothers and sisters.

You and I are now in the family of God. It is only natural that brothers and sisters in the same family love each other. The *family of God* is a *family of love* headed by a *God of love*. Let us therefore be consistently loving (1 Peter 1:22-25).

We derive our spiritual nourishment by daily feeding upon God's Word.

A newborn baby craves his or her mother's milk, which brings nourishment to the newborn. Likewise, we as Christians need to daily feed upon the milk of God's Word (1 Peter 2:1-3). If we fail to do so, spiritual malnourishment is the inevitable result.

Make Jesus the foundation of your entire life.

Our foundation for life is not found in a self-help book. It is not based on human philosophy. It is not rooted in the opinions of other human beings. It is not based on the teachings of some spiritual guru. Rather, our foundation is Jesus *and no other* (1 Peter 2:4-10). Jesus is our All. Because He is our All, we ought to *live* like He is our All, 24/7.

Because we are just temporary residents on earth, we must avoid worldliness and live righteously among unbelieving neighbors.

When we see strangers walking in our neighborhoods, we often keep a close eye on them. We, as Christians, are strangers upon the earth, and we are being

---

A Bible Promise

"In his great mercy he has given us new birth into a living hope through the resurrection of Jesus Christ from the dead, and into an inheritance that can never perish, spoil or fade—kept in heaven for you."
—*1 Peter 1:3-4 (NIV)*

Be Ready!

"Christ hath told us He will come, but not when, that we might never put off our clothes, or put out the candle."

—*William Gurnall (1617–1679)*

"Leave not off reading the Bible till you find your hearts warmed…Let it not only inform you, but inflame you."

—*Thomas Watson (1620–1686)*

1 Peter

carefully watched by the world. In view of this, we must purposefully live upright lives so God is glorified in our lives (1 Peter 2:11-12).

We Are Temporary Residents

- Peter refers to Christians as exiles (1 Peter 2:11), meaning "temporary residents."
- "Our citizenship is in heaven" (Philippians 3:20).
- God's people are "strangers and exiles on the earth," and they "desire a better country, that is, a heavenly one" (Hebrews 11:13-16).

The Christian life is a life of submission.

Submissiveness is Christlike. Peter talks a lot about submission to various kinds of authorities in his epistle. For example, he says Christians give a good testimony of their commitment to the Lord by their submission to government authorities (1 Peter 2:13-17). We may not agree with all the policies of our government, but God nevertheless calls us to be submissive—just as the apostles were submissive to pagan Roman emperors.

Peter also indicated that Christian servants give a good testimony of their commitment to the Lord by their submission to their masters (1 Peter 2:18-25). Likewise, Christian wives show their godliness in submitting to their husbands, just as Christian husbands show their godliness by honoring their wives (3:1-7).

Most important of all, Peter says, Christ is Lord of all, and we must therefore always submit to Him and honor Him (1 Peter 3:15). We might say that all other forms of submission (to government, within the family, and the like) grow out of our prior, foundational submission to Jesus Christ as Lord.

> "There is no argument like a holy life."
>
> —*Robert Murray M'Cheyne* (1813–1843)

As Christians walk in submission to the Lord, they will likely experience increased opposition, in response to which they must remain respectful and be ready with an answer.

Christ is our Lord, our Master, our Sovereign. As we walk in submission to the Lord, we will likely experience increased opposition from unbelievers. We must therefore always be ready to give an answer for our faith and conduct, but with respect (1 Peter 3:15-16).

Peter affirms that if Christians must suffer at all, it ought to be for the sake of righteousness and not because of sin (1 Peter 3:17-22). And through it all, they must keep a clear conscience.

Suffering has a purifying effect on our lives.

No one likes to suffer. But because of the involvement of the sovereign Lord in our lives, such suffering is used by God to purify us and shave off the "rough edges" (1 Peter 4:1-6). Just as fire burns the dross out of precious metals, so fiery trials burn the sinful rubbish out of our lives. Trials ultimately result in us becoming more Christlike.

> **Through Our Suffering, God**
> - trains us to obey Him (Hebrews 5:7-8);
> - disciplines us when we go astray (Hebrews 12:3-11);
> - helps us to learn patience (Romans 5:3) and humility (2 Corinthians 12:7-9); and
> - teaches us about His ways (Psalm 119:65-71).

We as Christians need to be there for each other!

Biblical love is an action-oriented kind of love. We don't just *feel* love in our hearts and let it remain isolated there. Rather we openly demonstrate our love by the things we do. More specifically, we as Christians ought to pray for each other, be hospitable to each other, and use our spiritual gifts to bless each other (1 Peter 4:7-11). *That's* Christian love!

Humility is good. Pride is bad. We as Christians are called to serve each other in humility.

Peter says, "Clothe yourselves, all of you, with humility toward one another, for 'God opposes the proud but gives grace to the humble'" (1 Peter 5:5). Pride is self-focused; humility is God-focused. Pride is self-exalting; humility is God-exalting. Pride distances one from God; humility draws one near to God.

> "Nothing sets a person so much out of the devil's reach as humility."
>
> —*Jonathan Edwards*
> *(1703–1758)*

My friend, here's a little something I've learned in the school of life: God loves you too much to allow you—one of His children—to remain in unrepentant pride. If you don't choose humility for yourself, God will take the necessary steps to humble you through discipline (Hebrews 12:5-11). Learn it well: Christians will either respond to God's light or they will respond to His heat.

Beware: Satan is always looking for opportunities to injure you. Stay strong in your faith.

Christians need to be on guard against the devil. Satan tried to defeat Christ, but failed (Matthew 4:1-11). Satan tried to defeat Peter, and succeeded (Luke 22:31-34). Peter was therefore speaking from hard experience when he warned his readers, "Be sober-minded; be watchful. Your adversary the devil prowls around like a roaring lion, seeking someone to devour. Resist him, firm in your faith" (1 Peter 5:8-9). The comparison to a roaring lion depicts Satan's strength and destructiveness. He is a powerful foe.

Elsewhere in Scripture, we read of the believer's armor against the devil (Ephesians 6:10-20). Here's the catch: *you must put the armor on for it to work.* "Putting on" the armor means that our lives must be characterized by such things as righteousness, obedience to the will of God, faith in God, and an effective use of the Word of God (compare with Matthew 4:1-11). These are what spell D-E-F-E-A-T for the devil.

A Thought to Anchor in Your Heart

The more you anchor yourself on the absolute sovereignty of God, the less distressed you will be when trials surface.

2 Peter

Beware of false teachers.
They'll lead you on a sure path to destruction.

Peter wrote his second epistle around AD 66. He wrote it to the same group as his first epistle with a view to warning about the emergence of false teachers within the church.

These teachers taught dangerous doctrines. Scoffing at the idea that there would be a second coming of Christ and a future judgment, they taught that morality was unimportant. Peter emphasized not only that Christ was coming again, but that the pursuit of moral excellence, knowledge, self-control, perseverance, godliness, brotherly kindness, and selfless love was God's will for all believers.

Peter strongly urged growth in Christian knowledge for his readers. He knew the best antidote to false teachings is a mature knowledge of the truth.

Following are key applicational concepts in 2 Peter:

False teachers will not only lead you astray doctrinally, they will lead you into immorality.

Peter knew his death was near. Knowing his time was short, he spoke against false teachers who had emerged from within the church, thereby putting the flock in danger—both doctrinally and morally (2 Peter 2:1-3). These false teachers were anti-authority, sought self-gratification, denied the Lord by the way they lived, and exploited others for monetary profit. Peter affirmed that the false teachers had a dire punishment awaiting them from God (2:4-22).

Timeline
29—Jesus calls Peter as a disciple.

33—The resurrected Jesus appears to Peter. Peter later preaches at Pentecost.

49—Peter attends the Jerusalem Council.

63–64—Peter writes his first epistle.

66—Peter writes his second epistle.

66—Peter is crucified upside-down.

Descriptions of Death in the Bible
- Putting off of the body (2 Peter 1:14)
- Dismissal from earthly life (Luke 2:29)
- Depart to be with Christ (Philippians 1:23)
- Tent (or body) is destroyed (2 Corinthians 5:1)
- The physical body "sleeps" (Acts 13:36)

2 Peter

The Word of God—the Bible—is your sole barometer of truth, not the mystical ideas of false teachers.

> "The original documents of the Bible were written by men, who, though permitted to exercise their own personalities and literary talents, yet wrote under the control and guidance of the Spirit of God, the result being in every word of the original documents a perfect and errorless recording of the exact message which God desired to give to man."
>
> —Benjamin B. Warfield
> (1851–1921)

In contrast to the false teachers who derived their ideas from mysticism, Peter pointed to the Word of God as our only barometer of truth. Peter affirmed, "No prophecy of Scripture comes from someone's own interpretation. For no prophecy was ever produced by the will of man, but men spoke from God as they were carried along by the Holy Spirit" (2 Peter 1:20-21).

The phrase "carried along" in this passage is intensive in the original Greek. The writers were literally "borne along" by the Holy Spirit. Luke uses this same word in the book of Acts to refer to a ship being "borne along" or "carried along" by the wind (Acts 27:15,17). The experienced sailors on the ship could not navigate the ship because the wind was so strong.

The ship was being driven, directed, and carried about by the wind. Likewise, the Holy Spirit drove, directed, and carried the human authors of the Bible as they wrote (2 Peter 1:20-21). The word is a strong one, indicating the Spirit's complete superintendence of the human authors. Scripture can therefore be trusted as authoritative. Unlike the doctrines of the false teachers, Scripture carries the authority of God because it came from God.

Moreover, Peter asserted, Scripture is based on eyewitness testimony. "We did not follow cleverly devised myths when we made known to you the power and coming of our Lord Jesus Christ, but we were eyewitnesses of his majesty" (2 Peter 1:16). The real myths are the ideas taught by the false teachers.

The Deity of Christ in 2 Peter

"Our God and Savior Jesus Christ" (1:1).

"Our Lord and Savior Jesus Christ" (1:11; 2:20; 3:18).

Dear Christian, let's learn an important lesson here: always stay anchored in the Bible!

The more you grow in spiritual knowledge by feeding upon the Word of God, the less vulnerable you are to the deceptions of false teachers.

Peter desired that his readers come to a true knowledge of Jesus Christ (2 Peter 1:1-2). This includes the recognition that believers are recipients of great and precious promises (1:3-4). In view of God's promises and blessings, believers ought to divorce themselves from the corruptions of the world, instead pursuing Christian virtues (1:5-7). Doctrinal beliefs must give way to virtuous practice (1:8-11).

Peter's motive in sharing all this was his conviction that the best way to fight false teaching (with its subsequent immoral behavior) was to grow in the true knowledge of Jesus Christ (with its subsequent holy behavior—see 2 Peter 3:17-18). Let's commit to pursuing life-changing knowledge of Jesus Christ on a daily basis.

> ### God Is a Promise Keeper
>
> - God has made "precious and very great promises" (2 Peter 1:4).
> - "Has he spoken, and will he not fulfill it?" (Numbers 23:19).
> - "Not one word has failed of all the good things that the Lord your God promised concerning you" (Joshua 23:14).

False teachers often scoff at the suggestion of God's judgment. Christians know better.

The false teachers were *this-world* focused (earth). Peter was *next-world* focused (heaven). The false teachers said people should live it up in this world because there will be no accountability in the next. Peter said there most certainly *will* be accountability in the next.

These false teachers had a false sense of immunity because they did not believe God intervened in world affairs. Peter responded forcefully. He pointed to how God created the world (2 Peter 3:5) and then destroyed the world of humanity through the flood (except Noah and his family—3:6). How's that for intervention?

Just as the Lord intervened in the past, so the prophesied interventions of the future will also come to pass—including God's destruction of the present heavens and earth, and the future judgment and destruction of the ungodly (2 Peter 3:7). The false teachers have no ground to stand on.

The reality of Christ's second coming—and the judgment that follows—is an impetus to moral living.

The false teachers were scoffers, holding that Christ had not come yet, and there was no reason to think He'd come in the future. Peter, however, spoke with certainty of Christ's future return (2 Peter 3:1-18). In fact, God's Word universally assures us it will happen

> "If the Lord is coming soon, is this not a very practical motive for greater missionary effort? I know of no other motive that has been so stimulating to myself."
>
> —J. Hudson Taylor (1832–1905)

2 Peter

(see, for example, Matthew 24:42,44,46-50; Acts 1:9-11; Revelation 1:7; 19:11-16). If it seems God is delaying the second coming, it is an act of mercy, for God desires that there be plenty of time for people to be saved (2 Peter 3:8-10).

Meanwhile, let the reality of Christ's future coming be a strong incentive to spiritual commitment (2 Peter 3:11-18; see also 1 Thessalonians 5:23; 1 Timothy 6:13-15).

There's a new world coming. Hold tight to an eternal perspective.

A divine renovation is coming. Peter speaks of this glorious future reality in 2 Peter 3:13—there's going to be a "new heavens and a new earth." You and I can look forward to living eternally in a magnificent domain where both heaven and earth unite in a glory that exceeds the imaginative capabilities of the finite human brain.

> "In the consummation of all things, God will renovate the heavens and the earth, merging His heaven with a new universe for a perfect dwelling-place that will be our home forever. In other words, heaven, the realm where God dwells, will expand to encompass the entire universe of creation, which will be fashioned into a perfect and glorious domain fit for the glory of heaven."
>
> —*John MacArthur*

Finally the prophecy of Isaiah 65:17 will be fulfilled, where God promises, "Behold, I create new heavens and a new earth, and the former things shall not be remembered or come into mind." And finally the prophecy of Revelation 21—verses 1, 3 and 5—will be fulfilled: "Then I saw a new heaven and a new earth...And I heard a loud voice from the throne saying, 'Behold, the dwelling place of God is with man. He will dwell with them, and they will be his people, and God himself will be with them as their God. He will wipe away every tear from their eyes, and death shall be no more, neither shall there be mourning, nor crying, nor pain anymore, for the former things have passed away.' And he who was seated on the throne said, 'Behold, I am making all things new.'"

My friend, choose to live *now* in view of *then*. Live on earth with your eyes focused on the future reality of heaven. Life on earth is short—like a dot. Life in heaven is long—like a line. Live for the line, not for the dot.

Judgment awaits false teachers.

Second Peter 2:9 tells us the Lord knows how to "keep the unrighteous under punishment until the day

Two Judgments

The wicked dead will face Christ at the great white throne judgment (Revelation 20:11-15).

Christians will face Christ at the judgment seat of Christ, for the purpose of receiving (or losing) rewards (2 Corinthians 5:10).

2 Peter

of judgment." The word "keep" in this verse is a present tense, indicating that the wicked (nonbelievers, false teachers) are held captive *continuously*. Peter is portraying them as condemned prisoners being closely guarded in a jail while awaiting future sentencing and final judgment. While God holds them there, He is continuing their punishment. Eventually, the wicked dead will be resurrected and then judged at the great white throne judgment, after which time their eternal punishment will begin in the lake of fire (Revelation 20:11-15).

A Thought to Anchor in Your Heart

Live for the line, not for the dot.

1 John

You and I have the awesome privilege of
daily fellowshipping with God.
John instructs us about the conditions,
characteristics, and blessings of such fellowship.

God in 1 John

- God is light—1:5
- God is love—4:8
- God is life—5:11,13,20

John wrote this letter around AD 90. By this time, Christianity had existed for some 50 years. Though Christ had now long been in heaven, John continued to enjoy a blessed and delightful daily fellowship with Him and the Father. John wanted the same for his readers.

When you think about it, the idea of daily fellowshipping with God staggers the mind. In this fallen world where so many things go wrong and so many things hurt us, we can count on enjoying blessed fellowship with God, day in and day out. Don't let anything stand in the way of it.

Following are key applicational concepts in 1 John:

Your fellowship with God hinges on walking in the light as He is in the light.

John emphasizes that to enjoy ongoing fellowship with the Father and Jesus, certain conditions must be met. For example, we must "walk in the light" (1 John 1:5-7). By "light," John points not only to God's truth, but also to *living one's life according to that truth*. This means our daily fellowship with God hinges on repenting of sin and choosing to live righteously. Put another way, we cannot live in "darkness" (in willful sin) while seeking to fellowship with the God of light (2:3-6).

Dear Christian, choose this day to walk in the

light. Choose this day to live God's way. From this day forward, make it your goal to enjoy unbroken fellowship with God. Your life will be immeasurably enriched!

If you fall into sin and fall out of fellowship with God, confession to God is the remedy that will restore your fellowship.

As Christians, we all still have a sin nature within us, and can subsequently still fall into sin (Psalm 51:5; Ecclesiastes 7:20; Jeremiah 17:9; Mark 7:21; Romans 3:23; Galatians 5:17; Ephesians 5:8; 1 John 1:10). Such sin dampens our fellowship with God. John says the remedy that restores fellowship with God is the confession of that sin to God (1 John 1:8-10).

> "Christianity is not a theory or speculation, but a life; not a philosophy of life, but a living presence."
>
> —*Samuel Taylor Coleridge (1772–1834)*

> "The way to *cover* our sin is to *uncover* it by confession."
>
> —*Richard Sibbes (1577–1635)*

The word "confession" simply means "to agree with God." Confession involves agreeing with God—not only that sin is sin, but that we ought to make efforts to avoid it. Once we confess our sin, our fellowship with God is instantly restored (1 John 1:8-10; see also Psalm 32; 51).

My friend, if there is sin in your life right now, don't wait another moment. Confess it to God. Restore your blessed fellowship with Him!

When you sin, Jesus is your defense attorney, and He never loses a case in God's court. Your fellowship with God is thereby protected.

In 1 John 2:1-2, John reveals something glorious. He tells us that when we as Christians fall into sin, Jesus Christ is our divine Advocate who pleads our case with the Father: "If anyone does sin, we have an advocate with the Father, Jesus Christ the righteous. He is the propitiation for our sins."

The word "advocate" means defense attorney. A defense attorney becomes necessary when someone accuses us of a wrongdoing. Our accuser is Satan— "the accuser of our brothers" (Revelation 12:10; see also Job 1–3).

Word Study: Propitiation

Propitiation means Jesus's death on the cross provided full satisfaction of all God's holy demands (Romans 1:18; 2:5,8; 3:5).

1 John

Remember, *Jesus is your defense attorney*. Never forget this. Jesus is on your side. He will always defend you. Because of Jesus, the believer is always *accepted* by the Father, even if his or her *behavior* is not always acceptable. Because Jesus is your defense attorney, Satan will never be able to break your fellowship with God. Rejoice in this fact.

Fellowshipping with God goes hand in hand with loving your Christian brothers and sisters.

> *"God loves...Go thou and do likewise."*
>
> —*Erwin Lutzer*

John's Big Ideas

- Conditions of fellowship (1:1–2:14)
- Things that hinder fellowship (2:15-27)
- Characteristics of fellowship (2:28–4:12)
- Results of fellowship (5:1-21)

John emphasizes that a Christian cannot claim to be walking in the light and fellowshipping with God while at the same time hating a Christian brother or sister (1 John 2:7-14). Loving others naturally accompanies fellowship with God.

The love John speaks of involves not mere lip service, but rather shows itself in active deeds. One's love for God actively spills over into acts of love for others.

Fellowshipping with God can actually motivate us to love others *as Christ loved us* (1 John 4:7-12). Jesus said there is no greater love than to sacrificially lay down one's life for his friends, which is what Jesus did for us (John 15:13). As we fellowship with God, sacrificial love for others overflows from our lives.

Fellowship with God is thwarted by love for the world system.

Effects of Love for the World

- Alienation from God—James 4:4
- Corruption by sin—2 Peter 1:4
- Deception—1 John 4:1

Satan and the World

- Satan is the "prince" of the world (John 12:31 NIV).
- Satan is the "god of this world" (2 Corinthians 4:4).

John says love for the world can hinder our fellowship with God (1 John 2:15-17). In John's theology, the "world" refers to an anti-God system. "All that is in the world—the desires of the flesh and the desires of the eyes and pride of life—is not from the Father but is from the world" (2:16). Such things can distract us from seeking God and fellowshipping with Him.

My friend, please take my word for it: short-lived worldly pleasures are simply not worth it because they hinder our rich and fulfilling fellowship with God. It's a terrible trade-off. Don't let it happen. Watch out for Satan's enticing lures.

1 John

False beliefs about Jesus can thwart your fellowship with God.

John says holding false views about Jesus can thwart our fellowship with the Father and Son (1 John 2:18-27). In John's day, the primary doctrinal error related to Gnosticism. Gnostics believed "Jesus" and "Christ" were two distinct entities—Jesus being a human, and "the Christ" being some kind of cosmic spirit who indwelt Jesus for a short time. John countered this idea with the biblical truth that Jesus *is* the Christ.

How does this relate to fellowship with God? If we do not believe in the true and genuine person of Jesus Christ (who is God), there can be no genuine forgiveness and fellowship with God. In John's theology, one depends on the other. So let's not get this wrong!

Fellowshipping with God has a transforming effect in your life.

John draws a close connection between fellowshipping with God and righteous living. First John 3:6 tells us, "No one who abides in him keeps on sinning; no one who keeps on sinning has either seen him or known him." This verse does not demand sinless perfection in the Christian life. Recall that earlier in John's letter, he emphasized the folly of denying that we, as redeemed Christians, are sinful (1 John 1:8). This is one reason John calls believers to confess their sins to God (1:9; see Romans 7:18-21).

So what is John saying? John relates living righteously to abiding in Christ and living in accordance with one's new nature. Contextually, we are told in verse 5 that there is no sin in Christ. Then in verse 6 we are told that those who abide in Christ do not sin. As we move down to verse 9, we are told that the new natures within Christians—natures that are pure and holy, like Christ—do not sin. These verses seem to indicate that insofar as the believer continues to abide in Christ and express his or her new nature in daily experience, he or she will not sin. If the believer *does* sin, it is an indication that he or she is not presently abiding in Christ and not living in accordance with the new nature.

The "fix" in such cases is straightforward. Confess the sin to God, thereby restoring one's fellowship

> **Choosing Rightly in 1 John**
> - Choose light, not darkness—1:5-7; 2:9-11
> - Choose truth, not deception—1:8-10
> - Choose obedience, not disobedience—2:3-6
> - Choose love for God, not love for the world—2:15-16
> - Choose righteousness, not lawlessness—3:4-9
> - Choose the true Jesus, not a counterfeit—2:18-27

> **A Bible Promise**
> "This is the testimony, that God gave us eternal life, and this life is in his Son. Whoever has the Son has life; whoever does not have the Son of God does not have life" (1 John 5:11-12).

1 John

with—and one's "abiding" in—God, and then live in subsequent victory over sin (1 John 1:9; see also 5:1-5).

Fellowshipping with God gives you an assurance of salvation.

Pastors have long noticed that Christians engulfed in sin often doubt their salvation. Toward the end of his epistle, John tells us how we can have an assurance of salvation. "I write these things to you who believe in the name of the Son of God that you may know that you have eternal life" (1 John 5:13). What are "these things"? "These things" are John's instructions about fellowshipping with God. Communing with God naturally makes one feel like a member of God's household. Glorious!

A Thought to Anchor in Your Heart

The Christian who fellowships with God enjoys rich relationships, rich blessings, and a rich hope for the future.

---

2 John

Our love for God reveals itself in obedience to His commands and standing for doctrinal purity.

John wrote his second epistle shortly after writing his first epistle, around AD 90. He emphasized that merely *feeling* love for God is not enough. Our love must show itself concretely in our obedience to Him and in standing for His truth.

Following are key applicational concepts in 2 John:

Let your love for God show itself in your obedience to His commands—especially the command to love one another.

It appears that John in this epistle is personifying a particular church as an "elect lady" and her members as "children." After all, we are told that "all who know the truth" love this "lady" (2 John 1:1). Moreover, the exhortation in verse 5 to "love one another" seems strangely inappropriate as an exhortation to a woman and her children, but would be perfectly fitting in a church context. The closing greeting—"the children of your elect sister greet you" (verse 13)—also makes sense in terms of members of one church sending greetings to another church.

John apparently wrote in this way to protect church members in the event that the epistle was intercepted by Roman persecutors. If the letter were discovered, the Romans would view it as a private letter to a friend, and the church would remain safe.

With that backdrop in mind, here is John's exhortation: *Our love for God must show itself in our obedience to His commands*—especially the command to love one another (2 John 1-6). My friend, our love for one another demonstrates that we are living in the truth, and that the truth lives in us. Starting today,

Timeline

90—Early gnostic heresies emerge.

90—Later this year, John writes 2 John to warn his readers about this heresy.

95—John is exiled to the isle of Patmos (a penalty for evangelizing).

97—John returns to Ephesus.

98–100—John dies at Ephesus.

Your Spiritual Walk

Walk in the light (1 John 1:7). Walk in the truth (2 John 4).

Walking is a step-by-step, moment-by-moment process.

Biblical Love

It is an active, demonstrative love based on God's truth.

It is *not* a naive, undiscerning kind of love that is hospitable to false teachers.

2 John

resolve to *truly* love your brothers and sisters—not just those who personally appeal to you, but also those who may seem unlovable. This cold world needs warm-hearted Christians.

Let your love for God show itself by consistently standing for His truth.

It appears that John was battling an early strain of Gnosticism (2 John 7-11). Gnostics taught that the spiritual and material (physical) realms are entirely separate and have nothing to do with each other. They believed spirit is good but matter is evil. This led them to conclude that the spiritual Christ could not have actually become human (with a material body).

Active Nature of Truth

It is not enough to *know* the truth. One must *live* ("walk in") the truth.

John's goal in the second half of his epistle was therefore to warn against deceivers who taught heresy concerning Christ. He urged that those who teach such things should not be assisted, encouraged, or even be shown hospitality by Christians who love and fellowship with God (verse 10). After all, right belief about Jesus Christ is a pre-condition to a right relationship with God (verse 9).

So, dear Christian, commit to showing your love for God by boldly standing for the true Jesus in an anti-Jesus culture. Don't be shy about it!

A Thought to Anchor in Your Heart

Don't play games with a lip service kind of love for God. Make your love for Him patently obvious in the way you live your life.

2 John

3 John

Godliness shows itself in being *other-person* centered.
Moreover, the pursuit of goodness is an
"ID Card" of God's children.

John wrote this epistle in about AD 90, shortly after he wrote 1 and 2 John. This is the shortest book in the Bible. You might recall that John in his second epistle warned against showing hospitality to heretics. Now in this third epistle, he condemns the lack of hospitality shown to true and faithful ministers of the Word.

Following are key applicational concepts in 3 John:

A key evidence of godliness is being *other-person* centered.

Gaius—a godly and generous man (3 John 2-8)—is a model for us. He selflessly engaged in loving deeds to traveling missionaries, even though they were perfect strangers to him. He apparently provided them with money, food, shelter, and other things. Resolve to be a Gaius-imitator—a God-loving and selfless missionary-supporter. If we welcome God's truth, we will also welcome God's people.

Timeline

90— John writes 3 John to emphasize goodness and love among his followers.

95— John is exiled to the isle of Patmos (a penalty for evangelizing).

97— John returns to Ephesus.

98–100— John dies at Ephesus.

Following a Good Model

Our *vertical* relationship with God shows itself in our *horizontal* relationships with other people (1 John 2:7-17; 3:11-24).

Gaius is an ideal model for each of us (3 John 5-8). John—with good reason—called Gaius "beloved" four times (3 John 1, 2, 5, 11).

Ungodliness is characterized by pride, arrogance, and self-exaltation. Avoid such behavior.

Unlike Gaius, Diotrephes was full of pride and ambition (3 John 9-11). He loved to be preeminent among the people. He arrogantly refused to recognize John's apostolic authority, and he refused hospitality to faithful ministers of the Word. He even expelled members of his own church who showed these missionaries hospitality.

The only person who should be preeminent in the church is Jesus Christ

3 John

(Colossians 1:18). Don't you agree? It seems to me that John the Baptist had it right. He said, "He must increase, but I must decrease" (John 3:30). Let's all be content to "decrease" as Christ alone is exalted in our churches.

The Pride of Life

Love for the world shows itself in the "pride of life" (1 John 2:16). Closely related to this, Chrysostom (AD 347-407) warned, "Nothing will divide the church so much as the love of power." The "pride of life" and the love of power were modeled by Diotrephes.

Humility is the better policy (Psalm 25:9; Proverbs 3:34; Matthew 11:29; Philippians 2:3; Colossians 3:12; James 4:6; 1 Peter 5:5-6).

Gaius	Diotrephes
Lived the truth	Did not live the truth
Was humble	Was prideful
Was obedient	Was disobedient
Was loving	Was unloving
Was hospitable	Was inhospitable

Doing good to others is an "ID Card" that proves we are members of God's family.

Recall John's earlier teaching that one cannot claim to walk in the light while at the same time hate a brother or sister (1 John 2:7-14). Diotrephes may have claimed to be walking in the light, but he proved by his attitude and actions against John and the traveling missionaries that he wasn't.

Never forget that if you are walking with the God of goodness and love, you will show the goodness and love of God to others.

A Thought to Anchor in Your Heart

Humility, goodness, and love. These are the attributes that ought to characterize each of our lives as Christians. Pursue them relentlessly.

3 John

Jude

God's forgiveness is not a license for Christians to sin without fear of judgment.

Jude, the Lord's half-brother, wrote this short epistle between AD 67 and 68. Though he had earlier rejected Jesus as the divine Messiah (John 7:1-9), he was now a committed servant of Christ (Jude 1; compare with Acts 1:14). His epistle debunks some serious false ideas that had penetrated the church.

Following are key applicational concepts in Jude:

Beware: God's forgiveness is not a license for Christians to live in immorality without fear of judgment.

False teachers had wormed their way into the church. They were teaching that being saved by grace opens the door for Christians to freely sin, since these sins will no longer be held against them by God. Jude's goal was therefore to exhort his readers to contend for "the faith" once-for-all delivered to the saints (Jude 1-4). "The faith" refers to the body of Christian truth handed down by the true apostles.

> "Dim or indistinct views of sin are the origin of most of the errors, heresies, and false doctrines of the present day."
>
> —J. C. Ryle (1816–1900)

Dear Christian, the true faith does not turn the grace of God into a license to sin. Rather, it points to a perpetual life of submission to the Master, the Lord Jesus Christ. Never forget it.

God's past judgment against evil humans and angels is a warning to us all.

Jude asserted that God would punish and destroy false teachers. He reminded his readers of God's past dealings with those who felt free to sin, including the unbelieving Israelites, the wicked people of Sodom and Gomorrah, and even the wicked angels (Jude

Fallen Angels
- Lucifer rebels against God (Isaiah 14:12-15; Ezekiel 28:12-15).
- One-third of the angels join him in the rebellion (Revelation 12:4).
- Lucifer becomes Satan.
- The fallen angels are demons.

Jude

5-7). Friends, don't take this lightly. Woe unto *anyone* who remains flippant about sin.

Beware: rebellious people who care for nothing except satisfying their sensual cravings and love for money are ripe for judgment.

The false teachers apparently claimed their ideas were based on dreams from God, seeking to bring authority to their perverted ideas. They were physically immoral, intellectually insubordinate, and spiritually irreverent. Jude thus emphasizes that their rebellious path will lead straight to judgment (Jude 8-13).

Beware: God will settle all accounts in the prophetic future.

Jude cited Enoch—esteemed among the Jews—in support of the severe judgment that awaits false teachers in the prophetic end times (Jude 14-16). The wicked will be judged at the great white throne judgment, over which Christ Himself will preside (Revelation 20:11-15). Christians will face the judgment seat of Christ (Romans 14:10-12).

As a protective measure, God calls Christians to build their lives on the Christian faith, be obedient to God, and rescue less-mature believers.

Jude reminded his readers the apostles had warned that false teachers would emerge (Jude 17-19). He encouraged them to stay grounded and guard against the onslaught of apostasy (20-21). As they continued to mature in the Christian faith, remaining obedient to God, they would be able to rescue others from false doctrine (22-25).

False Teachers in Jude

- teach false doctrines (Jude 3);
- are godless (4,10);
- are corrupt (10);
- are arrogant (16); and
- are worldly (19).

God in Jude

- Loving (Jude 1-3,21)
- Gracious (4)
- Glorious (24-25)
- Wise (25)

A Thought to Anchor in Your Heart

Don't try to play games with God.
His gracious forgiveness of your sins should never be
taken as a license to continue sinning!

Revelation

God is in control of human history. In the end,
He will bring immeasurable blessing to His people,
while quarantining the wicked forever.

The book of Revelation was written around AD 95. It is the only apocalyptic book in the New Testament. The apostle John had been exiled on the isle of Patmos in the Aegean Sea for the "crime" of sharing Jesus Christ with everyone he came into contact with (Revelation 1:9). It was on this island that John received the "revelation."

The recipients of the book were undergoing severe persecution, with some of them even being killed. Things were about to get even worse. John wrote this book to give his readers a strong hope that would help them patiently endure in the midst of suffering.

Following are key applicational concepts in Revelation:

Those who study and obey God's message are blessed.

Revelation 1:1-4 affirms that obedience brings blessing. Hearing without heeding won't cut it (compare with James 1:22-25). Only those who heed are blessed. The word "blessed" means "spiritually happy." So obeying God's message in Revelation brings spiritual happiness.

You can trust Jesus with the circumstances of your future death and what lies beyond it.

Jesus affirmed, "I have the keys of Death and Hades" (Revelation 1:18). This implies that Jesus—*as*

Timeline

81–96—Domitian, the emperor of Rome, demands emperor worship—a crisis faced by John's readers.

90—John writes three letters to instruct believers in the crises they face—1, 2, and 3 John.

95—John is exiled to the isle of Patmos, in the Aegean Sea, for the "crime" of sharing the message about Jesus Christ (Revelation 1:9).

95—John later writes the book of Revelation to encourage his readers in the face of increasing persecution.

Obedience to God brings

- blessing (Revelation 1:3; Luke 11:28);
- long life (1 Kings 3:14; John 8:51);
- happiness (Psalm 112:1; 119:56);
- peace (Proverbs 1:33); and
- well-being (Jeremiah 7:23).

God—has the authority to grant entrance and exit from the realms of death and Hades (compare with John 5:21-26; 1 Corinthians 15:54-57; Hebrews 2:14; Revelation 20:12-14). This means Jesus sovereignly decides *who lives, who dies, and when*. It also means you and I don't have to worry about our future deaths because it's all in Jesus's hands. Glorious!

Doctrinal accuracy and moral purity are important, but that's not enough. Supreme love for God and others is also necessary.

> "O for a thousand tongues to sing my great Redeemer's praise!"
>
> —*Charles Wesley (1707–1788)*

The church at Ephesus was strongly committed to doctrinal accuracy. However, they lost the love they once had (Revelation 2:1-7). Thirty years earlier, they were commended for the love they showed to the Lord and to others (Ephesians 1:15-16). Their love had since waned. They now needed to renew their love (compare with Matthew 22:37-38; John 14:21,23; 1 Corinthians 16:22).

My friend, we learn a good lesson here. Christianity is more than just being doctrinally correct. It involves an ongoing love relationship with the Lord.

You need not fear what Satan and unbelievers can do to Christians on earth. We are destined for eternal life in heaven.

Don't Worry About the Future
Deuteronomy 10:14 • 1 Chronicles 29:12 • 2 Chronicles 20:6 • Psalm 33:8-11 • 47:2 • Isaiah 46:10 • John 14:1-3

Jesus warned believers at the church of Smyrna that they would suffer at the hands of unbelievers and Satan (Revelation 2:8-11). But Jesus urged them, "Be faithful unto death, and I will give you the crown of life" (Revelation 2:10). Scripture reveals that the crown of life is given to those who persevere under trial, and especially to those who suffer to the point of death (James 1:12).

Don't sweat over earthly troubles. Our destiny in heaven is secure. Rejoice!

The Fruit of Repentance
Christians are to "bear fruit in keeping with repentance" (Matthew 3:8). They are to "repent and turn to God, performing deeds in keeping with their repentance" (Acts 26:20).

Your loyalty to Christ must show itself in avoiding compromising behavior.

Believers at the church in Pergamum were loyal to Christ. And yet they also succumbed to false teaching that led to inappropriate behavior (Revelation 2:12-17; see also verses 18-29). The false teaching promoted license in Christian conduct. Jesus strongly urged them to repent. We, too, must repent of all compromising behavior. Do it now!

Don't give the outward appearance of spirituality while in truth you are spiritually barren on the inside.

Members of the church in Sardis gave the outward appearance of being spiritual while in truth they were spiritually barren on the inside. Jesus told them, "You have the reputation of being alive, but you are dead" (Revelation 3:1). There was no spiritual vitality in this church, even though there were a few genuine believers left (verse 4).

> **Jesus Perfectly Evaluates**
> - He commends (Revelation 2:2-3,6,9,13,19; 3:4,8).
> - He rebukes (2:4-5,14-16,20-23; 3:1-3;15-20).

It seems that these church members were very much like the Pharisees, who gave the outward appearance of spirituality but on the inside were spiritually dead (Matthew 23:27-28). Don't be a faker. Be the real thing.

Beware: take steps to avoid spiritual lethargy and spiritual blindness.

Members of the church in Laodicea were spiritually lethargic and spiritually blind. Jesus told them, "You are neither cold nor hot" (Revelation 3:15). This is an allusion to the underground aqueduct where water was piped in from hot springs south of the city, becoming lukewarm in transit to Laodicea. Just as a resident of Laodicea recognized that the water piped in was neither cold nor hot, so Christ recognized that church members were neither cold nor hot. The church was not spiritually dead, but neither did it have spiritual zeal. Jesus told them if they did not rectify this situation, discipline was imminent (3:14-22).

What a relevant message this is for today. Make every effort to avoid spiritual lethargy. Jesus abhors it. Keep things nice and hot!

Just as God is gloriously enthroned in heaven, so He must be enthroned upon your heart.

Human language is inadequate to describe the glory of God in His throne room. John uses jewels in an attempt to portray the matchless beauty of what he beheld (Revelation 4:3). There is also reference to a

> **Trusting God**
> God knows the future (Isaiah 46:9-10). We should therefore trust God with our futures (Psalm 37:5; Proverbs 3:5-6).

rainbow (4:3) and flashes of lightning (4:5), both pointing to the awesome glory of God upon His throne.

My friend, God's throne points to His majestic rule over all affairs on earth (Proverbs 19:21; 21:30; Ecclesiastes 7:13; Isaiah 14:24; 46:10; Lamentations 3:37; 1 Timothy 6:15). We can infer from this that His desire is to be enthroned upon our hearts as well—with absolute obedience on our part. What are you waiting for?

Jesus is worthy to be exalted in our hearts, for He brought us salvation. Praise His name!

A Bible Promise

"Never again will they hunger; never again will they thirst… God will wipe away every tear from their eyes."
—*Revelation 7:16-17 NIV*

John said, "I saw a Lamb standing, as though it had been slain" (Revelation 5:6). "Lamb" refers to Christ's first coming and His death on the cross. Christ is called a Lamb 27 times in Revelation. Those in heaven sang a new song, which emphasized that Jesus the Lamb is worthy because He shed His blood— of inestimable value—for the sins of the world (John 3:16-17; 1 Peter 1:18-19). All in heaven exalted the Lamb. He ought to be exalted in our hearts as well.

Because unrepentant sin brings ever-intensifying judgment, your first best choice is to always pursue righteousness.

"Those who will not deliver themselves into the hand of God's mercy cannot be delivered out of the hand of His justice."

—*Matthew Henry (1662–1714)*

The book of Revelation reveals that human suffering will steadily escalate during the future tribulation period. For example, as Jesus breaks each of the seven seals, a new divine judgment is unleashed upon the earth. Included are bloodshed, famine, death, economic upheaval, a great earthquake, and cosmic disturbances. Following the seal judgments are the trumpet judgments and bowl judgments. These increasingly intense judgments correlate with the increasing hardness of hearts among humans on earth (Revelation 6–8).

How much better it is to choose righteousness—the path to blessing (Psalm 1).

Let your light shine!

During the future tribulation period, in which God's judgments will fall upon the earth, God will also raise up a force of 144,000 Jewish men to act as His witnesses of light during this period of darkness on earth. A great multitude will become believers as a result of their ministry (Revelation 7:9-10).

> "We were made to be prisms refracting the light of God's glory into all of life."
>
> —John Piper

You and I today are called to be witnesses of Jesus (Matthew 28:19-20). Resolve to let your light shine (Matthew 5:14-16).

You are targeted by Satan. Always be prepared for spiritual warfare.

In Revelation 12 we read about how Satan the dragon sought to kill the promised Messiah at birth but was unsuccessful. We are also told that in the middle of the future tribulation period, the Jewish people will be persecuted by the antichrist, who is empowered by Satan.

You and I are also targets of the evil one. "Be sober-minded; be watchful. Your adversary the devil prowls around like a roaring lion, seeking someone to devour" (1 Peter 5:8). A word to the wise: keep on your spiritual armor (Ephesians 6:11-18).

Because we know our ultimate destiny is serene rest in heaven, you can face whatever difficulties come your way on earth.

John heard a voice from heaven say, "'Blessed are the dead who die in the Lord from now on.' 'Blessed indeed,' says the Spirit, 'that they may rest from their labors, for their deeds follow them!'" (Revelation 14:13). No matter what pains we may face on earth, blissful rest awaits us in the afterlife. Always seek to maintain an eternal perspective.

> "Death should not be viewed as a terminus but as a tunnel leading into an ampler and incredibly more wonderful and beautiful world. The death of a believer is a transition, not a final condition."
>
> —J. Oswald Sanders (1902–1992)

False religion can victimize God's people.

In the book of Revelation, the false religious system that emerges is described in metaphoric language as a prostitute. The woman—the false religious system—is said to be drunk with the blood of the saints and Christian martyrs (Revelation 17:6; Matthew

> "We are refugees from the sinking ship of this present world order, so soon to disappear; our hope is fixed in the eternal order, where the promises of God are made good to his people in perpetuity."
>
> —F. F. Bruce (1910–1990)

Revelation

24:21). This includes the blood of God's two prophetic witnesses (Revelation 11:10) as well as all who refuse to receive the mark of the beast (13:15).

Dear Christian, even today we witness advocates of false religions persecuting and even murdering Christians around the world. This will no doubt continue—and even increase—until the glorious appearing of Jesus at the second coming (Revelation 19). Never forget that there is great reward ahead for all persecuted believers (Matthew 5:10-11; 2 Timothy 3:12).

Good news: the relationship of believers with Christ in heaven is one of incredible intimacy.

Your True Citizenship
- Philippians 3:20
- Ephesians 2:19
- Hebrews 11:16

Scripture often refers to the relationship between Christ and His church using a marriage motif, with Christ being the Bridegroom and the church being the bride (Revelation 19:6-10; see also Matthew 9:15; 22:2-14; 25:1-13; Mark 2:19-20; Luke 5:34-35; 14:15-24; John 3:29). The church is presently pictured as a virgin bride awaiting the coming of her heavenly Bridegroom (2 Corinthians 11:2; Ephesians 5:22-33).

Here's a point not to miss, my friend: While the bride (the church) awaits her divine Groom, she is called to keep herself faithful and pure, unstained from the world. Is this not a motivation to live righteously? Don't compromise!

If you are concerned about the problem of evil in the world today, take heart in the reality that Christ will overthrow all of it at the second coming.

The description of Christ's second coming is majestic (Revelation 19:11-21).

Jesus as King
Jesus is called the King of kings and Lord of lords (Revelation 19:16). As King, He sovereignly oversees all that comes into our lives. Because He is sovereign, we are never victims of our circumstances.

Christ rides a white horse, fitting for the glorious Commander-in-chief of heaven's armies. He is called Faithful and True, returning to earth just as He promised (Matthew 24:27-31). On His head are many diadems, representing total sovereignty and royal kingship. He comes as the "King of kings and Lord of lords" (1 Timothy 6:15). He will overthrow all evil and set up His glorious kingdom (Revelation 20). Rejoice in what lies ahead!

Exciting news: a new day is coming.

Following the second coming, Christ will set up His 1000-year millennial kingdom on earth (Revelation 20:1-7). Satan will be imprisoned in the "bottomless pit" (Luke 8:31; 2 Peter 2:4), and there he will remain for the duration of the millennial kingdom.

An Eternal Perspective
- Matthew 6:19-34
- Colossians 3:1-2

The millennial kingdom will feature an enhanced physical environment, plenty of food for all, harmony with the animal kingdom, longevity among humans, illnesses removed, prosperity, and joy.

At the end of the millennial kingdom, Satan will be loosed and lead one final rebellion against Christ (Revelation 20:7-9). Fire instantly destroys the rebels (20:9). Satan will be cast into the lake of fire. From this point forward, gone forever will be the assaults from Satan and demons.

How awesome it will be! I can't wait for this new day to come.

Finally, the wicked will be judged at the great white throne judgment.

The wicked aren't getting away with anything! Revelation 20:10-15 makes reference to the great white throne judgment. The dead—that is, all the *wicked* dead, both great and small—will be forcefully brought before the divine tribunal. A strong sense of dread will be pervasive. God's "books" will detail the lives of the unsaved. Every action, word, and even thought will be "recorded." These books will provide the evidence to substantiate the divine verdict of a destiny in the lake of fire. These books will also be used to determine degrees of eternal suffering in the lake of fire (Matthew 10:14-15; 11:22; Mark 12:38-40; Luke 12:47-48). The wicked will be eternally quarantined from God and His people. No more evil!

You and I will have resurrected bodies, live in a resurrected city (the New Jerusalem), that rests upon a resurrected earth, in a resurrected universe (new heavens and new earth)—and we will be face-to-face with God forever (Revelation 21–22). Rejoice in this!

No More Tears (Revelation 21:4)
- Isaiah 25:8
- Isaiah 60:20
- Jeremiah 31:12

Before the eternal kingdom can be made manifest, God must deal with this present earth that has been tainted by sin and Satan (Genesis 3:17-18; Romans 8:20-22). The present (old) heavens and earth will pass away (Psalm 102:25-26; Isaiah 51:6; Matthew 24:35), and then God will create new heavens and a new earth (Revelation 21–22). The New Jerusalem is the eternal city we will one day inhabit on the new earth. Christ Himself is creating it (John 14:1-3). God will live directly with redeemed humankind (compare with Deuteronomy 12:5).

> "The heavenly country is full of light and glory; having the delightful breezes of divine love, and the comfortable gales of the blessed Spirit."
>
> —John Gill (1697–1771)

Here at last we find unfettered companionship between the Creator and His creation. The crowning feature of heaven is that we will see God face-to-face (Revelation 22:4; see also 1 Corinthians 13:12; Psalm 17:15).

How awesome it will be.

A Thought to Anchor in Your Heart

Let your knowledge of what awaits you in the afterlife be a perpetual motivation for you to live in joyful anticipation.

Revelation

Postscript:
Be Transformed

From Genesis to Revelation, we have explored numerous applicational concepts that are strategically engineered to spiritually transform your life. As our journey through Scripture comes to a close, I think it is helpful for us to be reminded that it is God's will that we be transformed. To God, our personal transformation is a big deal.

Perhaps the best verse on this in the New Testament is Romans 12:2, where the apostle Paul instructs, "Do not be conformed to this world, but be transformed by the renewal of your mind." The word "conformed" in this verse carries the idea to "be patterned after, fashioned after, molded after." We are not to be patterned after the world, but rather transformed by the Word of God. The word "transformed" literally means "changed in form, molded." The Word of God *changes us*!

The Expanded Bible reflects a proper understanding of these words in its rendering of Romans 12:2: "Do not be shaped by [conformed to; pressed into a mold by] this world [age]; instead be changed within [transformed] by a new way of thinking [or changing the way you think; the renewing of your mind]." The Amplified Bible likewise renders the verse, "Do not be conformed to this world (this age), [fashioned after and adapted to its external, superficial customs], but be transformed (changed) by the [entire] renewal of your mind [by its new ideals and its new attitude]." These new ideals and new attitudes come to us from the Word of God, as directed by the Holy Spirit.

When I wrote this book, I did so with the idea that the applicational concepts would help facilitate this personal transformation as guided by the Holy Spirit. In view of this, my prayer for you—now that you have finished the book—is that it would continue to be a source of transformational inspiration for you in the years to come. It can only be good to review these concepts from time to time, continuing to make them a part of your daily fabric.

May the Lord bless you in your continued growth as a Christian. And may the Lord be glorified in the transformation each of us experience.

> To Him Who ever loves us
> and has once
> [for all] loosed and freed us from our sins by His own blood,
> And formed us into a kingdom (a royal race),
> priests to His God and Father—
> to Him be the glory and the power
> and the majesty and the dominion
> throughout the ages
> and forever and ever. Amen
> (Revelation 1:5-6 AMP).

Other Great Harvest House Books
by Ron Rhodes

BOOKS ABOUT THE BIBLE

40 Days Through Genesis

The Big Book of Bible Answers

Bite-Size Bible® Answers

Bite-Size Bible® Charts

Bite-Size Bible® Definitions

Bite-Size Bible® Handbook

Commonly Misunderstood Bible Verses

The Complete Guide to Bible Translations

Find It Fast in the Bible

The Popular Dictionary of Bible Prophecy

Understanding the Bible from A to Z

What Does the Bible Say About…?

BOOKS ABOUT THE END TIMES

8 Great Debates of Bible Prophecy

40 Days Through Revelation

Cyber Meltdown

The End Times in Chronological Order

Northern Storm Rising

Unmasking the Antichrist

BOOKS ABOUT OTHER IMPORTANT TOPICS

5-Minute Apologetics for Today

1001 Unforgettable Quotes About God, Faith, and the Bible

Answering the Objections of Atheists,
Agnostics, and Skeptics

Christianity According to the Bible

The Complete Guide to Christian Denominations

Conversations with Jehovah's Witnesses

Find It Quick Handbook on Cults and New Religions

The Truth Behind Ghosts, Mediums, and Psychic Phenomena

Secret Life of Angels

What Happens After Life?

Why Do Bad Things Happen If God Is Good?

Wonder of Heaven

THE 10 MOST IMPORTANT THINGS SERIES

The 10 Most Important Things You Can Say to a Catholic
The 10 Most Important Things You Can Say to a Jehovah's Witness
The 10 Most Important Things You Can Say to a Mason
The 10 Most Important Things You Can Say to a Mormon
The 10 Things You Need to Know About Islam
The 10 Things You Should Know About the Creation vs. Evolution Debate

QUICK REFERENCE GUIDES

Halloween: What You Need to Know
Islam: What You Need to Know
Jehovah's Witnesses: What You Need to Know

THE REASONING FROM THE SCRIPTURES SERIES

Reasoning from the Scriptures with Catholics
Reasoning from the Scriptures with the Jehovah's Witnesses
Reasoning from the Scriptures with Masons
Reasoning from the Scriptures with the Mormons
Reasoning from the Scriptures with Muslims

LITTLE BOOKS

Little Book About God
Little Book About Heaven
Little Book About the Bible

AVAILABLE ONLY AS EBOOKS

Book of Bible Promises
Coming Oil Storm
Topical Handbook of Bible Prophecy

To learn more about Harvest House books and
to read sample chapters, visit our website:

www.harvesthousepublishers.com

HARVEST HOUSE PUBLISHERS
EUGENE, OREGON
